FARMERS AND FISHERMEN

PUBLISHED FOR THE

INSTITUTE OF EARLY AMERICAN

HISTORY AND CULTURE,

WILLIAMSBURG, VIRGINIA

BY THE UNIVERSITY OF

NORTH CAROLINA PRESS

CHAPEL HILL AND LONDON

DANIEL VICKERS

FARMERS & FISHERMEN

TWO CENTURIES OF WORK IN

ESSEX COUNTY, MASSACHUSETTS,

1630–1850

The Institute of Early American History and Culture is sponsored
jointly by the College of William and Mary and the
Colonial Williamsburg Foundation.

The paper in this book meets the guidelines for permanence and durability
of the Committee on Production Guidelines for Book Longevity of the
Council on Library Resources.

Library of Congress Cataloging-in-Publication Data
Vickers, Daniel.
Farmers and fishermen : two centuries of work in Essex County,
Massachusetts, 1630–1850 / by Daniel Vickers.
p. cm.
Includes bibliographical references and index.
ISBN 0-8078-2148-9 (alk. paper)—ISBN 0-8078-4458-6 (pbk. : alk. paper)
1. Essex County (Mass.)—Social life and customs. 2. Farm life—
Massachusetts—Essex County—History. 3. Fishing—Massachusetts—Essex
County—History. I. Institute of Early American History and Culture
(Williamsburg, Va.) II. Title.
F72.E7V58   1994
974.4'5—dc20   93-36514
CIP

This volume received indirect support from an unrestricted publication grant
awarded to the Institute by the L. J. Skaggs and Mary C. Skaggs Foundation
of Oakland, California.

98 97 96 95 94   5 4 3 2 1

To my mother,

my sister,

and the memory

of my father

PREFACE

The idea for this book was hatched in a graduate seminar, when John Murrin drew my attention to the puzzle posed by Evsey Domar regarding the absence of slavery in northern colonial regions like New England, where free labor obviously was scarce.[1] On one level, the puzzle was easy to solve; since they had no highly profitable staple export, New Englanders could not afford to own slaves. I was still left with a problem, however: explaining how these northerners managed to deal with the labor scarcity they so frequently deplored. I conceived the possibility of writing a coherent history of New England's preindustrial development around the theme of three successive adaptations: first, the English encounter with the frontier and their adjustment to the risks and costs of operating in an environment short of labor and capital; second, the passing of that frontier and the accommodations that resulted as productive wealth and manpower began to accumulate within the region; and third, the changes that were set in motion by the commercialization that began at the end of the eighteenth century. As a case study, this book describes these broad developments within a rather limited compass. For practical purposes I have limited myself to one particular region (Essex County), two significant occupations (fishing and farming), and that half of the population who left behind the vast majority of work-related records (men). My story has implications for other areas and different occupations, and it tries to remain sensitive to the issue of gender by not univer-

1. Evsey D. Domar, "The Causes of Slavery or Serfdom: A Hypothesis," *JEH*, XXX (1970), 30.

salizing from male behavior. Yet because it asks questions for which evidence is not easily forthcoming from all subsets of early American society, it focuses by necessity on two groups that are particularly well documented—the farmers and fishermen of Essex County. The single question that governs most of what will follow—who worked for whom and under what terms—is one about which historians of the colonial north might well be more precise. By trying to be careful about how I answer this question, I hope to suggest a way in which others, examining different regions, a variety of trades, and above all the other sex, can complement or contest my findings and arguments.

The other important influence on this book, wholly undreamt of when I began, has been the experience of living in Newfoundland. Perched not in central Canada, where I grew up, or in Princeton, where I was trained, but here on the easternmost fringe of the North American continent, New England looks different. Living in a society where industrialization has never happened, where chronic underemployment remains the rule, and where most people still have to cobble together a sufficiency from a wide variety of sources, the important question seems now to explain why the Puritan colonies developed at all. It brings me back to Andre Gunder Frank's call for a history of the New World where the northern United States and the "peculiarities" of its comparatively happy economic experience are not the yardstick but the exception in a broader story of economic change in which development is not assumed.[2] I join with other historians in trying to illustrate what can be gained when America is examined from the outside.

Reporting currency values in a book that covers early modern England, colonial Massachusetts, and nineteenth-century America is a complicated matter. I have tried to keep to the following guidelines. For English values (in Chapter 2), I have assumed sterling values throughout. For colonial Massachusetts (in Chapters 2–5), I have reported all values in their sterling equivalents (using John J. McCusker, *Money and Exchange in Europe and America, 1600–1775* [Chapel Hill, N.C., 1978], 138–142). For the post-Revolutionary period (in Chapter 6), I have presented all figures in dollars, assuming that between 1751 and 1775 £1 in Massachusetts Lawful

2. Andre Gunder Frank, *World Accumulation, 1492–1789* (New York, 1978), 192.

Money equaled $3.33. Wherever confusion might arise from this method, I have tried to address the problem in the footnotes. In a few cases, especially when citing contemporaries and modern historians, the standard used in the source was impossible to determine; here I have reported the money values as I found them recorded.

ACKNOWLEDGMENTS

Over the sixteen years since the research for this book began, I have accumulated a great many debts—some to individuals whose names I never learned, others to people whose names I cannot recall, and still others to people I know well but who are altogether too numerous to mention individually here. It is in the nature of publishing that authors get credit for work that others perform, and to all of them I would like to express my appreciation. They saved me from numerous errors; those flaws that remain are naturally my responsibility.

The project began as a doctoral dissertation at Princeton University under the direction of John Murrin. A model supervisor, he sparked my initial interest in early American history, went to bat for me when necessary, and above all demonstrated to me that humor, kindness, and good companionship are compatible with serious study. On a more formal level, I owe a debt to the various institutions that supported me through my graduate and postgraduate careers. For financial assistance, I would like to single out Princeton University, the Social Sciences and Humanities Research Council of Canada, the Mellon Foundation, the American Philosophical Society, the American Council of Learned Societies, and the Institute of Early American History and Culture. To the Institute, which awarded me a two-year postdoctoral fellowship in 1981–1983 and has sponsored my scholarly career in all sorts of informal ways since, I am especially grateful. The universities where I have taught during these years—the College of William and Mary, the University of Wyoming, Harvard University, and especially the Memorial University of Newfoundland—have all contributed in dozens of ways, large and small, to the production of this book. Their college libraries and interlibrary loan services helped immeasurably; their administrations often funded travel and student assistance when necessary; and the academic communities I encountered at each continually pushed me to improve my product.

I have used the resources of many libraries and archives in this study, including the Massachusetts State Archives, the British Public Record Office, the Probate Record Office and Registry of Deeds in Essex County, the Maritime History Archives at Memorial University, the Massachusetts Historical Society, the Baker Library of Harvard University, the Society for the Preservation of New England Antiquities, the Cape Ann Historical Association, the Beverly Historical Society, the Lynn Historical Society, the Wenham Historical Association and Museum, the Lynnfield Public Library, the Salem Public Library, and above all what used to be known as the Essex Institute but now calls itself the James Duncan Phillips Library of the Peabody Essex Museum. From the fall of 1978, when I was first introduced to the library's marvelous early American collection, up to the production of illustrations for the present book, successive generations of staff have been unstinting in their assistance. Eugenia Fountain, Prudence Backman, Richard Fyffe, Will La Moy, Jane Ward, Mary Fabiszewski, Nancy Heywood, and the remarkable Irene Norton are only a few of those who deserve mention. What is so extraordinary about the library is that it has never mattered who worked there; the standards of service and consideration—not just to me but to all the other patrons I observed around me—have never wavered.

The book publications department of the Institute of Early American History and Culture guided my manuscript to press with all the care for which it is justly known. Fredrika Teute performed an honest and thoughtful job of substantive editing; John McCusker, Stephen Innes, and especially John Brooke offered advice of their own on improving the manuscript; Gil Kelly coordinated the editorial process in such a way as to cause me a minimum of anxiety; Cynthia Carter Ayres with the assistance of the Institute's editorial apprentices did a sensitive and painstaking job of copy editing; and Ruth Vaughan transferred everything into final computer-readable form. Thanks also to the computer services staff at Memorial University for assisting me with the graphs and to Gary McManus of the Memorial University Cartographic Laboratory for supervising the preparation of maps 1 and 2.

Among the many scholars who lent me moral, practical, and intellectual help over the years, I would like to single out for special thanks the late Robert Harney, John Beattie, Len Rosenband, Robert Darnton, John

Gruenfelder, Marcus Rediker, Phil Morgan, Ed Ayres of Yorktown, Fred and Virginia Anderson, Skip Fischer, Jim Lemon, Vince Walsh, Jerry Bannister, and Rosemary Ommer. To Carol Hannauer, whose generosity, companionship, and high standards have accompanied my studies since their beginning, I am especially grateful. My mother, my sister, and my late father always encouraged me without question in the path I chose, and to them I acknowledge an even deeper debt.

No one, however, has contributed as much to this endeavor as my wife, Christine. Continually she offered me her research and editorial skills; particularly she helped me in the use of statistics and the presentation of evidence in tables and graphs; and above all, she lent me the power and attention of an unusually clear mind. All readers of this book are in her debt.

CONTENTS

ILLUSTRATIONS AND TABLES

SHORT TITLES AND ABBREVIATIONS

CSPC	W. Noel Sainsbury *et al.*, eds., *Calendar of State Papers, Colonial Series, America and West Indies*, 40 vols. (London, 1860–1939)
Essex Co. Court Recs.	George Francis Dow and Mary G. Thresher, eds., *Records and Files of the Quarterly Courts of Essex County, Massachusetts*, 9 vols. (Salem, Mass., 1911–1975)
Essex Co. Court Recs., Verbatim Transcriptions	Archie N. Frost, comp., *Verbatim Transcriptions of the Records of the Quarterly Courts of Essex County, Massachusetts, 1636–1694*, 57 vols. (Salem, Mass., 1939)
Essex Co. Prob. Recs.	Probate Records of Essex County, Massachusetts, Probate Record Office, Registry of Deeds and Probate Record Office Building, Salem, Mass.
Essex Co. Prob. Recs., BV	Essex County Probate Records, Bound Volumes, Probate Record Office, Registry of Deeds and Probate Record Office Building, Salem, Mass.
Essex Co. Prob. Recs.	George F. Dow, ed., *The Probate Records of Essex County, Massachusetts, 1635–1681*, 3 vols. (Salem, Mass., 1916–1920)
Essex Deeds	Essex County Deeds, Bound Transcriptions, vols. I–XX, Registry of Deeds and Probate Record Office Building, Salem, Mass.
Files ICCP	Files of the Essex County Inferior Court of Common Pleas, property of the Supreme Judicial Court, Division of Archives and Records Preservation, on deposit at the James Duncan Phillips Library, Peabody Essex Museum, Salem, Mass.

JDPL	James Duncan Phillips Library, Peabody Essex Museum, Salem, Mass.
Jefferson, "Report on Fisheries"	"Report on the American Fisheries by the Secretary of State," Feb. 1, 1791, in Julian P. Boyd *et al.*, eds., *The Papers of Thomas Jefferson* (Princeton, N.J., 1950–), XIX, 206–236
JEH	*Journal of Economic History*
Recs. of Mass. Bay	Nathaniel B. Shurtleff, ed., *Records of the Governor and Company of the Massachusetts Bay in New England*, 6 vols. in 5 (Boston, 1853–1854)
"Salem Town Records"	William P. Upham, ed., "Town Records of Salem, 1634–1659," Essex Institute, *Historical Collections*, IX (1868), 1–242
Trelawney Papers	James Phinney Baxter, ed., *The Trelawney Papers*, vol. III of Maine Historical Society, *Collections*, 2d Ser. (Portland, Me., 1884)
Winthrop, *History of New England*	James Kendall Hosmer, ed., *Winthrop's Journal: "History of New England," 1630–1649*, 2 vols., Original Narratives of Early American History (New York, 1908)
WMQ	*William and Mary Quarterly*

FARMERS AND FISHERMEN

A Map of Essex County, comp. James G. Carter (circa 1830).
Courtesy of the Peabody Essex Museum, Salem, Mass.

INTRODUCTION

Between 1630 and 1642, thousands of English men, women, and children crossed the Atlantic to build on its far western shores a new England. With the purpose of founding a society that would answer God's commandments and their human needs as English people more fully, they sold their homes in the old country, packed up their movable goods, and found passage to Massachusetts. Similar enough in geography to the land they were leaving behind that they might expect to support themselves in the English manner, this country was devoid of the people and problems that had made life in England so difficult. For twelve summers, shiploads of colonists disembarked in Boston harbor, thanked God for delivering them from the terrors of the ocean crossing, and turned to the practical problems of converting the wilderness that stretched before them into a home.[1]

Although most of the Puritan colonists were townspeople with trades, they moved to New England in search of propertied independence and fully expected to support themselves by working the soil. Much of the practical information they sought after they had waded ashore and found their bearings in Boston, therefore, pertained to the business of settling themselves on the land. Which towns possessed adequate soil and sufficient meadowland to provide fodder for their animals? Which were still admitting newcomers into the town proprietorship as legal inhabitants, and on what terms? Were some communities more likely than others to serve as peaceable homes with neighbors ready to "entertain each other in

1. See Virginia DeJohn Anderson, *New England's Generation: The Great Migration and the Formation of Society and Culture in the Seventeenth Century* (Cambridge, 1991).

brotherly affection"? With the best answers they could obtain to these and other questions, the new colonists moved on, usually within a year or two, fanning out northward and southward along the Atlantic coast and up the major river valleys to search out sites that answered their needs.[2]

A few thousand of these immigrants headed for the North Shore of Massachusetts, where they founded the original ten towns of Essex County (see map 1). Salem was the first: occupied in 1626 by planters who had abandoned the Dorchester Company project on Cape Ann, reinforced by fifty or sixty immigrants sent by the New England Company in 1628, the town was incorporated the following year. This community together with Lynn, founded next to Salem in 1631, constituted one hub of settlement in the southern reaches of the county. During the mid-1630s, another wave of colonists scouted out the fertile coastal plain that stretched from the base of Cape Ann northward to the mouth of the Merrimack River and founded the towns of Ipswich, Newbury, and Rowley. From this second cluster of settlements, other groups pushed up the Merrimack to plant Salisbury and Haverhill and north along the coast to found Hampton. With the incorporation of Gloucester on Cape Ann in 1642 and Andover across the Merrimack from Haverhill in 1646, the territory of Essex County was completely set off into towns.

Even then, of course, the region was far from wholly settled. The original town jurisdictions were large, and the founders generally built their first homes clustered about a town center close to the ocean or along a navigable waterway. Almost immediately the press of land-hungry house-holders—maturing children together with latecomers excluded from the first proprietorships—overwhelmed the limited supply of coastal and riverine land, causing many to cast their eyes toward the as yet unsettled upland of the county's interior. As early as 1638, Salem was granting home lots far enough from the harbor to prompt proposals for the establishment of three different villages within its bounds, and in 1643 the General Court recognized the initiative by ordering the incorporation of Wenham. The process repeated itself in every corner of the county throughout the remainder of the seventeenth century as settlers sought out undeveloped land and requested from town and colony the right to establish themselves into proprietorships. Manchester, Marblehead, and Beverly were

2. Anderson, *New England's Generation*, 31–32. Quotation is from John Winthrop, "A Model of Christian Charity" (1630), in Alan Heimert and Andrew Delbanco, eds., *The Puritans in America: A Narrative Anthology* (Cambridge, Mass., 1985), 91.

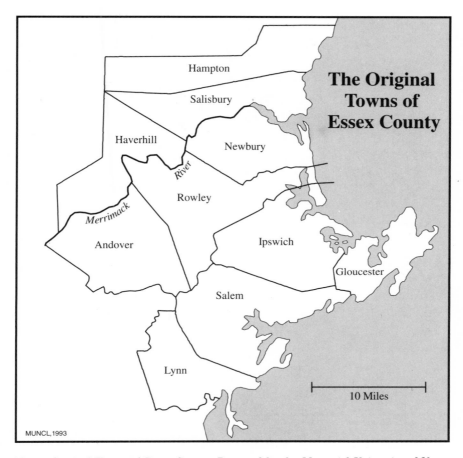

Map 1. Original Towns of Essex County. Prepared by the Memorial University of New-foundland Cartographic Laboratory

settled in the 1630s, then carved out of Salem and incorporated as town-ships between 1645 and 1668; the western corner of Ipswich became Topsfield in 1650; Amesbury separated from Salisbury in 1666; and Row-ley gave up its western lands to Bradford in 1675 and to Boxford in 1685 (see map 2). Cutting back forest, constructing farm buildings and fences, laying out land, and building roads: the conversion of Essex County from wilderness into settled farmland continued at a steady pace until the reserves of uncleared forest were finally exhausted in the eighteenth cen-tury.

The extraordinary process of colonization demanded everywhere an extraordinary application of human toil—far beyond what the settlers

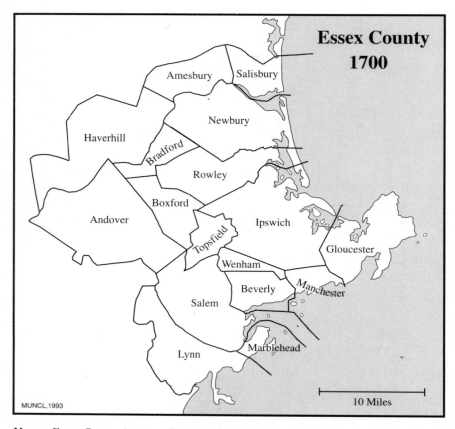

Essex County 1700

Amesbury
Salisbury
Newbury
Haverhill
Bradford
Rowley
Boxford
Andover
Ipswich
Topsfield
Gloucester
Wenham
Beverly
Manchester
Salem
Marblehead
Lynn

MUNCL,1993

10 Miles

Map 2. Essex County in 1700. Prepared by the Memorial University of Newfoundland Cartographic Laboratory

themselves were anxious to expend. The Puritans had the example of other colonies in the Americas, so they were undoubtedly familiar with the various ways their predecessors had dealt with the problem. The more astute among them grasped quickly an essential truth about organizing labor in the New World: whenever free men could acquire property to develop for themselves, they rarely wished to work for anyone else. Accordingly, those who needed help generally had to depend on those who were not free to share in the opportunities that the conquest and settlement of the continent presented.

The wide range of unfree labor systems that Europeans designed to exploit the New World was a testimony to human inventiveness. In the plantation economies of Brazil and the West Indies, where a valuable staple such as sugar could justify the cost and where there was no significant idle season, the system of preference was slavery. In regions with less dynamic staples, where planters could not afford to purchase slaves, as in the Chesapeake tobacco colonies of the early seventeenth century, indentured servitude prevailed. In the bureaucratic Spanish and Portuguese empires, owners of mines and haciendas enlisted state power to manage the labor supply directly through a regular draft of native labor, or repartimiento. Of course, the organization of production did not hinge on demand factors alone; conditions of labor supply were equally important. The attraction of slavery rested on the possibility and low cost of capturing Africans and transporting them across the Atlantic. Indentured servants were only to be found when times were hard enough in Europe to prompt young men and women to sell off several years of their lives in return for passage to the Americas. Repartimiento could work only where there remained Indian communities with manpower to tap. Yet these three systems shared the fact of legal bondage; when colonists could both afford and practically manage labor that was legally bound, this was the strategy of choice.[3]

Slaves and servants needed close supervision, however, and in some economies this was out of the question. Ranching and fishing, for example, usually required the successful hand to range over many miles of land and water far beyond the master's view. Under these conditions, provided that the profitability of the staple was high enough, estate owners and merchants normally dealt with the scarcity of labor by creating a clientele of dependent producers through the measured extension of credit. Debtors were never slaves; like those who indentured themselves into servitude, they chose their fate. Yet once in debt they were less than free to negotiate the terms on which they worked—especially in isolated regions where alternative employers were few. From the fishing outports of Newfoundland to the haciendas of New Spain, credit served an important function in recruiting and controlling help.[4]

3. The range of legal bondage systems across the New World is covered by John J. McCusker and Russell R. Menard, *The Economy of British America, 1607–1789* (Chapel Hill, N.C., 1985), 117–188, 236–245, and in the individual essays in Leslie Bethell, ed., *The Cambridge History of Latin America*, vol. II: *Colonial Latin America* (Cambridge, 1984), esp. 219–229.

4. Stephen Antler, "The Capitalist Underdevelopment of Nineteenth-Century Newfoundland," in Robert J. Brym and R. James Sacouman, eds., *Underdevelopment and Social Movements in Atlantic Canada* (Toronto, 1979), 191–192; James K. Hiller, "The Newfoundland Credit System: An Interpretation," in Rosemary E. Ommer, ed., *Merchant*

Nowhere did free labor disappear entirely. Especially in cases where individuals commanded special skills or in seasons when the demand for help was unusually heavy, labor was often engaged by the day or by the task. At Potosí in Peru, for example, Indians who had mastered the tricky business of smelting ultrarich silver ore always negotiated with the mine owners as free agents. Skilled workers throughout the New World built ships, erected farm buildings, tailored suits, and delivered babies for pay. In colonies like Pennsylvania where many householders depended on indentured help, a market in free labor emerged from the efforts of former servants to earn through waged employment the means to acquire property and escape their dependence. The less successful among them gradually formed a class of property-poor laborers on the model of the Old World.[5] Yet the broad contrast between Old World and New remains valid. Whereas over the centuries western Europe had been tending to organize production around manpower recruited by the year, week, or day, North and South America moved rapidly in the opposite direction, toward a range of labor regimes in which the freedom of those who worked for others was somehow circumscribed.

Where did New Englanders fit in this scheme of things? Like settlers throughout the New World, they began the project of colonial development short of the human help and productive equipment that the job required. Relative to the abundance of land and the task ahead, labor and capital were both in short supply. Slaves or indentured servants were possible sources of assistance, but could the Puritan settlers afford the cost? Without precious metals to plunder or tropical crops to raise and export, the only workable solutions would have to be inexpensive. The first half of this study examines the scarcity of labor and capital within the rural and maritime economies of Essex County and investigates the pro-

Credit and Labour Strategies in Historical Perspective (Fredericton, N.B., 1990), 86–101; Robert M. Lewis, "The Survival of the Planters' Fishery in Nineteenth and Twentieth Century Newfoundland," *ibid.*, 102–113; David A. Macdonald, "They Cannot Pay Us in Money: Newman and Company and the Supplying System in the Newfoundland Fishery, 1850–1884," *ibid.*, 114–128; Rosemary Ommer, *From Outpost to Outport: A Structural Analysis of the Jersey-Gaspé Cod Fishery, 1767–1886* (Montreal, 1991), chaps. 2, 5; Bethell, ed., *Colonial Latin America*, 153–188, 230–232; Chapter 3, below.

5. Bethell, ed., *Colonial Latin America*, 127; Paul G. E. Clemens and Lucy Simler, "Rural Labor and the Farm Household in Chester County, Pennsylvania, 1750–1820," in Stephen Innes, ed., *Work and Labor in Early America* (Chapel Hill, N.C., 1988), 106–143; Billy G. Smith, "The Vicissitudes of Fortune: The Careers of Laboring Men in Philadelphia, 1750–1800," *ibid.*, 221–251.

cess by which farmers and fishing merchants constructed labor systems adequate to their needs.

The second half of the book takes up the subsequent history of the county's socioeconomic maturation and tries to explain why the development strategies employed there and throughout New England served the region so well. During the first century and a half of settlement, there was nothing particular about the local economy to excite envy elsewhere. Throughout the New World colonies, Europeans were able to open the wilderness and raise its productivity to a high level in fairly short order—indeed, often with considerably more profit than the New Englanders could manage. For the most part, however, the benefits that settlers derived from learning the local environment, making initial improvements on the land, and exploiting that land were swiftly earned and rarely improved upon thereafter. In the wake of the advancing frontier the rate of economic growth per capita usually leveled off.[6] As long as untapped resources were waiting over the next hill or beyond the next headland to be mined, fished, cut, grazed, or brought under the plow, there was little advantage to developing already settled land or improving existing technology. Better, ran the general consensus, to employ capital in purchasing or parental authority in controlling a labor supply to capture and exploit new resources. Brazilian sugar planters thus preferred to purchase slaves for the clearing of new acreage rather than invest in draft animals, fertilizer, or farm equipment. Likewise, merchants in the Newfoundland fishery saw more to be gained by multiplying the number of boat crews they outfitted on credit than by building larger and more efficient vessels. The capital that colonists tied up in the control of their labor supply earned a handsome return, but it represented economic power that could not be used for other purposes. For this reason above others, the unfree labor practices so useful in tackling the wilderness and then operating developed lands and waters at high productivity generally failed to promote the linked development of supporting industries that was a feature of the ultimately more successful economies of western Europe.[7]

6. McCusker and Menard, *Economy of British America*, 60; Allan Kulikoff, *Tobacco and Slaves: The Development of Southern Cultures in the Chesapeake, 1680–1800* (Chapel Hill, N.C., 1986), 81–83; Gloria L. Main, *Tobacco Colony: Life in Early Maryland, 1650–1720* (Princeton, N.J., 1982), 95.

7. This argument is inspired in part by Gavin Wright, *The Political Economy of the Cotton South: Households, Markets, and Wealth in the Nineteenth Century* (New York, 1978), chaps. 3, 4.

Particularly in the more dynamic sectors of the early modern economy—ironworking, clothmaking, shipbuilding, and shipping itself—most parts of the New World lagged badly. West Indian planters clothed their slaves in skirts and drawers tailored out of blue cloth imported from England. Fishermen in the Gulf of St. Lawrence sent their hauls to market in ships owned in the Channel Islands. Burros hauled European ironwares into the hills of Peru—one of the richest mining areas of the world. One can overstate this dependency, for most colonial households, plantations, and haciendas made some effort to reduce their imports of European wares. But the greater truth remains that economic diversification with its attendant positive impact on regional per capita development rarely happened when high productivity staple production operated within reach of the frontier.[8]

Viewed in this light, the experience of Essex County, New England, and the American northeast was exceptional, for this corner of the New World eventually escaped the common colonial fate. Certainly, the earliest settlers there as elsewhere encountered shortages of manpower and productive wealth; and we shall see how they responded by structuring production in such a way that their reliance on free markets in capital and labor was minimized. Furthermore, on this frontier as on others, the lure of unexploited resources caused economic growth to proceed at first along extensive lines, with rapid settlement but little interest in further improvement.[9] What is striking about New England and the American northeast generally, however, is that the classic colonial pattern was outgrown. First in the maritime economy and later in the countryside, regional markets in capital and labor surfaced and the older extensive brand of growth gave way to more intensive development involving real gains in productivity and paving the way to industrialization.

To successfully search out and describe the historical relation between the maturation of New England's fishing and farming economies and the

8. Richard S. Dunn, *Sugar and Slaves: The Rise of the Planter Class in the English West Indies, 1624–1713* (Chapel Hill, N.C., 1972), 283–284; Bethell, ed., *Colonial Latin America*, 105n; Ommer, *Outpost to Outport*, chap. 6; Andre Gunder Frank, *Dependent Accumulation and Underdevelopment* (New York, 1979), 43–91.

9. Terry L. Anderson, "Economic Growth in Colonial New England: 'Statistical Renaissance,'" *JEH*, XXXIX (1979), 243–257; Gloria L. Main and Jackson T. Main, "Economic Growth and the Standard of Living in Southern New England, 1640–1774," *JEH*, XLVIII (1988), 36–45; Jackson Turner Main, *Society and Economy in Colonial Connecticut* (Princeton, N.J., 1985), 239; Chapter 2, below.

region's early transition to industrial capitalism requires that one take seriously both terms of the phrase *New England*. Like every other colonial project, this one began by being new. In the beginning, the founders were forced to alter their economic behavior in novel ways to cope with the unanticipated consequences of developing the frontier. More than most New World colonies, however, this one eventually succeeded in replicating many of the mother country's basic characteristics—by becoming English. One can easily take this argument too far; in significant particulars, clearly there was much to distinguish the new England from the old. But in its economic diversity, urbanization, institutional infrastructure, resident merchant class, and gradual development of efficient internal markets in capital and labor, New England achieved a structural similarity to the mother country that enabled it eventually to imitate England's industrial thrust. This book cannot tell that whole story. Instead, it takes two significant groups of male New Englanders—the farmers and fishermen of Essex County—and tries to reconstruct the social relations that governed their working lives between 1630 and 1850. First, it investigates the manner in which they restructured their economic ways in response to the exigencies of developing America's first frontier; then it charts the pattern by which the world they inhabited developed so as to make possible the industrial transformation of the nineteenth century.

Such a study, covering the history of so many people over so much time, cannot hope to be wholly inclusive. In fact, though the implications of its argument are broad, the compass of its research is narrow. In short, the book treats only the working lives of men in certain trades in a single county and confines itself to the single question: who worked for whom and under what terms? The decision to restrict the research to the social relations of production among men in two distinct lines of work imposes difficulties and creates opportunities to which the reader ought to be alerted.

A defining feature of this study is the long period it covers. Productive relations did not alter quickly in structure during preindustrial times, and measuring change of any sort demands that one take the long view. Even a hundred years may not be a sufficient span of time to place these developments in their proper perspective, and all too often this has caused historians to represent minor adaptations or changes in degree as revolutions in the very structure of society. The debate over the transition to capitalism in America, for example, has been plagued by this type of error. What were clearly the final stages in an extended process that began centuries earlier in Europe are often mistaken for the transformation itself.[10] At the same time, however, the decision to cover so broad an expanse of time imposes problems of its own. Most important, it leads one frequently to pass over specific events—especially political ones—and to ignore the real impact they had on the people of the day. The conflicts, both domestic and international, that arose from and intruded upon the working lives of farmers and fishermen receive short shrift in this book, even though such events obviously mattered deeply to the very people I am studying. Such is the cost of taking the long view, and I can only hope that my work will set the context of those political struggles in a more accurate light.

Why concentrate on farming and fishing? Partly my choice reflected the simple truth that in Essex County, those were the dominant trades. Until the arrival of industrialization, they constituted the economic core of every town within the county's bounds, save Salem and Newburyport. Indeed, farming and fishing are the only two occupations in which productive relations are consistently documented throughout the three centuries touched on in this study. More important, the task of measuring the impact of initial scarcity and subsequent accumulation of capital and labor on the county's economy demanded that I adopt a comparative perspective. The fishing industry imported from the West of England in the seventeenth century was already thoroughly capitalist in its productive relations; the agricultural system the colonists brought with them was still largely household based. Placing the two in a comparative light suggests a range of possible responses to the practical economic problems involved in building a new England in America.

To study productive relations seriously, one must catch working people in the act; this study is scrupulous in limiting itself to documented work experiences. It is a history of people who were working on an actual date in a known town at an identifiable task. The core of my research consists

10. It is impossible to explain the transition to capitalism in America without reference to the origins of that change in late medieval and early modern Europe. See Stephen Innes, "Fulfilling John Smith's Vision: Work and Labor in Early America," in Innes, ed., *Work and Labor in Early America*, 3–10; Allan Kulikoff, "The Transition to Capitalism in Rural America," *WMQ*, 3d Ser., XLVI (1989), 124–125, 133–134; Daniel Vickers, "Competency and Competition: Economic Culture in Early America," *WMQ*, 3d Ser., XLVII (1990), 3–29; and James T. Lemon, "Early Americans and Their Social Environment," *Journal of Historical Geography*, VI (1980), 118–119.

sources

of several thousand descriptions, drawn from journals, account books, and legal documents, of men and boys performing stretches of farming and fishing labor. Around these documented work experiences, usually recorded in terse entries, I have tried to paint in the background—adding details of the age, economic status, ethnicity, family, social origin, and future careers of the participants. This tack was chosen out of a suspicion, borne out by research, that men might perform different sorts of work under different terms of employment at different points in their lives. A man identified as a fisherman at the time of his death might not have worked on the deep for thirty years; another who termed himself a farmer might have been a wheelwright in earlier life; still another might call himself a shoemaker when in fact he spent every second summer handlining for cod on the Grand Banks. It is hoped that by being careful about describing the context in which farming and fishing labor took place, we can learn more about it.

The decision to begin not with parents, children, landowners, taxpayers, or inventoried decedents but with those caught in the act of physical labor required that I focus on a crowd of New Englanders who have never attracted much attention—less out of willful indifference than because so little is known about them. Most came to my notice when the work they performed was recorded in a farmer's accounts, when they chose to outfit themselves for a summer's fishing with a merchant whose records have survived, or when they passed through the background of a deposition. Discovering anything certain about these people involved complexities of record linkage that frequently defeated me. Sometimes they were simply too poor, too young, or too transient to make an impact on the record system of the county. In other cases they bore common names, shared by at least one other person around town, that prevented me from linking them with any certainty to other sources. Handling data of this sort places any historian in a difficult position. Naturally, one should not base one's findings on mistaken identities, yet neither should one systematically exclude certain social types just because they are difficult to identify. There is no simple solution to this problem, but I tried always to err on the side of caution, the net consequence of which was to reduce from many thousands to several hundreds the effective size of the fishing and farming populations I actually analyzed. The relatively small data base evident in the tables and notes signifies care, and not haste, in method.

Readers who expect to find a systematic portrayal of work and economic life in Essex County are bound to be disappointed. The decision to

cover an entire county over more than two centuries forced me to economize somewhere, and here I was guided by the nature of my sources. The
men and boys who worked as farmers and fishermen constitute my subject of study largely because their history is sufficiently documented to
answer the questions posed. One could well address the same questions
to other occupations—shipwrights, sawyers, shoemakers, housewives, or
maidservants—and certainly each has a history of productive labor that
matters every bit as much as the one told here. At different times I considered incorporating all of these into the study but drew back ultimately on
the grounds of insufficient evidence. Work experiences involving women
or craftsmen did not emerge in sufficient quantity, nor could their context
be determined in sufficient detail to enable me to say much about them
that is statistically significant. The result is an interpretation of two masculine lines of work that tries both to recognize their occupational and
gendered specificity and to advance hypotheses that might be extended by
other historians to as yet untested social groups.

In no way, therefore, does this book attempt to provide a complete
social history. Indeed, it focuses on what probably is the most thoroughly
studied county in all of early American history, precisely because so much
of that history has been written. Many of the farmers and fishermen
investigated here have already surfaced as immigrants, church members,
landowners, taxpayers, householders, or witches in other books; the historian of Essex County is fortunate to be able to build on this foundation of
earlier research. These men and boys are reexamined here because the
working lives that consumed most of their time and energy have usually
been taken for granted. Michael Walzer has written that Puritans found in
work "the primary and elemental form of social discipline, the key to
order, and the foundation of all further morality."[11] The social history of
New England looks different when work is privileged, as every Puritan
knew it ought to be.

11. Michael Walzer, *The Revolution of the Saints: A Study in the Origins of Radical
Politics* (Cambridge, Mass., 1965), 211.

IMPROVING
THE LORD'S GARDEN

The whole earth is the Lord's garden and he hath given it to the sons of men, with a general condition, Genesis 1:28, *increase and multiply, replenish the earth and subdue it*, which was again renewed to Noah. The end is double moral and natural, that man might enjoy the fruits of the earth and God might have his due glory from the creature—why then should we stand here striving for places of habitation . . . and in the mean time suffer a whole continent, as fruitful and convenient for the use of man, to lie waste without any improvement?—JOHN WINTHROP, 1629

Improving the Lord's garden: with these words John Winthrop reminded himself that the Puritan colonization of Massachusetts Bay was a project of human labor in which spiritual and material ends were conjoined. The construction of a new England on the far side of the Atlantic would have to honor this double purpose. But how exactly did the prospective settlers envision the natural and moral ends of human toil? Certainly, they worried about how their lives would be ordered in the days to come. While they reflected openly about the economic morality and the organization of work proper to a Christian commonwealth, they ruminated in silence on the ambitions they harbored for themselves and their families. Such aspirations, along with the relations of production and exchange that were their natural companions, may be termed an economic culture. A complex of values and behavior, it was born in England and carried to America in the Great Migration.

goals of the people

No element of this culture mattered more to the development of New England than the ambition of most working men to establish themselves and their offspring in comfortable independence. In an age of nascent capitalism when the fates of households hung as never before on their success or failure in the market, it was a natural concern. Comfortable independence was chiefly a masculine ideal. Mothers and daughters on both sides of the Atlantic certainly contributed to and shared in whatever economic well-being a family might enjoy. Yet because men of the seventeenth century defined independence in such a way as to exclude women, the latter may well have felt ambivalent about the pursuit of something they could never fully enjoy. To understand the encounter between immigrant Englishmen and the frontier garden they intended to improve, we must first investigate the value men placed on the ideal of comfortable independence or, in the language of the day, competency.

COMPETENCY

Most householders who moved to Massachusetts in the 1630s and 1640s had been accustomed to life in the middle ranks of English society. Although laborers and aristocrats were included in their numbers, the converted were chiefly distinguished not by extremes of wealth but by their standing as propertied producers. Judging by passenger lists of the 1630s, the majority were craftsmen and farmers of middle age and moderate prosperity. Close to 60 percent of all settlers in New England came from homes well enough off to employ servants, and many of the rest belonged to families so large that servants were unnecessary. That so many could afford the costs of freight and passage—about £25 sterling a family—and arrive in New England under no indenture binding them to servitude marked them further as men of some property. Weavers, carpenters, husbandmen, and others combined skilled training and hard work with the management of property to enable their families to live in a modicum of comfort.[1]

More than most of their countrymen these householders could claim a measure of independence: the ability to employ themselves and their families relatively free of outside control. They possessed sufficient skill and property to ensure that neither they nor their spouses regularly had to look abroad for employment; they could usually launch their offspring into life with something of an inheritance or at least an apprenticeship in a useful and rewarding craft; and they could usually escape the worst effects of hard times and the enclosure of agricultural lands, which in the early seventeenth century had scattered many of the poorer sort across England in search of work. Independent householders were not self-sufficient; indeed, they depended on commercial production to assemble cash and property with which to endow their children. But they were self-employed. Most could approach their neighbors for the exchange of goods and services on an equal footing, because for the basic opportunity to earn a living throughout the working hours that dominated life they depended on nobody.[2]

Although actual independence was not a common lot in seventeenth-century England, it retained power as an ideal—not just to the Puritans but among working people in general. In the franchise requirement of forty shillings freehold, it remained central to political power and responsibility. "Day labourers," Sir Thomas Smith had observed in 1565, "have no voice nor authority in our commonwealth, and no account is made of

1. Virginia DeJohn Anderson, *New England's Generation: The Great Migration and the Formation of Society and Culture in the Seventeenth Century* (Cambridge, 1991), 31–34, 61–62. Of 205 settlers who embarked on one of three voyages to New England from Sandwich and Great Yarmouth, 125 belonged to families who owned servants; see Charles Boardman Jewson, ed., "Transcript of Three Registers of Passengers from Great Yarmouth to Holland and New England, 1637–1639," Norfolk Record Society, *Publications*, XXV (1954), and Eben Putnam, ed., "Two Early Passenger Lists, 1635–1637," *New England Historical and Genealogical Register*, LXXV (1921), 217–226. On the social standing of English Puritans, see David Underdown, *Revel, Riot, and Rebellion: Popular Politics and Culture in England, 1603–1660* (Oxford, 1985), 42.

2. Peter Laslett, *The World We Have Lost: England before the Industrial Age*, 2d ed. (New York, 1971), 45–47; Keith Wrightson, *English Society, 1580–1680* (London, 1982), 31–36, 134–139. An interesting description of the meaning of independence to one particular Londoner can be found in Paul S. Seaver, *Wallington's World: A Puritan Artisan in Seventeenth-Century London* (Stanford, Calif., 1985), 76–78, 115–116.

them but only to be ruled." In their own towns and villages Englishmen ranked themselves similarly by their ability to employ themselves. The husbandman stood midway up the social ladder between the laborer below and the yeoman above, according to Robert Reyce of Suffolk, because "though hee thriveth ordinarily well, yett he laboreth much." The necessity of seeking work outside the home for a certain portion of the year situated him on a particular rung within the community. Independence was thus a matter of degree. A few individuals possessed enough property to be entirely self-employed, and on many more the stigma of wage labor rested the year round. The majority of householders, however, were situated along a fine hierarchy in between. Although the pattern of wealth holding was markedly more attenuated in 1630 than it had been a century before, the producing ranks of English society can more usefully be envisioned as a spectrum of wealth and power rather than as a system of distinct classes. Even the question of property was never a matter of absolutes: a few family heads owned the means of production outright, but most gained access to lands or raw materials either by lease or on credit. The terms of such agreements ate in various ways into the freedom of householders to manage their own affairs, and these imposed further qualifications on their relative status. The greater his ability to labor for himself, however, the further a propertied English householder was distanced from the "rascabilitie of the popular."[3]

Skill and capital were important to the English understanding of independence, but landownership was the key. Trade and manufacture may have supported a growing proportion of the population in the seventeenth century and provided the most obvious route to acquiring new wealth; still, these fields of enterprise lacked the historic prestige and political privileges attached to land. The greatest estates in the country were still those of the landed aristocracy; Parliament was overwhelmingly a rural

3. Sir Thomas Smith, *De Republica Anglorum* (1565), quoted in Christopher Hill, *Change and Continuity in Seventeenth-Century England* (London, 1974), 224; Mildred Campbell, *The English Yeoman under Elizabeth and the Early Stuarts* (New Haven, Conn., 1942), 27–32 (Robert Reyce, *Breviary of Suffolk* [1618], quoted on p. 31); C. W. Chalklin, *Seventeenth-Century Kent: A Social and Economic History* (London, 1965), 230–245; Alan Everitt, "Farm Labourers," in Joan Thirsk, ed., *The Agrarian History of England and Wales*, vol. IV: *1500–1640* (Cambridge, 1967), 397; Margaret Spufford, *Contrasting Communities: English Villagers in the Sixteenth and Seventeenth Centuries* (Cambridge, 1974), 37–39; David Levine, *Reproducing Families: The Political Economy of English Population History* (Cambridge, 1987), 86–87; Underdown, *Revel, Riot, and Rebellion*, 24–28.

and landed institution; and in spite of their commercial concerns and a willingness to apprentice younger sons into the more prestigious trades, the gentry still defined themselves primarily by the tenure of manors and the accompanying political and military obligations. Working people, too, judged land to be the soundest foundation of independence. Positions of local influence on juries and vestries—presumably awarded to those considered first among local freemen—were much more commonly filled by farmers than by craftsmen. Obviously this was less true in the larger urban centers, but considering the country as a whole, William Harrison observed in 1577 that the fundamental line dividing those of sufficient independence to play a role in governance from those with "neither voice nor authority in the commonwealth" was the ownership of land.[4]

Although true yeoman status was beyond the means of most, some small measure of economic independence was generally within plausible reach, and working Englishmen considered the pursuit or protection of this status to be a central organizing principle of economic life. Boys went out to service in their teenage years so that they might begin saving early on toward the acquisition of productive wealth, upon which households of their own could later be established. As young men, they delayed marriage until their late twenties in the hope of accumulating the means to protect their families-to-be as far as possible from having to look abroad for work. Later in life, they sought to prevent their posterity from that fate by acquiring lands and passing them on to their sons in units large enough to guarantee them a living. If their access to productive property was rooted in traditional rights that were under attack, they might well go to law or even take the law into their own hands to protect whatever standard of independence these guaranteed. All such strategies testify to the truth that throughout those ranks of English society where physical labor was a necessity, personal status hung to a large extent on possessing the means of self-employment. Thus Edward Johnson could promote the quality of life in New England to readers back home by pointing out that there were few "Towns in the Country, but the poorest person in them hath a house and land of his own, and bread of his own growing."[5]

4. William Harrison, *The Description of England*, ed. George Edelen (Ithaca, N.Y., 1968), 118. See generally *ibid.*, 115–121; and Wrightson, *English Society*, 31–37.

5. Wrightson, *English Society*, 67–70, 111–112, 173–179; Ann Kussmaul, *Servants in Husbandry in Early Modern England* (Cambridge, 1981); Levine, *Reproducing Families*,

The property that successful English householders possessed conveyed more than independence; it also implied a degree of material well-being. John Winthrop made precisely this point when he observed that among his English countrymen the better sort of people were distinguished by their capacity "to live comfortably by theire owne meanes duely improved."[6] One can certainly make an analytic distinction between independence and comfort, but in a preindustrial economy where regular paid employment the year round was difficult to come by, control over the means of production provided the best assurance of both. Seventeenth-century writers were careful not to promote materialism too vigorously, and Puritans especially believed that covetousness was to be denounced or suppressed, not baldly asserted. In their hearts, however, even the godly were prone to the attractions of wealth. In 1634, William Wood chose to emphasize the colonists' satisfaction with basic necessities, but this did not preclude him from observing also their taste for good wines, fine cloth, glass windowpanes, housewares of pewter and brass, and "all kinds of grocery wares." When Francis Higginson advised his English friends that planters in New England would need "meal for bread, malt for drink, woolen and linen cloth, and leather for shoes, and all manner of carpenter's tools, and a good deal of iron and steel to make nails and locks for houses, and furniture for plows and carts, and glass for windows," he also had in mind a sense of legitimate prosperity.[7]

As ideals, material comfort and independence were equally imprecise. Every householder defined them within an understanding of realistic possibilities that was itself a product of family history. The upwardly mobile yeoman thus had far more demanding standards for an acceptable farmholding than did the poor husbandman struggling to make ends meet and to settle his children on lands that even he found barely sufficient. Even within individual households these standards could vary, over lifetimes or from year to year, as family fortunes rose and fell. They were not infinitely expandable, for even the most ambitious and successful house-

75–88; J. Franklin Jameson, ed., *Johnson's Wonder-Working Providence, 1628–1651*, Original Narratives of Early American History (New York, 1910), 210.

6. John Winthrop, "A Modell of Christian Charity," *Winthrop Papers*, 5 vols. (Boston, 1929–1947), II, 283.

7. William Wood, *New England's Prospect*, ed. Alden T. Vaughan (Amherst, Mass., 1977), 68, 71–72; Francis Higginson to his friends at Leicester, July 1629, in Everett Emerson, ed., *Letters from New England: The Massachusetts Bay Colony, 1629–1638* (Amherst, Mass., 1976), 27.

holder normally reached a point in life when his thirst for property fell prey to diminishing psychic returns. Nor could standards be lowered below the point where they described at least some element of control over one's working life, if only a few rights in the commons. Although material comfort and independence were never strictly definable as practical ideals, this did not make them any less real—just humanly variable.

The pursuit of comfortable independence was mostly a family affair. Marriage was, in the words of William Perkins, "the foundation and seminary of all other sorts and kinds of life in the commonwealth and in the church." It may be true, as Alan Macfarlane has argued, that individuals could legally dispose of their property, seek out work, and move about the country as they wished. In practice, however, householders and their families normally chose to organize their working lives around collective strategies. The marital cooperation that divided chores and responsibilities between husband and wife was based on this principle, as was the patriarchal authority that made men the stewards of the households they had helped to form. Necessity often forced children in particular to fend for themselves as individuals—entering service, going to sea, or heading off to London—but this was primarily a mark of their parents' inability to support them at home. Middling householders of the sort that dominated the Great Migration took pride in their ability to protect their offspring from such dangerous courses. Not everyone in the family shared equally in the rewards of competency, for fathers and favored sons obviously gained the most. But to the degree that even women and children shared in the fruits of a household's overall achievements, competency had an undeniably collective family dimension.[8]

To those of Puritan leanings, the idea that householders could legitimately aspire to comfortable independence was doubly significant. Not only did it square with their human desires, but it also seemed to answer the commands of Scripture. "God chargeth the master of the family with all in the family," read one religious tract, and it surely followed that

8. William Perkins quoted in Wrightson, *English Society*, 67; Alan Macfarlane, *The Origins of English Individualism* (New York, 1978), chap. 3. Macfarlane emphasizes the extremes of individualist behavior (e.g., disinheritance) that the law tolerated, but he ignores the family obligations that customarily prevailed. See Lloyd Bonfield, "Normative Rules and Property Transmission: Reflections on the Link between Family and Inheritance in Early Modern England," in Lloyd Bonfield, Richard M. Smith, and Keith Wrightson, eds., *The World We Have Gained: Histories of Population and Social Structure* (Oxford, 1986), 155–176.

householders ought to possess the means to assure those under their responsibility a settled and orderly life. Reformed preachers and their lay brethren equally understood that the household was society's chief disciplinary tool, and insofar as piety depended on sustained instruction, family government was basic to its growth. The swelling throng of vagrants and beggars, "wild creatures, ruffians, vagabonds, Cains and the like," who seemed to dwell in undisciplined and sinful poverty, demonstrated to the satisfaction of Puritan commentators that godliness prospered best in settled families of sufficient estate. "When men will live as they list, without any over them, and unfit to rule themselves, I much doubt whether this be according to God," wrote Thomas Shepard. Relations of economic dependency were divinely ordained and socially necessary, but they worked to the profit of society only when confined within the household. There under a watchful eye, observed the governors of the Massachusetts Bay Company in 1629, "disorders may be prevented, and ill weeds nipt before they take too great a head." Excessive riches could be just as dangerous, as the spiritually sorry state of the English aristocracy proved only too well. The ungodly state of the plantation colonies confirmed the same truth. As John White of Dorchester explained, "If men desire to have a people degenerate speedily, and to corrupt their mindes and bodies too, and besides to tole-in theeves and spoilers from abroad; let them secke a rich soile, that brings in much with little labour." "Nothing," he concluded, "sorts better with Piety then Compete[n]cy."[9]

The ideal of competency took ship with the Puritan emigrants and disembarked in America. They were willing to chance their removal to the wilderness only on the promise of "land and means of livelihood," which the founders had extended to all comers of good quality.[10] As practical people, the Puritans organized systems of landholding that rewarded

9. John Dod and Robert Cleaver, *A Plain and Familiar Exposition of the Ten Commandments*, 19th ed. (1662), and Richard Sibbes, *The Returning Backslider* (1639), quoted in Christopher Hill, *Society and Puritanism in Pre-Revolutionary England* (London, 1969), 443, 472; John Albro, ed., *The Works of Thomas Shepard*, 3 vols. (Boston, 1853; reprint ed., New York, 1967), III, 350; *Recs. of Mass. Bay*, I, 397; John White, *The Planter's Plea* (London, 1630), in Peter Force, comp., *Tracts and Other Papers, Relating Principally to the Origin, Settlement, and Progress of the Colonies in North America, from the Discovery of the Country to the Year 1776*, 4 vols. (Washington, D.C., 1836–1846), II, 18; Anderson, *New England's Generation*, chap. 4, deals with this issue in more detail.

10. Richard Saltonstall to Emmanuel Downing, Feb. 4, 1631, in Emerson, ed., *Letters from New England*, 92.

those who bore the initial costs and labors of town founding and reaped dividends in the form of subsequent land divisions. Yet among an immigrant population that counted so many of moderate wealth, this was not a recipe for marked inequality. Few early town proprietorships were so oligarchical as to exclude the majority of householders.[11] In most farming settlements the majority of first inhabitants thus could expect to receive a house lot of several acres, as much again in the fields and marshes beyond, perhaps 20 to 50 acres more within the first decade, and double or triple that amount if they settled permanently.[12] In port towns, where land was less plentiful but opportunities for tradesmen greater, the land divisions were smaller, but even among the inhabitants of Boston and Salem house lots and gardens remained the rule into the middle of the century.[13] Those who were not proprietors in any town and not eligible to participate in regular land divisions were obviously not as well situated, but even they were free to apply for individual grants of land, transactions that constituted much of town business in the earliest decades.[14]

11. John Frederick Martin, *Profits in the Wilderness: Entrepreneurship and the Founding of New England Towns in the Seventeenth Century* (Chapel Hill, N.C., 1991). In chap. 6, Martin argues for the exclusiveness of town proprietorships and the inequality of land-ownership, largely on the basis of the discrepancy between the number of proprietors and the number of resident householders in the towns that he studied. Granting this reality, it is important not to overstate the case. In the towns for which Martin presents evidence (Hartford, Dedham, Watertown, and Ipswich), close to or sometimes more than half of the householding population were proprietors. These proportions were especially high when towns were in the process of being founded. In 30 of the 63 towns he studied, Martin reports no evidence of residents being excluded from the proprietorship during the first decade of settlement. See *ibid.*, appendix 6.

12. David Grayson Allen, *In English Ways: The Movement of Societies and the Transferal of English Local Law and Custom to Massachusetts Bay in the Seventeenth Century* (Chapel Hill, N.C., 1981), 31–32, 65, 111, 127–129; Kenneth A. Lockridge, *A New England Town, the First Hundred Years: Dedham, Massachusetts, 1636–1736* (New York, 1970), 71; Philip J. Greven, Jr., *Four Generations: Population, Land, and Family in Colonial Andover, Massachusetts* (Ithaca, N.Y., 1970), 46, 51, 58–59, 59n; Sumner Chilton Powell, *Puritan Village: The Formation of a New England Town* (Middletown, Conn., 1963), 229–232; Douglas R. McManis, *Colonial New England: A Historical Geography* (New York, 1975), 55.

13. Darrett B. Rutman, *Winthrop's Boston: Portrait of a Puritan Town, 1630–1649* (Chapel Hill, N.C., 1965), 195; Richard P. Gildrie, *Salem, Massachusetts, 1626–1683: A Covenant Community* (Charlottesville, Va., 1975), 60.

14. Martin, *Profits in the Wilderness*, 199–200. The claim that town records were mostly concerned with the granting of land from the time of settlement applies to Salem up to the mid-1650s, Topsfield to about 1675, and Manchester to about 1690. See "Salem Town

The founders' decision to promote the distribution of land to those of sufficient means resulted in the dispersal of the early inhabitants across a wide expanse of territory. William Bradford had already noted the "scattering" tendency of English settlers in Plymouth Colony, but the experience of Massachusetts proved just as telling.[15] The town of Lynn, observed Edward Johnson, was "but thin of Houses, the people mostly inclining to Husbandry, have built many Farmes remote there." In Newbury and Salisbury, homesteads were "very scattering" and "much distanced" from one another. Only a few years after its foundation, Haverhill was already stretched out along ten miles of the Merrimack River, "there being an over-weaning desire in most men after Medow land."[16] Even towns composed originally of clustered dwellings soon experienced the same inclination to disperse.[17]

It would be wrong to assume that town and colony authorities were entirely pleased with this development. William Bradford, for one, feared that drawing the community of settlers apart might be "the ruin of New England, at least of the churches of God there."[18] Yet for all the public discussion over the dangers of dispersal, the arm of government did more to facilitate than to prevent it. Occasionally, as in the case of Salem Village, an outlying precinct of the town of Salem, colonial authorities might refuse a grant of town status to petitioners from isolated parts. Within communities, inhabitants who debated the proper method of land division may have temporarily halted the formation of new farms in outlying areas.[19] Most of the time, however, the colony threw up no practical barriers to settlers intent on parceling out the wilderness into new pro-

Records"; George Francis Dow, ed., *Town Records of Topsfield, Massachusetts, 1659–1778*, 2 vols. (Topsfield, Mass., 1917–1920), I, 1–18; and *Town Records of Manchester, from the Earliest Grants of Land, 1636, when a Portion of Salem, until 1736* (Salem, Mass., 1889), 1–43.

15. William Bradford, *Of Plymouth Plantation, 1620–1647*, ed. Samuel Eliot Morison (New York, 1952), 253.

16. Jameson, ed., *Johnson's Wonder-Working Providence*, 73, 99, 189–190, 234–235.

17. James T. Lemon, "Spatial Order: Households in Local Communities and Regions," in Jack P. Greene and J. R. Pole, eds., *Colonial British America: Essays in the New History of the Early Modern Era* (Baltimore, 1984), 92–94.

18. Bradford, *Of Plymouth Plantation*, 254. Peter N. Carroll, *Puritanism and the Wilderness: The Intellectual Significance of the New England Frontier, 1629–1700* (New York, 1969), contains the most thorough treatment of this sentiment.

19. Paul Boyer and Stephen Nissenbaum, *Salem Possessed: The Social Origins of Witchcraft* (Cambridge, Mass., 1974), 39–45; Powell, *Puritan Village*, 119–123.

prietorships. Even the migration of numerous families to distant Connecticut in the mid-1630s, though certainly troubling to the Puritan leadership, never met with official obstruction. The economic fact "that all towns in the bay began [as early as 1635] to be much straitened by their own nearness to one another" persuaded even a reluctant Winthrop that the removal was justified. The "want of accomodation for their cattle" had created "a strong bent . . . to remove thither"; to resist an Englishman's preference for a competent living was neither possible nor proper.[20]

COMMERCE

Outside of the privileged classes no English householder could hope to acquire his reasonable share of life's amenities or to settle all his children in independent circumstances without raising or manufacturing a surplus to sell. In fact, dealing for profit was a wholly ingrained habit among propertied Englishmen of the day. By the early seventeenth century, the economy of the mother country was moving as never before to the rhythm of unseen market forces assembled from the millions of privately and freely transacted bargaining decisions of her inhabitants. A householder could now look almost anywhere for help, apart from certain well-organized portions of the craft economy, at wages that he was free within understood limits to negotiate. He could lease land and buildings throughout the country for rents that altered with each renewal. He could exchange commodities with a growing crowd of private dealers at prices that were settled in accordance with supply and demand. And with collateral, he could borrow money for any of these purposes at fluctuating but generally falling rates of interest. England was not yet a capitalist country in the fullest sense of the word, for a great many people were still petty producers for at least a portion of their lives and the accumulation of productive wealth was still limited by the human, and therefore finite, needs of those who controlled the basic units of production. Yet with the number of rural and urban laborers on the rise, a national commodity market in formation, and a system of land tenure based increasingly upon private rights, it was not entirely a pre-capitalist society either.[21]

20. Winthrop, *History of New England*, I, 132, 151; Carroll, *Puritanism and the Wilderness*, 144; Stephen Foster, *Their Solitary Way: The Puritan Social Ethic in the First Century of Settlement in New England* (New Haven, Conn., 1971), 50–51.

21. On the mobility of labor, see Kussmaul, *Servants in Husbandry*, 49–67; Wrightson, *English Society*, 41–44; Richard Lachmann, *From Manor to Market: Structural Change in*

As one slid down the scale of economic independence, free markets met with less enthusiasm and the demand for regulation grew. At these social levels, the tradition of moral economy was still much in evidence, supported by a host of ancient arguments and the very real interests of those who stood to suffer in a world of open competition. The marketplace clearly worked best for individuals with the economic strength to withstand its storms. For those without—the small craftsmen, wage laborers, and poor husbandmen with little land or capital—the regulation of prices, the maintenance of commons rights, and other customary privileges antithetical to free markets were often vital to whatever remnants of independence or scanty creature comforts they hoped to conserve. The property-poor and their supporters repeatedly cried out for restrictions on the principle of economic freedom, believing it to be the guise that permitted the economically powerful to pursue selfish ends at the expense of the weak. Naturally the poor attempted whenever they could to employ market opportunities to their own advantage—when bread prices fell or when the possibility of supplementing the cottage economy by spinning or woodcutting presented itself. In general, however, those poor in property were less than enthusiastic about the spread of market relations.[22]

If the principle of the regulated economy survived in the mother country because so many householders depended on it to make ends meet, then it was unlikely to flourish in a New World colony where access to resources was easier. Although the founders of New England certainly believed in distinctions of wealth, they had also taken steps to ensure that all settling families could be economically independent, and to people in such secure circumstances the operations of the free market held relatively little danger. Since even the wealthy and ill intentioned rarely could cause serious trouble for a householder who possessed the means of self-

England, 1536–1640 (Madison, Wis., 1987), 138–141; and Stella Kramer, *The English Craft Gilds: Studies in Their Progress and Decline* (New York, 1927), 101–138. On leasing, see Peter Bowden, "Agricultural Prices, Farm Profits, and Rents," in Thirsk, ed., *Agrarian History*, IV, 674–694. On markets, see Alan Everitt, "The Marketing of Agricultural Produce," *ibid.*, 466–592. On borrowing, see Gordon Batho, "Landlords in England," *ibid.*, 299–301. On financial markets, see Sidney Homer, *A History of Interest Rates* (New Brunswick, N.J., 1977), 126–127, 133–134, 142.

22. Everitt, "Farm Labourers," in Thirsk, ed., *Agrarian History*, IV, 403–409, 458–465; Robert W. Malcolmson, *Life and Labour in England, 1700–1780* (London, 1981), 23–35; Wrightson, *English Society*, 173–179; Seaver, *Wallington's World*, 113–117; Richard L. Greaves, *Society and Religion in Elizabethan England* (Minneapolis, Minn., 1981), 622–628.

employment, the rationale for restrictions disappeared. The godly could be sharp dealers, certainly, but they seldom dealt with one another across a social gulf so wide that either party would insist upon public protection.

It was in the expectation of relative economic freedom, therefore, that the colonists in Massachusetts Bay set about breaking the land and improving their estates. "That this Wilderness should turn a mart for Merchants," as Edward Johnson phrased it, was evidence of God's providence, but it also described exactly the immigrants' plans. When Johnson cataloged the early settlements of the colony, he used as a key measure of suitability their access to markets. Whereas Malden was "the more comfortable for habitation" because of its "neerness to the chief Market Towns," Andover occupied a more questionable site because of its "remoteness . . . from Towns of trade . . . [inconveniencing] the planters, who are inforced to carry their corn far to market." Even Dedham, whose founders had stated the spiritual purpose of their settlement in the most uncompromising terms, sat near enough to Boston that the lure of "coyne and commodities" commonly drew its inhabitants "to make many a long walk." As Winthrop concluded in 1640 with a mixture of realism and regret, it was "the common rule that most men walked by in all their commerce, to buy as cheap as they could, and to sell as dear."[23]

That public policy placed few encumbrances on trading in land and commodities, historians generally admit. By ordering that property transactions be recorded, providing for swift civil justice in the courts, establishing market days in the major towns, and refraining except in rare instances from price regulation, the founders gave practical support to the acquisitive instincts of the colonists and their belief in the justice of the marketplace.[24] The General Court did fine Robert Keayne in 1639 for taking *excessive* profits; however, the special animus against this particular Boston merchant arose not from the idea of profit (legitimized by the colony in several orders) but from his reputation as a "hard dealer" and a "Cormorant" who preyed on those weaker than he.[25] The deputies singled

23. Jameson, ed., *Johnson's Wonder-Working Providence*, 179, 247, 249, 250; Lockridge, *New England Town*, 4–7; Winthrop, *History of New England*, II, 20.

24. *Recs. of Mass. Bay*, I, 113, 127, 169, 306–307, 325–326. Richard B. Morris, *Government and Labor in Early America* (New York, 1946), 55–84, lists several examples of price regulation in early New England, but I am more impressed by their short duration and scattered quality.

25. *Recs. of Mass. Bay*, I, 111, 142, 159–160; Winthrop, *History of New England*, II, 65; Ezekiel Rogers to John Winthrop, Nov. 3, 1639, in Foster, *Their Solitary Way*, 118.

him out for punishment not because he responded to market scarcities by raising prices ("the common practice, in all countries," as was generally admitted), but "because he was wealthy and sold dearer than most other tradesmen." His fault lay not in haggling for a high price but in abusing the power he possessed in a thin and easily manipulated market (as Boston was in the 1630s) to extort an even higher one. "Where there is a scarcity of the commodity," John Cotton had noted at the time, "there men may raise their price; for now it is a hand of God upon the commodity, *and not the person* [my italics]." In the opinion of his contemporaries, Keayne was such a person, and his behavior did call for punishment. But it was the threat of monopoly he himself represented rather than the principle of market activity in all its forms that suffered the defeat.[26]

Did free bargaining equally characterize the world of work? The impressive catalog of wage and production controls assembled by Richard Morris certainly suggests quite the opposite: that the hand of government fell with some force on the labor market. On closer examination, however, this picture dissolves. At the colony level, Massachusetts set fixed maximum limits on wages only twice: for six months in 1630–1631 and again between 1633 and 1635. After this, the General Court experimented for thirteen months with discretionary wage controls and then in 1636 passed on the responsibility for devising further regulations to the towns.[27] A few towns took the trouble to establish general maximums, but most did not.[28]

26. Winthrop, *History of New England*, I, 316–318. Two good descriptions of the Keayne trial are Bernard Bailyn, "The *Apologia* of Robert Keayne," *WMQ*, 3d Ser., VII (1950), 572–577, and Foster, *Their Solitary Way*, 116–119. See esp. *ibid.*, 119n, for evidence of the infrequency of similar trials; see also Cleve v. Winter, *Trelawney Papers*, 212, 215, 240, where the courts decided in a merchant's favor on the grounds that regulating a man's trade was not proper. The peculiar market conditions that plagued Boston during the period and framed the Keayne trial were spelled out to me in a draft version of Stephen Innes's soon-to-be-published study of economic development in early New England.

27. Morris, *Government and Labor*, 71–78; *Recs. of Mass. Bay*, I, 74, 76, 79, 84, 109, 159, 182. The Connecticut colonies maintained regulatory orders somewhat longer, but the evidence for extensive enforcement is not strong; see Morris, *Government and Labor*, 78–84.

28. In Essex County, the town records of Salem for 1634–1659, Topsfield for 1659–1685, and Manchester for 1664–1685 revealed no wage (or price) regulation of any kind: see "Salem Town Records"; Dow, ed., *Town Records of Topsfield*, I, 1–58; and *Town Records of Manchester*, 17–27. Rowley, however, did pass one wage order in 1651; see Benjamin P.

Nor was the record for enforcement impressive. Presentations before the quarterly courts of Essex County for excessive wages were never common, and they disappeared entirely after 1660. In the decade following 1655 the town of Rowley employed herdsmen at several pence per day above the maximum for "labouring men" it had itself set a few years before. Springfield passed similar regulations in 1650, but though actual wage levels remained within the legislated limits most of the time, violations were frequent and seldom punished.[29] Finally, although nearly all the recorded New England codes pegged daily wages of farm laborers at twelve to eighteen pence in the winter and eighteen to twenty-four pence in the summer, the actual rates paid, in Essex County at least, never dipped below twenty-four pence at any time during the seventeenth century, regardless of the season.[30] Though admittedly scant, the evidence for seventeenth-century wages as they were paid suggests that legislated rates were not important. The conviction that the price of labor ought to be sorted out in private overwhelmed any impulse subjecting wages to effective government control.

What, then, were the regulations meant to achieve? The words of those who supported them bring us back in an odd way to the idea of protection against the excesses of sinful men; indeed, the justification for controls employed language similar to that used to condemn the merchant Robert Keayne. The General Court, for example, defended its regulatory order of 1633 by claiming that it had responded only to "great extortion used by divers persons of little conscience." In 1636, it described offenders as "ill disposed persons as may take liberty to oppresse and wronge their neighbrs."[31] In the eyes of the court, therefore, the problem lay not in the

---

Mighill and George B. Blodgette, eds., *The Early Records of the Town of Rowley, Massachusetts, 1639–1672* (Rowley, Mass., 1894), 72.

29. The only presentations before the Essex County courts for taking excessive wages and practicing extortion (that may have been wage related) can be found in *Essex Co. Court Recs.*, I, 3, 34, 49, 57, 247, 281, II, 119, 152; Mighill and Blodgette, eds., *Early Records of Rowley*, 72, 92, 156; Stephen Innes, *Labor in a New Land: Economy and Society in Seventeenth-Century Springfield* (Princeton, N.J., 1983), 307–335, 370–379, 461; and Joseph H. Smith, ed., *Colonial Justice in Western Massachusetts (1639–1702): The Pynchon Court Record* (Cambridge, Mass., 1961), 221–387.

30. For specific examples of wage codes, see Morris, *Government and Labor*, 59, 65–66, 71–72, 78–81. For sources on 17th-century wages in Essex County, see Chapter 2, below.

31. *Recs. of Mass. Bay*, I, 109, 160.

principle of the labor market as a whole, but in the occasional machinations of sinful individuals. New Englanders were quite prepared to see wages rise in response to the scarcity of labor; even their legislated maximums exceeded the levels paid in England.[32] What the deputies wanted to regulate were not high wages but "excessive" ones—instances where ungrateful individuals had taken advantage of their favorable bargaining position in the primitive and inefficient labor market that prevailed in the earliest days of settlement to swindle honest householders "to their utter ruein and undoeing."[33] We of the twentieth century might be willing to forgive the laborer before the merchant, but the householders of the Bay Colony depended on both and stood to lose when either gained an unusual bargaining advantage.

If the markets in goods and labor were subject to some regulation in New England, the colonial authorities had, in fact, very limited intentions. Although complaints over the high price of help were common among those who had to pay for it, especially in the first decade, the Bay colonists believed the workings of supply and demand to be in God's hands and so not to be tampered with. When it came to devising workable legislation and enforcing it, they turned away from general controls and sought only to punish sinners who interfered in an institution that was ultimately the Lord's handicraft. If competency was a blessing to be desired, and no Puritan would have denied this, then God conveyed it to propertied Englishmen in measurable portion through the marketplace.

CONTRADICTION

The first generation of New Englanders hoped to organize their working lives around the pursuit of comfortable independence through household production in a generally free economy. How could such aspirations not find fertile soil on a stretch of the North American coastline where land and resources were ample and there was no one (who could not be pushed

---

32. Compare the wage codes listed in Morris, *Government and Labor*, 56–66, 71–72, 78–81, with the English wages recorded in E. H. Phelps Brown and Sheila V. Hopkins, "Seven Centuries of Building Wages," *Economica*, n.s., XXII (1955), 205; James E. Thorold Rogers, *A History of Agriculture and Prices in England, from the Year after the Oxford Parliament (1250) to the Commencement of the Continental War (1793)*, 7 vols. (Oxford, 1866–1902), V, 668–669, 817; and Thirsk, ed., *Agrarian History*, IV, 864.

33. Bill introduced before the Massachusetts General Court, May 17, 1670, in Morris, *Government and Labor*, 64.

out of the way) to interfere with their development? If the Lord's garden was to be planted anywhere by men and women, surely this was the place.

Individually, these aims might have flourished in the New World, but together in this frontier environment, they clashed. Stated in its most basic terms, the problem was this: how could a group of English families go about the task of economic development in a frontier environment without a supporting cast of dependent labor? Much of the affluence Puritan householders had enjoyed in the mother country rested on the exploitation of thousands of servants, day laborers, journeymen, and apprentices, separated from the means of production by the boundaries of property. But in frontier Massachusetts, where an Englishman's thirst for landed independence could be slaked, the mass poverty that generated an adequate supply of labor did not exist. Emmanuel Downing drew attention to this shortage of help in 1645, when he advised John Winthrop that "our Childrens Children will hardly see this great Continent filled with people, soe that our servants will still desire freedome to plant for themselves, and not staye but for verie great wages."[34] The importation of slaves could remedy the shortage, or so Downing suggested; but how could a fledgling economy with no staple exports of any value sustain the cost of their purchase? The founders of the Bay Colony can be excused for not anticipating the transforming effect of the wilderness upon the institutions familiar to them, but what were they to do? The history of work in colonial Massachusetts begins with the tale of how these Puritan middle-class Englishmen adjusted their expectations to the realities of the frontier.

34. Emmanuel Downing to John Winthrop, ca. Aug. 1645, *Winthrop Papers*, V, 38.

FARMERS

1 6 3 0 – 1 7 0 0

Nothing was more reassuring to prospective immigrants to Massachusetts than the widespread report that it resembled the country of their birth and could be "manured and husbanded" in the same manner to yield everything necessary, in their English judgment, "for the comfortable sustenance of man's life." The first comers managed to persuade their friends and cousins at home to join them in the New World, not with tales of exotica, but with plain reports of "goodly woods" and "open lands . . . [where] grass and weeds grow up to a man's face."[1] The natural wealth of such a colony was not to be had without labor, of course. The new Canaan, like England and the old Canaan of biblical times, would be a land of corn and wine—not an El Dorado but a country where ordinary people could with application procure a competent living. It was certainly not one of those "fertile places in . . . hot climates," observed William Bradford, nor was it like Virginia, where nature brought forth abundance seemingly

1. Thomas Graves, Sept. 1629, and Francis Higginson to his friends at Leicester, Sept. 1629, in Everett Emerson, ed., *Letters from New England: The Massachusetts Bay Colony, 1629–1638* (Amherst, Mass., 1976), 34, 39.

"without any great labour or art of man." But Massachusetts was a land that would respond in a familiar way to the honest toil of those who brought "bodies able and minds fitted to brave the first brunts, which the beginnings of such works necessarily put men upon."[2] Here, English grains could be raised, animals pastured, and hay mowed just as they had been in the old country. Stretching the truth, John Winthrop went so far, upon first seeing Massachusetts, as to inform his son by letter that "for the Country it selfe I can discerne little difference betweene it and our owne."[3] The first governor's eyes may have been blinkered by enthusiasm, but what he said mirrored the expectations of his fellow colonists.

Massachusetts did not seem to be lacking in natural endowments, nor were these first settlers wanting in direction. On the surface, nothing seemed simpler than to concentrate the human resources and economic power of the mother country on this undeveloped wilderness and so create a new England in America. Yet it was not to be that simple. The English rural economy had developed in an environment where people and productive wealth were abundant and land was scarce—the opposite of conditions in America. The Bay colonists, like other Europeans in the New World, had to scramble in the first decades of settlement to discover sources of labor and capital and to devise strategies of managing them efficiently. Unlike planters in the tropical colonies, New Englanders did not rely heavily on slaves or indentured servants, but neither could they depend on the free market to deliver the help necessary to develop the land. In order to confront and overcome the special problems of the northern frontier, the first colonists adjusted the traditions of rural economy that they brought with them from the mother country.

THE RURAL ECONOMY OF ENGLAND

The intention to replant England overseas was plain enough, but which part of that country did the Puritan emigrants have in mind? A central truth about English society in the early modern period was its local diver-

2. William Bradford, *Of Plymouth Plantation, 1620–1647*, ed. Samuel Eliot Morison (New York, 1952), 28; Richard Saltonstall to Emmanuel Downing, Feb. 4, 1632, in Emerson, ed., *Letters from New England*, 92.

3. John Winthrop to John Winthrop, Jr., July 23, 1630, *Winthrop Papers*, 5 vols. (Boston, 1929–1947), II, 307. See also Edward Johnson's characterizations of New England in J. Franklin Jameson, ed., *Johnson's Wonder-Working Providence, 1628–1651*, Original Narratives of Early American History (New York, 1910), 210, 234.

sity, and we can fairly assume that emigrants from different regions and even parishes led working lives that varied enormously in their particulars. An important though almost wholly unrecorded experience in the great reshuffling of families that was the Great Migration must have been the discovery by new colonial neighbors that their respective notions of rural economy did not always agree. Nevertheless, as English people they did possess some ground in common—their system of husbandry, the social organization of their work, and the structure of the economy within which they farmed. Because these points of shared experience served as building blocks in the construction of New England's first agricultural labor system, they deserve our attention.[4]

The farming regime that prevailed where most of these emigrants had grown up, in the south and east of England, combined arable husbandry with the raising of livestock. The actual mix of wheat and barley, sheep and cattle, and alternative crops such as hops, flax, rapeseed, and turnips, as well as market gardening, was a matter of local preference, decided by conditions of soil and climate and by the farmer's need both to spread work across as much of the year as possible and to conserve the fertility of the land. Farmers on the light, dry soils of coastal Norfolk thus rotated their fields between small grains and sheep pasture; their counterparts in Hampshire and Dorset, where more rain fell, generally assigned most of their land to dairying or the fattening of livestock and grew wheat and barley only for home consumption. Although the details of husbandry could never be shared among an emigrant population gathered from across the entire country, the English held in common a general commitment to mixed farming.[5]

4. David Grayson Allen's tracing of cultural connections between specific towns or regions of England and the villages in Massachusetts to which their inhabitants removed is ingenious (*In English Ways: The Movement of Societies and the Transferal of English Local Law and Custom to Massachusetts Bay in the Seventeenth Century* [Chapel Hill, N.C., 1981]). I suspect, however, that if the Bay colonists moved about frequently during the first years after their arrival, as has been shown by Virginia DeJohn Anderson, *New England's Generation: The Great Migration and the Formation of Society and Culture in the Seventeenth Century* (Cambridge, 1991), 100–122, a great many peculiarly local continuities were, in reality, ironed out. That individual English householders hoped to reestablish the ways with which they were familiar is convincing enough; that it was possible to accomplish this, except in such highly homogeneous towns as Rowley and Hingham, is more difficult to accept.

5. Joan Thirsk, "The Farming Regions of England," in Joan Thirsk, ed., *The Agrarian History of England and Wales*, vol. IV: *1500–1640* (Cambridge, 1967), 1–112, but esp. 42–

This English agricultural system generated an annual work cycle that rose and fell with the seasons only in mild waves. When the land was tilled and planted (in autumn or in the early spring, depending on the crop), when sheep were washed and shorn (in June), at mowing time (in midsummer), and during harvest (in August and September), long hours and steady employment were the rule. Between these peaks the pace slackened, especially once the crops were in. Still, English winters were not cold enough to drive men indoors entirely, and there were always some farm tasks, especially of maintenance, that could be shifted into the emptier days of December, January, and February. Not only were there fields to be plowed and manured, grain to be threshed, hedges to be trimmed, trees to be pruned, and timber to be cut, but there were animals to be delivered, tended, and slaughtered and produce to be marketed. Furthermore, when the year's supply of farm work was truly exhausted, employment was often available in rural industry. Clothmaking and woodcutting were probably the most important, but a wide range of trades across the countryside provided work once agriculture tapered off for the year. This was a seasonal economy, therefore, but not of the pronounced variety that colonizers would have to construct in the more continental climate of New England.[6]

By the early seventeenth century, however, English husbandry consisted of more than the endless recycling of an annual routine. The techniques that defined it were in a state of continuous if gradual development, driven principally by the opportunities for sale and profit. By contemporary European standards the English were progressive farmers, who managed with every passing generation to raise their arable yields, institute new crops, support greater numbers of stock, and ultimately generate more produce for the market. The specific direction of these improvements shifted in accordance with the economic conditions of the day. Prior to 1640, when the prices of standard farm products—wool and grain in particular—had been on the climb, innovative farmers concentrated on developing existing methods. They invented more intensive rotations, manured their lands with greater care, began to irrigate their meadows,

---

46 and 67–69; Virginia DeJohn Anderson, "Migrants and Motives: Religion and the Settlement of New England, 1630–1640," *New England Quarterly*, LVIII (1985), 356–357, 361–364.

6. Alan Everitt, "Farm Labourers," in Thirsk, ed., *Agrarian History*, IV, 431; Thirsk, "Farming Techniques," *ibid.*, 166–197.

and increased their tillage by reclaiming waste and converting pasture. When the prices of staple products began to level off and even decline after 1640, improvers switched directions and pursued alternative projects. Rather than buck the declining returns of a sheep-corn husbandry that met with ever softer markets, they began to experiment with new crops—fruits, vegetables, rapeseed, hops, hemp, flax, and the different dye plants, to name a few—for which demand seemed more promising. The principle of improvement had numerous promoters in every generation, and although ancient farm practices and the bent for mixed husbandry were not casually abandoned, English agriculture in general did become markedly more specialized and efficient with the passage of time.[7]

Here, then, was a rural economy that was mixed, moderately seasonal, and growing in productivity—but how exactly did society organize the labor by which it operated? There is no single answer to that question, but it does appear that within the middling social ranks represented in the Great Migration, farmers usually worked the lands they occupied in household units, of which nuclear family members constituted the core. The most basic lines of economic power, certainly among the modestly propertied, were those that linked parents with their children and organized daily work among them.[8] Indeed, without the willingness of youth to do their elders' bidding—helping at plow, fetching cattle, working on

7. The most thorough treatments of this theme are Thirsk, "Farming Techniques," in Thirsk, ed., *Agrarian History*, IV, 161–199, and Eric Kerridge, *The Agricultural Revolution* (London, 1967). But see also Joan Thirsk, "Patterns of Agriculture in Seventeenth-Century England," in David D. Hall and David Grayson Allen, eds., *Seventeenth-Century New England* (Colonial Society of Massachusetts, *Publications*, LXIII [Boston, 1984]), 39–54; M. A. Havinden, "Agricultural Progress in Open-Field Oxfordshire," in W. E. Minchinton, ed., *Essays in Agrarian History*, 2 vols. (Newton Abbot, 1968), I, 152–157; E. L. Jones, "Agriculture and Economic Growth in England, 1660–1750," *ibid.*, 206–208; A. H. John, "The Course of Agricultural Change," *ibid.*, 243–244; and Ann Kussmaul, "Agrarian Change in Seventeenth-Century England: The Economic Historian as Paleontologist," *JEH*, XLV (1985), 1–30. A useful comparison of the different national agricultures in Europe can be found in Jan de Vries, *Economy of Europe in an Age of Crisis, 1600–1750* (Cambridge, 1976), 30–83.

8. There has been some lively theoretical discussion of the problem, for example, in Richard M. Smith, "Some Issues concerning Families and Their Property in Rural England, 1250–1800," in Richard M. Smith, ed., *Land, Kinship and Life-Cycle* (Cambridge, 1984), 6–38. A good deal of empirical demographic work has powerful implications for the history of work (see the other contributions in the above collection), but few empirical studies of family labor are based on the records of the work experience itself.

the family account for a neighbor, or going into service—most farming would have been next to impossible. The moral imperatives of fear, love, and custom, as well as hunger and the implicit understanding that children would receive a portion of the family estate, powered an enormous segment of the English rural economy. This is not to deny the reality of class. These households were neither isolated from one another nor equivalent in wealth. The fences and hedges that carved the land surface of the country into unequal holdings and the legal system that defended this division did confer upon wealthier families the power to organize the labor of others. Still, the lines of authority functioned most effectively within households, not between them. To the degree that farming was still profitable on a moderate scale, the great lords and gentlemen who actually owned the land surface of England generally preferred to exploit it in ways that employed the household economy as a unit.

This they accomplished by delegating the responsibility of operating their lands to a vast array of tenant farmers through a complicated system of leaseholding. By 1630, tenancy was not nearly as universal as it had been at the end of the Middle Ages. For close to a hundred years, landlords had been chipping away at the customary rights of peasant families and, by the beginning of the seventeenth century, had dispossessed about half of them. Freeholders, whose fixed and inheritable leases were protected under common law, usually defended themselves well enough. They tended to become the yeomen of the early modern period, and their home farms grew substantial enough to absorb not only the labors of their own households, but also those of the parish poor. Copyholders, by comparison, held their lands only by local custom as defined in the declining manorial courts and possessed no such security. Some of them managed to retain their holdings on traditional terms, but more and more were forced to negotiate new leases at the market rate. Many were made responsible for repairs on the property, and some were now obligated to add improvements. Throughout the sixteenth century, when rents were soaring, the position of copyholders had deteriorated; now, especially if they were small and relatively inefficient, the threat of eviction hung constantly over their heads. Yet tenancy persisted into the seventeenth century, for not only did it permit the ruling classes to realize a tidy rental income from their holdings free from the difficulties of labor supervision, but it also allowed the middling sort of rural household to gain a living without having to scatter its members abroad in search of employment. Nowhere was tenancy simple, nor was it lacking in regional variation, but throughout the early modern period it continued to frame the work experience across rural England.[9]

Another mechanism that enabled willing hands poor in property to obtain access to a living was the institution of service in husbandry. A few farmers counted just enough natural offspring to handle the regular labor requirements of their landholdings, but this was uncommon. Young families, especially those with property, often found it necessary to take in servants until their own children had reached a useful age. More mature households, particularly the poorer ones, had to send their sons and daughters into service simply to rid themselves of mouths they could not feed. Differences in wealth based on class and age, therefore, channeled productive offspring into households where labor was in demand. Young men in particular followed this route. From their early teens to their mid-twenties, they hired themselves out by the year to more prosperous farmers and lived as members of their households. While serving an apprenticeship in husbandry, a young man earned his keep plus a small annual wage, ranging from twenty shillings for a new lad to seven or eight pounds for a man in his prime, which could be spent or set aside for the future.[10] Servants in husbandry were an important part of the English rural society that the Puritan emigrants had known at home. Counting across the entire early modern period and including both men and women, farm servants amounted to about 13 percent of the population and about 60 percent of those between fifteen and twenty-four years of age. Indeed, 72 percent of yeomen and 47 percent of husbandmen retained at least one servant on their farms. Of the families that left England for the Bay Colony in the 1630s, 56 percent had servants, and servants composed almost 17 percent of the total emigrating group.[11]

9. E. L. Jones, "Introduction," in E. L. Jones, ed., *Agriculture and Economic Growth in England, 1650–1815* (London, 1967), 14; Leslie A. Clarkson, *The Pre-Industrial Economy in England, 1500–1750* (New York, 1972), 61–68; F. M. L. Thompson, "The Social Distribution of Landed Property in England since the Sixteenth Century," *Economic History Review*, 2d Ser., XIX (1966), 505–517; Peter Bowden, "Agricultural Prices, Farm Profits, and Rents," in Thirsk, ed., *Agrarian History*, IV, 674–694; Richard Lachmann, *From Manor to Market: Structural Change in England, 1536–1640* (Madison, Wis., 1987), 102–114.

10. Ann Kussmaul, *Servants in Husbandry in Early Modern England* (Cambridge, 1981), is authoritative on farm service in this period, but see also Smith, "Some Issues," in Smith, ed., *Land, Kinship and Life-Cycle*, 32–38.

11. These figures include male and female servants. See Kussmaul, *Servants in Husbandry*, 11–22; Peter Laslett, "Mean Household Size in England since the Sixteenth Century,"

At regular points in the year, there were particular activities—tilling land, shearing sheep, and taking the corn harvest, for example—that even households with children and servants could not handle without additional paid help. Of necessity, farmers turned to their poorer neighbors—laborers cut off from the means of production by their poverty—and hired them, individually or in gangs, by the day or the week, until the job was done. This tradition stretched back into the Middle Ages, but by the early decades of the seventeenth century, especially in southern and eastern England, waged labor living apart from the master or employer was growing in significance. At the same time that rising prices were driving up the cost of maintaining help within the home, growing numbers of married men beyond the age of service, whose ability to employ themselves had been handicapped by enclosure or eviction, were coming to farmers for work. Arable farmers with large holdings, like Robert Loder of Berkshire and Nicholas Toke of Kent, probably relied more on outside hands—plowmen and harvesters especially—than on household members; at least the proportion of labor by the day and task within their wage bills suggests as much. Some workmen rented cottages on the fringes of large farms that could offer them daily employment; others dwelt on small holdings in the forest and migrated seasonally to regions where their help was in demand; still others simply drifted up and down the countryside, selling their services on a casual basis. In the English lowlands at the time of the Great Migration, families laboring chiefly for others accounted for between one-quarter and one-half of the rural population.[12]

---

in Peter Laslett and Richard Wall, eds., *Household and Family in Past Time: Comparative Studies in the Size and Structure of the Domestic Group over the Last Three Centuries in England, France, Serbia, Japan and Colonial North America, with Fuller Materials from Western Europe* (Cambridge, 1972), 154; Anderson, *New England's Generation*, 24, 223; and Everitt, "Farm Labourers," in Thirsk, ed., *Agrarian History*, IV, 436–437.

12. Smith, "Some Issues," in Smith, ed., *Land, Kinship and Life-Cycle*, 31–32, 36–38; Peter Laslett, *The World We Have Lost: England before the Industrial Age*, 2d ed. (London, 1971), 1–22; Everitt, "Farm Labourers," in Thirsk, ed., *Agrarian History*, IV, 396–465; Bowden, "Agricultural Prices," *ibid.*, 661–663, 668–670; David G. Hey, *An English Rural Community: Myddle under the Tudors and Stuarts* (Leicester, 1974), 169–175; Keith Wrightson and David Levine, *Poverty and Piety in an English Village: Terling, 1525–1700* (New York, 1979), 33, 35–36; Mildred Campbell, *The English Yeoman under Elizabeth and the Early Stuarts* (New Haven, Conn., 1942), 211–212; Keith Wrightson, *English Society, 1580–1680* (London, 1982), 33–34. Robert Loder, whose holdings of close to 300 acres (half in tillage) would have placed him among the wealthier yeomen of his day, spent about £80 sterling a year between 1612 and 1617 on outside help and roughly £25 to £45

Wage labor, farm service, tenancy, and family production: is it fair to say that these different elements describing the social organization of work in seventeenth-century England were bound together in a functioning labor market? There were certainly a great many obstacles preventing its free operation. The Elizabethan Poor Laws may have created a multitude of local labor markets by tying evicted tenants to the parishes where they were legally settled and discouraging them from seeking new leaseholdings elsewhere, but the same logic prevented these local pools from swelling into an efficient national market until the laws were overturned in 1834. The preference of workmen for their native parts, the less than accurate information that circulated throughout every region regarding opportunities elsewhere, and the difficulty of transporting oneself to alternative employment reduced even further the efficiency that market forces could bring to bear on labor. That few rural Englishmen moved beyond the county of their birth either in their years of farm service or later as adult laborers is ample evidence of this.[13]

For large spheres of the economy, moreover, supply and demand operated on the price and allocation of labor indirectly at best. Within the family, it was obviously parental fiat and not monetary incentive that decided who would perform which tasks; only age or the consent of a father could launch a son into the labor market, and then only into the highly qualified freedom of service in husbandry. Within the community, the maintenance of common land for the support of the poor erected another nonmarket arena for labor power that might otherwise have been put up for sale. Even in the world beyond, such seemingly open negotiations as those between a farmer and his prospective hand over the price of a day's threshing were subject to customary social restraints. Notions

sterling a year (board included) on servants. The size of his farm and its orientation toward arable husbandry suggest that his ratio of waged help to servant help constituted something close to the extreme case in English agriculture. On Nicholas Toke's holdings in Kent, servant labor in sample years accounted for 57% (1627–1628), 36% (1646–1647), and 44% (1678–1679) of the estate's total wage bill. See G. E. Fussell, ed., *Robert Loder's Farm Accounts, 1610–1620* (Camden Society, *Publications*, 3d Ser., LIII [London, 1936]), table IV (facing p. xxvi), 22–23, 54–55, 72, 90, 107–108, 123, 136–137, 152, 172; and Eleanor C. Lodge, ed., *The Account Book of a Kentish Estate, 1616–1704* (London, 1927), xxxvii–xxxix, 97–108, 208–213, 372–379.

13. Lachmann, *From Manor to Market*, 138–141; Kussmaul, *Servants in Husbandry*, 65–67; Everitt, "Farm Labourers," in Thirsk, ed., *Agrarian History*, IV, 434; Wrightson and Levine, *Poverty and Piety*, 76–81.

about what constituted fair pay, reasonable hours, and adequate refreshment were often resistant to change and within a given region might not be altered for decades.[14]

This said, one cannot gainsay the role that market forces did play in organizing social labor. In every corner of the English countryside, laborers searched from farm to farm for waged employment—servants did the same, although only once or twice a year and mainly for room and board. Their earnings were negotiable, moreover, with age, experience, character, physical strength, the nature of the work performed, and the time of year. Henry Best of Yorkshire advised his readers in 1641 that he "usually" paid his hands certain basic rates, but he also admitted that in practice the hiring process was largely a matter of open negotiation. When dealing with servants, he warned, a farmer should "talke privately with them concerninge theire wage," perhaps at "the backe side of the church," where the public scrutiny that might encourage undue generosity was at a minimum. Best alerted farmers to be especially careful at harvest, when the price of labor was more than half again the normal summer rate, for any hand who knew that a prospective employer was "in a case of necessity" to get in his crops was likely to ask for a penny or two extra.[15]

14. E. H. Phelps Brown, *The Economics of Labor* (New Haven, Conn., 1962), 131–132; E. H. Phelps Brown and Sheila V. Hopkins, "Seven Centuries of Building Wages," *Economica*, n.s., XXII (1955), 197, 202, 203, 205; E. J. Hobsbawm, "Custom, Wages, and Work-load in Nineteenth-Century Industry," in E. J. Hobsbawm, *Labouring Men: Studies in the History of Labour* (London, 1964), 345–350; Thirsk, ed., *Agrarian History*, IV, 864, table XV.

15. Lachmann, *From Manor to Market*, 17; Everitt, "Farm Labourers," in Thirsk, ed., *Agrarian History*, IV, 435–438; Henry Best, *Rural Economy in Yorkshire in 1641, Being the Farming and Account Books of Henry Best, of Elmeswell, in the East Riding*, ed. C. B. Robinson (Surtees Society, *Publications*, XXXIII [Durham, 1857]), 134, 142. From 1620 to 1660, Toke paid a harvest wage that was 50% higher than his normal summer rate; in the 1640s, Henry Best paid 67% more and some of his neighbors paid 100% more than the summer rate; to get in his crops in 1619, Robert Loder of Berkshire had to lay on an 80% surplus. Ten 17th-century wage assessments describe official harvest rates that were on average 50% higher than normal. The evidence is thin, but one might speculate that the surplus of actual over official rates also indicates the presence of market forces. See Lodge, ed., *Account Book of a Kentish Estate*, xxxiv; Best, *Rural Economy in Yorkshire*, 140–142; Fussell, ed., *Loder's Farm Accounts*, 167; James E. Thorold Rogers, *A History of Agriculture and Prices in England, from the Year after the Oxford Parliament (1259) to the Commencement of the Continental War (1793)*, 7 vols. (Oxford, 1866–1902), V, 622–625, VI, 692; A. E. Bland, P. A. Brown, and R. H. Tawney, eds., *English Economic History: Select Documents* (London, 1914), 346–347; and H. E. S. Fisher and A. R. J. Jurica, eds., *England from 1000*

Over the longer term, market influences were clearer still. The fall in real wages during the hundred years prior to the Great Migration was obviously a function of rising population and labor supply, just as the movement of English men and women to America was prompted by the elevated levels of New World demand. Even the type of labor that employers preferred could be shaped by the market. When the population of England leveled off in the second half of the seventeenth century and real rates of daily labor began to rise, a great many farmers switched over to year-round servant help, which was now less costly to maintain. The same improved conditions served to slow the immigration of indentured servants to Maryland and Virginia, where planters turned to the importation of African slaves.[16] The labor market in early modern England was certainly inefficient (by modern standards) and its influence scarcely touched some economic relations, but it mattered a great deal to the growing portion of Englishmen who had to survive without any land.

In spite of its considerable local variation, the farming regime that the New England settlers left behind possessed a number of defining qualities. As an agricultural system it was seasonal in character, progressive in technique, and increasingly oriented to the market, especially in the regions from which the Puritan emigrants came. Though tending in the direction of specialization, this system retained a considerable mix of activities that served to satisfy domestic needs, maintain soil fertility, and extend the working year. As a set of social relations, moreover, it recognized households as the basic units of production but placed them within a hierarchy of wealth, forcing those poor in property to market a portion of their labor among people of greater means. Such was the rural economy that the first New Englanders expected to reestablish in America.

SETTLEMENT

The reality of the American wilderness directed the rural history of Massachusetts along a somewhat different course. The mixed farming, agri-

to 1760, vol. I of B. W. Clapp, H. E. S. Fisher, and A. R. J. Jurica, eds., *Documents in English Economic History*, 2 vols. (London, 1976–1977), 524.

16. Kussmaul, *Servants in Husbandry*, 97–101; Russell Menard, "From Servants to Slaves: The Transformation of the Chesapeake Labor System," *Southern Studies*, XVI (1977), 355–390. David W. Galenson, *White Servitude in Colonial America: An Economic Analysis* (Cambridge, 1981), is the most thoroughgoing attempt to argue for the freedom of labor markets in the early modern Anglo-American world.

cultural techniques, market production, and many beasts and crops traditional to England were, indeed, transplanted to the Bay Colony with tolerable success. The way New Englanders organized themselves to operate this frontier economy, however, was different. Like all other colonists in the Americas, they discovered that the relations of production that powered the developed economies of Europe had to be adjusted in a land that was empty of Europeans. Unlike their contemporaries in the plantation colonies, New Englanders did not seize upon any general form of servitude to solve their labor problems, but neither did they leave the social relations of farm production unaltered. Presently, we will investigate the actual changes they made; let us begin by discovering why they were necessary at all.

English farming did not survive the Great Migration intact partly because Massachusetts was a different type of country geographically. One ought not to exaggerate the transatlantic distinctions, but insofar as they forced certain adaptations on the colonists they cannot be ignored. Take the character of New England's soil and topography. A patchwork of amazing diversity, the region possessed a lot of acreage that was plainly ill suited to English farming practices. Much of the country was stony and resistant to the plow, and that which was arable swiftly lost its nutrients through erosion. Native plants were accustomed to tree cover and unused to being trampled by domesticated livestock; when Englishmen removed trees and instituted animals the ground was dried out and trodden down, losing much of its ability to support crops of any kind. Even the more fertile bottom lands along the banks of streams and rivers, whose nutrients were replenished by flooding every spring, tended to lose more than they gained when water coursed over their newly disturbed surfaces.[17]

The continental climate of the new land also came as something of a surprise. In terms of annual average temperatures, the Bay Colony was no colder than southern England, but the winters were more severe than the settlers had previously known and the danger of frost lingered over the land from November to April. Wrote Thomas Gorges with some literary license, "you must looke uppon us as prisoners from the end of 9ber till the beginning of Aprille." The dunging and plowing that employed husbandmen in the Old World during the months of February and March

17. William Cronon, *Changes in the Land: Indians, Colonists, and the Ecology of New England* (New York, 1983), 27–31, 122–125, 141–151.

were simply not possible in frozen soil. Livestock that were used to spending almost the entire year in pasture now were penned up for four to five months, consuming fodder that had to be grown in the summertime.[18]

If New England's geography tested the colonists, however, it was not wholly unfamiliar. It neither forced them to abandon the crops and beasts they had grown up with nor permitted them much experimentation with tropical or northern staples that might have met with a healthy market overseas. Most of England's colonial projects in the New World sat in southerly latitudes, where the export of tropical and semitropical produce prevailed. In New England, where the four seasons followed one another in recognizable fashion—with amounts of rainfall, frost, snow cover, and summer heat that bore some resemblance to the land left behind—such an export economy was not possible. This did not dismay the Puritan settlers; that was why they had chosen New England in the first place. Although most of the land they encountered could not match the old country in fertility, it could nonetheless nurture English grains, vegetables, and fodder with marginally acceptable yields—and so it did. In basic produce and seasonal rhythms, therefore, the mixed husbandry of the mother country migrated to Massachusetts with the colonists.

The real novelty of this new country was not the character of its geography but the simple quantity of it. Nothing about the Puritans' adopted homeland struck them with greater force. "I am told," marveled Francis Higginson of Salem, as did many others, "that about three miles from us a man may stand on a little hilly place and see divers thousands of acres of ground as good as need to be, and not a tree in the same." Curiously, the very abundance of what English farmers had come to find—the land that could guarantee them the independence they cherished so highly—resulted in the most profound adjustments. For while land was plentiful, the means of bringing it into production were not. Forests had to be cleared, barns and mills erected, fences built, sod turned, and animals bred to populate this "good ground"—all from scratch, which demanded the application of more manpower, livestock, and equipment than most early

18. Thomas Gorges, *Letters*, quoted in Karen Ordahl Kupperman, "Climate and Mastery of the Wilderness in Seventeenth-Century New England," in Hall and Allen, eds., *Seventeenth-Century New England*, 11, but see also *ibid.*, 11–19; Cronon, *Changes in the Land*, 138; Howard S. Russell, *A Long, Deep Furrow: Three Centuries of Farming in New England*, abridged by Mark Lapping (Hanover, N.H., 1982), 87; and John Winthrop to Nathaniel Rich, May 22, 1634, Winthrop to the earl of Warwick, Sept. 1644, *Winthrop Papers*, III, 167, IV, 492.

settlers could readily obtain. "Great pity it is," wrote Higginson, "to see so much good ground for corn and for grass as any is under the heavens, to lie altogether unoccupied." What was needed was "the good company of honest Christians to bring with them horses, kine, and sheep" and make use of it.[19] As long as the rural economy of the region was substantially occupied in the work of farm construction, productive wealth and labor power would remain in short supply.

The scarcity of productive wealth meant shortages of all kinds in the earliest years. Throughout the 1630s colonists wrote home about the need for iron and steel to manufacture farm implements, the inadequacy of livestock, the lack of seed and fodder, and the cost of obtaining any of these in Massachusetts. John Winthrop's interest in the arrival of ships from abroad and their cargoes—especially the head of cattle on board— speaks to the worries that even a prominent booster had concerning the dearth of capital goods in the new colony.[20] Yet the Puritan immigrants were not poor, and some of these items could be imported to or even produced within the colony. By the third quarter of the seventeenth century, judging from tax lists and farm inventories, the settlers possessed herds of livestock and a range of basic farm implements that compared favorably with those of their English cousins.[21] The types of productive wealth most obviously lacking in the Bay Colony, and into the creation of which the settlers had to throw the greatest part of their energies, were

19. Francis Higginson to his friends at Leicester, Sept. 1629, in Emerson, ed., *Letters from New England*, 30, 36.

20. Higginson to his friends at Leicester, Sept. 1629, John Pond to William Pond, Mar. 15, 1631, anonymous letter, early 1637, in Emerson, ed., *Letters from New England*, 27, 64– 65, 214–215; John Winthrop to Nathaniel Rich, May 27, 1634, in *Winthrop Papers*, III, 166; Winthrop, *History of New England*, I, 65, 66, 80–81, 100, 102, 107, 111, 126, 134, 140, 152, 161, 178. See also Edward Johnson's description of the founding of Concord in Jameson, ed., *Johnson's Wonder-Working Providence*, 114–115.

21. Compare the data from New England sources collected in Percy Wells Bidwell and John I. Falconer, *History of Agriculture in the Northern United States, 1620–1850* (Washington, D.C., 1925), 26, 28, 30, 32, 34–35; Terry Lee Anderson, "The Economic Growth of Seventeenth Century New England: A Measurement of Regional Income" (Ph.D. diss., University of Washington, 1972), 90, 96, 103; and Jackson Turner Main, *Society and Economy in Colonial Connecticut* (Princeton, N.J., 1985), 77–80, 203, 212–213, 215, 218, 222, with the English values in Margaret Spufford, *Contrasting Communities: English Villagers in the Sixteenth and Seventeenth Centuries* (Cambridge, 1974), 64–65, 98–99, 131–133; Wrightson, *English Society*, 32; and Bowden, "Agricultural Prices," in Thirsk, ed., *Agrarian History*, IV, 655–656.

improvements upon real property. Chiefly by clearing land and constructing farm buildings, decade after decade, New Englanders tried to replicate the agricultural system of the mother country. The steadily rising value of these improvements from the middle of the seventeenth century onward —measured in acreage, the price of land, and the worth of houses and outbuildings—certainly testifies to the labor invested by the settlers; but it also underlines the extent of the original scarcity, at least relative to the potential of an untapped wilderness, that the colonists sought to remedy.[22]

The shortage of labor power was just as great a problem and elicited even more comment. Simply growing food in a new community, wrote Edward Johnson upon the founding of Concord, required "every one that can lift a hawe [hoe]." The General Court declared in 1634 a "necessity of husbanding mens time in this country," and this broad truth bore heavily on agriculture.[23] So much "labour and service was to be done about building and planting," complained William Bradford in 1642, that "such as wanted help in that respect, when they could not have such as they would, were glad to take such as they could." Servants who had completed their indentures, John Winthrop declared with obvious annoyance in 1645, learned swiftly that they inhabited a seller's market and "could not be hired . . . but upon unreasonable terms."[24] Busy farmers in England could count on the assistance of their less affluent neighbors, but in a thinly settled country where a family head could acquire an independent freehold with relative ease, help was in short supply and rather expensive.

In their use of time and equipment, farmers tried to be as sparing as possible. They cleared the forest largely by girdling trees and waiting for nature to rot away the trunks and roots. As soon as repeated croppings had looted the ground of its nutrients, farmers moved tillage from one field to the next, in order to economize on the time that serious manuring and crop rotation would have occupied. Wooden fences were favored over hedges and stone walls, for they were quickly constructed and easily moved as farmers shifted the locus of their cultivation. Indian corn swiftly became the breadstuff of choice in spite of English distaste. Not only did it grow well, but it could be sowed among the stumps of newly cleared fields

22. Main, *Colonial Connecticut*, 207; William I. Davisson, "Essex County Wealth Trends: Wealth and Economic Growth in 17th Century Massachusetts," Essex Institute, *Historical Collections*, CIII (1967), 317–325; Anderson, "Economic Growth of Seventeenth Century New England," 89–92, 96, 102–103.

23. Jameson, ed., *Johnson's Wonder-Working Providence*, 114; *Recs. of Mass. Bay*, II, 47.

24. Bradford, *Of Plymouth Plantation*, 321; Winthrop, *History of New England*, II, 228.

and cultivated without a plow and team, and it produced higher yields for the labor invested than any of its European competitors. The colonists made do with a more basic range of implements than they had employed in England and, when possible, used wood instead of iron in their construction. Since outbuildings were also kept to a minimum, farmers often wintered their livestock out of doors.[25]

Short of time and poor in capital goods, the first Bay colonists never adhered to the tidiest of farming practices. There are no contemporary accounts to guide us here (like those of the eighteenth-century observers who remarked on the sloppy husbandry they saw in New England), but the colonists themselves apparently recognized the problem.[26] During the first three decades of settlement, the General Court complained of grain that was improperly ground; fences that failed to prevent animals from roaming at large; sheep that were carelessly washed in muddy or brackish water before shearing; hides that were cast aside after slaughtering and never sent to the tannery; and even bridges that collapsed under the weight of farmers driving their teams on private business when they should have been maintaining the public way. Town meetings and county magistrates echoed these concerns.[27] Massachusetts husbandmen were certainly not lazy, but the nature of their task and the paucity of means to perform it gave their farming an unpolished appearance. The scrubby

25. Bidwell and Falconer, *History of Agriculture*, 9–10, 25, 31, 115; Russell, *Long, Deep Furrow*, 82–83, 87, 101–107; Cronon, *Changes in the Land*, 116–117, 119–120, 150–153; Richard L. Bushman, "Opening the American Countryside," in James A. Henretta, Michael Kammen, and Stanley N. Katz, eds., *The Transformation of Early American History: Society, Authority, and Ideology* (New York, 1991), 243–244; Thomas Coram to Benjamin Colman, July 9, 1737, Benjamin Colman Papers, 1641–1763, Massachusetts Historical Society, Boston.

26. On 18th-century assessments of New England agriculture, see Bidwell and Falconer, *History of Agriculture*, 70–125.

27. *Recs. of Mass. Bay*, I, 215, 241, 305, II, 14–15, 190, 228–229, III, 298, 319, IV(i), 322; George Francis Dow, ed., *Town Records of Topsfield, Massachusetts, 1659–1778*, 2 vols. (Topsfield, Mass., 1917–1920), I, 8, 12, 15, 17, 20, 36, 42; "Salem Town Records," 40, 64, 68, 85, 86, 106–107, 110, 127, 130, 136, 137, 143, 144, 145, 152, 185, 199, 211; Benjamin P. Mighill and George B. Blodgette, eds., *The Early Records of the Town of Rowley, Massachusetts, 1639–1672* (Rowley, Mass., 1894), 55, 74, 75, 86–87, 88, 91, 145–146, 147, 148, 224; *Town Records of Manchester, from the Earliest Grants of Land, 1636, when a Portion of Salem, until 1736* (Salem, Mass., 1889), 7, 8, 33–34; *Essex Co. Court Recs.*, I, 25, 28, 50, 51, II, 376, IV, 164. These constitute a small sample of the far larger body of town orders and court citations arising from hasty agriculture.

countryside of early New England—a product of hasty workmanship and makeshift equipment—is the best testament to the scarcity of labor and capital with which these frontier farmers had to contend.

Scarcity is, of course, a relative term. Labor and capital were scarce only in relation to the requirements placed upon them, and it is important to be precise about where the demand originated. Commercial farming and the settlers' early efforts to profit by it could account for some of the scarcity. Most farmers in seventeenth-century Massachusetts lived within a day's travel under sail or by foot from Boston or Salem, and a great many took advantage of this fact by selling surplus produce there. As early as 1650, craftsmen, fishermen, and merchant seamen by the dozens were established in coastal towns, and most were consumers of regional produce. Moreover, by midcentury seaport merchants were beginning to locate additional markets for agricultural produce and lumber overseas—in Madeira, the Azores, the Canaries, the Iberian Peninsula, Newfoundland, and the Caribbean—where the Bay colonists competed for a share of the trade. Winthrop, Bradford, Johnson, and later Edward Randolph all drew attention to the commerce in grain, livestock, salted meat, and wood products, and they exempted hardly a town in New England from its attractions.[28] Not everyone dealt in the market, but merchant account books like those kept by George Corwin in the 1650s suggest that involvement was fairly broad. Although Corwin lived in Salem and was interested chiefly in the local fishery, he provisioned his mariners with wheat, dried peas, Indian corn, beef, pork, cheese, and butter purchased from numerous farmers in the surrounding hinterland. Although the majority were Salem neighbors, the remainder hailed from almost every town in Essex County within fifteen miles of Corwin's warehouse; young farmers and those of lower status may have been a little less likely to make the trip, but every social grouping was represented among his suppliers.[29]

28. Darrett B. Rutman, *Winthrop's Boston: Portrait of a Puritan Town, 1630–1649* (Chapel Hill, N.C., 1965), 180–189; Winthrop, *History of New England*, II, 91, 341; Bradford, *Of Plymouth Plantation*, 252–253; Jameson, ed., *Johnson's Wonder-Working Providence*, 246–248; "Answer of Edward Randolph to several heads of inquiry concerning the present state of New England," Oct. 12, 1676, *CSPC*, IX, 466.

29. George Corwin Account Book, 1652–1655, JDPL. The names of 134 suppliers of farm produce were drawn from this source, and their ages and towns of origin were established from *Essex Co. Court Recs.*, the account book itself, and a wide variety of secondary sources in the local history collection of the James Duncan Phillips Library, Peabody Essex Museum, Salem, Mass. Corwin noted when customers were from out-of-

Still, this was not commercial agriculture along the pattern of the plantation colonies or even the mother country. The plain interest of the colonists in finding a vent for their produce notwithstanding, no substantial market existed for which they possessed any sustained comparative advantage.[30] Local markets were handy but limited by the widespread ownership of farm property. Within the region, the only urban centers of any size were Boston and Salem, and they counted no more than a few thousand souls. And since so much of what local farmers were able to wring from the stubborn soil could be grown at similar cost in Europe—closer to the principal markets—the possibilities for export were limited. Once their domestic needs had been met, nothing prevented settlers from dispatching whatever they could spare townward for export to the Caribbean, the Chesapeake, or Newfoundland—but given the limited productivity of the soil, there was little to encourage them either. Although in certain parts of New England (especially Rhode Island and portions of Connecticut) this surplus was significant, Essex County was typical of most of the region in not producing much more than was consumed within its own shores.[31]

A greater strain upon local supplies of capital and labor was generated by the internal needs of families. These demands were serious—much more so than the original immigrants had guessed—for simple reasons of demography. At the beginning of settlement, the majority of immigrants were able-bodied adults, physically equipped for the task. More than two-

town, and they accounted for 42% of those with whom he dealt. Of the 79 whose ages could be estimated, 16% were aged 20–29, 31% were aged 30–39, 33% were aged 40–49, and 20% were aged 50 or above. Establishing status was more difficult, but individuals whose names appeared in the Ipswich tax list of 1648 and the probate records of Essex County to 1665 included those of both healthy and modest estate. See "Ipswich Proceedings," *New England Historical and Genealogical Register*, II (1848), 50–52; and *Essex Co. Court Recs.*, vols. I–IV. Another 17th-century account book that deals with agricultural produce is that of Samuel Sewall for 1685–1689, Baker Library, Harvard Business School, Boston.

30. Timber products constituted a partial exception here—but only until farmers had cleared their lands of trees.

31. Russell, *Long, Deep Furrow*, 33–38; Bidwell and Falconer, *History of Agriculture*, 40–48; Carl Bridenbaugh, *Fat Mutton and Liberty of Conscience: Society in Rhode Island, 1636–1690* (Providence, R.I., 1974), 25–60; Karen J. Friedmann, "Victualling Colonial Boston," *Agricultural History*, XLVII (1973), 189–205; Stephen Innes, *Labor in a New Land: Economy and Society in Seventeenth-Century Springfield* (Princeton, N.J., 1983), 33–34.

thirds of this population was between fifteen and sixty years of age, and the ratio of dependents to active producers was .475, much lower than the .674 of contemporary England. By the end of the seventeenth century, however, the high fertility and low mortality of Massachusetts had lifted the colonial ratio to at least .900—considerably higher than its English equivalent. At first glance a large family might seem the answer to the scarcity of labor. In reality, maintaining this growing number of children and grandparents was a difficult task, which fell more heavily upon productive family members with every passing decade. Although on a societal level population growth obviously did play a role in alleviating the labor problem, individual families experienced the press of numbers as a further strain on their resources.[32]

The other extraordinary demand on the immigrant colonists' time and capital equipment was the work of farm formation: the construction of buildings; the manufacture of farm implements; and, most of all, the clearing and fencing of land. Such activities naturally were most important during the first decade or so. Given the large numbers of children who grew to maturity and the rate at which existing fields were worked to exhaustion, however, the demand for new land proved more or less continuous up to the end of the seventeenth century. Clearing forests and enclosing fields alone consumed close to one-quarter of the working year throughout this period.[33] Much of this activity did not compete directly with other agricultural tasks, since it could normally be tackled during the slacker periods of the summer or, better yet, deferred until after harvest.

32. The dependency ratios represent the number of people under 15 and over 59 divided by the number of those aged 15–59. See Anderson, *New England's Generation*, 25n. The figures for the later 17th century in Massachusetts were calculated from the model life tables presented in Robert Paul Thomas and Terry L. Anderson, "White Population, Labor Force and Extensive Growth of the New England Economy in the Seventeenth Century," *JEH*, XXXIII (1973), 652–653. They ranged from .886 to .912 for men and from .956 to .975 for women (upper and lower bound estimates). The model tables employed by Thomas and Anderson compared quite closely (as far as could be measured) to the age tables constructed from empirical data for different adult male populations in 17th-century New England. See table 2, below. The same argument has been made for the 18th century by Jim Potter, "Demographic Development and Family Structure," in Jack P. Greene and J. R. Pole, eds., *Colonial British America: Essays in the New History of the Early Modern Era* (Baltimore, 1984), 144–145.

33. Out of 167 instances of farm work performed by men in 17th-century Essex County, drawn from the sources in Appendix 1, 38 involved cutting wood, hauling it, and fencing in the cleared land.

Still, it was a type of work that reshaped the labor system of seventeenth-century New England into something new.

How was the farming year actually structured? In Essex County, the work of breaking up, fertilizing, and harrowing the soil normally began late by English standards, at the end of March or the beginning of April. Next to mowing time and corn harvest, this was the busiest part of the agricultural year. Not until the end of April or early in May were men ready to sow their fields and women to plant their gardens. Shortly thereafter sheep would have to be washed and sheared, but then the tending of animals and crops slackened, and for a month or two, family members had only to weed the garden from time to time and hoe or plow around the cornstalks in the fields beyond. For a few weeks, their attention could turn to the myriad tasks of farm improvement—constructing new fences, enlarging barns, and the endless job of grubbing out stones and rotten stumps from previously cleared land. Beginning with the start of mowing in July, the normal routines of husbandry intensified again. Hoping for dry and windy weather, men and boys spent long hours in meadow and marsh, mowing and raking hay cut from salt and English grasses, turning it several times on the ground before piling it into ricks to dry, and then finally carting it home at summer's end. Late in August began the harvest of grains (by men) and garden vegetables (largely by women), and until the last ear of corn was husked in October all hands were employed about the crops. Harvest time never stood apart as a period of special intensity in New England as it had in the old country, where gangs of laborers toured the countryside working long days at good wages to make up for the days earlier in the year when they had been unable to find work. In the Bay Colony of the seventeenth century, the basic work of homesteading kept most people busy from spring to autumn, and so the long working days of July and August did not stand out as much in comparison. Nor did the end of harvest give anyone much immediate pause for rest. As the days shortened and winter approached, all the family turned to tasks that in the busier months of the growing season had been laid aside. An acre or two of land could be cleared, animals slaughtered, barns improved or repaired, and the fruits of the harvest processed. Only when the first snowfalls in December announced the arrival of truly frigid weather did most outside work come to an end. For about three months, New Englanders were frozen out of gardens, fields, and forests in a way that their English cousins were not. The entire family was confined chiefly to the house and yard, threshing grains, dressing flax, fixing tools, chopping wood, and tending the animals that had been driven in from the fields. Not until March, when frost relaxed its hold upon the soil, would the pace of work recover and the farming year begin again.[34]

The continuous pressure that homesteading placed on time and capital resources combined with the limited size of local markets led most colonists who settled in the countryside to set aside their previous craft training and forgo the tradition of by-employments that had been so important in the economy of rural England. This is not to say that they lost their abilities, but apart from employing the rough carpentry skills that became commonplace across the countryside, the great majority found little time for anything other than clearing, improving, and working the land. This was not universally true, for it is clear from estate inventories that certain farmers did practice a craft on the side. John Cheney of Newbury owned forty-two lasts and a set of shoemaker's tools; William Law of Rowley owned a "cotton loum with furneture to it"; and Wymond Bradbury of Salisbury set his fishing net in the Merrimack River. Farmwives and their daughters, moreover, performed a great variety of manufacturing tasks within the same households. Thus by comparison with the plantation colonies of the seventeenth century, the rural diversification of Essex County was reasonably impressive. For the male members of farming households, however, the tradition of by-employments weakened considerably in the transition from old to New England. Exceptional cases notwithstanding, most farmers possessed little equipment beyond their "implements of husbandry" and a few woodcutting tools. In legal records from the first century of settlement rural householders rarely styled themselves by any specific calling—craft or agricultural—because the business of founding farms that occupied so much of their lives made them consider themselves planters foremost. This would continue until the eighteenth century, when the availability of capital and labor relative to land began to increase.[35]

34. Darrett B. Rutman, *Husbandmen of Plymouth: Farms and Villages in the Old Colony, 1620–1692* (Boston, 1967), 50–52; Robert Blair St. George, "'Set Thine House in Order': The Domestication of the Yeomanry in Seventeenth-Century New England," in Jonathan L. Fairbanks and Robert F. Trent, eds., *New England Begins: The Seventeenth Century*, 3 vols. (Boston, 1982), II, 175–176, 325; Innes, *Labor in a New Land*, 106–117. St. George suggests less variation in seasonal work load, but his evidence is drawn from the milder climate of coastal Connecticut, where the growing season was longer than in most parts of New England, including Essex County.

35. The evidence on tools is drawn from a sample of 36 farm inventories (defined here as

The first generation or two of farmers in Essex County were short of time and help, oxen and outbuildings, therefore, not because the rhythms of the agricultural cycle made special demands at peak seasons, but because the basic work of farm formation required so much energy throughout the year. Had a sizable market developed in or outside the colony for the produce New Englanders could raise in quantity, the strain on local resources of labor power and productive wealth would have been more seasonally specific and even more severe. Fueled by English credit, the region would have attracted many more indentured servants who, upon achieving their freedom, might have provided the rural economy with a supply of property-poor laborers. As matters stood in New England, the proximity of the frontier in a region with limited agricultural potential created problems that local communities had to grapple with on their own.

LABORERS, SERVANTS, AND EXCHANGING WORKS

"It is not an easy matter to gett workmen to goe for new England," wrote a London merchant in 1652; he might have added that it was even harder to find them among the inhabitants themselves.[36] Even planters with enough foresight to have brought additional help with them soon discovered that paid assistance of any kind melted away on the Massachusetts shore. Having grown up in a world where servants and laborers played a significant role in agriculture, the Puritan colonists would have to learn to do without in the course of the seventeenth-century pioneering experience. How, then, were the different elements of farm labor familiar to early modern Englishmen reorganized on this particular stretch of America's first frontier?

On the question of access to a regional labor market where they could hire hands by the day or by the task, Essex County farmers were of one mind. Laborers, they complained, were both expensive and difficult to

---

those containing land, cattle, and some farming equipment) taken from *Essex Co. Prob. Recs.*, II. For the three examples cited, see *ibid.*, 55–56, 110–112, 170–171. Compare with my findings for the 18th century in Chapter 5, below, and with information for Maryland in Gloria L. Main, *Tobacco Colony: Life in Early Maryland, 1650–1720* (Princeton, N.J., 1982), 77–78. That 17th-century colonists in Essex County rarely styled themselves by occupation, whereas those of the 18th century did so increasingly, is obvious from even a cursory examination of the county land, probate, and court records described in Appendixes 1–4.

36. *Essex Co. Court Recs.*, II, 88–89.

find. Ecclesiastical synods, sessions of court, town meetings, and private individuals alike took account of labor's cost, although they spoke of it more as testimony to moral failing than as evidence of market forces. "Extortion" and "oppression" were the preferred terms, echoing repeatedly through the end of the seventeenth century.[37] In a sense these commentators were right: the twenty to thirty pence per day (in English currency) that agricultural labor commanded in seventeenth-century Essex County was an unusually hefty wage. By the contemporary English standard of ten to twenty pence per day, such earnings quite understandably provoked attention, although they were primarily indicative of the favorable bargaining position that labor commanded.[38] By 1641 the General Court had abandoned any effort to regulate wages. Workmen, explained John Winthrop, "for being restrained . . . would either remove to other places where they might have more, or else being able to live by planting and other employments of their own, they would not be hired at all."[39]

One exception to this general truth was on the agricultural periphery of Salem, where a number of farms that were large by local standards did operate with the help of hired men, some of whom commuted to the fields from the town. These individuals were less established than most and not simply because of their youth, for many who were in their thirties and

37. Morris, *Government and Labor*, 55–78.

38. For Essex County rates, see *Essex Co. Court Recs.*, II, 328, 363–364, IV, 107, VI, 87, VII, 208, VIII, 64, IX, 80; "Salem Town Records," 197; Winthrop, *History of New England*, I, 112; Mighill and Blodgette, eds., *Early Records of Rowley*, 92, 156; Dow, ed., *Town Records of Topsfield*, I, 36; and various pre-1700 accounts in the Thomas Barnard Account Book, 1688–1708, JDPL. In Springfield, the mean daily wage ranged from 14.5 pence in the winter to 20.2 pence at harvest; across the year, it averaged out at 19 ($N = 202$). See Innes, *Labor in a New Land*, 307–335, 370–379. Throughout this chapter, Massachusetts currency has been converted into British sterling. For English equivalents, see the account books and wage assessments listed in n. 15, above, as well as David W. Galenson, "Labor Market Behavior in Colonial America: Servitude, Slavery, and Free Labor," in David W. Galenson, ed., *Markets in History: Economic Studies of the Past* (Cambridge, 1989), 89; and Innes, *Labor in a New Land*, 74–75. There are no good price series for 17th-century Massachusetts that might enable us to make accurate transatlantic comparisons. An examination of the price ranges given by Innes in *Labor in a New Land*, 464, and of the tables in William Henry Beveridge *et al.*, *Prices and Wages in England from the Twelfth to the Nineteenth Century*, vol. I: *Price Tables: Mercantile Era* (London, 1939), suggests, however, that after 1645, the cost of living was, if anything, lower in Massachusetts than in England.

39. Winthrop, *History of New England*, II, 24.

forties can confidently be placed in the poorer half of the town's population. Indeed, it seems that they toiled for others out of simple poverty—just as workmen did in England.[40] John Blany from Lynn, a fifty-year-old widower trying to provide for his six children with a single cow and the "money . . . received for wood or timber or for the work of his team," was probably typical. Turned out in 1677 by his father-in-law, with whom he had lived for twenty-eight years, possibly after a spree with the bottle, Blany found shelter for his family with friends. The next year, with his children suffering "for food and raiment," he remarried, and soon after they all moved into a little house across the line in Salem. At no time did Blany appear to have any income beyond what he made by plowing and carting for farmers in the neighborhood.[41] A similar story was that of John Glover, who came to Salem in the 1650s and worked on local farms, either as a tenant or as a hired hand, for the rest of his life. When he died in 1695, not yet sixty years old, he owned only a tiny cottage, a few tools of husbandry, and two pigs—worth together a mere £24 sterling.[42] Blany and Glover were laborers on the English model; the hinterland behind Salem where they found employment contained less than 20 percent of the county's rural population, but 32 percent of the farming day labor represented in the seventeenth-century county court records worked there.[43] Being a seaport, Salem possessed a local market sufficient to support more commercial agriculture than most towns in the county. Given the healthy wages that a few local farmers could afford to pay, some of the migrant crowd drawn to the town through its maritime connections chose to settle permanently and support themselves as farm laborers.

Beyond the environs of Salem, however, this was not common, and the

40. The median age of employees from Salem and Lynn in 54 such instances was 34. Of the 19 whose wealth status could be established, 13 belonged to the poorer half of the population and were scattered in age from 24 to 50 years. Of the 24 employers for whom the same information was available, 22 were wealthier than average and 12 ranked in the top wealth decile of the town. See Appendix 1.

41. Essex Co. Court Recs., VI, 300, VII, 23–25, VIII, 179, 198, IX, 317; Sidney Perley, The History of Salem, Massachusetts, 3 vols. (Salem, Mass., 1924–1928), III, 421.

42. Essex Co. Court Recs., II, 12, III, 276, IV, 102, 278; Perley, History of Salem, III, 18–19, 420; Estate of John Glover (1695), Probate No. 11025, Essex Co. Prob. Recs.

43. See Appendix 1 and Evarts B. Greene and Virginia D. Harrington, American Population before the Federal Census of 1790 (New York, 1932), 20. Salem's hinterland is defined here as the two agricultural wards of the town (including the village) as well as Lynn.

occupational description "laborer" almost vanished. No resident in the 1678 town listings for Beverly and Gloucester had such a designation.[44] Of course farmers might periodically hire artisans—carpenters, blacksmiths, and millers, for example—to perform specialized tasks. In a year when a major project like a house raising was undertaken, such craftsmen would play a critical role. But in the regular round of field chores, woodcutting, and property maintenance, it was the rare husbandman who hired laborers by the day.[45]

That a class of laborers failed to materialize in most of Essex County did not distress the colonists; they had planned the Bay Colony as a society where men could enjoy a modest independence and support themselves without working for others. Insofar as the poverty that forced people into the labor market was in the Puritan view a source of disorder and ungodliness, they were pleased to be rid of it. Those who anticipated a need for extrafamilial help expected to depend not on day laborers but on domestic servants, and they brought hundreds into the county during the Great Migration.[46] But did farm servants play a more significant role in the agricultural economy? For the large estates situated on the richer soils of the Merrimack Valley or in the coastal marshlands of Ipswich, Rowley, and Newbury, servant labor did matter.[47] Families such as the Bradstreets, Appletons, Gardners, and others—all of whom generally scorned physical

44. *Essex Co. Court Recs.*, VI, 400–402. A quick glance at the "occupations" entries in the indexes of vols. I–VIII confirms this claim for the entire county.

45. Stephen Innes has calculated, however, that in Springfield, a town where property concentration, soil productivity, commercial orientation, and hence labor demand were unusually large, more than half of the population in any given year worked at least a month for John Pynchon, the community's only major employer. This is, I would argue, the significant exception that proves the rule. It should be remembered, too, that he was the primary source of income for fewer than 20% of Springfield's 17th-century inhabitants. See Innes, *Labor in a New Land*, 38, 72.

46. This is an estimate, based on Anderson, *New England's Generation*, 15, 24.

47. Farm servants are defined here as those performing agricultural labor for employers with whom they lived. Considering the county as a whole, Ipswich, Rowley, Newbury, and Haverhill together accounted for 62% of all farm servants but only 41% of the county population, whereas the poor upland farming towns accounted for 10% of farm servants and 26% of the population. Some towns were not considered in this calculation, notably (1) Salem, Lynn, and Marblehead, which are treated separately above; and (2) Salisbury and Amesbury, for which the court records that form the basis of the servant sample are sparse. See Appendix 1 and Greene and Harrington, *American Population before 1790*, 20.

labor themselves—employed servants on their lands throughout the seventeenth century, though rarely more than two or three at a time.[48] Samuel Symonds of Ipswich, who owned a farm that was later valued at more than £2,000 sterling, expected to be left helpless in 1661 when Philip Welch and William Downing, "all the men he had," threatened to desert him in midsummer. Some years later, an estate of similar size belonging to Henry Short of Newbury was managing with only Daniel Musselway "of the Irish bloud," a Welshman named John Ewen, and Robin Mingo, an African slave.[49] Elsewhere in New England larger estates supported more of these young men. In Springfield, Massachusetts, for example, John Pynchon employed several servants about his extensive lands to cultivate wheat, raise cattle, and cut timber for shipment abroad.[50] Most husbandmen in Essex County, however, did not employ help of this kind. Once servants who accompanied the original migrants of the 1630s had served out their time and dispersed, the English system of farm service entered a speedy decline. Estimating the numerical importance of servants is tricky; but considering men only and working from those mentioned in the court records, even if we assume that at least one was to be found on each of the county's wealthiest farms, their proportion to the rural population as a whole was something less than 5 percent.[51] A 1687 tax list from Topsfield

48. That wealthy New Englanders did not work is suggested by the fact that in 83 work experiences from Ipswich recorded in court depositions, only one involved a member of the town elite in manual activity. See Appendix 1; and Edward Spaulding Perzel, "The First Generation of Settlement in Colonial Ipswich, Massachusetts, 1633–1660" (Ph.D. diss., Rutgers University, 1967), 171–172.

49. Perzel, "First Generation in Ipswich," 184; *Essex Co. Court Recs.*, II, 295, IV, 179–180, V, 167.

50. Innes, *Labor in a New Land*, 6–10, 110–112.

51. This maximum figure for the proportion of male servants within the farm population of 17th-century Essex County was derived as follows. First, in the agricultural work experiences described in the records of the county court involving masters identifiably in the top wealth decile of the population and their menservants ($N = 24$), the ratio of servants to masters (S/M) was 1.33. Second, the ratio of servants belonging to masters in the top wealth decile to the servants of all other masters (10/90) was .96 ($N = 49$). Assuming that all householders in the top wealth decile of the population owned at least one servant, and also that the ratio of population to householders was 6, it follows that in a hypothetical community of 100 householders and a total population of 600, the 10 wealthiest householders would have kept 13.3 servants, and the remaining 90 would have kept 13.9. A total of 27.2 menservants constituted 4.5% of the population. When the same calculation is performed under the more optimistic (and almost certainly incorrect) assumption that the wealthiest 15% of the population of each town kept servants, S/M remains at 1.33, 10/90

that lists male dependents and distinguishes between sons and "men" allows us to place the actual figure for this particular town at less than 2 percent.[52] Considering that in seventeenth-century England male servants composed more than 8 percent of the entire farming population (including laboring families) and about 14 percent of the members of

climbs to 1.65, and the resultant maximum percentage of male servants within the population still reaches only 5.4. Even these percentages, however, must be regarded as maximums, since it is certain that some of the householders in the top decile did not keep any menservants, and since the multiplier of population/household of 6 is likely too low. Philip Greven, for one, reports an average family size of 5.94 for Massachusetts in 1764 and suggests that 17th-century levels were probably higher. See Philip J. Greven, Jr., "The Average Size of Families and Households in the Province of Massachusetts in 1764 and in the United States in 1790: An Overview," in Laslett and Wall, *Household and Family in Past Time*, 553–557. Moreover, if Main is correct in *Colonial Connecticut*, 8n, that 4.5 to 5 is the best multiplier for population/polls, and if we can assume on the basis of the town rates cited below that the ratio of households to polls in 17th-century Essex County was 1.33, then an average household size of greater than 6 may well be more accurate. See Appendix 1.

52. The Topsfield list mentions 5 male servants, 62 households, and 91 polls. Even if we allow a low multiplier of 4.5 for population/polls, and increase the number of servants by 20% to allow for those under the age of 16 whom the assessors would have missed, the *maximum* proportion of male servants to the entire town population would have been 1.5%. See "Taxes under Gov. Andros: Topsfield Town Rate, 1687," *NEHGR*, XXXV (1881), 34–35. It is assumed here, following an 18th-century valuation list for this town that mentions only 4% of its householders as being craftsmen without farms and a further 12% as craftsmen with farms, that for practical purposes all the inhabitants of Topsfield were primarily agriculturalists. See Topsfield Valuation List, 1773, Microform Edition of the Tax and Valuation Lists of Massachusetts Towns before 1776, roll 6. All references to 18th-century Massachusetts tax and valuation lists, unless otherwise specified, are to the microfilm edition compiled by Ruth Crandall and published in 1971 by the Charles Warren Center for Studies in American History at Harvard University, which filmed the originals housed in town record offices. In Dedham, Massachusetts, servants of both sexes accounted for less than 5% of the population, according to Kenneth A. Lockridge, *A New England Town, the First Hundred Years: Dedham, Massachusetts, 1636–1736* (New York, 1970), 72. Of these, 61% were male (*N* = 28), and no household possessed more than two. See Don Gleason Hill *et al.*, eds., *Early Records of the Town of Dedham, Massachusetts*, 7 vols. (Dedham, Mass., 1886–1968), V, 121–122. In a census of Rhode Island taken in 1708, "white servants" accounted for only .8% of the total population. John Demos reports much higher percentages for the town of Bristol, but I suspect that most of his "servants" were actually African slaves. See Abbot Emerson Smith, *Colonists in Bondage: White Servitude and Convict Labor in America, 1607–1776* (Chapel Hill, N.C., 1947), 316; and John Demos, "Families in Colonial Bristol, Rhode Island: An Exercise in Historical Demography," *WMQ*, 3d Ser., XXV (1968), 43.

those households headed by the husbandmen and yeomen who were the old country equivalents of colonial farmers, the measure of this transatlantic contrast is plainly evident.[53] Whether maidservants were equally scarce we do not know. Certainly, mistresses were just as quick as their husbands to complain about the difficulty of finding assistance. As Elizabeth Saltonstall learned from her mother, "to keep a great dairy" was impossible if you were "forced to hire all your help." New Englanders complained endlessly about the unreliability of their hired hands, and it seems that those of either sex could, indeed, be difficult when they knew how difficult it would be to replace them.[54]

This was not, moreover, service on the English model. It is true that in age these young men ranged for the most part between fifteen and twenty-five, and the same seems to have held true for their female counterparts. All of them hoped to establish a means of marrying and settling down—much as they had in the mother country.[55] But whereas Old World farmers had recruited hands from nearby villages, the great majority of farm servants whose names entered the court records of Essex County pos-

53. "Farming households" are defined here as those headed by yeomen, husbandmen, or laborers. These figures were calculated from the data for 11 English rural villages, 1599–1705, in Kussmaul, *Servants in Husbandry*, 12, allowing for a male/female sex ratio of 1.07 and an average household size of 5.5 for husbandmen and yeomen, and 4.5 for laborers. See Laslett, *World We Have Lost*, 72, 262–263.

54. Quotation from *Saltonstall Papers, 1607–1814* (1972), in Laurel Thatcher Ulrich, *Good Wives: Image and Reality in the Lives of Women in Northern New England, 1650–1750* (New York, 1982), 74. A catalog of servants' misdemeanors and masters' complaints can be found in Edmund Morgan, *The Puritan Family: Religion and Domestic Relations in Seventeenth-Century New England*, rev. ed. (New York, 1966), 123–131, and in Lawrence William Towner, "A Good Master Well Served: A Social History of Servitude in Massachusetts, 1620–1750" (Ph.D. diss., Northwestern University, 1954), chaps. 5, 7, 8.

55. The calculation was as follows. Of 44 menservants whose ages could be determined, each was counted only once. If the period of recorded service spanned several years, an individual's age was appropriately prorated across the time frame. Of those identified, none was younger than 10; 17% were aged 10–14; 29% were aged 15–19; 32% were aged 20–24; 7% were aged 25–29; 14% were aged 30–34; and 2% were 35 or older. See Appendix 1. Of the 58 menservants uncovered in the court records, at least 22 (38%) eventually married within Essex County. A good many more disappeared from the local records but almost certainly managed to marry elsewhere in the colonies or returned to England and married there. The best information on the ages of maidservants is in Lyle Koehler, *A Search for Power: The "Weaker Sex" in Seventeenth-Century New England* (Urbana, Ill., 1980), 111.

sessed no local kin of any kind.[56] Some were ethnic outsiders: prisoners of war or captives in slavery, who were victims of English imperialism. John King, Philip Welch, and William Downing, all from Ireland, had been "stollen . . . in the night out of theyr beds" by Cromwell's soldiers in 1654, clapped into prison ships, and transported across the Atlantic "by order of the State of England" to be sold. From Africa, in chains of a different sort, came Chuza and Wonn: two of several black slaves delivered to Essex County farmers in the seventeenth century, probably by way of the Caribbean.[57] Numerically more significant were the individuals who were serving out indentures that they or their parents had contracted in England. In 1638, when he was thirteen, Richard Coy and several other boys were taken from Boston in Lincolnshire to London by a Mr. Whittingham, who then shipped them across the ocean at a cost of £8 sterling a head for seven to ten years service in the colony.[58] Yet, as Edward Randolph reported in 1676, neither Africans nor indentured servants were really important in this corner of the New World. From one end of Massachusetts to the other, he told the Lords of Trade in London, there were "not above 200 slaves," and no bound servants beyond "a few who serve four years for the charge of being transported thither."[59]

More common, Randolph quite accurately observed, were the single and unattached residents—perhaps former indentured servants—who now toiled "on hired wages" by the month or year and lived with the masters for whom they worked.[60] William Dellow, having arrived in Essex

56. Of servants who entered the records between 1645 and 1700 ($N = 48$), only 12 (25%) had families in Essex County; few others (although identification becomes difficult over the wider area) appear to have had relatives anywhere in New England. See Appendix 1.

57. *Essex Co. Court Recs.*, II, 294–296, IX, 326. For other examples of non-English servants, see *ibid.*, II, 218, 358, IV, 179, 180, VII, 329, VIII, 173, and Smith, *Colonists in Bondage*, 154–155. In the Rhode Island towns scattered around the shores of Narragansett Bay, where a number of wealthy farmers bred livestock for the market, "black servants" outnumbered "white servants" by more than seven to one. See Smith, *Colonists in Bondage*, 316; Bridenbaugh, *Fat Mutton*, 19; and Wilfred H. Munro, *The History of Bristol, R.I.* (Providence, R.I., 1880), esp. 111–112, 367.

58. *Essex Co. Court Recs.*, I, 381–382. See also *ibid.*, VI, 156, 158–160; Dorothy Flute to John Winthrop, May 5, 1640, *Winthrop Papers*, IV, 236–237; and Towner, "Good Master Well Served," 51–74.

59. "Answer of Edward Randolph to several heads of inquiry concerning the present state of New England," Oct. 12, 1676, *CSPC*, IX, 464–465.

60. *Ibid.*, 464.

County about 1650, probably under indenture, was still a servant in 1659, when he appeared in the court records at thirty-one years of age, loading wood in Ipswich for his master, Richard Shatswell. Five years later, Dellow had moved to Rumney Marsh on the north shore of Boston harbor to work for Samuel Bennet, a carpenter of some means who owned a large farm there. Evan Morris, another servant, drifted around Essex County—from Salisbury to Topsfield and Rowley and finally to Newbury—throughout most of his adult life. In 1682, at the age of seventy, he was still keeping sheep for the Newbury proprietors, but he commuted from Topsfield and "never settled in one family for more than a few weeks."[61] Morris and Dellow obviously resembled the farm servants of the mother country in a way that their Irish and African workmates never could. Yet they shared one central trait with most other servants: a want of kindred in America.

Insofar as the rural economy of Essex County employed farm servants at all, therefore, it recruited them among outsiders—those without personal links to the founding population and least able to profit by opportunities that family connections afforded. Nobody planned this; but in a colonial world where labor was scarce and children rarely put out into neighboring homes, except sometimes to learn a skilled trade distinct from agriculture, the few farmers who could afford to hire help had to depend on imported labor and the unattached. In this particular corner of early America, therefore, service in husbandry became quantitatively less important and socially more peripheral than Englishmen would have expected.[62]

When family labor resources were inadequate for their immediate requirements, farmers turned to one another. The exchange of labor could assume many different forms, but in essence it reflected the functional needs of the households concerned and did not radically divide the rich from the poor or the young from the old. As far as can be measured, both parties to such arrangements tended to be between the ages of twenty and fifty, drawn from across the relatively limited spectrum of local wealth. Typically, on several occasions in the 1680s and 1690s, Henry Trussler of Salisbury employed younger men, Joseph Lancaster and John Foot, as

61. On Dellow, see *Essex Co. Court Recs.*, I, 227, II, 113, 147, III, 159, IV, 113. On Morris, see *ibid.*, I, 95, 97, II, 358, IV, 243–245, 386, VIII, 291–292. For other instances of servants on wages, see *ibid.*, I, 423–424, V, 301, VI, 28, and *Essex Co. Court Recs., Verbatim Transcriptions*, XLVIII, 99 (iii).

62. For a rather different and somewhat misleading evaluation of farm service in early New England, see Morgan, *Puritan Family*, 75–78, 109.

well as an older neighbor, Joseph Pritchett, to help mow his fields. In the 1640s John Hazeltine of Haverhill helped fence the lands of Thomas Nelson, one of Rowley's largest landholders and twenty years Hazeltine's senior; in 1665, Hazeltine was plowing the fields of Stephen Webster, a young householder fifteen years his junior. Four years later, Webster himself was mowing hay for John Emery of Newbury, aged seventy-one.[63] True, men like Emery in their sixties and seventies were more likely to ask for help than to offer it. A scattering of gentlemen-farmers had frequent need of paid labor because they did not work themselves. But the network of labor exchange among seventeenth-century households in the farming villages of Essex County did not reflect any marked social distinctions.[64] Women, too, helped out their neighbors—spinning, washing, shelling peas, and tending children—though unlike their husbands they rarely recorded their obligations in diaries or account books, at least any that have survived.

How much time did labor exchanges among households really occupy? Unfortunately, their significance is impossible to measure for the simple reason that almost everyone at one time or another worked for somebody else. The majority of men employed by their neighbors were in their twenties and thirties, but then so was most of the county's adult population. Indeed, only the very wealthy and the very old seem to have spared themselves entirely from this type of work. Men who swapped chores on an occasional basis thus cannot, like servants and laborers, be dismissed as an insignificant portion of the population. Nor, since this sort of casual help may have occurred only a few times a year, can we be certain that it *was* important. Because the court records, which provide most of the surviving evidence on seventeenth-century farm labor, generally describe disputes between households and not within them, they would seem to privilege extrafamilial over intrafamilial labor relations. One must be careful, therefore, not to overestimate the importance of labor exchanges

63. Bartlett v. Trussler (1715), Box 15, Files ICCP; *Essex Co. Court Recs.*, II, 17, III, 276–277, IV, 228.

64. Outside of Salem and Lynn, 60% of those hiring help by the day or task, and 86% of those being hired, were aged 20–49. Of those who can be confidently ranked by wealth, 9 of the 12 employers were above average in estate and 6 of the 11 employees were below average in estate. However, given the small numbers of those so identified and the likelihood that the process of identification would tend to highlight the well-to-do, it seems probable that virtually anyone could be an employer and that anyone save the aged and the rich could be an employee (see n. 40, above, and Appendix 1).

that figure so prominently in these records. Solid evidence that might allow us to move beyond random illustration does not exist for the seventeenth century, so any certain answer must await a later period and another chapter.

What is quite certain, however, is that whenever these Bay colonists did seek extrafamilial assistance, they did so within a network of exchange that operated differently than the labor market of seventeenth-century England. The pattern of seasonal wage variation in Essex County and other regions of New England was flatter than that of the mother country and more sensitive to seasonal variations in the length of the working day than to market pressures. Local authorities on both sides of the Atlantic agreed that the regulation of daily pay should be adjusted to fit the three generally accepted seasons of the agricultural year: winter, when the days were short and the pace of work dullest; summer, when the days lengthened and farming activity picked up; and mowing time or harvest, when work continued from dawn to dusk. Over the wage that was appropriate to each season, however, England and Massachusetts diverged. In the mother country, extrapolating from ten surviving assessments, judges on average pegged daily summer rates at 20 percent and harvest wages at 81 percent higher than those of winter, whereas the average of three ordinances from the Bay Colony (including one from Rowley) hiked summer wages by 32 percent but those at harvest by only 58 percent. Actual payments from account books state the contrast with even greater force. Two English farmers, Robert Loder and Henry Best, recorded winter to summer rises of only 14 and 33 percent, but at harvest their wages soared 107 and 144 percent above the slack season. John Pynchon's account books from Springfield in the Connecticut Valley, by contrast, showed a 25 percent summer to winter increment but no more than a 33 percent increase at harvest. In short, the Massachusetts wages rose in the spring in consonance with the longer workday, as they had in England, but at mowing time and harvest they scarcely climbed any further: enough, perhaps, to recompense the hired hands for their added hours of toil but not to raise the actual value of their labor.[65]

65. Calculations were based on Innes, *Labor in a New Land*, 307–335, 370–379, 461–462, the town assessments recorded in Morris, *Government and Labor*, 72, and the English account books and wage assessments listed in n. 15, above. The ratios for Connecticut and New Haven, which can be calculated from Morris, *Government and Labor*, 78–81, were very similar to those in Massachusetts. About actual hours of work in different seasons we know very little, but the assumption is that they were generally governed by the sun and,

Why was the seasonal wage curve in Massachusetts so much flatter than that in England? One reason was the changed seasonality of labor demand. Harvest time was full of activity in New England, but so was the rest of the year—at least between spring thaw and freeze. As we have seen, there could be no slack period in a frontier community as long as the weather was warm enough to allow the work of farm formation to proceed. Wages failed to rise at harvest, therefore, because the demand for labor was already high throughout the rest of the growing season. Had local farmers ever found a sizable market for their produce, they could have paid the cost of importing servants and supported a class of hired laborers; they would have needed gangs of extra help at harvest, and seasonal wage patterns would have come closer to resembling those of the old country. Something like this actually happened in the more fertile countryside of colonial Pennsylvania, where the business of raising wheat for export developed during the eighteenth century and seems to have generated a distinguishable laboring class.[66] In most of Massachusetts, however, the land was so stinting in its yields that families constantly had to clear new fields just to sustain themselves in an independent competency, and the limited surplus they generated could not justify the cost of paying outside help at harvest.

Where commercial production was not important, moreover, farmers understood that there was little point in John charging Zerubbabel double time one day, if Zerubbabel was going to ask the same rate of John the next. Wages rose at English harvest because wealthier farmers quickly outstripped the labor capacities of their own households and had to recruit additional labor power: help that was not necessarily local and had other possible means of employment. Laboring men who were rarely if ever employers themselves had everything to gain by bargaining for the highest wage they could. In most New England communities, where more householders were independent landowners and just as likely to ask for as to offer assistance, the same logic did not hold. Haggling for a better return on one's time was not likely to produce any long-run advantage,

therefore, varied by the season. See Morris, *ibid.*, 65, 72, 81; Innes, *Labor in a New Land*, 461; Statute of Artificers (1563), in Fisher and Jurica, eds., *England from 1000 to 1760*, 492–493; Robert W. Malcolmson, *Life and Labour in England, 1700–1780* (London, 1981), 37; and Best, *Rural Economy in Yorkshire*, 32, 33, 44, 52, 82–83, 115, 138.

66. Paul G. E. Clemens and Lucy Simler, "Rural Labor and the Farm Household in Chester County, Pennsylvania, 1750–1820," in Stephen Innes, ed., *Work and Labor in Early America* (Chapel Hill, N.C., 1988), 106–143.

and the damage to one's reputation that it generated might even cost the farming household by leading neighbors to excuse themselves from lending hands at all. Market forces impinged indirectly on labor exchanges by prompting individual households to drop dealings that were plainly not to their advantage; but the free negotiation of terms that defines labor markets under capitalism was not a feature of these local dealings.[67]

The drive to create competent farmholdings out of the wilderness placed local farmers in a double bind. On the one hand, the tasks of farm development left them chronically short of help; on the other hand, the limited commercial product of their farms did not allow them to hire or purchase the labor they could have used. Neither hired hands nor indentured servants were locally available at costs farmers could afford, and neighborly assistance could not be called upon repeatedly when all households were in the same predicament. This was the price New Englanders paid for their insistence on fashioning a society of independent households in a land that could not support wholesale export agriculture. To tame the land and work it farmers required a dependable but cheap labor force, and this was supplied by their sons.

FATHERS AND SONS

When Essex County farmers left for the fields at sunup on seventeenth-century mornings, they generally walked alone or in the company of their boys. But what do we actually know about the work relations connecting fathers with their sons? Throughout most of the New World, Europeans had adopted systems of bound labor to cope with the peculiar risks of producing surpluses along the frontier. The returns of agriculture in coastal Massachusetts were too meager to allow farmers the luxury of imported help; so in working the fields and forests that were the male responsibility within New England's rural economy, they exploited with doubled intensity the only labor resource available to them—their sons. The other labor relations discussed in this chapter all have their historians, as does the domestic round of chores that was the province of mothers and daughters, and much that has been written on fathers and sons addresses topics other than work. The character of productive relations within the male branch of the New England family, however, has

67. This point is informed by the treatment of Melanesian trading patterns in Marshall Sahlins, *Stone Age Economics* (Chicago, 1972), 312.

never received extended study.[68] Let us then examine the farm boy, as a laborer under parental direction, from early childhood to the point at which he achieved an independence of his own.

Young boys in Essex County, much like their sisters, shortly after their fifth birthday began to help their parents. It was at that age, admitted John Cogswell of Ipswich in an account he placed before the courts, that the net cost of supporting his two grandsons had begun to drop, and we can only assume that he was appealing to some normal understanding of childhood productivity.[69] At first, the work consisted of tasks closely supervised by parents, brothers, and sisters. "Little boys" and "children" fetching tools, guarding holes in the fence against wandering cattle, and helping to drive the animals home from the fields—always in the company of elders and rarely mentioned by name—form a rather misty backdrop to many scenes of labor described in the court testimony of the day.[70] If five was, indeed, the customary point of entry, it would be tempting to consider the possibility that New Englanders pushed their offspring into the world of work at a younger age than had been customary in the mother country. Certainly at Sunday meeting they were urged in that direction, and the demand for labor inherent in the pioneer life would have given parents in the Bay Colony every incentive to hurry along the training of their children. Still, in the absence of hard comparative information, we cannot know for sure.

The farm boy began to acquire a workman's identity of his own about the age of ten. Neighbors started to notice him in the fields and recognize him by his face. His father now trusted him to assist in heavy work and even to take on independent responsibilities, especially in the tending of livestock. Occasionally, the courts might summon him to testify on specific matters of husbandry with which he was familiar; certainly they trusted the memories of older deponents to recall with some precision the farming routines of these early years. Thus, soon after turning eleven, Nathaniel Ingersoll of Salem was helping his father at plow, and Abraham Adams of Newbury knew the family cattle well enough that he could describe to the magistrates a missing steer, down to its hastily cut and "crookedish"

68. The most useful treatments of this topic to date are Morgan, *Puritan Family*, 66–79, and Richard S. Dunn, "Servants and Slaves: The Recruitment and Employment of Labor," in Greene and Pole, eds., *Colonial British America*, 183–188.

69. *Essex Co. Court Recs.*, VI, 161. Interestingly, the cost of support fell more swiftly for the two boys than for their sister. See also Morgan, *Puritan Family*, 66–67.

70. *Essex Co. Court Recs.*, II, 22; Boardman v. Perkins (1695), Box 3, Files ICCP.

earmark. Similarly, John Pingry, Jr., could remember the "cutting and carrying of hay, wood, timber, and hoop polls" for his father from about this age. To extrapolate slightly from Cogswell's account, parents could no longer regard their sons as a drain on the family economy by the time they reached thirteen or fourteen at the latest. Having acquired the skills and physical strength to produce as much as they consumed, they were pulling their own weight and more.[71]

Up to this point, young New Englanders followed much the same path in life as did their counterparts on the far side of the Atlantic. In their teens, however, they encountered a fork in the road. Just when English youths were beginning either to fend for themselves in the world of service or to learn to cooperate with servants brought onto the farm from outside, their Essex County cousins were still spending the vast majority of their waking hours working on their fathers' lands in the company of family members alone. Indeed, as these young colonists matured, their labor commitment did not shift away from the parental estate; it intensified. Putting up fences or cutting wood at their fathers' request, Richard Jacob and John Atkinson, Jr., each fourteen years of age and beginning to shoulder the work load of a man, were investing in family property the labor that most English youths of the same age would be starting to market outside the home. Now, too, either youth might well be dispatched to complete a wide variety of tasks by himself. "Sent by my father to put up our cattell"; "mowed grass . . . at his fathers orders"; "set to work in his . . . [father's] field": such phrases convey both the range of responsibilities and the hand of authority that were still a part of nuclear family life.[72] It is true that from time to time teenage boys might be hired out to neighbors and the earnings posted to their fathers' accounts. Thomas Putnam of Salem Village remembered that at fifteen he had been "implyed wth my Fathers Team . . . to draw Timber for William and John Trask." Another farmer from Haverhill recalled that he was even younger when he was assigned to assist a friend of the family "by taking up after him that wch he mowed" and helping him "fech hom a load." Yet, com-

71. *Essex Co. Court Recs.*, I, 212, III, 151, VI, 161, VII, 14, 201, VIII, 410; Wainwright v. Farley (1709/1710), Box 12, Files ICCP. That English farmers would keep young servants and sometimes pay them a small wage at this age suggests that they constituted no net expense; see Kussmaul, *Servants in Husbandry*, 37–38.

72. *Essex Co. Court Recs.*, IV, 88, VII, 219, 297, VIII, 284; *Essex Co. Court Recs.*, *Verbatim Transcriptions*, XLVIII, 98 (iii).

pared to work performed at home, the exchange of male teenage labor between households occupied relatively little time.[73]

The roles of farming sons shifted gradually as they matured, but one has to be patient to pick up the first glimmerings of real independence. Responsibility landed on them certainly enough, but chiefly it was responsibility toward family and family property, not in any direct sense toward themselves. A particular obligation that began to occupy more time in their later teens was the supervision and training of younger brothers. When Robert Cross of Ipswich agreed in 1657 to tend thirty sheep belonging to a wealthy landowner from neighboring Andover, the actual work of shepherding devolved upon his eldest son, Robert Jr., then about to turn sixteen. For at least the next two summers, not only did he look after the flock, but he also directed his younger brother Stephen, his junior by almost five years, in the same task. A few years later, the town flock in Ipswich was being minded by sixteen-year-old John Potter, charged by his father to look after the sheep while managing his younger brother Edmund. Teams of boys, with the eldest usually in charge, set off almost every day to work at one corner or another of most farms, under the general orders of their father.[74] Having learned what husbandry was about, they could be trusted not only to work by themselves, but even in certain ways to contribute their own ideas to the running of the farm.

On their twenty-first birthdays these young colonists finally crossed something of a watershed in their relations with their fathers, not only in law but in the real experience of working life. Walter Fairfield told the county court that his father had "set me at liberty from his service to trad[e] worke and acte for myself" before reaching this age, but his case

73. *Essex Co. Court Recs., Verbatim Transcriptions*, LIV, 35 (i/ii); Swan v. Ayres (1694), Box 1, Files ICCP. Of the 47 instances of day labor (as distinct from service) performed by teenage sons in the court records prior to 1700, 31 were directed by fathers on family property; 7 were directed by fathers on the property of others; and 9 were directed by non-family members. See Appendix 1. These figures overstate, probably by a considerable amount, the relative importance of labor exchanges, since testimony describing internal household events was inherently less likely to surface in legal disputes.

74. *Essex Co. Court Recs.*, III, 396, IV, 82–83; see also *ibid.*, II, 51, III, 46, 151, IV, 47, 88, VI, 261, VII, 257, 295, VIII, 405, IX, 108, 470; *Essex Co. Court Recs., Verbatim Transcriptions*, LV, 119 (i); Corwin v. Hovey (1695), Box 2, Clark v. Wainwright (1696), Box 3, Dwinnell v. Lake (1699), Box 5, Files ICCP; and Mighill and Blodgette, eds., *Early Records of Rowley*, 156.

was exceptional.[75] Most of his companions would have gained the freedom to collect wages on their own accounts, purchase animals that were not their fathers', contract leases, pay taxes, acquire land, or live apart in dwellings of their own only when they turned twenty-one. On coming of age most young Englishmen already possessed some cash of their own, a couple of animals purchased from their servants' wages, or at least the experience of contracting work on their own account. But in this region of Massachusetts, as far as we can gather from court records, valuation lists, and account books, farm boys did not even begin to act on their own behalfs until they had reached twenty-one.[76]

What were the actual consequences of legal majority? In evidence presented to the courts, sons aged twenty-two to twenty-six were only half as likely to be working under paternal command as those aged seventeen to twenty-one. The older group may have continued to toil on family property, but they no longer told the magistrates that they were doing so at their fathers' behest. At the same time, there was a 23 percent increase between the same two age cohorts in the frequency with which they were observed working on the farms of neighbors, almost certainly on their own account. At this point in their lives some young men obtained work from the town, hiring themselves out to the proprietors as herdsmen on the town common. Leaseholding, too, though more important for unattached young immigrants than for locally born sons, was nearly four times more common among young men aged twenty-two to twenty-six than among those aged seventeen to twenty-one. A realm of activity relatively free of paternal control was gradually being carved out.[77]

Actual property ownership of the type that meant real independence, however, came far more gradually. As is plain from tax valuation lists,

75. *Essex Co. Court Recs., Verbatim Transcriptions*, LVI, 9 (iii).

76. Of the hundreds of Essex County farm inhabitants recorded as owning land and livestock (in tax valuations and court records), contracting leases (in court records), living apart from their parents (in tax valuations), or earning wages on their own account (in Thomas Barnard Acct. Bk.), only three individuals were under the age of 21. Compare with Kussmaul, *Servants in Husbandry*, 39, and Everitt, "Farm Labourers," in Thirsk, ed., *Agrarian History*, IV, 459.

77. The proportions reported in this paragraph were calculated from the 35 examples of father-son work relationships, 40 examples of extrafamilial work relationships, and 30 man years of recorded tenancy. See Appendix 1. For town herdsmen, see Mighill and Blodgette, eds., *Early Records of Rowley*, 84, 92, 94, and George Brainard Blodgette and Amos Everett Jewett, *Early Settlers of Rowley, Massachusetts* . . . (Rowley, Mass., 1933), 150, 305–306, 322.

Table 1. Male Owners of Taxable Farm Property in Salisbury, Newbury, and Topsfield, 1682–1688 (in Percents)

Age	Property					
	Cattle	Horses	Land	Houses	Sheep	Oxen
17–20	0	1	0	0	0	0
21–24	6	7	6	6	5	3
25–28	36	32	21	23	24	20
29–32	63	62	53	49	33	43
33–36	93	85	84	79	67	57
37–60	96	84	95	90	85	68

Note: These are percentages not of taxable householders but of the estimated total male population in each age group and are, therefore, intended to be approximate. It was assumed that all men aged 33 to 60 were taxpayers. The percentages of men aged 17 to 32 owning property had to be adjusted to allow for the many (especially in the youngest age brackets) who were living at home and not listed on the rolls as taxpayers at all. This adjustment was made using the life tables in Robert Paul Thomas and Terry L. Anderson, "White Population, Labor Force and Extensive Growth of the New England Economy in the Seventeenth Century," *Journal of Economic History*, XXXIII (1973), 654. These percentages should be understood as maxima, since obviously there were a few men aged 33 and older who were *not* taxpayers and who, if included in the calculations of estimated men, would raise the number in all age cohorts. The three lists contain a total of 352 taxpaying householders, 228 of whom could be identified as aged 17 to 60.

Sources: "Taxes under Gov. Andros: Town Rate of Newbury, Mass., 1688," *New England Historical and Genealogical Register*, XXXII (1878), 156–164; "Taxes under Gov. Andros: Topsfield Town Rate, 1687," *NEHGR*, XXXV (1881), 34–35; George Francis Dow and Mary G. Thresher, eds., *Records and Files of the Quarterly Courts of Essex County, Massachusetts, 1636–1686*, 9 vols. (Salem, Mass., 1911–1975), VIII, 390–393. Ages of taxpayers were identified from sources in Appendix 1.

most young men did not begin to acquire taxable land and livestock until their late twenties or early thirties (see table 1). Court testimony bears out the same pattern. In the first three decades of settlement, not a single animal mentioned in the county court records belonged to a colonist identified as younger than twenty-five.[78] The achievement of formal eco-

78. Of the 53 individuals who could be identified as animal owners and by age, 11% were in their twenties, 40% were in their thirties, 23% were in their forties, and 26% were 50 or older. *Essex Co. Court Recs.*, vols. I–II; see also Appendix 1.

Table 2. Age Distribution of Males Performing Farm Labor, 1630–1699 (in Percents)

| | All Males over Age Twenty | | | |
Age	Migrant Population, 1630s (N = 213)	Rowley Males, 1645–1685 (N = 186)	Male Population, 1690	Working Males, 1630–1699 (N = 243)
20–29	48	43	35	42
30–39	33	26	25	31
40–49	14	14	18	18
50–59	5	9	12	6
60–69	1	5	7	3
70+	0	3	4	1
Total	101	100	101	101

Note: The majority of these age determinations were based not on published vital records but on references to age in the county court records. This protects the population from the charge that it is biased toward youth because of any supposed dependence on birth records that only began with the Great Migration. A test of those in the sample from Ipswich revealed missing ages for 17% of the 18 original settlers (including sons born before emigration) and for 32% of the 44 sons and grandsons born after immigration. This would suggest that, if anything, our population is biased away from youth.

Sources: For sources of work performed, see Appendix 1. Age tables for the adult male population as a whole were obtained from Virginia DeJohn Anderson, *New England's Generation: The Great Migration and the Formation of Society and Culture in the Seventeenth Century* (Cambridge, 1991), 222; my own calculations for Rowley— taking the five sample years 1645, 1655, 1665, 1675, and 1685 and computing a composite age table out of those five—using George Brainard Blodgette and Amos Everett Jewett, *Early Settlers of Rowley, Massachusetts . . .* (Rowley, Mass., 1933); and the estimates for 1690 in Robert Paul Thomas and Terry L. Anderson, "White Population, Labor Force and Extensive Growth of the New England Economy in the Seventeenth Century," *Journal of Economic History*, XXXIII (1973), 652. Virginia Anderson reports age cohorts in units of 21–30, 31–40, and so on. This means that in her presentation of the data the population seem slightly younger than if she had reported them in the 20–29, 30–39 format.

nomic freedom, therefore, did not by any means launch these young New Englanders toward self-employed independence. How, then, did they oc-cupy these years? Without property to work themselves or much paid em-ployment to keep them busy, what exactly were they doing? They were working, for in the recorded instances of men performing work undirected by others those in their twenties surface frequently—mowing, carting, driving sheep, sharpening scythes, and carrying out dozens of other tasks, just as one would expect from farming people in their physical prime.[79] We can only surmise that most young men of this age were continuing to labor on family land, but no longer necessarily on their fathers' orders (see tables 1 and 2). As they matured, the operation of the family farm acquired a less authoritarian and more cooperative character. Only if this were true, for example, would John Ingersoll of Salem have recalled that at the age of twenty-one he had been "partner with his father" in the hiring of a farm.[80] On a less formal plane, it is easy to imagine family labor patterns becoming so routine that a maturing son would know what to do on a given day without a word of command. It was also quite possible that in the course of his twenties he would come to an informal understanding with his father about what part of the family estate—most likely an undeveloped corner—would form his wedding portion. Like Henry Dow of Hampton, who was "at work in his lot" when he was only twenty-one and not yet married, he might begin clearing and readying his land to support a future household.[81]

The passing on of this portion marked the first crucial step toward self-employed independence. A few families preferred to manage the transfer by means of a legal conveyance, and a small number of surviving deeds gave married sons a formal title. More commonly, however, these arrangements appear to have been casual: sons simply moved onto whatever lands they had been promised and started to improve them.[82] Coinciding

79. In the instances of farm work performed by adults aged 20 and over, in which the laborer was acting under no apparent orders, 33% involved men in their twenties—a proportion roughly equivalent to their importance in the population. See Appendix 1.

80. *Essex Co. Court Recs., Verbatim Transcriptions*, XLIX, 15 (ii). See also *Essex Co. Court Recs.*, V, 176.

81. *Essex Co. Court Recs.*, IV, 185.

82. This claim is based on evidence concerning 125 sons drawn from a sample of 17th-century wills in *Essex Co. Prob. Recs.*, vols. I–III, and the unpublished Essex Co. Prob. Recs. ($N = 53$). Frequency of land transfer was measured from evidence in the wills themselves and in land transfers recorded in Ipswich County Deeds, Bound Transcriptions, vols. I–V, Norfolk County Deeds, Bound Transcriptions, vols. I–IV, and Essex County Deeds, Bound Transcriptions, vols. I–XX, Registry of Deeds and Probate Record Office Building, Salem, Mass. Only 20 sons received portions before their fathers' deaths, and just one of them could be identified as unmarried. See also Linda Auwers, "Fathers, Sons, and Wealth in Colonial Windsor, Connecticut," *Journal of Family History*, III (1978), 141. A few examples of the legal conveyance of marriage portions can be found in *Essex*

with marriage as it did, this event would have occurred for most young men between the ages of twenty and thirty-five. In the countryside of seventeenth-century New England, male colonists chose to marry at an average age of twenty-five to twenty-seven—slightly younger than their contemporary English equivalents but older than in maritime Massachusetts or in the tobacco colonies to the south.[83] A number of factors may have borne on this decision: the availability of women and the legal freedom to marry are two that historians frequently cite. Ultimately, however, access to the means of production and the possibility of supporting a family weighed heaviest in the balance. The sons of farmers may have married later than local fishermen (who rarely stood to inherit productive property anyway) or planters in the Chesapeake (where rates of mortality ensured that inheritances would be passed on without much delay), but from a transatlantic perspective they were joining, if cautiously, in the general American trend toward forming families at an earlier age, for the simple reason that land was available.

Indeed, the more pertinent question might be: why did they wait as long as they did? For householders in Essex County were cautious by American standards, not only in encouraging their sons to marry, but even about facilitating each new couple's independence. Young husbands were generally paying poll taxes soon after their weddings, but the acquisition of horses and cattle did not come until a year or so later and that of oxen and sheep not until half a decade after that. Some young farmers may have been assigned a portion of family property when they married, but most developed this land into something of assessable value only after they turned thirty. Throughout these years a good many sons continued to

---

Co. Court Recs., III, 236, V, 177, and in Ipswich Deeds, III, 157–158, 159–160, 264–265. Only one of the 53 testators, however, had a deed to this effect formally recorded by the county.

83. The data for rural and maritime New England created by Philip Greven, John Demos, Linda Auwers Bissell, Daniel Scott Smith, Kenneth Lockridge, Susan Norton, and Douglas Jones are nicely assembled in Douglas Lamar Jones, *Village and Seaport: Migration and Society in Eighteenth-Century Massachusetts* (Hanover, N.H., 1981), 72–73. See also E. A. Wrigley and R. S. Schofield, *The Population History of England, 1541–1871* (Cambridge, Mass., 1981), 255; Darrett B. Rutman and Anita H. Rutman, " 'Now-Wives and Sons-in-Law': Parental Death in a Seventeenth-Century Virginia County," in Thad W. Tate and David L. Ammerman, eds., *The Chesapeake in the Seventeenth Century: Essays on Anglo-American Society* (Chapel Hill, N.C., 1979), 158; and Daniel Blake Smith, "Mortality and Family in the Colonial Chesapeake," *Journal of Interdisciplinary History*, VIII (1978), 424–425.

work family land "to the halves" with their fathers or to cooperate with them, fencing or cutting timber in the woods. In partnership, fathers and sons might lease plots of tillage or pasture from their neighbors or share responsibility for the care of each other's animals. Finally, if older minds and bodies began to fail, it was common for at least one son to assume responsibility for the operation of parental land. And all of this could well persist long after they had ceased to dwell in the same house.[84]

Would it be accurate to characterize these families as patriarchies, in which fathers successfully managed their adult sons through marriage and beyond? This was certainly so in the sense that control over the farm remained ultimately in the father's possession. Clearly, most sons were spending a portion of their lives that was unusually long by seventeenth-century standards working on family property that was not theirs to command. But it is important to remember that they did this not simply because they were dependent on their fathers, but more accurately because the two were interdependent on each other. Both father and son had something to gain by prolonging the relationship. For the parent, it was manpower—something scarce in developing New England that he could not afford to import, given the unexceptional quality of the farmland he was likely to own. For the child, it was security of employment—a natural concern in an economy with little concentrated capital that might set him to work outside the family fold. It made no sense either to put sons out to labor when their fathers were short of hands or to encourage sons to replicate the pioneering hardship of the first comers by trying to carve new homesteads out of the wilderness immediately after marriage. In an environment where the demand for labor and capital was high, less from the expectation of immediate income than from the overwhelming and realizable desire to settle one's family in landed independence, it was better economics for fathers and sons to prolong this cross-generational interdependence and not to scatter family members across the landscape at too early an age.

Patriarchal relationships were common enough in the seventeenth century. What distinguished those of Essex County was not their existence or even their power; rather it was their longevity. Nothing confirms this as much as the evidence from wills. Characteristically, land was seldom

84. For examples of these activities, see *Essex Co. Court Recs.*, II, 288, IV, 224, 348, VIII, 416–417; *Essex Co. Court Recs., Verbatim Transcriptions*, XLVII, 43 (i), L, 66 (ii); *Essex Co. Prob. Recs.*, II, 2–4; and Putnam v. How (1695), Box 2, Files ICCP.

passed from father to son in a legal conveyance before the father's death. The wills that did describe parcels of land already in the possession of the younger generation clearly intended to confirm what had been originally informal gifts. This was land that "he is now possessed of," "now lives upon," or "doth improve to the halfes," but land, nonetheless, that had yet to be transferred formally. Married sons who occupied farms on this basis almost certainly operated them day by day with considerable latitude, but they were not free to sell them and remained available to their fathers as laborers. Knowing, moreover, that both the land they were working and the land their fathers continued to manage would eventually combine to form a patrimony from which they would benefit, sons tolerated the arrangement. In the English countryside, propertied farmers generally apportioned their lands (or at least legally admitted a son to part-ownership) by the time they died and did not feel the compulsion to compose a will for the purpose as frequently as did their New England equivalents. The contrast with Massachusetts is striking, especially considering the longer life expectancy in the New World and the greater likelihood that offspring would have reached the age of marriage. Once again, it underlines the strength of the colonial frontier strain of cross-generational interdependence.[85]

When fathers reached the age of fifty, they began to withdraw from active labor. Although one might happen upon a man in his sixties or

85. Examples of these provisional gifts can be found in *Essex Co. Prob. Recs.*, II, 2–3, 230–232, 291–294, III, 2–5, 162–163; Estate of Richard Jacob (1672), Probate No. 14725, Estate of Stephen Flanders (1684), Probate No. 9588, Estate of Theophilus Wilson (1691), Probate No. 30150, Essex Co. Prob. Recs. This explanation seems consistent with evidence presented in Philip J. Greven, Jr., *Four Generations: Population, Land, and Family in Colonial Andover, Massachusetts* (Ithaca, N.Y., 1970), 72–99, and Auwers, "Fathers, Sons, and Wealth," *Jour. Family Hist.*, III (1978), 141, 141n, 142, 147–148. For English comparisons, see Margaret Spufford, "Peasant Inheritance Customs and Land Distribution in Cambridgeshire from the Sixteenth to the Eighteenth Centuries," in Jack Goody, Joan Thirsk, and E. P. Thompson, eds., *Family and Inheritance: Rural Society in Western Europe, 1200–1800* (Cambridge, 1976), 169–176; Richard T. Vann, "Wills and the Family in an English Town: Banbury, 1550–1800," *Jour. Family Hist.*, IV (1979), 352–356, 361–363; Keith Wrightson, "Kinship in an English Village: Terling, Essex, 1550–1700," in Smith, ed., *Land, Kinship and Life-Cycle*, 325, 328–329; and Lloyd Bonfield, "Normative Rules and Property Transmission: Reflections on the Link between Marriage and Inheritance in Early Modern England," in Lloyd Bonfield, Richard M. Smith, and Keith Wrightson, eds., *The World We Have Gained: Histories of Population and Social Structure* (Oxford, 1986), 171–175.

seventies cutting wood, driving swine, or carrying grist to the mill, he would have been exceptional (see table 2).[86] The position ought not to be overstated, because for much of the seventeenth century the population itself was rather young. But since most of the evidence in table 2 dates from after 1660, when the older portion of the population was swelling quickly, the abrupt break at fifty does suggest a real point of retirement. This is not to say, of course, that they withdrew from the active management of their lands; fully two-thirds of the fathers documented as directing their sons at work were fifty or older. Indeed, fathers continued to surface commonly in the court records until their middle sixties, sending their charges off to complete the physical work of farming while they handled the affairs of the family: buying and selling, arranging for the borrowing of hands and equipment, and generally keeping their sons in line. At this point in life, men would be making critical decisions governing the future welfare of their families: assisting their sons in their choice of callings; marrying off their eldest children; and settling land on them. Nonetheless, they were now primarily managers, and the daily routine of chores, field work, and woodcutting was in their past.[87]

Did Essex County fathers and grandfathers ever retire completely? Occasionally they gave over responsibility for all their lands to the younger generation and settled down in a corner of the kitchen to sit out their remaining years in quiet. In February of 1666, for example, Thomas Safford granted the ownership of his farm in Ipswich to his son, Joseph, in return "for love and affection and his care." Joseph was to reserve for his father "one-half the benefit of the farm to be paid him yearly," promise to support his mother should she be widowed, and pay out portions to his three sisters. This was an exceptional case, however. Within a few weeks the elder Safford was lying on his deathbed, and doubtless when he resolved upon the transfer he had anticipated the same. His conveyance was in effect a will, and his story reflects the general truth that older men were reluctant ever to withdraw entirely from the operation of the family es-

86. *Essex Co. Court Recs.*, V, 29, VIII, 74, 179; *Essex Co. Court Recs.*, *Verbatim Transcriptions*, XLIX, 116 (iii), L, 60 (ii).

87. Of 54 fathers and grandfathers directing the labors of their sons and grandsons, 36 were aged 50 or older. See Appendix 1. Evidence for a later age of retirement, but of a type that does not distinguish clearly between labor, management, and other activities, such as public service, can be found in John Demos, "Old Age in Early New England," in John Demos, *Past, Present, and Personal: The Family and the Life Course in American History* (New York, 1986), 166–171.

tate.[88] Even those in their seventies and eighties continued to pay taxes, to hold property, and even to direct the labors of their grown sons in numbers that reflected their importance in the population. And if writing a will implied that there was still authority to be handed down, then at least by English standards these grandfathers remained men of importance until they died.[89]

None of this should strike American audiences as surprising, for it is the familiar tradition of the family farm. For the first two or three generations in seventeenth-century Essex County, however, it was a new and striking adaptation of English values to a world in which the scarcity of labor and capital relative to land was precisely the reverse of the conditions they had known in England. Why were young men in New England reluctant to strike out on their own, especially when land was so easy to procure? The answer is straightforward: in a capital-short environment they could not afford to. Why were fathers unwilling to let them go? Again, where labor was scarce they would not risk it. The social relations that powered the rural economy of the mother country were largely those of class, mediated through a series of regional free-labor markets. The relations that drove production in the New England countryside were to a far greater degree those of parental command.

Here we have dealt with the sea change only as it was experienced by fathers and sons. It would be equally interesting to know whether mothers and daughters underwent the same, though there would seem no compelling logic to suggest that they did not. What probably distinguished all of the working arrangements that men and women organized for themselves within these New England families was the unusually limited portion of their working lives in which they acted as free agents, independent of parental control. This was not the easiest environment in which to grow up; ultimately, the great majority of children chose to stand by their fathers or mothers and work together in the development of family prop-

88. *Essex Co. Court Recs.*, III, 401–402.

89. Those 70 or older composed about 12% of the adult male population aged 45 years or above in 1690 (obviously the maximum for the century) and still accounted for 11% of fathers directing their sons ($N = 54$). In the tax valuations for Newbury, Salisbury, and Topsfield, the 15 householders aged 70 years and over represented 6% of all taxpayers ($N = 241$), and their mean holdings totaled 2.5 oxen, 7.5 cattle, 11 sheep, and 33 acres of land. See Appendix 1; and Thomas and Anderson, "White Population, Labor Force and Extensive Growth," *JEH*, XXXIII (1973), 652.

erty. Nor should we assume that it was always simple for aging parents to stay on top of household matters and attempt to prevent their children from succumbing to the attraction of inexpensive land. Both parties submitted themselves, often with difficulty, to a work regime that demanded a powerful degree of cooperation, and they did so to cope with the natural exigencies of developing the frontier.

TENANCY

Can a characterization of work that emphasizes family production be squared with the equally important fact of economic inequality? The first New Englanders had grown up in a class society, and we know that their leaders took pains in the distribution of colonial land to re-create the different "Condicion[s] of mankinde" with which they were familiar. At the foundation of most Essex County towns, close to half of the apportioned property was assigned to the wealthiest 10 percent of the population, who controlled community affairs.[90] Virgin land, however, did not translate into income automatically. Given that laborers and servants were never numerous in Essex County and that the wealthiest landowners shunned physical work themselves, one might well wonder who actually brought their holdings into production. In fact, although the history of rural New England has tended to slight their importance, the agents of development on the larger holdings of this county were usually tenants.[91]

Tenancy was one feature of the English countryside that the American colonists successfully transplanted into portions of the new continent where mixed husbandry aimed at the market was important—notably Maryland, Pennsylvania, New Jersey, and the Hudson and Connecticut river valleys. Estate owners, who had been attracted to these regions by the prospects for agriculture, discovered that the lands were most profitably managed when they were rented out to propertyless farming families. Obliged by their agreements to pay annual rents and frequently to im-

90. John Winthrop, "A Modell of Christian Charity," *Winthrop Papers*, 5 vols. (Boston, 1929–1947), II, 282; Allen, *In English Ways*, 32, 111; Greven, *Four Generations*, 46; Richard P. Gildrie, *Salem, Massachusetts, 1626–1683: A Covenant Community* (Charlottesville, Va., 1975), 57.

91. Two major works that have emphasized tenancy in New England are Innes, *Labor in a New Land*, and John Frederick Martin, *Profits in the Wilderness: Entrepreneurship and the Founding of New England Towns in the Seventeenth Century* (Chapel Hill, N.C., 1991).

prove the property as well, these tenants proved to be the most effective agents for the transfer of English agricultural custom to the larger land-holdings of the northern colonies.[92]

Throughout the parts of Essex County where adequate land with easy access to the centers of consumption made commercial agriculture a possibility, the same logic held. In and around Ipswich, with its large tracts of "very good Land for Husbandry," assigned at the time of settlement to a number of well-to-do immigrants, tenancies were common, as they were in the countryside surrounding the markets of maritime Salem and Marblehead. Although it is impossible to calculate their importance with any real precision, a cautious estimate would place leaseholders and their families at between 5 and 15 percent of the county's farming inhabitants. Tenancy, in short, cropped up under the same conditions that favored farm service and day labor, but probably more often.[93]

That leaseholding should have prevailed over direct operation on the larger estates of the county says a good deal about its rural economy. From the lessee's standpoint, the chief advantage of the arrangement was access

92. Gregory A. Stiverson, *Poverty in a Land of Plenty: Tenancy in Eighteenth-Century Maryland* (Baltimore, 1977); James T. Lemon, *The Best Poor Man's Country: A Geographical Study of Southeastern Pennsylvania* (Baltimore, 1972), 94–96; Sung Bok Kim, *Landlord and Tenant in Colonial New York: Manorial Society, 1664–1775* (Chapel Hill, N.C., 1978); Ned C. Landsman, *Scotland and Its First American Colony, 1683–1765* (Princeton, N.J., 1985); Innes, *Labor in a New Land*, 44–71.

93. Jameson, ed., *Johnson's Wonder-Working Providence*, 96. The data in this and the following paragraphs on farm tenancy draw on a file of 52 tenants and their landholders, created from the sources in Appendix 1. The estimate of the quantitative importance of tenancy was derived as follows. In the rental agreements described in the court records involving landlords in the top wealth decile and their tenants, the ratio of tenants to landlords was 1.41 and the ratio of tenants of these landlords to tenants of landlords in the remaining nine wealth deciles was .42. If we assume that each of the 10 wealthiest landowners had at least one tenant, then in a hypothetical community of 100 householders, the 10 wealthiest would have had 14.1 tenants and the remaining 90 would have had 5.9: a total of 20 in all. If we assume only three-quarters of the top decile to have kept tenants, then the overall figure falls to 15; allowing only one-quarter to have had tenants on their lands lowers it to 5. If tenant families were approximately the same size as landowning families, we can convert 20 leaseholders into 20% of the population; if not, then their importance in the community would have been somewhat less. See Appendix 1. For the same connection between tenancy, service, and wage labor—imbedded sometimes in the same contracts—see Clemens and Simler, "Rural Labor and the Farm Household in Chester County, Pennsylvania," in Innes, ed., *Work and Labor in Early America*, 106–109, 112–113.

to a qualified form of independence. Not every householder who came during the Great Migration succeeded in gaining entry to the proprietorship of a New England village, and latecomers found it even harder. Indeed, almost half of the farm tenants who appear in the court records arrived in Essex after 1642, when most of the county had already been carved up into towns and the undivided land reserved to the legal inhabitants.[94] Some latecomers apparently expected to rent, and they moved into tenancy directly upon their arrival. Others began life in the Bay Colony as servants and took up leaseholding only after serving out their time. Richard Coy arrived in 1638 as an indentured teenager; twenty years later as a married man he was renting a farm in Wenham. Similarly, Cornelius Kent of Ipswich extracted himself legally from the service of John Whipple in 1661 to take up a tenancy from Thomas Bishop, which he held until his death.[95]

What all tenants lacked in common was productive wealth, especially such improvements to real estate as houses, barns, and cleared fields upon which they could employ themselves and their families. For if virgin land was cheap and plentiful, at least on the still relatively accessible frontier, developed farms were not, and it was upon these that prospective tenants—usually single men or recently married couples with no grown children and few resources of their own—set their gaze.[96] Accordingly, they approached the greater landowners of the county and negotiated rentals—normally for cleared farmland with buildings and often livestock as well. For relatively short terms (usually ten years or less) they agreed to a stated rent, a form of payment in kind, and a series of minor obligations—all with the intent of supporting themselves while they saved toward an independent freehold of their own. Only a few ever achieved any real prosperity. John West, who first appeared in Ipswich about 1640 as an eighteen-year-old tenant of the wealthy Daniel Denison and died forty years later in

94. Of 49 farm tenants who could be identified from the file, 23 arrived after 1642—a minority, but significant when one remembers how limited immigration to New England was after 1642. The remaining 26 were either original immigrants or their descendants. See Appendix 1 and Martin, *Profits in the Wilderness*, chap. 6.

95. On Coy, see *Essex Co. Court Recs.*, I, 381–382, III, 207–208. On Kent, see *ibid.*, II, 318–319, V, 135–136.

96. Of those tenants whose ages are known ($N = 34$), 59% made their first appearance in the court records as leaseholders when they were 34 years of age or younger. Some of those who were 35 or older, moreover, almost certainly began their leasing careers in the younger bracket. See Appendix 1.

Beverly, a landowner in his own right with an estate worth £320 sterling, was exceptionally successful. Most tenants, however, did find a living sufficient to maintain them in the county for several decades, often until the end of their lives. The experience of Robert Wallis, who agreed in 1653 to lease an Ipswich farm in partnership with William Smyth, may be typical of others who took the same route. Although Wallis never grew rich, his family managed to support themselves on this land for a number of years, and they eventually acquired a little property of their own. When Wallis died in 1674, he left to his two sons, Nicholas and Simon, a part of a house and a small number of animals, valued together at £76 sterling. This was enough, so he judged in his will, to support one household but not two; as the elder son, Nicholas received the housing and livestock, and Simon had to make do with a portion of £16 sterling. Here was a level of competency that was modest, indeed, yet it marked an achievement for someone who began with next to nothing.[97]

From the landlord's point of view, the leasing of property provided an alternative to the trouble and expense of direct operation. In the earliest decades of settlement, tenancy could serve a developmental purpose, for the owners of estates sometimes succeeded in settling families on their lands by offering to give them credit for any improvements they carried out. In 1658, for example, Peter Palfrey leased his farm on the Ipswich-Wenham line to a tenant who was to pay his rent in grain but could claim a deduction for "whatever building or fencing" he added to the property.[98] Other agreements, though presumably based on a reduction in rent, left the leaseholder no choice and required him to develop the property in a specified way. Thus William Goodhue of Ipswich required his tenants "to break up twelve acres of ground, crosscut it and harrow it . . . and fence in the farm" as part of a lease that he drew up in 1653. Emmanuel Downing, who had been granted an estate on the periphery of Salem in 1629, went even further by obliging George Norton "to build upon the farm a strong

97. In 70% of farm leasing arrangements found in the court records ($N = 44$) the landlord was in the top wealth decile of the town in which he lived. Of 30 farm tenants whose subsequent careers can be traced with any confidence, only 3 had disappeared from the county within a decade of their appearance as leaseholders in the court records. The median value of 12 ex-tenants' estates at death was £80 sterling. See Appendix 1, but esp. *Essex Co. Court Recs.*, I, 148–149, III, 77–78, 286, VI, 343, VIII, 420–421, IX, 129, and the wills and inventories in Probate Nos. 3458, 8609, 12894, 13782, 17355, 24820, Essex Co. Prob. Recs. On Robert Wallis, see *Essex Co. Court Recs.*, I, 125, 368, V, 313.

98. *Essex Co. Court Recs.*, III, 208; see also VII, 115, VIII, 257–258.

and sufficient house . . . and . . . to leave the house tenantable at the end of the term," in addition to his annual payments.[99] Yet in fairly short order, certainly within two or three decades of settlement, once the greater tracts of uncleared forest had begun to recede, the developmental provisions in farm leases slackened considerably. Henceforth, paying the annual rent, repairing the housing and fences as needed, and assuming the liability for damages due to negligence constituted all of the tenant's obligations.[100]

The same scarcity of productive wealth and manpower that drew landowners and leaseholders together also encouraged a surprising number of tenancies-in-partnership. Of the twenty-four renters mentioned in the fully detailed leases that have survived in the court records of the period, ten entered their agreements in pairs. So it was that Thomas Rowell and Robert Collins together signed their names to a 1656 lease that allowed them the use of a farm in Ipswich with its two oxen, two plows, cart, sled, yokes, and chains for a term of seven years. Robert Savery and William Bolton were prepared to share a house in Rowley for twenty years when they rented the farm on which it stood from Philip Nelson in 1662. Like most other tenants, leaseholders-in-partnership were usually young householders—married but poor in family members and productive wealth. Farming in common, they could split the rental, share the cleared land, draft animals, and equipment they needed, and be sure of each other's help. Short of productive wealth and labor power, by working in partnership they could lay claim to a readier supply of both than would be possible on their own.[101]

For those founders of the colony who had been granted substantial estates, sometimes many hundreds of acres, tenancy was thus the most effective means of putting land under the plow and obtaining a revenue. It was simply easier to hand over the development and operation of these tracts to tenant households than to seek out the numerous servants and

99. *Ibid.*, I, 368, III, 286; see also II, 31, 275. The developmental leases with significant labor requirements, which Innes, *Labor in a New Land*, 49–52, describes as typical of Springfield, were less common in Essex County and generally easier in their terms.

100. *Essex Co. Court Recs.*, IV, 220, VI, 130, 356–357, IX, 259, 466–467; Wainwright v. Healey (1694), Wainwright v. Clements (1695), Box 1, Files ICCP. An examination of detailed leases surviving in the court records reveals that before 1656, 5 of the 10 leaseholders who signed agreements accepted developmental obligations, whereas only 2 of the 14 who signed agreements after that date accepted such obligations.

101. *Essex Co. Court Recs.*, I, 368, II, 177, 361, IV, 220, VI, 130. Of the 10 who signed leases-in-partnership, 7 were married, and their median age was 28.

hired hands needed to farm them directly. Of course, potential lease-holders might also prove difficult to find; both the Winthrops and the Downings complained of this problem.[102] But the shortage of tenants never sparked the degree of comment that the other labor problems of the Bay Colony did. The measurable if qualified degree of independence that tenancy conferred upon householders without developed land and productive equipment of their own was attractive enough to ensure a ready supply of willing men. Arising from the fact of economic inequality, tenancy was a power relationship like farm service or free labor; it survived the trip to America better because it could be accommodated more easily to a world where manpower and productive resources were scarce.

In the middle of the seventeenth century, an unknown Englishman observed: "Virginia thrives by keeping many servants, and these in strict obedience. New England conceit they and their Children can doe enough, and soe have rarely above one Servant."[103] His point was plain: children served the farm economy of New England as servants did the plantations of the Chesapeake. My point is similar: the contrast with southern servitude should not lead us to imagine that the labor force of seventeenth-century New England was predominantly free. Children differed from servants in many ways, but as laborers they possessed little liberty. A rural economy that operated chiefly on child labor was to a significant degree responding to precisely the same pressures that created systems of slavery, servitude, and peonage elsewhere in the Americas. Where labor was in light supply and heavy demand, the impetus to recruit from those unable to bargain for a better return was irresistible.

The founders of New England had crossed the Atlantic with the intention of establishing themselves in comfortable independence. In the old country, with its abundance of productive wealth and its throngs of underemployed laborers, propertied families such as those that joined in the Great Migration had pursued this goal by learning how to deal in the marketplace of labor. Fathers could try to accumulate material goods and secure for their households a modicum of independence by enlisting the

102. Emmanuel Downing to John Winthrop, Sept. 29, 1648, Adam Winthrop to John Winthrop, May 3, 1649, *Winthrop Papers*, V, 261, 340; *Recs. of Mass. Bay*, I, 114; Winthrop, *History of New England*, I, 144.
103. Quoted in Smith, *Colonists in Bondage*, 29.

inexpensive help, when it was needed, of non-family members; sons could find work outside the home, in service or otherwise, from a host of different employers. Success in economic matters was never simple, but it resulted, or failed to result, in important ways from choices made by individuals within a regional free-labor market. In Essex County, however, where labor power and productive wealth were in shorter supply than they had been at home, that market gave way to a system of family labor governed far more by cross-generational interdependence. In a world where so many men had realized the English dream of landownership, where laborers and servants were few, and where farms were initially poor in livestock, equipment, buildings, other improvements, and commercial worth, fathers and sons discovered that the path to material accumulation required a degree of cooperation for which little in their experience would have prepared them. They could be comfortable and they could be independent, but only if they defined each term as an intergenerational family possession.

CHAPTER 3

FISHERMEN

1 6 3 0 - 1 6 7 5

The first Europeans to wring a living from the coast of New England were not farmers but fishermen. They came from the West Country of England in the earliest years of the seventeenth century on the advice of voyagers like George Waymouth, who had cruised the coast in 1605. He brought back reports of cod "so plentifull, so great, and so good, with such convenient drying as can be wished," that the fishery there was said to be even better than at Newfoundland.[1] These bold words were accurate in one regard: the most immediately profitable resource that New England possessed was undoubtedly cod. Fish might seem "a mean and base commoditie," John Smith admitted in 1614, but it would in time give rise to

1. James Rosier, *A true relation of the most prosperous voyage made this present yeere 1605, by Captain George Waymouth, in the discovery of the land of Virginia* (1605), in David B. Quinn and Alison M. Quinn, eds., *The English New England Voyages, 1602–1608* (Hakluyt Society, *Publications*, 2d Ser., CLXI [London, 1983]), 287. See also John Brereton, *A briefe and true relation of the discoverie of the North part of Virginia . . . Made this present yeere 1602* (1602), *ibid.*, 171; *A Voyage set out from the citie of Bristoll . . . Under the command of Martin Pringe* (1625), *ibid.*, 216, 226; and Rosier, *True relation*, 301.

other employments, and it was the "maine Staple" the country had to offer.[2]

Those who first attempted to develop a fishery on the North Shore of Massachusetts had also to confront the colonial scarcity of capital and labor; indeed, the problem was even more severe in the maritime economy than in the countryside. Put simply, New Englanders had planted themselves in a part of the world where fishing seemed likely to provide the most obviously profitable export commodity, but as landsmen almost none of them knew how to fish or cared to learn. Furthermore, where land was easy to obtain, there was no incentive to pursue the hard and frequently disagreeable work that fishing involved. How did merchants and fishermen come to terms with this dilemma? The productive relations that eventually prevailed within the fishery differed in many ways from those that triumphed on the farm, but in one important respect they were similar. Responding to the scarcity of capital and labor that prevailed on the periphery of the European world system, merchants and fishermen, anxious to minimize the risks each had to face, combined into tight though unequal relations of interdependence.

THE RISE OF THE NORTH ATLANTIC FISHERIES

Cod and herring in particular had long been popular in the diet of maritime Europeans, especially on the Iberian Peninsula, because they furnished people of moderate means with an affordable alternative to meat. In sixteenth-century Seville, for example, of all the common foodstuffs only beans and brown bread could compete with fish in cost, and in Barcelona the midday meal of a common laborer was said always to include a salted herring. Even in Valladolid, over one hundred miles from the sea, fish carried overland from the Galician coast cost less than locally produced meat and sold in nearly comparable quantities. Dried cod was somewhat pricier than other fish, but it was common fare among artisans and shopkeepers and enjoyed a regular market in the Roman Catholic hospitals, colleges, monasteries, and convents that served it on Fridays.[3]

2. Edward Arber, ed., *Travels and Works of Captain John Smith, President of Virginia, and Admiral of New England, 1580–1631* (Edinburgh, 1910), I, 194.

3. Earl J. Hamilton, "American Treasure and Andalusian Prices, 1503–1660: A Study in the Spanish Price Revolution," *Journal of Economic and Business History*, I (1928), 21–25; Walter Minchinton, "Patterns and Structures of Demand, 1500–1750," in Carlos M. Cipolla, ed., *The Fontana Economic History of Europe*, vol. II: *The Sixteenth and Seven-*

The demand for this plain food was, therefore, sensitive to population growth, and as the swelling number of hungry mouths pushed its price steadily upward after 1500, merchants from Bergen to Genoa began to cast their eyes farther and farther afield to answer their customers' requests.[4] When John Cabot returned from his explorations in 1497 with the news of rich virgin grounds off the North American coast, European merchants were ready to take advantage. As early as 1517, fifty ships were reportedly working on the Newfoundland banks, and by 1578 England, Spain, Portugal, and France together were dispatching 350 sail to the region every year.[5]

Many nations fished for cod, but their methods differed according to the availability of salt and the nature of the markets they supplied. Those who could procure salt at a reasonable price and catered to northern palates accustomed to generously pickled foods worked the so-called green fishery from large vessels in the deeper waters offshore. There they sought the larger cod, salted it liberally out on the banks, and carried it home wet in the belly of the ship. Breton and Norman fishermen, able to purchase sea salt inexpensively from the Bay of Biscay and to market their produce in Rouen and Paris, rapidly made the green fishery a French preserve. The dry fishery, by comparison, employed smaller vessels along the Newfoundland coast to catch the lesser cod. After a light sprinkling of salt these could be cured to rock hardness in the open air along the shore

teenth Centuries (Glasgow, 1974), 121; Bartolomé Benassar, "L'alimentation d'une capitale espagnole au XVIe siècle: Valladolid," in Jean-Jacques Hémardinquer, ed., Pour une histoire de l'alimentation: Recueil de travaux présentés par Jean-Jacques Hémardinquer (Cahiers des annales, XXVIII [Paris, 1970]), 55–56; Frédéric Mauro, Le Portugal et l'Atlantique au XVIIe siècle, 1570–1670: Etude économique (Paris, 1960), 287–289; A. R. Mitchell, "The European Fisheries in Early Modern History," in E. E. Rich and C. H. Wilson, eds., The Cambridge Economic History of Europe, vol. V: The Economic Organization of Early Modern Europe (Cambridge, 1977), 172–178; Laurier Turgeon, "Consommation de morue et sensibilité alimentaire en France au XVIIIe siècle," Canadian Historical Association, Historical Papers (1984), 23–34. For statistics on nourishment, see Robert Philippe, "Une opération pilote: L'étude de ravitaillement de Paris au temps de Lavoisier," in Hémardinquer, ed., Pour une histoire de l'alimentation, 65, 66.

4. In Andalusia, one of the prime fish-consuming regions on the Continent, the price of cod rose 929% between the periods 1500–1520 and 1595–1605; over the same span, Earl Hamilton's Index of General Prices rose only 713%. See Hamilton, "American Treasure and Andalusian Prices," Jour. Econ. and Bus. Hist., I (1928), 20–26.

5. Mitchell, "European Fisheries," in Rich and Wilson, eds., Economic Organization of Early Modern Europe, 155–161.

and then shipped to the markets of southern Europe, where the warm climate precluded the presence of any moisture in the finished product. It was in this fishery that the English, relative latecomers to the North American grounds, carved a place for themselves toward the end of the sixteenth century. With no domestic market for green Newfoundland cod or any noteworthy sources of native salt, the English could compete only in foreign markets that favored the dry cure, notably Spain and Portugal. Accordingly, the West Country fishermen developed an interest in any part of the North American coast where productive inshore grounds, suitable harbors, and ample reserves of timber adjoined one another.[6]

Dozens of bays and coves along the Newfoundland coast fit this description admirably, and by 1600 thousands of Englishmen were fishing the inshore grounds there in what had become a well-established annual routine. Every March small ships of between thirty and eighty tons burden, manned by crews of twenty to forty men and boys, weighed anchor in Plymouth, Dartmouth, and other West Country ports and made for the fog-enshrouded island across the Atlantic. In their holds the ships carried salt, provisions, fishing equipment, nails and boards for the construction of boats, and a wide variety of necessary tools. Upon arriving about two months later, the crews set about first to find a suitable harbor close to the fishing grounds, preferably flanked by dense evergreen forests to provide timber and rimmed with a rocky beach where the cod could easily be dried. There each company moored its vessel, erected a temporary fishing station, assembled the fishing boats, and—when the cod struck in along the coast, normally in June—began to fish. The vessels usually launched one boat for every five crew members: three to work at sea with hook and line and two to remain ashore splitting, salting, and tending the fish while it dried in the summer air. Two or three months of uninterrupted labor would generally fill the hold, and by autumn most ships were safely back in England.[7]

By seventeenth-century standards, this was enterprise on a big scale, demanding quantities of capital and labor that could be assembled only in the marketplace. Recruiting the crew could be quite a headache, and the

6. Harold A. Innis, *The Cod Fisheries: The History of an International Economy*, rev. ed. (Toronto, 1954), 30–51; Charles de la Morandière, *Histoire de la pêche française de la morue dans l'Amérique septentrionale*, 3 vols. (Paris, 1962–1966), I, 145–157, 185–195.

7. Innis, *Cod Fisheries*, 32, 34, 53–54, 56–59, 60–61.

West Country merchants who owned and outfitted a fishing ship usually preferred to delegate that task to the master. He might have business connections in the country towns willing to send along potential fishermen; often he visited hiring fairs himself hoping to find the men he needed; and, of course, he picked up others who had heard of the opportunity by word of mouth. Using some combination of these methods, the master normally recruited his crew within a region stretching twenty to twenty-five miles inland of the port from which he sailed. Generally the men were young—fifteen to twenty-five years in age—and interested less in maritime service as a career than in the possibility of saving up toward some small measure of propertied independence near to home. This labor market was very similar to that within which farm servants circulated; indeed, the two probably overlapped considerably.[8]

In financial organization, the voyage was typically a joint venture between a consortium of merchant investors and the crew. Before the vessel sailed, the parties involved negotiated an agreement determining the price of the fish to be caught and a method of apportioning shares. When it returned, the ship's owner claimed the catch; its value would be calculated according to the predetermined price, balanced against the cost of the outfit, and divided into the appropriate shares. Generally, the crew received a third of the proceeds divided into equal portions, in addition to fixed wages that varied by rank. Once the crew members had been paid and dismissed, the vessel owner and his outfitters claimed the balance to cover costs and provide a return on their investment. The system of payment in shares created an element of common interest in the voyage. Not only did it serve to diminish the individual risk inherent in an unusually risky industry, but it also gave the fisherman a personal interest in his efforts. Nevertheless, relations between merchants and their men remained in substance those of capital and labor. Merchants still garnered the lion's share of the profits (and bore most of the losses); they retained complete ownership of the vessel, provisions, and gear throughout the

8. Keith Matthews, "A History of the West of England–Newfoundland Fishery" (D. Phil. diss., Oxford University, 1968), 6–9, 20; W. Gordon Handcock, *Soe longe as there comes noe women: Origins of English Settlement in Newfoundland* (St. John's, Nfld., 1989), 60–64, 185–196; Gillian T. Cell, *English Enterprise in Newfoundland, 1577–1660* (Toronto, 1969), 15–16; Ann Kussmaul, *Servants in Husbandry in Early Modern England* (Cambridge, 1981), 49–67.

voyage; and they could do with their capital what they wished once the fish had been sold. By early modern standards of economic organization, this transatlantic fishery was a distinctively capitalist institution.[9]

Although companies from the west of England based their summer labors on the Avalon Peninsula of Newfoundland, there was no good reason why the dry fishery could not flourish equally on other coasts. So when the merchants of Bristol and the lesser western outports began hearing from voyagers to New England of "Codes . . . so large & great" that Englishmen had never seen "the lyke . . . beffor," some of the more adventurous began to redirect their ships toward the Gulf of Maine. At first only a few parties a year cared to chance these unknown waters, but by 1621 their number had grown to ten or twelve, and by 1624 to forty or fifty. Most of the fleet congregated at the "rounde high Ile" of Monhegan, but by 1625 at least a dozen harbors in common use were scattered along the coast between Cape Cod and Penobscot Bay.[10]

Thus when John Winthrop composed "The grounds of settling a plantation in new England" on the eve of his departure in 1629, fish was "a knowen and staple Commoditie," which the Puritan emigrants fully intended to exploit. "Codfish hath been the enrichment of other nations," announced William Wood in 1634, "and is likely to prove no small commodity to the planters"; John White urged the colonists in the same direction, saying that fishing would be "the first means that will bring any income into your lande."[11] It was true that earlier fishing colonies had an unenviable history. Sagadahoc at the mouth of the Kennebec River (1607–1608), Wessagussett on Massachusetts Bay (1622–1624), the Dorchester Company plantation on Cape Ann (1623–1624), and Mount Wollaston to the north of Plymouth (1623), each of which had tried to combine the fishery with farming and the fur trade, utterly failed to justify their costs and collapsed. Although a few hundred hardy souls clung on the year round at Newfoundland, the long-term prospects for develop-

9. Innis, *Cod Fisheries*, 34, 40–44, 60; Cell, *English Enterprise in Newfoundland*, 6–18.

10. William Strachey, "A Narrative of the North Virginia voyage and colony," in Quinn and Quinn, eds., *English New England Voyages*, 423; Arber, ed., *Travels and Works of Captain John Smith*, I, 206, II, 697, 745–748, 783, 941–943.

11. John Winthrop, "Sir John Eliot's Copy of the New England Tracts" (1629), *Winthrop Papers*, 5 vols. (Boston, 1929–1947), II, 145–146; William Wood, *New England's Prospect*, ed. Alden T. Vaughan (Amherst, Mass., 1977), 53; John White to John Winthrop, Nov. 16, 1636, *Winthrop Papers*, III, 322.

ment there were not encouraging either.[12] As John White reminded the emigrants of 1630, however, planting a colony was like building a house: although "the first stockes employed that way are consumed," just as "the first stones of the foundation are buried under ground . . . [yet] they serve for a foundation to the worke." In that year, as the price of cod climbed to its highest point in history, the founders of the Bay Colony began to put their enthusiasm to work.[13]

LAUNCHING THE FISHERY IN NEW ENGLAND

When the New England colonists set about organizing a fishery of their own, they drew upon the only relevant experience then available to Englishmen: the traditions of Newfoundland. The techniques of the dry fishery and a stock of men who understood them were West Country possessions, assembled over a century of practice on the North American grounds. Since the founders of Massachusetts were mainly landsmen from the south and east of England who had given little thought to the actual organization of an industry they scarcely understood, the Newfoundland example had to guide them.

The earliest initiatives, therefore, relied in the traditional manner on servants, who were recruited in the fishing ports of the West Country, engaged for the season to work under the supervision of a master appointed by the colonists, and paid in cash or a credit note upon their return. In 1629 nine servants, most of them from Dorset, agreed to a contract of this nature with Matthew Craddock and the Massachusetts Bay Company. Craddock and the company promised to supply the servants with victuals, salt, and equipment and ordered the governor of the colony

12. Charles M. Andrews, *The Colonial Period of American History*, vol. I: *The Settlements* (New Haven, Conn., 1934), 91–94, 329–332, 338–339, 342; Bernard Bailyn, *The New England Merchants in the Seventeenth Century* (Cambridge, Mass., 1955), 2–5, 10–13; Matthews, "West of England–Newfoundland Fishery," 99–129; Peter Pope, "Residence, Labour, Demand, and Exchange on the Seventeenth-Century English Shore of Newfoundland: The South Avalon Planters and Their Servants, 1630 to 1680" (Ph.D. diss., Memorial University of Newfoundland, 1991), 206–212.

13. John White, *The Planter's Plea* (London, 1630), in Peter Force, comp., *Tracts and Other Papers, Relating Principally to the Origin, Settlement, and Progress of the Colonies in North America, from the Discovery of the Country to the Year 1776*, 4 vols. (Washington, D.C., 1836–1846), II, 42. For the price of cod, see Hamilton, "American Treasure and Andalusian Prices," *Jour. Econ. and Bus. Hist.*, I (1928), 20–24.

and his council to direct their activities and keep a strict inventory of provisions. Two servants were discharged before the ship departed, for fear that "their ill lyfe might be prejudiciall to the plantacion," but the remainder continued on to New England, where they settled probably in Marblehead, housed for the summer in thatched cabins. For several months they carried on the company's business, "ether in harbor or upon the banke"; with the approach of autumn they returned to England and their catch was dispatched to market.[14] Two years later, Isaac Allerton, a merchant previously involved with the colony at Plymouth but now acting as an agent for a group of Londoners, established another station in the same harbor, and by 1634 he was directing the labors of close to thirty men.[15] In that year, William Wood spoke of "Marvill Head" as "a very convenient place for plantation, especially for such as will set upon the trade of fishing."[16]

In its infancy, the Bay Colony could never have maintained a fishery without imported servants. Free Puritan emigrants willing to labor for others were scarce enough, and those who knew how to handle a hook and line were rarer still. As late as 1635, Hugh Peter was bemoaning the absence of a resident fishing population, and John White reminded the governor a year later that there was hardly a fisherman—master or servant—settled permanently anywhere in the colony.[17] Any manager of a fishing operation that was short of men in these early years had to look to the mother country for recruits.

Almost as soon as it was launched, however, the servant fishery began to founder. Part of the problem lay with the founding fathers' second thoughts over its desirability as a permanent colonial institution. The men it attracted, for one thing, rarely met the standards of probity the Bay colonists were trying to maintain. The merchants and agents in control of

14. Governor and Deputy of the New England Company for a Plantation in Massachusetts Bay to Governor and Council for London's Plantation in the Massachusetts Bay in New England, Apr. 17, May 28, 1629, in *Recs. of Mass. Bay*, I, 395, 403, 404, 406; Winthrop, *History of New England*, I, 119; Sidney Perley, *The History of Salem, Massachusetts*, 3 vols. (Salem, Mass., 1924–1928), I, 233–234.

15. Winthrop, *History of New England*, I, 119; Perley, *History of Salem*, I, 232–233. Winthrop reported eight boats; with three fishermen and one man on shore per boat, the total was about thirty men.

16. Wood, *New England's Prospect*, ed. Vaughan, 64.

17. Winthrop, *History of New England*, I, 168–169; John White to John Winthrop, Nov. 16, 1636, *Winthrop Papers*, III, 322. See also White to Winthrop, ca. 1637, *ibid.*, 336.

the industry, such as Allerton, whose "covetousness" so appalled William Bradford of Plymouth, all too often favored sharp dealing over diligence and industry; Allerton's "wicked and drunken crue" of 1631 and the "stubberne" and "Idle" fishermen at Richmond Island in the Gulf of Maine never seemed to observe the servant's trinity of obligations—obedience, reverence, and fidelity—with sufficient respect.[18] In matters of religion, moreover, the itinerant fishermen at several plantations proved distressingly attached to the traditions of the High Church. Richard Gibson, in Winthrop's words a cleric "wholly addicted to the hierarchy and discipline of England" who by his sermons "did scandalize our government," ministered to receptive audiences near the fishing grounds from 1636 to 1642; servants at several places were willing to pay his salary.[19] Many of these abuses, it is true, occurred outside the bounds of the Bay Colony and beyond the reach of the local authorities, but to the Puritan leadership in Massachusetts they represented visibly the dangers of allowing ungodly and self-interested souls to determine the course of settlement.

The root problem of the servant fishery, however, was that it did not pay. The experience at Richmond Island, a plantation one hundred miles north of Boston belonging to Robert Trelawney and known to posterity by the correspondence he received from its manager, John Winter, was a case in point. As Winter explained in letter after letter, the returns of the local fishery could not justify the trouble and expense of finding enough men to keep his boats at sea. In the West Country, it was possible to find fishermen willing to hire themselves out on reasonable terms, Winter informed his employer, but not in New England. "Good, Carefull, plyable" servants could be recruited only at home, and Trelawney would do well to contract with them there on the strictest terms possible; "otherwise, when they Com heare, they will forget their promyse and slacke their busines." Men could so easily find different work on generous terms, other fishing masters were so desperate for hands, and the empty land to be cleared and farmed was so extensive that Winter found it quite impossible to keep the plantation adequately staffed. "Our men as their tymes Comes out do go away," he reported in 1639, echoing dozens of earlier complaints, "and so

18. William Bradford, *Of Plymouth Plantation, 1620–1647*, ed. Samuel Eliot Morison (New York, 1952), 237–244; John Winter to Robert Trelawney, June 28, 1636, May 18, 1642, *Trelawney Papers*, 91, 308.

19. Winthrop, *History of New England*, II, 61; Winter to Trelawney, June 23, 1636, *Trelawney Papers*, 86, 86n.

will all hear after except I will give them double hire, & I cannot Conceave how they will deserve it, nor hardly the wages the[y] now have; but they give men great wages heare in this Country."[20]

In 1641, after a group of fishing hands hired in England at £5 sterling a year refused to renew their indentures in the middle of the following season, Winter finally decided to try a new tack and allow them instead one-third of all the fish they took—a sum amounting that year to more than £9 sterling. Later, he began to direct more business to independent fishermen, some of them former servants who had taken up residence along the shore, paying them only for what they delivered to his wharf. The men at Richmond Island preferred these arrangements, which allowed them to profit by the healthy markets of the 1640s and to manage their own affairs. Why, as good Englishmen, should they prolong their dependence on Winter and Trelawney if, in a world where access to land and resources was fairly open, they could fend for themselves? Particularly in the Gulf of Maine, "a lawles Contry" where runaway hands were impossible to retrieve, a servant fishery was just not practicable.[21] Even in the settled regions of Massachusetts, however, the same logic prevailed. Hired men who knew there was inexpensive land to be had, were prey to its attractions, and suspected that they could not easily be replaced proved costly and difficult to manage. By 1635, therefore, the disquieting ways of imported servants and the labor problems they engendered had persuaded the Bay colonists (like Winter) to concentrate instead on the establishment of a resident fishery. That year, Hugh Peter and a number of civic-minded friends tried to organize a "magazine" that would furnish local seamen with inexpensive supplies and purchase the fish they brought in. Peter and his colleagues even persuaded the General Court to create a "stock" of public capital for the purpose with

20. These particular incidents are described in Winter to Trelawney, June 18, 1634, July 30, 1638, July 10, 1639, *Trelawney Papers*, 33, 136, 164; for other evidence of labor difficulties, see July 7, 1634, June 11, 1635, June 23, 28, 1636, July 8, 10, 29, Sept. 20, 1637, Aug. 27, 1638, July 10, 1639, and May 18, 1642, *ibid.*, 44–45, 56, 57, 86, 91–93, 108–109, 114, 120, 121–122, 137, 146, 164, 311.

21. Winter to Trelawney, July 29, 1641, June 8, 1642, *ibid.*, 281–282, 312. For a rather different account of the abandonment of a servant fishery in Newfoundland, see Gerald M. Sider, *Culture and Class in Anthropology and History: A Newfoundland Illustration* (Cambridge, 1986), 16–20. Here, as everywhere in Chapter 3, currency values are described in pounds sterling, converting Massachusetts currency into sterling, if necessary, using John J. McCusker, *Money and Exchange in Europe and America, 1600–1775: A Handbook* (Chapel Hill, N.C., 1978).

a committee to manage it, and eventually to exempt from taxation all colonial vessels engaged in the taking and transporting of fish.[22] Their point, as Winthrop explained, was not "to encourage foreigners to set up fishing among us, (for all the gains would return to the place where they dwelt,) but to encourage our own people to set upon it." Moral improvement, local development, and returns to capital, contended these promoters, were all within the reach of a fishery composed of settled and sober householders.[23]

The centerpiece of this new program, however, was a judicious policy of land grants. In 1635, the General Court decided to permit fishermen who settled in Marblehead "to plant and improve such grounde as they stand in neede of": an offer of considerable appeal to those with aspirations to self-employment. Indeed, for ordinary Englishmen, it was too appealing, for the land-hungry fishermen at once began to enclose all the acreage they could. As the established colonists soon discovered, those who acquired the means to economic independence on shore rapidly lost their taste for the sea. In 1637, therefore, the town of Salem (which had jurisdiction over Marblehead until 1649) declared that "the better furthering of the fishing" could not be reconciled with "the inconvenience . . . found by granting of land for fishermen to plant." Henceforth, a house lot and two acres of planting land were the most that a prospective fisherman might expect. Other towns made similar provisions. Ipswich set farming land aside for fishermen in 1641, but limited each "boat gang" (four or five men) to an acre apiece. The same year, the General Court granted to fishing crews willing to settle at Nantasket "such accomodations as the plantation will affoard," but the actual allowance amounted to no more than an acre per man plus meadowland for those with cattle. Such carefully measured parsimony, it was hoped, would induce fishing families to settle without leading them to stray from their calling. It would meet the expectations of precisely the sort of fishermen whom the Bay colonists hoped to attract.[24]

In practice, however, the attempt to construct a householding fishery of Puritan materials failed. Family heads with orthodox religious beliefs,

22. Winthrop, *History of New England*, I, 165, 169; *Recs. of Mass. Bay*, I, 158, 230.

23. Winthrop, *History of New England*, I, 310; *Recs. of Mass. Bay*, I, 257–258.

24. *Recs. of Mass. Bay*, I, 147, 326–327; "Salem Town Records," 15, 27, 28; Thomas Franklin Waters, *Ipswich in the Massachusetts Bay Colony, 1633–1917*, 3 vols. (Ipswich, Mass., 1905–1917), I, 80.

even when granted fishing lots, rarely followed the sea for long. Land was too easy for such men to acquire, and the order and security of life on shore too difficult to resist. Between 1636 and 1639, Salem attempted to draw into the fishery a number of local residents—mostly householding churchgoers with property elsewhere in town—by offering them half-acre lots at Winter Harbor for drying their hauls. It was hoped that these solid citizens would either organize the labor of their children and servants or follow the fishery themselves. But the town fathers miscalculated, for only a minority of the grantees apparently ever involved themselves in the fishery. Some died; others moved away; still others pursued careers on merchant vessels (usually in positions of command); but most simply returned to their old land-based trades, if, indeed, they ever went to sea at all.[25]

The small number of fishermen who did put down roots on the Massachusetts coast in the 1630s seldom resembled the type of settler that the Puritan fathers had envisaged. A few sober and pious individuals headed well-ordered families that fit easily into the mainstream of New England society. Pasco Foote, the recipient of a fishing lot in Salem who followed the sea almost to the day he died and raised up his sons to the same trade, never ran afoul of the courts and was accepted into the church in 1649. Similarly, Osmund Dutch labored among patently unreformed company for several decades from the shores of Gloucester harbor without ever losing his reputation for piety.[26] More often, however, resident fishermen turned out to be little different from the itinerant servants of earlier years and seemed equally wedded to the casual behavior that troubled Puritans most. Like their predecessors, they worked an erratic schedule and spent their leisure hours in the classic maritime diversions: drinking, smoking, carousing, and profaning the Lord. Matthew Nixon, a chronic debtor with a penchant for the bottle, fished out of Salem for almost forty years

25. "Salem Town Records," 16, 33, 36, 62, 78, 80, 83, 84, 88, 92. Of 21 grantees whose lives can be traced in the records, 12 had wives at the time the lots were granted and 8 of the remaining 9 were married within the next five years. See Appendix 2.

26. On Pasco Foote, see Perley, *History of Salem*, I, 368n; "Salem Town Records," 33; *Essex Co. Court Recs.*, IV, 398; and accounts of Pasco Foote, George Corwin Account Book, 1663–1672, Curwen Family Papers, 1641–1902, JDPL. On Osmund Dutch, see John J. Babson, *History of the Town of Gloucester, Cape Ann, including the Town of Rockport* (Gloucester, Mass., 1860), 83, 84; *Essex Co. Court Recs.*, III, 328, 350; and Edward E. Hale, ed., *Note-Book Kept by Thomas Lechford, Esq., Lawyer, in Boston, Massachusetts Bay, from June 27, 1638 to July 29, 1641* (Cambridge, Mass., 1885), 110–114.

without ever holding a town office, serving on a jury, or gaining membership to the church. John Bennet, who came with the Winthrop fleet in 1630 and settled in Marblehead, was so openly hostile or at least oblivious to Puritan sensibilities that he once lit his pipe during Sunday services and was fined for it. Even John Devereaux, one of the few fishermen who accumulated enough property to turn away from the sea and take up farming instead, was often dragged before the courts in his early years for crimes of drunkenness and violence. The evidence on these early residents is thin—chiefly because they were so few in number—but to the colony's leadership, they seemed a disorderly lot.[27]

The attempt to build a fishing industry on the backs of solid Puritan families was clearly misconceived. Put simply, free men who met the Bay Colony's standards of comportment and religious conviction generally received land and drifted away from the sea. Faced with choosing between the dirty job of catching fish largely to the profit of others and quietly cultivating ground of their own, householders tended naturally to the latter. Colonists of means and status came to regard the fishery as the preserve of second-rate men, and the effort to attract free and orthodox families into it proved largely a waste of time.

The 1630s, therefore, were a period of much experimentation in the Massachusetts fishery but little permanent achievement. As Hugh Peter, who had energetically promoted the industry a few years earlier, admitted in 1639, "fishing will not yet . . . [serve the] purpose."[28] Still, some lessons were plain. If the colony hoped to develop maritime industries in the future, it would have to learn to tolerate the presence of outsiders: foreigners in spirit if not in nationality, and hardly, as Winthrop put it, "our own people."[29] More important, the colony would need to accept the simple fact that fishermen—however exceptional they may have been in other ways—shared with their English brethren a reluctance to labor in the service of others. Virginia and Plymouth Colony had already learned that immigrants from the mother country required at least the promise of

27. On Matthew Nixon, see Perley, *History of Salem*, II, 73, III, 80; and *Essex Co. Court Recs.*, I, 123, 124, 231, II, 136, III, 15, IV, 178, 414, V, 348, VI, 87–88, VII, 249, 325, 425. On John Bennet, see Perley, *History of Salem*, I, 237, II, 2; *Essex Co. Court Recs.*, I, 74, 320, IX, 239–241; and *Essex Co. Prob. Recs.*, I, 415. On John Devereaux, see Perley, *History of Salem*, I, 218, II, 2; *Essex Co. Court Recs.*, I, 58, 77, 135, IV, 285; and Estate of John Devereaux (1693), Probate No. 7614, Essex Co. Prob. Recs.

28. Hugh Peter to John Winthrop, Apr. 10, 1639, *Winthrop Papers*, IV, 113.

29. Winthrop, *History of New England*, I, 310.

freehold property if they were to invest any real effort in the success of the settlement. Fishermen may have used terms more appropriate to the maritime setting to define independence, but they valued it every bit as much, and on America's first frontier they were equally interested in turning that ideal into reality. Most important, the local fishery needed a boost. Competing with the highly skilled and well-capitalized fisheries of western Europe for markets and with the developing rural economy of the Bay Colony itself for labor and capital was not going to be easy.

The event that truly launched the New England fishery on its successful trajectory of growth was the outbreak in 1642 of the English Civil War. Hitherto, Massachusetts trade had been financed with capital brought in by immigrant settlers, but in that year the flow of passengers stopped and the balance of trade turned against the colonists. As local prices collapsed and credit dried up overseas, necessity forced New Englanders to come up with marketable resources and pay their own way.[30] The political upheavals at home, ironically enough, made this task a little easier, for the disruption they caused in Britain's maritime economy, especially in the fisheries, undermined her position in foreign markets and provided room for competition. At Newfoundland the West Country fleet fell from 340 vessels in 1634, to 270 in 1644, to fewer than 200 by 1652; on the New England coast it vanished altogether.[31] Exports to southern Europe suffered, and prices there began to mount. In Seville, the cost of codfish climbed by 25 percent between the periods 1637–1642 and 1644–1648, and in Madeira, a particular preserve of the English, it rose over the same period by roughly one-half. In 1645 the price of cod at Richmond Island in the Gulf of Maine touched twenty shillings sterling per quintal (112 pounds), the highest level recorded in New England for the entire colonial period.[32] These developments presented enterprising fishermen in Massachusetts with a fine opportunity: not only had the value of their catch

30. Bailyn, *New England Merchants*, 32ff., 45–49.

31. D. W. Prowse, *A History of Newfoundland from the English, Colonial, and Foreign Records* (London, 1895), 159, 190; Innis, *Cod Fisheries*, 70; Winthrop, *History of New England*, II, 19; Bailyn, *New England Merchants*, 77; Cell, *English Enterprise in Newfoundland*, 118–119, 140–144.

32. Hamilton, "American Treasure and Andalusian Prices," *Jour. Econ. and Bus. Hist.*, I (1928), 24–26; Mauro, *Le Portugal et l'Atlantique*, 288; account of Robert Jordan, May 20, 1645, *Trelawney Papers*, 382; Daniel Vickers, "'A knowen and staple commoditie': Codfish Prices in Essex County, Massachusetts, 1640–1775," Essex Institute, *Historical Collections*, CXXIV (1988), 194, 198–202.

soared, but also they could now work in their harbors undisturbed. The Bay Colony had exported some fish every year since its founding, but only with this turn of events did the pace of trade accelerate. In 1641, reported Winthrop, 300,000 dry fish had been sent to market, an amount weighing 6,000 quintals and worth close to £5,000 sterling. By 1645, the value of the catch was said to have climbed to £10,000, and the following year the men of Marblehead alone took about £4,000 worth. Virtually all of this cargo was sent in English bottoms to Spain, Portugal, and the Wine Islands, where it was sold to English agents and helped to balance the colonists' accounts in the mother country.[33]

Unfortunately, the New Englanders could send to southern Europe only the portion of the catch that consumers there deemed "merchantable," that is, properly split and cured. Cod that was broken, undersized, oversalted, left out in the rain, or damaged in any other way Europeans termed "refuse" and unfit for consumption by free men; it sold for a far lower price if it could find purchasers at all. An outlet for this low-grade produce, however, appeared in the late 1640s with the first flush of the West Indian sugar boom. As Winthrop learned from Richard Vines, a Puritan planter from Barbados, the islanders were "so intent upon planting sugar that they had rather buy foode at very deare rates than produce it by labour." One by one, Barbados, the Leeward Islands, and Jamaica abandoned the serious production of anything but sugar, and with the rapid expansion of the slave economy, the islands became heavily dependent on imported foodstuffs. Merchantable cod was too costly, but the refuse product, though less appealing to the nose and palate, was equally nourishing and sold for two-thirds the price. Accordingly, beginning in 1647 Massachusetts sent large-scale shipments not only of fish but of farm and timber products as well to the tropical colonies, and this business overtook the trade to southern Europe sometime in the 1670s.[34]

The foundering of the West Country fishery during the English Civil War thus combined with the discovery of new markets to launch the New England fisheries into several decades of uninterrupted growth. In the

33. Winthrop, *History of New England*, II, 42, 321; Darrett B. Rutman, "Governor Winthrop's Garden Crop: The Significance of Agriculture in the Early Commerce of Massachusetts Bay," *WMQ*, 3d Ser., XX (1963), 403n; Bailyn, *New England Merchants*, 78–86.

34. Richard Vines to John Winthrop, July 19, 1647, *Winthrop Papers*, V, 172; Rutman, "Governor Winthrop's Garden Crop," *WMQ*, 3d Ser., XX (1963), 404; Charles F. Carroll, *The Timber Economy of Puritan New England* (Providence, R.I., 1973), 87–89, 142.

towns of Essex County, which dominated the industry, the maritime community expanded. Marblehead, the most important, had only 24 householders in 1637; by 1648 the number had climbed to 44, by 1675 it had risen to 116, and its share of the total Essex County population, calculated from conscript and militia rolls, doubled from 4 percent in 1637 to 8 percent by 1690. Gloucester, too, acquired a fleet of fishing boats, and by 1670 Salem was beginning to gain on them both. Between 1645 and 1675, the combined output for New England grew at an annual rate of between 5 and 6 percent, from roughly 12,000 to 60,000 quintals per year; by 1675 there were reportedly 440 boats and at least one thousand men working the coast between Boston and the Kennebec.[35]

MERCHANT PATRONS

The fishery succeeded in New England only because merchants and fishermen were able to minimize the extraordinary risks of doing business in a frontier world. The vast geographical network of the fishing trade, the scarcity of capital and labor in the new colony, and the powerful competition from Newfoundland in the open markets of Europe and the West Indies created unusual problems, which in the first decade of settlement New Englanders had failed to resolve. By combining in tighter relations of clientage during the 1640s and 1650s, local New England merchants and immigrant West Country fishermen managed to strike a productive if unequal compromise.

The merchant's problem was the organization of production and shipment to market. He alone possessed the business techniques, the personal connections, and the financial power to unite the sources of dried fish on the western shores of the Atlantic with the points of consumption in southern Europe and the plantation colonies. It followed that the overall strategy for the fishery could be planned only in the centers of international commerce where the wealthiest and best-connected merchants

35. "Salem Town Records," 63; William Hammond Bowden, ed., "Marblehead Town Records," Essex Institute, *Hist. Colls.*, LXIX (1933), 211; *Recs. of Mass. Bay*, I, 192; Evarts B. Greene and Virginia D. Harrington, *American Population before the Federal Census of 1790* (New York, 1932), 20; Rutman, "Governor Winthrop's Garden Crop," *WMQ*, 3d Ser., XX (1963), 403n; Order in Council, May 5, 1676, *CSPC*, IX, 362. Of the 121 fishermen referred to in the court records of Essex County between 1640 and 1679, 67 (55%) were from Marblehead, 26 (21%) were from Salem, 22 (18%) were from Gloucester, and 6 (5%) were from other towns. See *Essex Co. Court Recs.*, I–VII, and Appendix 2.

dwelt. The basic arrangements for each successive season originated, therefore, not in Marblehead, Salem, or even Boston, but in London. For their part, London merchants—usually tied to their colonial counterparts through blood or friendship and their common piety—normally agreed to furnish on credit the salt and productive equipment that the fisheries required and to provide the necessary shipping. In return, the merchants in New England contracted to prepare cargoes of dried cod for delivery to the London-owned transports when they dropped anchor off the Massachusetts coast.[36] In February of 1648, for example, William Bartholomew of the Bay Colony and his English partner, Nathaniel Eldred, bound themselves to a consortium of London merchants "for the Delivery of sixteene hundd Kint [quintals] of merchtble dry cod fish . . . aboard the shipp Swallow of London . . . wth in twenty working dayes after the arrivall of the sd shipp at the port of Cape Anne in New England." As it turned out, there was no fish at Cape Ann, so Bartholomew and Eldred were forced to lade the vessels at Marblehead and the Isle of Shoals, but otherwise they discharged their obligations. Had they been unable to deliver a cargo within the period specified, however, they would have been liable for the damages in dead freight and wasted time that the vessel owners had incurred. Worse still, the two merchants would have been saddled with an inventory of depreciating produce until they could negotiate the freighting with another carrier. Every week lost in New England meant a delay in arrival at market, and a tardy vessel ran the risk of encountering the seasonal glut, when prices might not even cover costs. The English traders knew that such credit arrangements were a less than perfect mechanism for extending their control into New England waters, but given the distance between London and Boston they were the best that could be managed.[37]

With the weight of these deadlines constantly on their minds, Massachusetts merchants devoted the winter to negotiating with local men for the delivery of fish the following season. Some merchants, particularly those who lived in the coastal towns of Essex County, preferred to bargain with the fishermen directly. George Corwin of Salem, for example, dealt at

36. Bailyn, *New England Merchants*, 34–37, 79–81.

37. "A Volume Relating to the Early History of Boston Containing the Aspinwall Notarial Records from 1644–1651," in Registry Department of the City of Boston, *Records Relating to the Early History of Boston*, XXXII (Boston, 1903), 217–218. See also *ibid.*, 24, 79, 222–223, 279–280, 261, 390; Bailyn, *New England Merchants*, 79–81; and Matthews, "History of West of England–Newfoundland Fishery," 21–22.

one time with almost every fisherman in the harbor. He sold them food, drink, and dry goods from England; he furnished them with salt and equipment; he rented them boats or advanced them the cordage and canvas to maintain their own; and at the end of every voyage he purchased their fish. Merchants in Boston and Charlestown, by comparison, generally preferred to operate through outport middlemen. During the late 1640s, for example, Valentine Hill of Boston arranged to procure his cod from the Marblehead farmer and fish dealer John Devereaux. Hill agreed to finance the cost of all supplies, pay for the rental of boats, and handle the expense of freighting the cod from the fishing grounds to Marblehead. Devereaux, in return for a small salary and one-third of the profits, assembled the material, hired the men, supervised their labor, dried the fish, and delivered it on Hill's account to the waiting transports at the end of the voyage. Here the risk was shared, but sometimes the exporting merchants passed it along to the outport dealers entirely. Corwin procured some of his fish from men like John Peach and William Nick of Marblehead—small outfitters who purchased their supplies wholesale from the Salem merchant, provisioned the voyages on their own, and paid back their debts in cod. Neither they nor Devereaux labored at sea themselves, but since they understood the workings of the industry and knew the fishermen as neighbors and clients, many of the commercial leaders of the Bay Colony found their services invaluable.[38]

The point of these arrangements at every level—from London to Boston to Marblehead—was to ensure the regular delivery of fish, for a merchant who lost his reputation for reliability could not survive in a trade where markets were open and highly competitive. Those who dealt in fish somehow had to devise a system by which the obligations and the time limits they had accepted could be shifted closer to the point of production, and eventually onto the men who actually gathered in the catch. This was a complicated undertaking, and nowhere more so than in the fishery itself. For one thing, fishermen carried on most of their business several hundred miles from Boston and Salem in small boats scattered along an enormous length of coastline; under such conditions, direct supervision was impossible. For another, fish dealers were competing over a finite catch. If they allowed their men to bargain away a relatively scarce re-

38. George Corwin Acct. Bks., 1658–1664, 1663–1672, esp. the accounts of William Nick and John Peach; *Essex Co. Court Recs.*, I, 214–217. See also *ibid.*, III, 330–333, V, 8–11, 246.

source, they risked coming up short of their promised cargoes at the end of the season. Finally, resident fishermen in a newly settled region might not feel the economic pinch that in the old country had driven them into the employ of others. Along the coastal margin of the county, many of them had obtained by a variety of means sufficient land to provide them with an element of independence. On such tracts, they could erect a cottage and some outbuildings, raise produce in sizable garden plots, pen an animal or two in the yard, or plant an orchard among the rocks. They could even hunt and gather fuel in the nearby woods. Most of the earliest settled fishermen did all of these things, and merchants had to be concerned that their men might treat fishing duties as a secondary obligation. Laborers who caught a whiff of independence could prove, as John Winter put it, to be "trouble-som people."[39]

Given these conditions, most local merchants and middlemen decided to engage their fishermen—as Winter had—under a local variation of clientage.[40] The individual outfitter advanced to each company of men the necessary provisions and equipment for the voyage; in return, they promised to sell him at current prices the entire catch. From the revenue derived, he deducted his expenses, divided the net profit or loss into equal shares among the crew, posted these sums to their individual accounts, and claimed the fish to meet his export obligations. Thus William Browne of Salem outfitted Michael Partridge, Thomas Hooper, and two other men in 1674 with "Beefe and nett," a shallop, and room to dry their fish on the condition that at the end of the voyage he would receive all their fish and oil and credit them with equal shares of the profits: about £9 sterling apiece.[41] For the merchant, this system had three advantages. First, his men had a vested interest in catching as much fish as possible; in an

39. Winter to Trelawney, July 8, 1637, *Trelawney Papers*, 108.

40. This was a New England variation of what in Atlantic Canada is usually termed the truck, or supply, system. See Innis, *Cod Fisheries*, 155–156, 359, 403–405, 494; Rosemary Ommer, *From Outpost to Outport: A Structural Analysis of the Jersey-Gaspé Cod Fishery, 1767–1886* (Montreal, 1991), 36–41, 123–135; Stephen Antler, "The Capitalist Underdevelopment of Nineteenth-Century Newfoundland," in Robert J. Brym and R. James Sacouman, eds., *Underdevelopment and Social Movements in Atlantic Canada* (Toronto, 1979), 191–192; L. Gene Barrett, "Underdevelopment and Social Movements in the Nova Scotia Fishing Industry to 1938," *ibid.*, 128–129; and Sider, *Culture and Class*, 18–23, 58–73, 86–88, 146–148.

41. *Essex Co. Court Recs.*, V, 372. The Corwin Acct. Bks. provide excellent documentation for this system.

industry so decentralized and difficult to oversee, some system of incentives was essential. Second, they had to meet the merchant's deadlines if they hoped to prosper by their labors. The price of codfish overseas, governed by the vast and seasonally fluctuating Newfoundland fishery, moved in a fairly predictable cycle, and New Englanders had to bend to its rhythms.[42] Shippers liked to dispatch their cargoes to Spain and the West Indies in April and November, catching the two New England seasons at their respective crests and beating the northern competition to market.[43] If a company of men managed to land, cure, and deliver their haul early in the season, when the merchants were still putting together their cargoes, prices would be healthy and the profits of the venture could be substantial; but if they arrived late, after the transports had departed and the price of fish had fallen, the value of their catch would similarly tumble and they would have to bear the deficit. Since most partnerships operated on profit margins smaller than 30 percent, a drop of as little as one shilling (6–8 percent) in the price of cod could put a significant dent in their earnings.[44] Finally, the system limited competition over the fruits of their labor. Had fishermen been at liberty to deal with whomever they chose, in an economy that was poor in manpower they easily could have found a fair selection of merchants willing to bid for their produce. Only by limiting this freedom could the individual outfitter be certain that the credit he had advanced at the season's beginning would be transformed by its end into the fish he needed to meet his export obligations.

Taken together, these three provisions imposed on fishermen a form of labor discipline that minimized the risk to capital in an unusually far-flung frontier industry. Only the last—limiting the producer's freedom to dispose of his catch—was a point of contention. Yet, to the client system it

42. On the fishing season at Newfoundland, the need for haste, and the dangers of arriving late at market, see Matthews, "History of the West of England–Newfoundland Fishery," 20–22.

43. Samuel Sewall Account Book, 1685–1689, Baker Library, Harvard Business School, Boston. Of the 16 departures from Boston of trading vessels laden with fish between 1685 and 1689, 5 sailed in November, 2 in October, 4 in April, and 2 in May.

44. Accounts of Robert Codner's boat, William Phillips and Company, William Oxman and Company, William Woods's Company, John Roads's Company, Edward Winter's Company, and Roger Wooland's Company, George Corwin Acct. Bk., 1658–1664; accounts of James Frude and Company, Samuel Causey and Company, William Cauley and Company, and Thomas Dill's Company, George Corwin Acct. Bk., 1663–1672. In the voyages described in these accounts, the net profit or loss amounted on average to 26% of the total outlay.

was the key, for no merchant would be willing to hand out a season's supplies to a company of men who were likely to hand over their fish to one of his competitors. He needed some assurance that his credit had bought the voyage. In 1662, John Jackson and John Bryers, a pair of fishermen from Cape Ann, provisioned themselves on credit from two different outfitters, Jacob Greene of Charlestown and Peter Duncan of Gloucester. With Greene, the two fishermen signed a written bond requiring them to hand over their entire catch in payment, but the only evidence of their obligation to Duncan was a debit balance in his books "to be paid in fish and mackerel" at an unspecified future date. As soon as the season was over and the catch had been cured, Greene and Duncan both demanded that it be carried to their respective wharves. They immediately discovered the nature of their conflicting claims, and soon after each brought a separate suit of debt against the two fishermen in order to establish prior right. Eventually, the courts decided that, bond or no bond, both merchants had equally valid claims and they both won their cases. The final judgment, however, is less important than the clear assumption on the part of both merchants that capital was advanced only to establish a lien on the entire haul.[45]

Sometimes formal agreements regarding the delivery of the fisherman's catch served to restrict the play of his hand. In 1672, for example, Joseph Elwell from Gloucester signed a bond for £37 sterling in goods received from an Ipswich merchant, Samuel Bishop, to the effect that "I the sd Joseph doe make over and confirme to the sd Samuel or his assignes all the sd share of [cod]fish, mackerel, & oile that I have or shall ketch of Season in ye 1672 under Samuel Elwell, No wayes neither Directly nor

45. *Essex Co. Court Recs.*, II, 386–387, 401–402; *Essex Co. Court Recs., Verbatim Transcriptions*, VII, 103, 104, 106, 141. For the custom of the fishery in Newfoundland, see Antler, "Capitalist Underdevelopment of Newfoundland," in Brym and Sacouman, eds., *Underdevelopment in Atlantic Canada*, 192; James K. Hiller, "The Newfoundland Credit System: An Interpretation," in Rosemary E. Ommer, ed., *Merchant Credit and Labour Strategies in Historical Perspective* (Fredericton, N.B., 1990), 86–101; Robert M. Lewis, "The Survival of the Planters' Fishery in Nineteenth and Twentieth Century Newfoundland," *ibid.*, 102–113; David A. Macdonald, "They Cannot Pay Us in Money: Newman and Company and the Supplying System in the Newfoundland Fishery, 1850–1884," *ibid.*, 114–128; Pope, "Residence, Labour, Demand, and Exchange," 469–471; Handcock, *Soe longe as there comes noe women*, 137, 232–235; and the discussion that supersedes all of the above in Sean Thomas Cadigan, "Economic and Social Relations of Production on the Northeast Coast of Newfoundland, with Special Reference to Conception Bay, 1785–1855" (Ph.D. diss., Memorial University of Newfoundland, 1991).

Indirectly ordering or disposing of the sd share or any part of it without per Samuell order."[46] Most arrangements did not have to be this explicit, however, for the rules were generally understood by each party. Sometimes the merchant required his client to subscribe a notation penned at the foot of a reckoning in the merchant's accounts: "to be paid in fish."[47] Often the debt would simply be acknowledged without any reference to the means of payment. Yet in all cases the understanding that governed the financing of the fishery was the same, for as the account books of the period clearly show, the produce of every voyage passed into the hands of the outfitting merchant.[48]

A system that legally restricted the fisherman's right to bargain obviously worked to the advantage of his creditors. Merchants could not arbitrarily name their prices or they would shortly run out of clients, but the upper hand was theirs as long as they maintained a common front. In other fisheries at other times—during the nineteenth century, for example, in Newfoundland, Nova Scotia, and the Gaspé region of Quebec—merchants were able to enforce a stricter version of the clientage relationship because their men were dispersed in numerous little settlements, each of which could support only a single dealer who normally commanded the local market and dictated terms.[49] But in New England the fishery was outfitted from a small number of sizable towns, clustered along the brief fifty miles of coastline between Boston and Portsmouth. A fisherman like John Meager, for example, could easily turn down the offer of a summer's work on a Gloucester boat when he knew that he could "ship winter and summer" out of Salem, only a few hours away.[50] Clientage could never operate as tightly under these conditions as it later did in the resident fisheries of the far northern colonies, but it did provide

46. *Essex Co. Court Recs., Verbatim Transcriptions*, XL, 138 (i). For other examples, see *ibid.*, VII, 141 (i), and *Essex Co. Court Recs.*, VI, 67.

47. Many of these can be found scattered throughout the George Corwin Acct. Bks., 1658–1664, 1663–1672, and the Philip English Account Book, 1678–1690, English/Touzell/Hathorne Papers, 1661–1851, JDPL.

48. George Corwin Acct. Bks., 1658–1664, 1663–1672; *Essex Co. Court Recs.*, V, 11, 372, 419–420, VI, 67; *Essex Co. Court Recs., Verbatim Transcriptions*, XL, 138.

49. I am indebted on this point to conversations with Rosemary Ommer, but see also Sider, *Culture and Class*, 68–70, as well as n. 45 above.

50. *Essex Co. Court Recs.*, III, 328. The boat owner replied, in terms that reinforce this sense of mobility, that Meager should stay in Gloucester anyway, "for we are all three young men and can Goe when wee will and Com when we will."

merchants with some protection as long as they agreed to refrain from competition.

We can infer a degree of tacit collaboration both from the regularity with which fishermen delivered their dried cod to the warehouses of their creditors and from the rarity of disputes between dealers as to the ownership of the fish.[51] But in one instance the court records actually describe how such consensus was reached. During the summer of 1666 a disagreement broke out at the Isle of Shoals when a group of dealers from the mainland, owing to the slowness of markets abroad, decided to lower their offer for merchantable cod from sixteen to thirteen shillings per quintal. The local fishermen were outraged and refused to hand over their hauls except on "ye termes they had payd it to one another," that is, the old price. The merchants then "generally agreed" that a public meeting was needed to resolve the difficulty, and at this gathering they "did positively declare" that the higher price would be reestablished only if shippers in Marblehead and Salem would match it. That night, "at the Lodgeing of mr James Whitcomb in company with most of ye Marchts," the spokesmen for the fishermen "proffered some small abatemt of the price which they formerly insisted on," but the traders would not be budged. The fishermen finally capitulated, and indeed no merchantable cod changed hands that season on any terms but those the merchants had collectively determined.[52]

These were obviously delicate negotiations. Whitcomb and his fellow dealers presented a united front to avoid a local bidding war, which might have boosted prices to a level they could not afford. In this sense, the market at the Isle of Shoals was certainly less than open. Yet neither was it entirely closed. For one thing, the statements of the fishermen regarding terms of exchange among themselves imply that not all of the fish was engaged to creditors; for another, the merchants' willingness to reconsider the old price if conditions in the export trade warranted suggests that they understood the long-term disadvantages of trying to reap a windfall from clients who might take their business elsewhere the following year. Most dealers would have preferred a tighter market, but under conditions that prevailed along the New England coast that sort of control was not possible.

51. The cases involving Greene, Duncan, Jackson, and Bryers cited above are the only lawsuits of this nature that I could find in *Essex Co. Court Recs.*, I–IX.

52. *Ibid.*, V, 6–12.

In the middle decades of the seventeenth century, all the prominent fish dealers of Essex County—George Corwin, William Browne, and Edmund Batter of Salem; Peter Duncan of Gloucester; Moses Maverick of Marblehead; and Francis Wainwright and Jonathan Wade of Ipswich—adopted this particular variant of clientage. By directing credit downward through the fishery, they created a structure of labor obligation that flowed upward in return. Although looser in construction than they might have wished, the client system enabled them to deal with the high cost of labor, the unforgiving time restraints of a seasonal economy, and the impossibility of directly disciplining workmen who had to scatter across hundreds of banks and ledges to carry on their job properly. It did so, moreover, in a manner that permitted the swift development of a resident fishery and the accumulation of capital in the merchants' own pockets.

FISHING CLIENTS

How did these arrangements appear from the perspective of the fisherman? Clearly, he lost something by being caught in the folds of clientage, but were there any compensating gains? While granting that merchants were the protagonists in the credit system, it is important to understand how fishermen became enmeshed in the system and whether it benefited them in any way.

The fisherman's position was defined first by his dependence on others for access to capital. At no stage of his career, even if he was among the fortunate minority who owned their boats, could he have financed the purchase of the necessary salt, timber, food, liquor, cordage, and canvas for even a single season's operations without credit. Nor could he, without merchant connections, have disposed of his produce overseas.[53] This was as true in New England as it was in all the commercial fisheries of the day. Yet within merchant capitalism there were certainly variations; what set

53. The cost of outfitting a four-man company (three fishermen and one shoreman) usually ran between £100 and £150 sterling per annum, the equivalent of one to two years' income for each man on board. See George Corwin Acct. Bks., 1658–1664, 1663–1672. For a differing view, see Rosemary E. Ommer, "'All the Fish of the Post': Resource Property Rights and Development in a Nineteenth-Century Inshore Fishery," *Acadiensis*, X, no. 2 (1980–1981), 107, and Antler, "Capitalist Underdevelopment of Newfoundland," in Brym and Sacouman, eds., *Underdevelopment in Atlantic Canada*, 193.

apart the Essex County industry, in the eyes of those who worked in it, were the comparatively favorable terms that it offered. In earnings, judging from a sample of accounts drawn from the period 1666–1671, local fishermen could expect to average about £20 sterling (room and board, such as it was, included) for work that never filled twelve months in the year.[54] Compared with the incomes of freeholding landsmen, this was hardly an enormous sum, but nowhere else in the North Atlantic region—on merchant vessels, on the London docks, on farms in the West Country, or even in the migratory fishery at Newfoundland—could common seamen have done as well.[55] "There being great wages given to men in New England," wrote one Newfoundlander in 1700, "makes men desirous to go there, and frequently attempts it."[56] The same could have been said for the entire period after 1640. Healthy markets and the local scarcity of maritime labor persistently forced New England merchants to enter the Atlantic labor market and to bid high.

Even more compelling to a fisherman, however, was the availability of easy credit. From his standpoint, the client system meant cordage and timber, rum and English cloth, advanced in quantities that might amount to several years' earnings, interest free, without collateral—on the sole proviso that he agree to deal with his creditor alone. Merchants were prepared, at least in the good times before 1675, to let these obligations stand for years, indeed for as long as the men who held them continued to deliver the fish. Farmers and artisans frequently received credit as well, but generally in much smaller sums. The records of probate reveal that 40 percent of active or recently retired fishermen who died before 1676 possessed debts in excess of £20 sterling, whereas the equivalent figure for

54. This average was calculated from a sample of 51 annual incomes drawn from the years 1666–1671 in George Corwin Acct. Bk., 1663–1672. These years were selected for their legibility in the account book and their representativeness of average prices over the entire period 1630–1675.

55. Ralph Davis, *The Rise of the English Shipping Industry in the Seventeenth and Eighteenth Centuries* (London, 1962), 135, 151–152; Innis, *Cod Fisheries*, 70n–71n, 101; Cell, *English Enterprise in Newfoundland*, 16; W. G. Hoskins, "The Farm-Labourer through Four Centuries," in W. G. Hoskins and H. P. R. Finberg, eds., *Devonshire Studies* (London, 1952), 424; Alan Everitt, "Farm Labourers," in Joan Thirsk, ed., *The Agrarian History of England and Wales*, vol. IV: *1500–1640* (Cambridge, 1967), 436–437. Peter Pope disagrees with me in his "Residence, Labour, Demand, and Exchange," 345–349.

56. Capt. Staffd. Fairborne, "Account of the Fishery at Newfoundland," Sept. 11, 1700, *CSPC*, XVIII, 522.

landsmen was only 23 percent.[57] Sampling the ledger balances of those who brought in fish and farm produce to George Corwin in 1658 and 1661 shows, in parallel fashion, that fishermen were behind an average of £35 sterling on their accounts—more than double the indebtedness of farmers.[58] Evidence from the county court points in the same direction: between 1664 and 1673, residents of Marblehead were responsible as plaintiff creditors for a mere 12 percent, but as defendant debtors for a full 35 percent, of all litigated debt. And whereas the non-fishing inhabitants of Essex County were sued for amounts averaging only £11 sterling, fishermen were in court for an average of £29 sterling.[59] Sometimes the amounts that Corwin and his competitors were willing to advance individual fishermen were staggering. John Slater, a young man of twenty-nine who lived with his new wife in a sparsely furnished house at Marblehead, died in 1665, owing Corwin almost £90 sterling, the equivalent of more than four years' wages. John Roads and Henry Trevett, both of whom worked for the same merchant between 1660 and 1675, were almost invariably between £75 and £200 sterling in debt.[60] Sums this high were unusual, but fishermen creditors were rarer still.

Indebtedness was not a function of poverty. It could be a short-term consequence of hard times: a year when the fish did not come in or when prices dipped, in which case fishermen needed credit to survive the win-

57. See Appendix 2. The probate inventories for the non-maritime sample ($N = 31$) were drawn at random, and for fishermen were identified as those with decedents active or recently retired at the time of their death.

58. George Corwin Acct. Bks., 1651–1662, 1658–1664. The figure for farmers was £14 sterling. Out of 30 men who fished for Corwin over two consecutive seasons during this period, 18 were indebted throughout, 10 had accounts that roughly balanced, and only 2 were consistently ahead.

59. Of four suits brought by fishermen in this period, the average debt was £7, whereas those entered by the 168 non-fishing inhabitants averaged £13. See *Essex Co. Court Recs., Verbatim Transcriptions*, X–XX. The names of plaintiff and defendant, their town of origin and occupation (if recorded), and the amount sued for were all abstracted from 235 surviving writs of debt in these volumes and were then combined with other biographical data drawn from the local history collection of the James Duncan Phillips Library. It should be remembered that these were not the final judgments, which frequently were somewhat smaller than the sums the plaintiffs claimed in the writs but too rarely recorded to be usefully analyzed.

60. Accounts of John Slater, John Roads, and Henry Trevett, George Corwin Acct. Bks., 1658–1664, 1663–1672; *Essex Co. Court Recs.*, III, 267–268; *Essex Co. Court Recs., Verbatim Transcriptions*, XX, 113 (ii).

ter. Merchants were less than enthusiastic, however, about advancing goods to unsuccessful clients, and the records of probate suggest that the property-poor were no further in the red than their relatively flourishing neighbors.[61] In fact, three of the five wealthiest fishermen in the probate records—William Charles, Job Hilliard, and Edmund Nicholson—were also among the five most indebted. William Nick, an outfitter and client of Corwin's, died in 1683 owning a well-appointed house, an orchard and a field, two stages, two boats, a fishyard, and a warehouse worth a total of £545 sterling; yet his liabilities, £204 sterling, were the most of any man involved in the fishery during this period. Merchants generally tolerated heavier indebtedness among their more substantial clients, whom they viewed as better risks.[62]

Some fishermen built moderately prosperous careers within the maritime community that would have been unthinkable without financial assistance. Had George Corwin refused him credit, Job Hilliard could never have bought in 1663 a share in the ketch *Mayflower*, nor could John Roads have purchased in 1662 the bricks, boards, hinges, and shingles with which he built a house. Similarly, Andrew Tucker needed advances first from Moses Maverick and then from William Browne to buy his house and yard on Marblehead Neck, erect a stage and warehouse, and purchase vessels for the fishery. Eventually, he was able to retire from the sea, earn his living as an outfitter, and leave his descendants enough property to ensure their security through the following century.[63] Tucker

61. See Appendix 2. Net indebtedness among fishermen who died within ten years of their last recorded voyage (the same group as in n. 57) was *positively* correlated with the value of physical estate ($r = .36$), although the low value of r and the small number of cases (20) suggest caution in interpretation. Rosemary Ommer has found that in the 19th-century Gaspé the negative balances on fishermen's accounts did rise during periods when fish were scarce, although not necessarily more for those in worse straits than for the better-off individuals. See her "Accounting the Fishery" (paper presented to the Thirteenth Conference on Quantitative Methods in Canadian Economic History, Waterloo, Ont., Mar. 16–17, 1984), 9–16.

62. *Essex Co. Court Recs.*, I–VI. On William Nick, see George Corwin Acct. Bks., 1658–1664, 1663–1672, and Estate of William Nick (1683), Probate No. 19545, Essex Co. Prob. Recs.

63. Accounts of William Woods, ketch *Mayflower*, Job Hilliard, and John Roads, George Corwin Acct. Bk., 1663–1672; Estate of Andrew Tucker (1692), Probate No. 28248, Essex Co. Prob. Recs.; *Essex Co. Court Recs.*, IV, 66, VII, 411, VIII, 194–195, IX, 199–200. For the history of the Tucker family in the 18th century, see the Marblehead Tax Valuation List, 1735, Microform Edition of the Tax and Valuation Lists of Massachusetts Towns before

was unusual, but almost every fisherman who settled locally and survived to the age of forty-five managed to accumulate at least a house and garden, a few animals, and sometimes a boat—amounting, after debts were paid, to an average of £66 sterling (see table 3). This was not a large sum, but given that many of these seamen had arrived in Massachusetts penniless, their achievement was considerable; not only did their estates surpass in wealth those of contemporary English farm laborers, but also they compared passably with those of immigrant servants and laborers elsewhere in the American colonies.[64] Cultivating a firm relationship with one's merchant creditor was of the utmost importance, therefore, to any fisherman trying to carve out even a modest place in a developing economy where capital was scarce.

Fishing merchants were not naturally openhanded. It cost George Corwin a good deal to cover the £1,000 sterling in debit balances that he had allowed to about eighty men "att the Estward" in the 1660s, and he only paid that price to gain leverage over them.[65] By financing a portion of the fishing community—not simply from voyage to voyage, but also the purchase of their vessels and land, the rebuilding of their homes, and even their daily bread—Corwin ensured that a crowd of indebted clients would troop down to his warehouse several times a year to provision themselves and sign away yet another season's catch. For years the services of fishermen like Job Hilliard, John Slater, and Henry Trevett were retained on credit; when they died, their liabilities were likely to be concentrated in Corwin's hands.[66] His account books constitute the only detailed record of

1776, roll 12. All references to 18th-century Massachusetts tax and valuation lists, unless otherwise specified, are to the microfilm edition compiled by Ruth Crandall and published in 1971 by the Charles Warren Center for Studies in American History at Harvard University, which filmed the originals housed in town record offices.

64. See Appendix 2. Of the 25 fishermen in this group, 24 owned real estate when they died, 16 owned livestock, and 6 owned at least a share in some vessel. For comparative figures on the inventoried estates of Maryland servants in this period, see Russell R. Menard, "From Servant to Freeholder: Status Mobility and Property Accumulation in Seventeenth-Century Maryland," *WMQ*, 3d Ser., XXX (1973), 40–42, 62–63. Fishermen in Essex County did somewhat worse than Maryland servants who arrived before 1660 and somewhat better than those who came after that date.

65. George Corwin, "Ann accompt of debts dew att ye Estward," Curwen Family Papers, 1641–1902, JDPL.

66. George Corwin Acct. Bks., 1658–1664, 1663–1672; *Essex Co. Court Recs.*, I–VI. A sample of 20 fishermen who began working for Corwin between 1659 and 1662 gave him on average 3.2 of their next 5 years, and 8 fished for him the entire time. It should be

Table 3. Mean Inventoried Estate Values of Essex County Fishermen, 1630–1675 (in Pounds Sterling)

| | Fishermen[a] | | |
	Immigrant[b] (N = 12)	Active[c] (N = 20)	Established[d] (N = 24)
Real wealth	£2.9	£27.5	£65.8
Personal wealth	£14.7	£22.6	£36.2
Debts	£14.2	£19.4	£38.2
Total wealth	£3.4	£30.7	£63.8

[a]Some fishermen fall within more than one category.
[b]Immigrant fishermen were those who died in Essex County before 1676, having arrived there less than ten years before.
[c]Active fishermen were those who died before 1676 and were recorded as actively fishing less than ten years before their death.
[d]Established fishermen were those who were recorded as fishing before 1676 and lived to be 45 or older.

Sources: See Appendix 2. The mean value of personal estates of contemporary English laborers has been estimated at £9 sterling; see Alan Everitt, "Farm Labourers," in Joan Thirsk, ed., *The Agrarian History of England and Wales*, vol. IV: *1500–1640* (Cambridge, 1967), 421.

clientage in the early fishery, but the broad pattern of indebtedness within Marblehead and the waterfront portions of Salem and Gloucester suggests that its workings were general. The long-standing credit connections between fishermen and their merchant outfitters gave the production of fish in outport Essex County its essential discipline.

Long-term credit never constituted an absolute claim on the debtor's labor. He was always free to negotiate other employment—mending nets locally, perhaps, or shipping as an ordinary hand on a West Indian voyage—and to have the earnings transferred to his creditor. He could purchase supplies from other members of the community and ask them to bill

---

remembered, moreover, that this continuity was broken just as often by death or departure from the county as by the decision to look elsewhere within the community. The records of probate offer another measure of clientage: of 14 fishermen who died before 1676 and were indebted to identifiable individuals at the time of death, 9 owed more than 50% of their debts to a single creditor.

the merchant to whom he owed his fish. He could try to persuade another outfitter to provision him for a fishing voyage on a brand-new account, or he might occasionally flog his share of the catch to another dealer in plain violation of the tacit rules of clientage. All these elements of freedom— almost unknown to the more closed truck systems of nineteenth-century Canada and Newfoundland—Essex County fishermen never lost.[67] Yet to try one of these tacks over any stretch of time was to court trouble. The primary creditor always had the power, through civil action, to bring financial ruin on any seriously indebted client who took too much of his business elsewhere, and this fact constantly stood between the two in their negotiations. When Walter Price of Salem brought suit for £34 sterling against Peter Joy, a local fisherman whose credit-worthiness had been compromised by frequent presentations for drunkenness, Price was threatening to take away most of what his client owned. Similarly, had George Corwin proceeded with an intended action for £400 sterling against Henry Trevett, his steady customer of fifteen years, Corwin could have seized all Trevett's chattels and turned him for practical purposes into a servant for life.[68] The wise fisherman thus thought twice before letting his interests stray too far from those of his creditor.

But merchants also had to be careful. Those who too readily dragged their indebted hands into court acquired a reputation for hard dealing

67. Evidence for fishermen directing the shoreman who dried the company's fish to deliver it to someone other than the outfitter can be found in *Essex Co. Court Recs.*, II, 386–387, V, 420, VII, 305–308, VIII, 412–415. The question of the relatively closed nature of these credit arrangements is important: to what degree did the financing of fishermen oblige them to provision themselves only through their creditors? Eight separate debit accounts from the period 1663–1685 reveal that on average fishermen received 78% of their credit in goods from the merchants' own stores, 20% in the covering of debts that fishermen had run up with other men, and only 2% in cash. Here as elsewhere, the evidence suggests that clientage operated more as a powerful constraint than as an outright prohibition on open dealing. See *Essex Co. Court Recs.*, III, 260, VII, 247, VIII, 74–75, 206–207, IX, 45, 199; and accounts of Daniel Jeggles and Thomas Cloutman, Philip English Acct. Bk., 1678–1690. For 19th-century comparisons in British North America, see Ommer, "Accounting the Fishery," 5–9, and the sources cited therein.

68. *Essex Co. Court Recs.*, *Verbatim Transcriptions*, XIV, 142 (iii), XX, 113 (ii). On Peter Joy, see *Essex Co. Court Recs.*, II, 343, IV, 43, 87, 88, 94, 170, V, 266, VII, 2; and Perley, *History of Salem*, III, 420. On Trevett, see George Corwin Acct. Bks., 1658–1664, 1663–1672. See Stephen Innes, *Labor in a New Land: Economy and Society in Seventeenth-Century Springfield* (Princeton, N.J., 1983), 41–42, 66–71, 89–90, 98–100, 101–104, 176–179, for the most thorough discussion of this theme.

that alienated the fishing community and damaged their business. Edmund Batter was one of this breed, complained Mary Hilliard of Marblehead in 1667: "a well known man of such a quick spirit that he will not allow any debt to stand . . . as witness the great trouble of the constables in this town."[69] Philip English, an immigrant fishing merchant from Jersey, was always ready to take on recalcitrant debtors at law and had his warehouse sacked by an angry crowd when he was accused of witchcraft in the 1690s.[70] Most fish dealers, however, even those with scores of clients, like Moses Maverick of Marblehead and William Browne of Salem, found that their interests were best served when they launched only a suit or two a year.[71] Fish dealers were probably more scrupulous about keeping their books in order and their customers in line than were the merchants whom the General Court chided rather ineffectually in 1669 for failing to reckon their accounts on a regular basis.[72] But there was little point in bringing down the force of law on clients whose hands were in effect tied already, particularly if one risked at the same time driving away new business.

Clientage was in this instance an exchange relationship employed by merchant capital to organize production on the periphery of the European world economy, where geographical distance made business an unusually risky affair and where capital and labor were scarce relative to land. This relationship flourished in New England during a period when markets were sufficiently healthy to draw in capital for development and transatlantic shipping links were erratic enough that credit seemed a viable way to regulate the delivery of produce. It made sense on the American frontier, where the chronic scarcity of manpower constantly pushed entrepreneurs into attempting to secure a captive labor force and limited capital forced fishermen to barter some of their freedom in ex-

69. *Essex Co. Court Recs.*, III, 445–446.

70. George F. Cheever, "A Sketch of Philip English, a Merchant in Salem from about 1670 to about 1733–4," Essex Institute, *Hist. Colls.*, I (1859), 160, 160n; David T. Konig, "A New Look at the Essex 'French': Ethnic Frictions and Community Tensions in Seventeenth-Century Essex County, Massachusetts," Essex Institute, *Hist. Colls.*, CX (1974), 174; Paul Boyer and Stephen Nissenbaum, *Salem Possessed: The Social Origins of Witchcraft* (Cambridge, Mass., 1974), 131–132.

71. *Essex Co. Court Recs.*, *Verbatim Transcriptions*, X–XX. Between 1665 and 1673, Browne was a plaintiff in 17 debt cases, and Maverick in 12.

72. *Recs. of Mass. Bay*, IV, ii, 422. For the history of the General Court's attempts to impose more regular accounting practices on the colony, see *ibid.*, IV, ii, 511, V, 28, 138, 212.

change for ready provisioning. And as long as the population of the colony remained small enough, outfitters could realistically collaborate to restrict competition. Up to a point, these different conditions hung on separate threads. Yet, in a basic way, they all derived from the logic of economic development in a frontier environment. Just as the challenge of development and the scarcity of production factors had caused the rural economy to reconstruct itself around the nuclear family, so they drew merchants and fishermen together into the interdependent if unequal bonds of clientage.

WORK

Interdependence in the organization of labor between the producers and those who controlled the means of production was common to the farm and the fishery. On land, however, this principle operated within households whose members held a common interest, whereas at sea it described a relation between households that were frequently at odds. This made a profound difference. In fact, structured as it was, the fishing industry acquired a flavor foreign to the experience of most mainland New Englanders. Labor at sea under any circumstance involved a level of danger, tension, and deprivation to which landed householders were rarely accustomed. But the fisherman's subordinate status within merchant capitalism placed constraints on his freedom that made the inconveniences natural to his trade even harder to bear.

The pace of activity in the fishery was determined by the seasons and the marketplace, and to some degree it had to follow the natural migration of the cod. By contrast to the inshore waters of Newfoundland, however, where the fishery operated only through a short and intense summer season, the New England grounds could be worked almost continuously. The Gulf of Maine was a maze of banks and ledges, shoals and deeps, all of which could sustain cod and other fish in their preferred environment through different portions of the year. As water temperatures changed, the cod moved about, but not in one enormous wave on and off the coast as at Newfoundland. Operations did peak twice every twelve months, in the spring and in the fall, but never did the fish desert the coast entirely.[73]

73. Richard Rathbun and Joseph W. Collins, "The Sea Fishing-Grounds of the Eastern Coast of North America from Greenland to Mexico," in Richard Rathbun, ed., *The Fishing Grounds of North America* (section III of George Brown Goode, ed., *The Fisheries and*

Foreign markets, however, did move in an annual pattern. With vessels lading in Boston and Salem for the earliest possible departure and exporters willing to pay for the swift delivery of their produce, companies of fishermen could not simply gear their work to the natural movements of the cod. Instead, they had to strive at all times to be ahead of their competitors: first out of port, first on the grounds, first to complete their loads, and first to be home.

As far ahead of impending deadlines as possible, therefore, fishermen had to set about securing work. The fortunate minority who owned shares in the vessels they operated had little to worry about. Commonly residents of some standing in the maritime community, they purchased and crewed their boats in company with friends or relatives and had only to hire possibly one extra hand and a shoreman to dry the fish.[74] The Nicholson brothers of Marblehead, for example, divided the ownership of their father's boat after his death in 1660 and operated as a team. John Codner of the same town agreed in 1663 to take on William Browne as a partner in the "shallop called the Black Besse," if Browne would marry his daughter.[75] Companies of this nature, composed of men who knew one another's habits, experienced a relatively stable working environment. Yet close to 60 percent of Essex County fishermen—including most of the recent arrivals—did not own an interest in the vessels on which they worked. As a result, they had to either sign on with an existing company that was short a man or, together with others in the same predicament, rent a boat in a partnership of their own. In both cases, the individual would participate in the company as an equal member, but he would be

Fishery Industries of the United States, 5 sections in 8 parts [Washington, D.C., 1884–1887]), 8–16, 26–46. For the best contemporary description of seasonal fishing on a given site, see Winter to Trelawney, June 18, July 7, 1634, July 11, 1635, July 10, 1639, _Trelawney Papers_, 26, 27, 44, 57, 169.

74. George Corwin Acct. Bks., 1658–1664, 1663–1672. In a sample of 29 voyages outfitted by Corwin between 1660 and 1664, 34 of 87 men (39%) owned shares in the boats they operated. Of 20 fishermen who died between 1645 and 1675 within five years of their last recorded voyage and whose inventories survive, 8 (40%) owned boats. Of the 13 who died in the same year as their last recorded voyage (in the very course of their work), 5 (38%) owned boats. See _Essex Co. Court Recs._, II, 290–291, 302, 344, III, 81, 181, IV, 40–41, 371–372, V, 69–70, 253, VI, 51. For other examples of boat-owning fishermen, see _ibid._, III, 40–41, and Hale, ed., _Note-Book Kept by Thomas Lechford_, 406–407.

75. _Essex Co. Court Recs._, II, 256, 290–291, III, 156–157; accounts of Edmund Nicholson and Christopher Nicholson, George Corwin Acct. Bk., 1658–1664.

charged by whoever owned the craft for "boat hire" at the end of the voyage.[76] In partnerships patched together for the season, where mere acquaintances and even total strangers brushed shoulders every day, loyalties were fragile and open conflict was common. In the spring of 1666, John Meager of Gloucester discovered that Samuel Dutch, with whom he had shipped on a mackerel voyage, was about to leave without him. In a fury Meager set out to track down the boat master and caught up with him at a neighbor's house, preparing to depart. Meager and a friend barred the two doors of the dwelling, but Dutch escaped through a window, raced down to the shoreline, and made it to the safety of his boat, moored in the harbor. The thwarted fisherman stood on the rocks and hurled abuse across the water, but Dutch retorted that if Meager approached, "he would throw him overboard." After the vessel weighed anchor without him, Meager sued his prospective partner for non-performance of an agreement; the court awarded him the case and ordered Dutch to take on Meager or pay him nearly £6 sterling in damages.[77] In every legal action brought before the quarterly courts in this period involving contests between members of the same fishing company in which the terms of the partnership were clear, at least one of the contending individuals owned no share in the vessel.[78] Although not all hired men were as quick to anger as John Meager, most were accustomed to approaching their problems in the same freewheeling manner; because at least in numbers they dominated the industry as a whole, hired fishermen lent to it the same unrestrained character.

Having banded together in companies, the fishermen next outfitted themselves for the season. Efficiency at the start was everything, and most partnerships, aware of looming deadlines, spent the last days before sailing in continuous preparation. If vessels needed work, their owners either hired a boatbuilder or, more frequently, went to their supplier for the sailcloth, cordage, or timber and did the job themselves. All the equipment—hooks, lines, leads, bait, salt, lumber, and carpenter's tools—then had to be assembled and carted down to the shoreline. Into the vessel the

76. See n. 74, above. Of 32 fishermen identified as owning a share in a boat, 16 (50%) had at that time been resident in their community for five years or more. Of the 63 who could positively be identified as boat renters, 18 (29%) had been in town for that period.

77. *Essex Co. Court Recs.*, III, 328, 350.

78. *Ibid.*, II, 188, 313, III, 102, 154–155, 209, 262, 328–329; John Noble and John F. Cronin, eds., *Records of the Court of Assistants of the Colony of Massachusetts Bay, 1630–1692* (Boston, 1901–1928), III, 29–63.

men loaded pots and pans, casks of bread and salted meat, bushels of dried peas and flour, jars of "salet oyle," barrels of brandy, cider, and beer, and usually a few live hogs. Against their own accounts, they purchased sea-boots, blankets, heavy waterproof clothing, perhaps some tobacco or chocolate, and any other items they thought necessary.[79] If all went according to plan, the vessel could be ready to sail within a week.

Some crews preferred for at least part of the year to base themselves at home and work the familiar waters off the Massachusetts coast. When the boat containing Elias Fortune, William Carter, and Francis Hooper was overrun and sunk in May of 1662 by a ship from Barbados, the three fishermen were tending their lines about twenty miles from Marble-head.[80] Parties from Salem sometimes chose to operate from Misery Island, a few miles from the harbor's mouth. John Ingersoll, Thomas Sallowes, and Paul Mansfield ran a fishing station on its shores in 1659, and a year later the General Court granted this and other neighboring islands to the town on the condition that any company could freely operate there.[81] Although the fishing on these home grounds often proved indifferent, they were handier, especially in the winter, and for a cautious man or one with family commitments their advantages were obvious.

The big money was to be made in more distant waters, however, and most who put out from Essex County set sail "to the eastward" into the Gulf of Maine.[82] For those with the patience to wait out bad weather, this was a straightforward enough journey, but the seaman in a hurry risked running into trouble. Especially for the lucrative late winter and early spring voyages, on which fishermen embarked in the knowledge that they had to get home before April, when cargoes were assembled for export, the pressure to chance an early departure and the storms of February and March bore on every company. This early in the year, when ice formed

79. Accounts of William Phillips and Company, William Oxman and Company, and Roger Wooland's Company, George Corwin Acct. Bks., 1658–1664, 1663–1672.

80. *Essex Co. Court Recs.*, II, 390–392; see also *ibid.*, III, 102–103, 209.

81. Perley, *History of Salem*, II, 240; accounts of John Ingersoll, George Corwin Acct. Bk., 1658–1664.

82. References to the local fishery and to the Gulf of Maine fishery in *Essex Co. Court Recs.* are roughly equal in number. Assuming that this source was biased toward local activity, it would seem that the gulf fishery was more important. That fishermen routinely bought their supplies from George Corwin in large amounts and that long intervals elapsed between their purchases suggest voyages of some length. See George Corwin Acct. Bks., 1658–1664, 1663–1672.

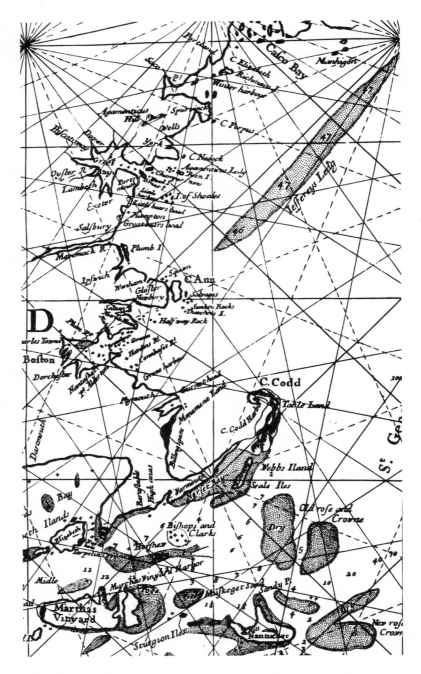

Part of New England (detail). From John Thornton and William Fisher, *The English Pilot,*
The Fourth Book (1689; reprint ed., Amsterdam, 1967)

easily on the rigging and driving snow could cut visibility to near zero, coastal travel in single-masted thirty-foot fishing shallops, half-decked at most and packed to the gunwales with provisions, could be dangerous. Having just weighed anchor for Pemaquid in the middle of January, a vessel from Piscataqua with a crew of eight was struck by a gale from the northwest and driven far out to sea. Two weeks later they recovered Monhegan Island, but not before four fishermen had perished from the cold. Most maritime disasters occurred at this time of year, and later in the colonial period both public authorities and private insurers took action to prevent such early departures.[83] Yet from the fisherman's standpoint, to wait until the weather improved would be to miss the beginning of the season and to return late, after the best markets had passed, so most partnerships bent their calendar to market forces and continued to risk winter travel.

When fair weather did prevail, companies could reach Monhegan, Damariscove, Matinicus, and the other important fishing sites in the gulf within a matter of days. There they erected stages, or platforms with sheds on top, at the water's edge where boats could lie to them and unload, and they put up flakes, or open-frame tables covered with boughs and birchbark, for drying the fish.[84] If the men were fortunate, they might happen upon the remains of a previous installation, which they were free by custom to occupy and repair; however, buildings on the coast, especially those that jutted into the sea, disintegrated quickly when unattended, so the men usually faced at least a few days of preparation on shore. Rights

83. William Hubbard, "A General History of New England, from the Discovery to MDCLXXX," Massachusetts Historical Society, *Collections*, 2d Ser., VI (1815), 421. For descriptions of these shallops, see Howard I. Chapelle, *The History of American Sailing Ships* (New York, 1935), 15, and William Avery Baker, "Vessel Types of Colonial Massachusetts," in Frederick S. Allis, Jr., ed., *Seafaring in Colonial Massachusetts* (Colonial Society of Massachusetts, *Collections*, LII [Boston, 1980]), 17. It was estimated in 1676 that the average New England "fisherboat" was of six tons burden. See "Inquiries given to Edward Randolph," Mar. 20, 1676, *CSPC*, IX, 362. On the construction of these shallops, see *Essex Co. Court Recs.*, IV, 254–255. On 17th-century winter fatalities at sea, see *Essex Co. Prob. Recs.*, I, 162, 359–364, II, 109–110, III, 241–242. On 18th-century attempts to regulate early departures, see "An Act for the Better Regulating the Fishery" (1757), in *The Acts and Resolves, Public and Private, of the Province of the Massachusetts Bay* (Boston, 1869–1922), III, 1030, and "Covenant for Mutual Insurance, 1774," in John J. Babson, *Notes and Additions to the History of Gloucester* (Gloucester, Mass., 1876), 141.

84. "Downing's Account of Fish, 1676," Maine Historical Society, *Collections*, 2d Ser., IV (1889), 374–375.

and usages around the harbor sometimes touched off considerable disagreement. Where the shoreline had not passed into private hands or been incorporated into towns, as was the case throughout most of the gulf and on several islands off the Massachusetts coast, any party of fishermen was free "to make use of such harbours and grounds . . . and to take timber and wood at their pleasure for all their occasions."[85] But once a company had established moorings, flakes, and a stage, the berth was considered its property for the season. Unfortunately, as in Newfoundland, the right to temporary usage was difficult to enforce. In a choice harbor, the competition over land and timber could be fierce, and with no magistrates or constables at hand, petty squabbles and incidents of trespass could flare up into major disputes at any time. A resident of Piscataqua complained in 1650 of "diverse fishermen . . . pulling downe, ruinateinge, and breakeing up of Stages, Flakes and other edifices," and reports of similar depredations filtered into the Maine courts throughout the period. Even in Marblehead, where property rights were more clearly spelled out, misunderstandings over moorings and rights around stages occasionally led to fisticuffs and legal suits.[86]

When the cod struck—which could be from early spring to early autumn, depending on the locale—the pace of work acquired a new urgency. As much as eighteen or twenty hours a day, sometimes even on the Sabbath, the men pushed themselves to the limit of endurance in the knowledge that the fish might depart at any time. Every hour was precious, the more so because there was no telling when storms might close down the harbor or how many days the foul weather might last. Records kept on larger and more seaworthy vessels that worked the Maine and Nova Scotia coast during the eighteenth century suggest that, most weeks, one to three full days were lost to the elements.[87] So whenever morning dawned with a fair promise of tolerable weather, the men, attired in heavy boots, woolen outerclothing, and thick canvas or leather aprons called barvels, rowed or

85. *Recs. of Mass. Bay*, II, 147.

86. Charles Thornton Libby *et al.*, eds., *Province and Court Records of Maine* (Portland, Me., 1928–1974), I, 51–53, II, 88, 98–99, 115, 132, 209. See also Babson, *History of Gloucester*, 38–39, and *Essex Co. Court Recs.*, III, 107–108, V, 109–110. On similar difficulties in Newfoundland, see Matthews, "West of England–Newfoundland Fishery," 21, 129–137.

87. Fishing Accounts, 1758–1769, Joshua Burnham (1736–1791) Papers, 1758–1817, Box I, Folder 1, JDPL. In *The Fisher-mans Calling* (Boston, 1712), Cotton Mather rebuked these seamen for both fishing and selling fish on the Sabbath (pp. 47–48).

sailed off to fish as early as they could. Three to a shallop—foreshipman, midshipman, and steersman—they headed for the nearest fishing place, usually a few miles from the harbor's mouth, hove out a stone anchor or iron grapnel, and settled down to fish.[88]

The actual landing of cod was tiring and tedious work. Every man used two or three fishing lines with two hooks on each, baited with capelin, herring, or salt mackerel. If the shallop was anchored in shallow water, say three fathoms deep, each man attached floats to his lines and counted on the weight of the bait to drag the hooks down to the bottom where the cod were feeding. A tug on either line meant a fish had bitten, and the fisherman hauled in the line, hand over hand, unhooked the creature, tossed it into the boat, rebaited the hook, and cast it out again. Experienced men could tell whether one or both of the hooks on each line were taken and could save themselves effort by waiting to pull in the line until they knew they had a pair. When a crew had to work in deeper waters of twenty, thirty, or even fifty fathoms, as was more common, they needed correspondingly longer lines with several pounds of lead attached to bear the baited hooks speedily down to the ocean floor. Casting out several hundred feet of sodden lead-weighted lines and then drawing one in with a pair of five- or ten-pound fighting cod on the end was no easy chore and probably consumed close to five minutes a line. When the fish were plentiful and the lines thrown out a hundred times a day or more, the labor could be almost continuous, and in cold weather totally exhausting.[89] But just as taxing on the nerves if not the body were the times when the fish were not biting at all, for every day lost brought the fisherman closer to the end of the season, when the cod would depart and his earnings would cease. Through the bitter winds of February or under the hot July sun, as the men sat idly waiting, they must have yearned for busier times. In a

88. "Downing's Account," Maine Hist. Soc., *Colls.*, 2d Ser., IV (1889), 374.
89. *Ibid.* Detailed accounts of the same handlining work in the 19th century can be found in G. Brown Goode and J. W. Collins, "The George's Bank Cod Fishery," in George Brown Goode, ed., *The History and Methods of the Fishery*, 2 vols. (section V of Goode, ed., *Fisheries*), I, 191–194; G. Brown Goode and J. W. Collins, "The Bank Hand-Line Fishery," *ibid.*, I, 127–129. For daily totals of fish caught per man, see *Essex Co. Court Recs.*, III, 103; "Downing's Account," Maine Hist. Soc., *Colls.*, 2d Ser., IV (1889), 374; Winter to Downing, June 11, 1635, *Trelawney Papers*, 57; Nicholas Denys, *The Description and Natural History of the Coasts of North America*, trans. and ed. William F. Ganong (Champlain Society, *Publications*, II [Toronto, 1908]), 261; Fishing Accounts, 1758–1769, Burnham Papers, Box I, Folder 1.

normal season the work routine swung between these extremes, and accommodating oneself to this erratic pace could be frustrating.[90]

Ever present, too, was the bald fact of physical danger. In foul weather, the shallops returned to the harbor as swiftly as possible, but sometimes storms blew up so quickly or from such an unfavorable direction that the men were forced to ride them out. At Richmond Island in February 1635, one company, "havinge a freat of Cold frosty weather," failed to make it home before they foundered. "The next day after," reported John Winter, "we found the boote ridinge to an anker full of water & the bootes maister & mydshipman dead in her, but what became of the foreshipman we did never yet know." If storms closed in with many boats at sea, the result could be disaster. The late winter gales of 1662, which carried at least five shallops and their crews to the bottom, were only the most dramatic of a number of similar incidents recorded by contemporaries. Fatal accidents could also occur just off the shore. Elias Whittee, the servant of a well-to-do sea captain from Salem named Robert Stone, lost his life in 1675 when he failed to make the land after tumbling out of the boat while unloading fish at Winter Island. Three years later, Edward Vinton "fell out of a fishing shallop in Marblehead harbor . . . was drowned . . . and [after] remaining in the water so long was much eaten by the fishes." Few fishermen were strong swimmers, and even if they had been, the weight of their enormous seaboots and their heavy outerwear would have swiftly drawn them under. All told, of the men who went to sea between 1645 and 1675 whose deaths were mentioned in the court records, more than half perished in accidents on the deep.[91]

If the day's fishing did pass without mishap, the crew returned to the harbor, heaved their catch up into the stage, and began splitting the fish. The man called the header laid the cod on a table, slit open the belly, chopped off the head, and stripped out the guts, reserving the liver for oil. He then pushed the fish across the table to the splitter, who sliced it in two from head to tail and, with a back stroke, removed the bone. The split fillet was then handed to the salter, who shoveled on the proper amount of salt and tossed it onto a pile, bringing the responsibility of the fishermen to a

90. See Fishing Accounts, 1758–1769, Burnham Papers, Box I, Folder 1, for daily patterns.

91. Winter to Trelawney, June 11, 1635, *Trelawney Papers*, 57; *Essex Co. Prob. Recs.*, I, 359–364, II, 255, 257–258, 402–403, III, 9–10; *Essex Co. Court Recs.*, I–VII, but see esp. II, 301–302, VII, 152, 241.

Men Landing and Drying Cod in Newfoundland. From Duhamel du Monceau, *Traité des Pesches* (Paris, 1772). Courtesy of the Peabody Essex Museum, Salem, Mass.

close.[92] At this point the product passed into the care of the shoreman, hired by the company to dry their catch. Over the course of the next four weeks or so, while his partners toiled at sea, he tended the fillets set on flakes by the shore, taking care especially to turn them skin side up every night before the dew fell or at the first hint of rain, for if "the fish [flesh] side . . . be much wett," reported one commentator, "its never almost good but spoyled discolourd and stinkes." Finally, when the cure was complete, the cod was sorted according to quality and then weighed and packed for shipment.[93]

Upon the shoreman, a fishing crew placed heavy responsibility. Stephen Daniel of Salem described his company's shoreman as a person "to whose trust we did Commit from tyme to tyme all the fish we cacht Dureing this our fishing voyadge . . . to be dried . . . to delyver and to give an account yr of."[94] If, at the end of the season, the fishermen decided that

92. "Downing's Account," Maine Hist. Soc., *Colls.*, 2d Ser., IV (1889), 374–375.

93. *Ibid.*, 375–376; *Essex Co. Court Recs.*, II, 291, V, 6, VIII, 415. An excellent, concise description of Newfoundland practice can be found in C. Grant Head, *Eighteenth Century Newfoundland: A Geographer's Perspective* (Toronto, 1976), 3–6.

94. *Essex Co. Court Recs.*, VIII, 414.

the shoreman had failed in his duty or that his accounts did not jibe with their own, tempers could flare. Francis Johnson and his company collided in this manner with Richard Bedford at Monhegan in 1672. Bedford, they argued before the courts, "by his drunkenness and neglect of his care and labor" had not only damaged about forty quintals of cod, which had to be sold as refuse, but also forced the crew to remain ashore at the height of the season just to save the remaining fish. As one witness reported:

> When the fishermen were at sea, Richard Bedford would make himself drunk, having runn up and down and got liquors, and would lie under the flakes or in one house or another and let the fish lie "upon spoiles." He would also get others to drink it with him, with the bottle in the knees of his breeches. Once twenty quintals of fish lay upon spoil in a rainy night with the fish side upwards.[95]

Johnson and his company sued Bedford for £24 sterling in damages and were awarded the case. More frequent than charges of incompetence were accusations of theft and fraud. In 1648, for example, a company from Ipswich complained to the court that the fish they had entrusted to Peter Pitford at Marblehead vanished while in his hands. Similarly, the Nicholson family of Marblehead persuaded the Salem magistrates in 1661 that John Devereaux, their shoreman on a voyage the previous spring, had delivered their catch to a ship, lading in the harbor, without rendering a true account.[96] Regardless of whether they had actually practiced deceit, shoremen were bound to be a focus of suspicion in the event of any difficulty.

Serviced by coasting vessels from Boston and Salem, these companies spent up to half a year at a time working out of temporary stations in the Gulf of Maine before returning home to reorganize. A typical venture was that of John Roads and Peter Greenfield. The two men had emigrated from England in the 1650s, married locally, and settled in Marblehead, and in 1659 they purchased for nearly £100 sterling an open-decked shallop that they employed on extended voyages to the eastward. In the late fall of 1661 George Corwin outfitted them for a voyage, and shortly after Christmas, along with a hired man named William Ford, Roads and Greenfield weighed anchor for Monhegan. There they set up camp, employed a shoreman to dry the fish, and worked until April, when they

95. *Ibid.*, V, 6.
96. *Ibid.*, I, 160–161, II, 290–291. See also *ibid.*, VII, 305–306, VIII, 412–415.

returned to Salem to deliver their catch and purchase more provisions. After completing their business, they returned to the gulf to take advantage of the remainder of the spring season. In June, the three returned for good, conducted their final reckoning with Corwin, saw that Ford was paid, and went their separate ways. Any man who signed on for a voyage to the eastward could expect the same: months of labor on an isolated stretch of shoreline in exclusively male company, punctuated only by visits from other fishermen or wine peddlers and by occasional trips home on business.[97]

Greenfield and Roads may have shipped out again immediately, but most fishermen chose to spend a week or two at home recuperating. Indeed, in midseason, when the fleet was out, even an ambitious mariner might have to spend time looking for a position; and once the spring or fall voyages had finished, the entire industry slowed down for a month or two before the next season began. The erratic alternation between work and inactivity, therefore, characterized not only the daily operations out on the grounds but the entire course of the fisherman's year. Many of these men, the General Court declared in 1674, "when they are at home, & not imployed in their callings, [tended] to be spectators, or otherwise ideling, gaming, or spending their time unproffitably, whereby such persons as attend their duty, & spend their time in that service, are discouraged."[98] Puritan colonists, who believed that work was pleasing to God only when performed in a regular and disciplined manner, obviously considered this alternation of frantic activity and idleness to be rooted in moral failing; in fact, the irregularity of work patterns was a necessary feature of this seasonal and market-oriented calling.

The fisherman's working life unfolded in a world where the focus of attention on markets and credit set him against the clock, against his competitors, and even against the partners who were helping him to earn his bread. Powered principally by self-interest, yet demanding strict cooperation in a hostile environment, the fishery generated levels of interpersonal friction that on extended voyages were difficult to defuse. Only one murder is recorded in the annals of these early years—in 1654 when

97. Accounts of Peter Greenfield, John Roads, and John Roads's Company, George Corwin Acct. Bk., 1658–1664. On Peter Greenfield, see Perley, *History of Salem*, I, 217, and *Essex Co. Prob. Recs.*, II, 310–311. On John Roads, see *Essex Co. Court Recs.*, IV, 255, VIII, 219–220. On itinerant wine peddlers, see John Josselyn, "An Account of Two Voyages to New England," Mass. Hist. Soc., *Colls.*, 3d Ser., III (1833), 351.

98. *Recs. of Mass. Bay*, IV, ii, 552.

Gregory Caswell, after "many fallings out," felled his employer "with the broad end of an Hamer" at Monhegan—but violent conflict, especially when inhibitions had been lowered by drink, was common.[99] Fully one-quarter of all the violent crimes reported to the Essex County courts in the seventeenth century were committed by residents of Marblehead—four times the rate one would expect from its population.[100] John Josselyn, who spent several years on the coast of Maine, advised men of "quality" to steer clear of fishermen under the influence, "for when *Wine* in their guts is at full Tide, they quarrel, fight and do one another mischief."[101]

Nothing testifies to the power of these internal strains as much as the instability of partnerships. Three years seems to have been the maximum lifetime for any company, and many, especially those whose members did not own the vessels they operated, broke up after one or two voyages. John Roads of Marblehead, whose career can be followed over a number of years, worked in at least seven different companies between 1655 and 1670; William Woods of the same town belonged to a minimum of four between 1659 and 1668.[102] So constant was this shuffling of personnel, even in midseason, that in 1679 the General Court ordered "that all fishermen that are shipt upon a winter & spring voyage shall duely attend the same" and that those who had signed on for the summer "shall not presume to breake off from said voyage before the last of October."[103] Nevertheless, while outlawing desertion, the court recognized that partnerships might legitimately be reorganized at least twice a year. Such latitude, unnecessary in a stable farming community, was essential to the highly competitive fishery.

Needless to say, the overwhelming majority of villagers in the Bay

99. Noble and Cronin, eds., *Records of the Court of Assistants of Massachusetts Bay*, III, 61.

100. *Essex Co. Court Recs.*, I–VIII. Of 42 cases of "assault," "battery," and "striking" recorded in the sample years 1640–1642, 1650–1652, 1660–1662, 1670–1672, and 1680–1682, 11 (26%) involved residents of Marblehead, a town that accounted for no more than 8% of Essex County's population. See Greene and Harrington, *American Population before 1790*, 19–21.

101. Josselyn, "Account of Two Voyages," Mass. Hist. Soc., *Colls.*, 3d Ser., III (1833), 352.

102. Accounts of John Roads and William Woods, George Corwin Acct. Bks., 1658–1664, 1663–1672; *Essex Co. Court Recs.*, II, 26. The longevity of 21 different companies was measured in Corwin's account books. Out of 14 companies composed of boat renters, none remained together more than 12 months; by contrast, of 7 companies in which one or more members owned the boat, 6 lasted 12 months or more.

103. *Recs. of Mass. Bay*, V, 212.

Colony would have found life in the cod fishery intolerable. The erratic pace of work, the flux in personnel, the peculiarly maritime hardships, the occasional necessity of toiling on the Sabbath, the enforced absence from home and church, and the ethic of aggressive competition fostered by the industry clearly would have grated on men who highly valued religion, discipline, and the maintenance of social order. Most important, proper-tied householders who took pride in managing their own affairs could never have accommodated themselves to a trade where the pattern of daily toil was so framed by personal and social dependency. The farmers and artisans of seventeenth-century New England regularly dealt in the marketplace too, but they usually did so from a position of economic competency on terms they helped to negotiate—and not generally as cli-ents. The movement of prices and the availability of credit informed their working lives but did not, as in the fishery, govern them. For farmers, the market provided opportunity; for fishermen it was also a master.

SOCIETY

On the ocean fringes of Essex County fishermen formed communities of their own. There, many of the factors that regulated society in the villages of the interior—the relative homogeneity of religion, the stress upon regu-lar work habits, the strengthening of the household, the stern standards of public authority, and the provision of economic independence for each family—were wholly inappropriate. It is true that fishing communities, like their rural counterparts, were molded by a common experience: the encounter of Englishmen with the frontier. And it is also true that the tight interdependence between those who controlled the means of production and those who labored under their direction was as characteristic of the maritime clientage system as it was of family patriarchy. The capitalism of the fishery lent a particular quality to this interdependence, however, and in the town of Marblehead and in the waterfront quarters of Salem and Gloucester created a distinctive way of life.

Who were the fishermen, and by what chain of circumstances did they come to work in the outports of the Bay Colony? This is not a simple question, for their names surface without warning in merchants' account books and frequently disappear just as quickly. Only about 11 percent of those who can be identified were part of the Great Migration, and the group contained no blacks, no Indian servants, and no more than a hand-ful of indentured Englishmen. Judging from surnames and the observations of contemporaries, it appears that the great majority of fishermen were drawn from a pool of British maritime laborers, chiefly West Countrymen, who made their living on the ocean and stopped in at the ports of Essex County not to escape political or religious persecution, but to fish.[104] "Marblehead," noted its inhabitants in a petition of 1667, "hath been a place of fishing for many yeares past, on which Accot divers persons from England, Newfound Land, and other places have [reso]rted thither."[105] Since established New Englanders were loath to work at sea when there was enough to keep them busy on land, the fishery had to draw its men from abroad.

Many of these early hands seem to have found their way into Essex County by accident. Stephen Griggs, for example, called in at Marblehead in June of 1664 as an ordinary seaman on board the ship *Black Eagle*. A few days after making port, John Dunkin, the ship's master, advised his hands that he intended to embark on a fishing voyage (for which they had not originally bargained) and that they could choose to come or not. When most of the crew declined, Dunkin ordered them "to Carry the shipe off to her moreings, and then every man For himselfe"; he then set out for Boston to drum up the men he needed, leaving his old hands to their fate. Though all the others disappeared from the records and likely made their way back to England, twenty-five-year-old Griggs, who was single, decided to stay behind and try his luck in the local fishery. Soon he was working for George Corwin, wooing a widow named Elizabeth Coombs who owned a house and land near the Salem ferry landing, and preparing to settle permanently in town.[106]

Another young seaman who ended up fishing out of Marblehead through unforeseen circumstances was a minister's son from Great Yarmouth in England. Job Tookey had gone to sea in his mid-teens as a shipmaster's apprentice, injured his hand off the New England coast in 1681, and had to be put ashore in Portsmouth. For six months he con-

104. The material in this section is based largely on the files of fishermen described in Appendix 2. Of 12 fishermen whose English origins are known, all but one hailed from either the counties of Dorset, Somerset, and Devon or from towns on the North Sea coast. For the geographic origins of Marblehead and Gloucester residents as a whole, see Christine Leigh Heyrman, *Commerce and Culture: The Maritime Communities of Colonial Massachusetts, 1690–1750* (New York, 1984), 214–215.

105. *Essex Co. Court Recs.*, V, 373.

106. *Ibid.*, III, 155, V, 49, 114, VII, 306–307, IX, 468–469; accounts of Stephen Griggs, George Corwin Acct. Bk., 1663–1672.

valesced at the home of Samuel Wentworth on an island in the Piscataqua River and ran up a debt "for Washing Lodging & Diet" of about £6 sterling. After recovering, he cast around for a means of repaying his obligation and decided to travel south to Marblehead for seven months' fishing with the merchant Richard Knott, who agreed to discharge his debts and pay him slightly less than £2 a month to boot. Tookey eventually left the sea, settled as a common laborer in Beverly, and was almost hanged as a witch in 1693; like Griggs he was typical of hundreds of mariners who drifted into the fishery in the course of their travels mainly by happenstance.[107]

Many mariners seem to have come by way of Newfoundland. West Countrymen who had signed on for a summer's fishing on that island often discovered at the end of the season that, to save on provisions and cargo space, their employers would rather "pack them away to New England" than carry them home. Shipmasters from Massachusetts who supplied the Newfoundland fishery were anxious for return freight and only too happy to offer the fishermen passage southward. As one British naval officer reported, "the New England traders . . . spirit away the inhabitants, to the mischief both of adventurers and planters. I myself saw one who came into St. John's with eleven hands and was sailing out with twenty." The drift of maritime labor from Newfoundland to New England first noted in the 1640s continued well into the eighteenth century.[108]

Unlike their Puritan neighbors, who had moved to the New World in

107. *Essex Co. Court Recs.*, VIII, 330–332, 337–338; Boyer and Nissenbaum, *Salem Possessed*, 206–208.

108. Winthrop, *History of New England*, II, 307; *Essex Co. Court Recs.*, V, 373; "Reasons for the settlement of Newfoundland and the trade under Government," ca. 1668, *CSPC*, V, 559; Capt. Davis to Mr. Wren, Sept. 9, 1671, *CSPC*, VII, 257; Captain Sir Robert Robertson to William Blathwayt, Sept. 16, 1680, *CSPC*, X, 600; Captain Daniel Jones to William Blathwayt, Sept. 12, 1682, *CSPC*, XI, 294; Capt. Leake, "Answers to the enquiries of the Council of Trade and Plantations," Sept. 17, 1699, *CSPC*, XVII, 440; Capt. Staffd. Fairborne, "Account of the Fishery at Newfoundland," Sept. 11, 1700, *CSPC*, XVIII, 522; Commodore Graydon, "Answer to the heads of Enquiries sent to Mr. Burchett, March 13, 1701," *CSPC*, XIX, 530; Commodore Taylor to the Earl of Sunderland, Nov. 18, 1709, *CSPC*, XXIV, 526; Commodore Ogle to Mr. Popple, Oct. 13, 1719, *CSPC*, XXXI, 235; Council of Trade and Plantations to Governor Shute, Mar. 17, 1721, *CSPC*, XXXII, 270; Commodore Cayley to the Council of Trade and Plantations, Jan. 2, 1724, *CSPC*, XXXIV, 2; Commodore Lord V. Beauclerk, "Answers to Heads of Enquiry relating to the Newfoundland Fishery," Oct. 14, 1729, *CSPC*, XXXVI, 507; "Governor Falkingham's Answers to Heads of Enquiry and Instructions, 1732," Oct. 4, 1732, *CSPC*, XXXIX, 225.

established family units, migrant fishermen were mostly young, single, and penniless. Two-thirds were under thirty years of age when they arrived; nearly all were unwed or at least alone; and like most young men, they came with little more than the clothes on their backs. When Edward Vinton drowned in 1678, he left to his creditors (for he had no family) only a few changes of apparel, an old chest, a bedsack, his fishing tackle, a Bible and some other books, nine shillings, and fifty pounds of salt fish. By contrast, Michael Partridge and Thomas Hooper owned portions of a shallop, Henry Muddle kept a heifer, and Thomas Dill attempted to support a wife and child in England with the earnings from his one-quarter share in the ketch *Prosperous*. But as often as not, investments such as these had been financed on credit and upon the fisherman's decease were seized to meet his obligations.[109]

Within a decade of their appearance in the fishery, roughly half of these men had disappeared. What became of Benjamin Barton, Jonas Moore, Christopher Labitt, and others like them, who worked for a season or two, took up a page in a merchant's books, and then vanished without making any further imprint on the colony? We have no way of knowing. Some probably died; others must have returned to their families in England; still others merely packed up and moved on to the next port. Whatever their subsequent history, "the concourse of many strangers especially in the summer season," as the Marblehead selectmen put it, certainly distinguished this outport society from most of the Bay Colony.[110] The con-

109. See Appendix 2. The age sample included 42 pre-1676 fishermen and the marriage sample counted 217, of whom 6 were certainly espoused at the time of their arrival and a further 31 were married at some point that *may* have preceded their coming to the county. For the inventories of Vinton, Muddle, Dill, Partridge, and Hooper, see *Essex Co. Court Recs.*, VII, 133, and *Essex Co. Prob. Recs.*, I, 359–360, II, 132–133, 402–403. For inventories of recently arrived fishermen, see *ibid.*, II, 255–256, 421, III, 9–10, 181, and *Essex Co. Court Recs.*, II, 344, III, 227, 267–268. The estates of 12 fishermen who died before 1676 and within ten years of their arrival in Essex County were inventoried at an average of £17.6 sterling in real and personal property and £3.4 in net wealth (after debts and credits had been paid and collected). See table 3.

110. *Essex Co. Court Recs.*, VIII, 318. The names of Barton, Moore, Labitt, and scores of other migrant fishermen can be found in George Corwin Acct. Bks., 1658–1664, 1663–1672, and in *Essex Co. Court Recs.*, I–IX. As often as not, the single reference to their fishing is the only record of their having lived in Essex County at all. Of 217 fishermen who worked in Essex County before 1676, 108 had vanished from the records within a decade of their arrival. See Appendix 2. On transiency in early Marblehead, see Heyrman, *Commerce and Culture*, 213.

tinual comings and goings of fishermen reflected their integration into a maritime culture that spanned the North Atlantic.

From time to time, however, one of the dozens of transient seafaringmen who boarded in the coastal villages of the county while fishing the New England waters chose to settle there. No factor weighed more in this decision than success in the marriage market. Women did not play a basic role in the fishery itself (as they did, for example, curing the catch in the planter fishery of Newfoundland), but from the individual fisherman's point of view, a wife and family not only gave meaning to toil, but made it easier as well.[111] By tending gardens, caring for chickens and swine, tailoring clothes from purchased cloth, cooking, and keeping the cabin in good order, a skilled helpmate vastly complemented the labors of any married fisherman. More important when the household head was frequently too far from home to manage business efficiently, most fishermen's wives had to take care of their husbands' business. Elizabeth Meek of Salem thus saw to the weighing of the fish and oil belonging to her husband and his company after they had returned to sea in the summer of 1682. Mary Tucker, a tough character who thought nothing of tossing a pushy Marblehead neighbor out of her house and "beating his head upon the stones," looked after the marketing of her husband's fish as far away as Boston. Some women took in boarders, of whom there were many in the bachelor-crowded waterfront; others helped to run taverns where the "concourse of . . . strangers" ate and drank.[112] Most important, however, a fisherman's spouse bore and raised the children who supported him when he retired from serious work at sea. Fishing communities like Marblehead became notorious for their hordes of children, and in an age when fathers normally assumed the supervision and training of boys, the delegation of this task to mothers imposed an unusual burden on them. Obviously, women were central to any male colonist's understanding of what settled householding meant—and no less so to these coastal inhabitants than to their rural neighbors.

Some prospective residents were already married, and for them the trick

111. The best description of this family fishery is Cadigan, "Economic and Social Relations of Production on the Northeast Coast of Newfoundland," chap. 5.

112. On Tucker and Meek, see *Essex Co. Court Recs.*, VIII, 195, 226, 227, 318, IX, 90, 521. For other evidence on the work of fishermen's wives inside and outside the home, see *ibid.*, II, 291, III, 333, VIII, 101–102, 194, and for the inventories of married fishermen, see *ibid.*, II, 256, III, 222–223, 267–268, V, 206–207, VI, 172, VII, 144–145, 232–233, 239–240, VIII, 359–360, IX, 60, 512–513, 559, and *Essex Co. Prob. Recs.*, II, 194, 310–311, 421.

was to persuade their existing families to join them in the New World. Robert Bray from Ipswich in England, for example, was working for George Corwin during the late 1660s when he called for his wife, Thomazin, and their two children to join him in Massachusetts. They made their home near Winter Island and founded a family of fishermen who skippered vessels out of Salem well into the nineteenth century.[113] For the unwed majority, however, the decision to settle rested chiefly on finding an eligible mate within the colony. This was no simple matter, for women were scarce in these early maritime communities, and fishermen did not always strike prospective fathers-in-law as desirable suitors. Yet every year a few lucky fellows managed to persuade older fishermen, small waterfront artisans, resident mariners, and even the occasional farmer to surrender their daughters, and very gradually they constructed the family basis for a native-born fishery.[114] Elias Fortune arrived in Marblehead in 1660 and, after fishing several years for Moses Maverick, married a local girl named Mary Pittman. The young couple erected an eighteen-foot-square cottage on town land, set up housekeeping, and managed in these cramped quarters to raise eight children. Similarly, Paul Mansfield came to Salem as a bachelor about 1650, married Damaris, the widow of Timothy Laskin, built a home on the South River, and maintained a modest household there by working the fishery off Misery Island in Salem Sound.[115] Although married or soon-to-be-married householders like Mansfield, Fortune, and Bray accounted for only 38 percent of immigrant fishermen before 1675, as long-term residents of the colony they played a relatively greater role in the fleet. Returning to the sea year after year, they filled slightly more than half of the positions available, a proportion that eventually increased as more seafaringmen decided to cease their wanderings and settle down.[116]

113. *Essex Co. Court Recs.*, VII, 30, IX, 145, 349; Perley, *History of Salem*, III, 48–49; accounts of Robert Bray, George Corwin Acct. Bk., 1663–1672.

114. See Appendix 2. Of 29 fishermen's spouses whose family origins could be traced in the records, 12 were the daughters or widows of fishermen or shoremen; 11 came from the families of artisans and tradesmen (including 4 shoemakers); 5 were farmers' daughters; and 1 was from a seaman's household.

115. On Fortune, see Estate of Elias Fortune (1705), Probate No. 9780, Essex Co. Prob. Recs.; *Essex Co. Court Recs.*, II, 390; and Sidney Perley, "Marblehead in the Year 1700, No. 6," Essex Institute, *Hist. Colls.*, XLVII (1911), 165. On Mansfield, see *Essex Co. Court Recs.*, I, 256, III, 14; Perley, *History of Salem*, I, 314, II, 13, III, 240; and Estate of Paul Mansfield (1696), Probate No. 17639, Essex Co. Prob. Recs.

116. See Appendix 2. Of 217 fishermen from the period before 1676, 83 (38%) were or

The Massachusetts fishermen of the seventeenth century tended to be older than their Newfoundland counterparts. Young men were found in both fisheries, of course. But whereas Newfoundland was dominated by fishing servants who generally quit the strenuous transatlantic fishery to marry and settle at home in the West of England in their late twenties and early thirties, the Massachusetts fishery employed many householding fishermen into their thirties and forties. The proximity of family was probably the critical factor, but it mattered too that the outports of Essex County were newly settled and not yet demographically self-sufficient. Berths remained open for older men past their physical prime because the number of vigorous native-born youths capable of taking their places was as yet very small. The distinctively middle-aged character of resident fishermen was that of recently settled immigrant householders.[117]

The households that married fishermen established on the maritime periphery, however, were different from those elsewhere in Essex County. For one thing, they were much less prosperous. Fishermen may have fared better in Massachusetts than did seamen elsewhere around the North Atlantic, but they were still among the poorest residents in the colony. The total value of their estates reached a mean of only £81 (Massachusetts currency), considerably less than the comparable figure of £281 (Massachusetts currency) for estates throughout the county as a whole over roughly the same period. Fishing families with estates valued close to the median usually owned a small house on a few acres of land, an animal or two, a couple of beds stuffed with feathers or silk grass, iron and brass cooking wares, a single table set with earthenware, woodenware, and pewter and a small number of chairs, a few carpenter's tools and a gun, possibly a Bible, and, of course, their clothes.[118] They ate well

---

later became householders; of 483 voyages undertaken in the period, however, 261 (54%) were conducted by such individuals.

117. Placing the common age of retirement at 50 years seems fair given that out of 157 voyages for which the ages of the fishermen involved could be determined, none involved teenagers; 48 (31%) were in their twenties, 60 (38%) were in their thirties, 37 (24%) were in their forties, and only 8 (5%) were in their fifties, sixties, or seventies. See Appendix 2. On the small number of native-born fishermen prior to 1675, see Chapter 4, n. 20, below.

118. For the period 1630–1675 there are only eight surviving inventories of active, married fishermen. All possessed livestock, all but one owned real property, and their estates ranged in value from £11 to £224 with a median of £75. See *Essex Co. Prob. Recs.*, I, 324–325, 388, 456–457, II, 16–17, 194–195, 310–311, 372–374, 421; also Donald Warner Koch, "Income Distribution and Political Structure in Seventeenth-Century Salem, Mas-

enough, and for the purchase of maritime gear there was credit in plenty, but the sizable land grants and the financing of farm development that underlay most of the prosperity in early New England were not within their reach. A modest estate supported by a steady income from fishing marked an improvement over what common seamen could have expected in England, but in the Bay Colony of the seventeenth century even the most prosperous households within the fishing community remained essentially dependent on their merchant patrons.[119]

The truest measure of limited opportunity was the infrequency with which fishermen managed to penetrate the agricultural interior. To the end of the colonial period such family names as Bartoll, Brimblecome, Pedrick, Trevett, Cally, Legros, Dolliver, and Meek, descended from these early seamen, were unknown in Massachusetts outside its coastal villages.[120] In Maine, where land was open for the taking, fishermen who

---

sachusetts," Essex Institute, *Hist. Colls.*, CV (1969), 56, 59. Koch reports a median estate value of £153 for Salem and £128 for Essex County outside Salem, which compares to £74 for married fishermen. The sums for fishermen were left in Massachusetts currency in this case in order to compare them with Koch's data. The median portable physical wealth of these fishermen of £44 compares reasonably with the estates of those whom Gloria Main terms the "poorer planters" of 17th-century Maryland in her *Tobacco Colony: Life in Early Maryland, 1650–1720* (Princeton, N.J., 1982), chap. 5.

119. The idea that the New England cod fishery was worked by "farmer-fishermen" is a misleading one with a curiously long genealogy. In 1880, Charles Levi Woodbury, in *The Relation of the Fisheries to the Discovery and Settlement of North America* (Boston, 1880), asserted that early Puritan farmers had occupied themselves in the slack winter season by fishing on the deep, furnishing their families thereby with "not merely a supply of food . . . but [also] an article which was a medium of exchange" (p. 23). What evidence he possessed for this claim is not clear; oddly enough, Bernard Bailyn picked up Woodbury's notion, combined it with his own cursory examination of some unrepresentative published inventories of the period, and included it in his otherwise excellent treatment of the cod fishery in *New England Merchants*, 78, 212, n. 6. On Bailyn's authority, the idea acquired intellectual respectability and has passed into general acceptance by early American historians including, most recently, John J. McCusker and Russell R. Menard, *The Economy of British America, 1607–1789* (Chapel Hill, N.C., 1985), 99, 312. Some farmers fished to satisfy household needs and a few fishermen of the householding variety owned a couple of animals, but the commercial cod fishery of the 17th century was overwhelmingly peopled by maritime laborers, not part-time agriculturalists.

120. Movement of these families out of Marblehead, Gloucester, and Salem was measured using Bettye Hobbs Pruitt, ed., *The Massachusetts Tax Valuation List of 1771* (Boston, 1978). The method is described in Daniel Frederick Vickers, "Maritime Labor in Colonial Massachusetts: A Case Study of the Essex County Cod Fishery and the Whaling Industry of

aspired to the security that land could offer were able to move into farming, of an admittedly hardscrabble nature, rather easily.[121] But in Essex County the price of acreage was higher and fishermen were unlikely to meet with the approval of town meetings authorized to dispense farm property. The access to quantities and varieties of wealth—especially land—that might effectively have reduced fishermen's reliance on maritime employment was severely circumscribed.

Fishing families were not only poorer and more limited in opportunity than other residents, but also more short-lived. Whereas most New England fathers of the seventeenth century lived into their seventies, the median age at death for married fishermen was fifty-nine. As we saw earlier, the high rate of mortality sprang in part from the natural hazards of life on the ocean. Yet accident could not have been the only factor, for most fishermen died between the ages of fifty and seventy, beyond the normal age of retirement from the sea. More likely, the constant importation of disease, common to all maritime centers, bore the heaviest responsibility for sending so many of these men to early graves. Whatever the cause, the net result of higher mortality was to hasten the breakup of households. Parental control of the sort historians have identified in rural New England families could not easily flourish among mariners given that most of them died when their sons were still in their twenties.[122]

Fishing families would probably not have acquired a patriarchal char-

Nantucket, 1630–1775" (Ph.D. diss., Princeton University, 1981), 142, n. 120. By 1771, of 61 descendants of 14 pre-1676 fishing families, 5 were living in non-maritime villages within Essex County, 7 dwelt in non-maritime villages elsewhere in Massachusetts, and a full 49 remained on the maritime fringe of the colony.

121. Edwin Arnold Churchill, "Too Great the Challenge: The Birth and Death of Falmouth, Maine, 1624–1676" (Ph.D. diss., University of Maine at Orono, 1979), 289–290. That fishermen in Newfoundland and the Gaspé shared with Nantucket whalemen this aspiration toward the ownership of farmland is clear from Ommer, "Accounting the Fishery," 6–7, 13–14; Gerald M. Sider, "The Ties That Bind: Culture and Agriculture, Property and Propriety in the Newfoundland Village Fishery," Social History, V (1980), 3–6, 9–13; and Daniel Vickers, "Nantucket Whalemen in the Deep-Sea Fishery: The Changing Anatomy of an Early American Labor Force," Journal of American History, LXXII (1985), 286.

122. The approximate dates of 27 fishermen's deaths were obtained from Essex Co. Court Recs., I–IX; Perley, History of Salem; and the unpublished probate records of the county. Their ages at death were then calculated from the sources in Appendix 2. Comparative statistics for rural New England are conveniently assembled in Susan L. Norton, "Population Growth in Colonial America: A Study of Ipswich, Massachusetts," Population Studies, XXV (1971), 441.

acter under any circumstances. The marked interdependence of fathers and sons in rural Massachusetts related clearly to the problems of controlling access to the land in a developing household economy, and fishing families were generally not working units. A few sons joined their fathers on voyages to the banks, and in-laws occasionally shared in the rental or purchase of a boat, but membership in a given company was governed far more frequently by other considerations—availability, convenience, friendship, mutual appreciation of talent, and so on—that had little to do with family structure. Farm boys worked within the households in which they had been raised until they were ready to start families of their own. Any young fisherman, by comparison, could secure a position simply by purchasing an outfit on credit and signing on with a vessel short of hands. Once he came of age, he did not have to work with his father (if, indeed, his father wanted him to, owned a vessel, or was even living in New England); he did not have to obtain his father's consent to work for somebody else; and he could keep his earnings for himself. This is not to say that fishermen were totally free: they depended heavily on others for access to productive equipment. But these "others" were merchant creditors, not their fathers. This fact above all—that the basic unit of production consisted not of the conjugal household, but of a partnership between the members of a company and their outfitter—underlay the relative insignificance of the family within seventeenth-century fishing society.

If family life was undeveloped in this outport world, the sense of community was feebler still. The disharmony that clouded relations among fishermen off to the eastward also characterized the tough waterfront neighborhoods at home—and for many of the same reasons. Among other things, they were peopled with strangers: Welsh, Irish, and Channel Islanders together with West Country Englishmen from a host of different parishes mixed uneasily around the fishing berths, at the boardinghouses, and in the ordinaries that ringed the harbors of Salem and Marblehead. Unfamiliar with one another's ways, they often failed, especially when drinking, to resolve their disagreements short of physical violence. Most fishermen were quite ready to reach for the nearest weapon at hand—a rock, a stick, an ax handle, or even a soup ladle—and bloody their neighbors' heads if ever they were crossed. Even in the smaller seaside villages the homes of fishermen witnessed a variety of ugly scenes. John West stormed into Abraham Whittier's cottage in Manchester in the fall of 1663 and, in the midst of a shouting match, grabbed the seventy-year-old man "by the throat, struck him across the arm and cheek, and pulling him by the jaw, brought blood in two places." Women, too, could be caught in the fray. A Marblehead resident reported in 1646 that when his neighbors William Barber and Jane James had fallen to heated words, Barber screamed, "get you out of doars you filthy ould Baud or elce I will Cuttle your hyde, you ould filthy Bagage," and threatened James with a firebrand.[123]

The rough language and physical violence of Essex County's fishing ports, although typical of most seafaring communities of the day, stood sharply illuminated by the unusually stable landward culture that surrounded them. Indeed, the tumult often associated with life on the ocean fringes of the colony persisted precisely because the forces that served elsewhere in New England to moderate open conflict were absent from communities like Marblehead. The steadying influence of family responsibilities never operated with the same effectiveness in this largely bachelor society, and outport women, few as they were, often created as much trouble for the constables as did their husbands. Nor was organized religion a powerful bond among fishermen, if their infrequent attendance at meeting and indifference to church membership are any indications of their commitment to formal Christian practice. Even political authority exerted little force on the maritime communities. Judging by the absence of colony regulation of the fishery, the General Court's lack of interest in matters relating to Marblehead, the inability of the town to form its own government before 1649, and the indifference of the inhabitants to town meetings thereafter, fishing society on the whole was left to settle its differences by whatever standards of rough-and-tumble justice it chose.[124]

Maritime society did form a collectivity of sorts, but mainly in its opposition to the rest of the colony. The combination of Anglican spirituality and English popular culture that fishermen favored was an affront to Puritan tradition. Though generally a failure, Robert Child's petition of 1646 call-

123. *Essex Co. Court Recs.*, I, 104, III, 221. On the tendency of Marblehead residents to end up in court for crimes of violence, see n. 100. Christine Heyrman draws a similar portrait of life in 17th-century Gloucester and Marblehead in *Commerce and Culture*, 39, 39n–40n, 212–230; see also Konig, "A New Look at the Essex 'French,'" Essex Institute, *Hist. Colls.*, CX (1974), 167–180.

124. Heyrman, *Commerce and Culture*, 39, 212–230. Marblehead had no church before 1684, and out of 66 fishermen who had settled there or in Salem before 1676, only 4 (6%) had joined any church before Marblehead formed one of its own. At least 11 of 29 Sabbath-breaking offenses (not clearly related to serious doctrinal disputes within the Puritan tradition) recorded in the county before 1663 were committed by residents of Marblehead. See Appendix 2.

ing for liberty of conscience and political rights for non-churchmembers
did attract the signatures, so the governor reported, of "fishermen of
Marblehead, profane persons, divers of them brought the last year from
Newfoundland to fish a season, and so to return again." By invoking the
names of saints, observing the rituals of seafaring tradition, or merely using
what Cotton Mather called "the Pagan Language of a *Good Fortune*" to
describe their "*Luck of Fish*," fishermen advertised the cultural gulf that
separated them from their Puritan neighbors.[125] Social drinking also drew
fishermen together in defiance of colonial norms. For both the number of
taverns they supported and the number of court presentations for drunkenness for which they were responsible, the maritime quarters of Salem
and Marblehead were notorious in the colony. Farmers drank as well—and
often to excess—but not to the point where intemperance struck contemporaries as a special feature of their calling. The rowdy conviviality of
drinking in company mattered to the maritime community, partly because
the smoke and crowded warmth of the tavern were a comfort to men who
worked in the cold and wet, but also because this waterfront tavern culture
defined a corner within New England society where Puritan teachings
were mocked. Resisting at every turn the magistrates' urgings of temper-
ance, fishermen refused to denounce illegal establishments, tossed constables out on their ears, and continued to imbibe as they pleased. As outsiders
they knew they could never earn Puritan admiration, but drunken comportment could at least intimidate the establishment enough to keep it at a
distance.[126]

125. Winthrop, *History of New England*, II, 307; Mather, *Fisher-mans Calling*, 19–20,
42–43. These works as well as Mather's *The Sailours Companion and Counsellour* (Boston, 1709) are very revealing of established New Englanders' estimation of maritime
society and its salient features. For English parallels, see Keith Wrightson, *English Society,
1580–1680* (London, 1982), 183–184, 199–205, 220–221.

126. Two petitions of the 1670s listed 14 "Ordinaries and publick drinking Howses" in
Salem, chiefly in the lower peninsula where most fishermen lived, and 8 more in Marblehead. See *Essex Co. Court Recs.*, V, 223, VII, 70–72; and Perley, *History of Salem*, III,
419–422. Of 63 presentations for drunkenness before the quarterly courts in the sample
periods 1650–1652, 1660–1662, and 1670–1672, at least 17 (27%) involved residents of
Marblehead; see *Essex Co. Court Recs.* For instances of the defense of this drinking culture
against regulation from outside, see *ibid.*, I, 107, V, 90–92, VII, 70–73, 109. See also
Richard P. Gildrie, "Taverns and Popular Culture in Essex County, Massachusetts, 1678–
1686," Essex Institute, *Hist. Colls.*, CXXIV (1988), 158–185, and Peter Pope, "Historical
Archaeology and the Demand for Alcohol in Seventeenth Century Newfoundland," *Acadiensis*, XIX, no. 1 (1989–1990), 72–90.

Rebelliousness alone, however, was a fragile basis for solidarity. The bonds of community, like those of family, were weak on the fishing periphery because they were not reinforced by the ties of economic interest defined by clientage. From the fishermen's standpoint, credit was something of a half-kept promise. It offered a relief from risk in the short run by financing them during periods when the fishery slumped; yet because fishermen received exactly the market value of their catch, the responsibility for the success or failure of the industry in the last analysis rested squarely on their shoulders. Clientage promised a kind of independence by allowing the purchase of productive equipment on credit, but in the process operators became saddled with debts, often too large ever to be paid off, that chained them to their creditors. In order to survive, fishermen had to compete with one another, stoop before their creditors, and march to the beat of the price cycle, frequently in opposition to the prescriptions of family and community interests.

At the heart of the social instability on the fishing periphery of Essex County stood the issue of power. Clientage, as it operated in the New England fishery, was calculated to deal with the problems of risk and the scarcities of capital and labor by reining in the aspirations for independence that seamen shared with all working Englishmen of their day. John Josselyn went so far as to call fishermen who entered into debt "for such things as they . . . [stood] in need off" no better than "the Merchants slaves."[127] This strong language did not do full justice to the complexity of clientage, but it did grasp one central truth. Massive indebtedness meant dependence of a very direct and personal nature, and the great majority of landed New Englanders were simply not willing to labor on those terms. The fishery in the Bay Colony thus had to recruit those whose unacceptable religious leanings, peculiar ethnicity, questionable behavior, single status, and poverty—in short, their class—disqualified them from enjoying the fruits of the Lord's garden as independent men. Clientage was the maritime equivalent to patriarchy; each served to organize production on the periphery of European settlement in the New World. But whereas most farm boys eventually outgrew their dependency, fishermen were often entangled for life. On America's first frontier, the logic of merchant capitalism demanded no less.

127. Josselyn, "Account of Two Voyages," Mass. Hist. Soc., *Colls.*, 3d Ser., III (1833), 352.

FISHERMEN

1 6 7 5 - 1 7 7 5

In the Hall of the Massachusetts House of Representatives hangs a model of a codfish. Samuel Eliot Morison drew it to our attention in 1921, and it survives for the same reason it was selected in 1784—as a symbolic memorial to the critical economic role the fishery played when Massachusetts was a colony.[1] For the men it employed, the profits it earned, the vessels and provisions it consumed, and the shipping business it fostered, the industry was without question the first leading sector in New England's remarkable history of economic development. It is hard to imagine how the carrying trades would have succeeded in Massachusetts without fish to ship, and equally hard to explain the colony's successful industrialization during the nineteenth century without the profits cleared in overseas shipping. As the brick and mortar walls of Lowell were rising in the 1820s, the wooden walls of Marblehead and Gloucester had chiefly served their historic purpose. But in their heyday they were at the center of affairs in a way that historians have too frequently forgotten.

1. Samuel Eliot Morison, *The Maritime History of Massachusetts, 1783–1860* (Boston, 1979), 134.

Elsewhere, the cod has rarely had as happy a reputation. Especially in neighboring Atlantic Canada, two centuries of trying to wring profits out of coastal waters have persuaded many that fishing and underdevelopment are unfortunately linked. Historically, if not inevitably, they may have a point. Many features that the New England fishery adopted in its primitive beginnings and later outgrew—especially the small scale and relatively low productivity of operations organized through clientage—persisted far longer in the outports of Nova Scotia, Newfoundland, and the Gaspé Peninsula. As late as the twentieth century, fishing merchants there followed a business logic that made sense near the margins of settlement—instead of investing in technological improvement, they continued to direct capital into the recruitment of new client operators through the credit system.[2]

The fishing industry of the Bay Colony, having embarked on this tack initially, sailed on it for several decades. Essex County merchants grew wealthy by learning the ropes in a specific business—the small boat fishery in the Gulf of Maine—and then outfitting it on a progressively larger scale. Between 1675 and 1725, however, with important consequences for the entire colony, the industry changed course. A new generation of entrepreneurs transformed its economic structure by making a clear distinction between capital and labor and exploiting local markets in each—creating a fishery, in other words, on the European model. This did not in any sense mark the transition *to* capitalism in New England's fishery. Capitalist relations of production had been important in all the major maritime industries of the North Atlantic since the sixteenth century. This change did, however, mark a developmental transition *within* capitalism, for by 1675 New England's maritime economy had matured to the point where the fishery could begin to shake off the garments of clientage. In the risky frontier environment of the earliest decades, those relations of economic interdependence had made good business sense. But as capital and labor accumulated in the colonial seaports, merchants discovered that they could recruit fishing hands without the expense of financing them on liberal credit terms; fishermen found that they could obtain provisioning without pledging their catch in advance; and the patron-client relations

2. For a good introduction to the fisheries of Atlantic Canada and their problems, see Rosemary E. Ommer, "What's Wrong with Canadian Fish?" *Journal of Canadian Studies,* XX, no. 3 (1986), 122–142.

that had first organized the industry withered. Merchants now recalled the capital that had supported the boat fishery and reinvested in larger and more productive deep-sea vessels of their own. Fishermen who had once worked the inshore grounds to haul themselves out of indebtedness to patron creditors now sold their labor in a free market to any local fishing employer needing hands. This transformation happened far more rapidly in Massachusetts than anywhere else in the Atlantic northeast. Though hardly at the root of all the future prosperity that New England would enjoy, this development was symptomatic of a pattern that would eventually cast the region in the image of the mother country and lay the way for the industrial transformation of the nineteenth century.

SHALLOPS TO SCHOONERS

The fishermen who settled on the waterfront of Essex County in the middle decades of the seventeenth century had made a living in small vessels. A young man standing on Rowland's Hill in Marblehead on the right morning in the spring of 1675 might have counted several dozen fishermen putting out to sea in a fleet of shallops from the various road-steads that stretched from the harbor below past Salem and Beverly to the eastward and Cape Ann. Had he returned to the same spot fifty years later, the whole marine landscape would have changed. The fishermen of 1725 now numbered in the hundreds; they hoisted sails on ketches and schoo-ners; and when they weighed anchor they were heading for deeper waters. In the half-century from 1675 to 1725 the Essex County fishing fleet had been transformed.

Most obvious to the eye was the simple transformation in the size and sophistication of the newer vessels. Ketches and schooners were two-masted oceangoing craft—thirty-five to sixty-five feet in length and fully decked with a raised forecastle or cabin abaft. Not only were they seawor-thy in the heaviest weather, but their holds could carry the supplies and store the fish necessary to keep a crew nourished and busy for weeks at a time. In burden they ranged from twenty to a hundred tons, and their price reflected their greater size. Brand-new, the vessels generally cost between £2 and £3 sterling per ton for the masted hull, and as much again for the rigging and fittings needed before they were ready to sail. The expense of constructing a shallop in the seventeenth century generally ran from £30 to £65 sterling; the earliest ketches cost between £100 and £250 sterling; and by the middle of the eighteenth century the initial outlay for a schooner could range, depending on its size, from £150 to £375 sterling.[3]

The rapidity with which these larger and costlier vessels were adopted varied from one harbor to the next, and Salem led the way. George Corwin had launched the town's first fishing ketch, the *Mayflower*, in partnership with three of his more enterprising clients in 1663, and by the mid-1670s such two-masted vessels were a common sight. Although many were employed primarily in the coasting trades, especially at first, their adaptability to deep-sea fishing was plain, and increasingly they were put to that use. When King William's War broke out in 1689, one Salem merchant later recalled, the town contained "about 60 fishing K[etches] & other Trading Ships." Local shipping suffered terribly during the subsequent conflict with the French and never fully recovered, but in the formation of Massachusetts's deep-sea fleet Salem's merchants and mariners had been first.[4] In Marblehead the shallop fishery hung on longer. Small craft still

3. Joseph A. Goldenberg, *Shipbuilding in Colonial America* (Charlottesville, Va., 1976), 94, 95; account of Jacob Eastman, Thomas Pedrick Account Book, 1760–1790, Marblehead Historical Society, Marblehead, Mass.; account of first cost of banker and small schooner, Ezekiel Price Papers, 1754–1785, Massachusetts Historical Society, Boston; account of ketch *Mayflower*, George Corwin Account Book, 1663–1672, Curwen Family Papers, 1641–1902, JDPL; account of ketch *John*, Philip English Account Book, 1678–1690, English/Touzell/Hathorne Papers, 1661–1851, JDPL; account of ketch *Swan*, John Higginson Account Book, 1678–1689, JDPL; account of schooner *Ranger*, Miles Ward Account Book, 1753–1764, Ward Family Papers, 1718–1945, JDPL; account of schooner *Cato*, Timothy Orne Ship Book, 1760–1767, Orne Family Papers, 1719–1899, JDPL. For used vessels, the mean value was £23 sterling for fishing shallops mentioned in 17th-century inventories; £155 sterling for ketches mentioned in 17th-century inventories; £197 sterling for schooners in 18th-century inventories; and £236 sterling for schooners mentioned in an insurance agreement signed in Gloucester in 1774. See William I. Davisson, "Essex County Wealth Trends: Wealth and Economic Growth in Seventeenth-Century Massachusetts," Essex Institute, *Historical Collections*, CIII (1967), 301–302; Estate of Ambrose Boden (1728), Probate No. 2820, Estate of Andrew Tucker (1740), Probate No. 28250, Estate of Joseph Tasker (1761), Probate No. 27284, Estate of James Freeman (1764), Probate No. 8921, Estate of Timothy Orne (1767), Probate No. 20104, Estate of Thomas Gerry (1774), Probate No. 10782, Estate of Jeremiah Lee (1779), Probate No. 16611, Essex Co. Prob. Recs.; John J. Babson, *Notes and Additions to the History of Gloucester*, 2 vols. (Gloucester, Mass., 1876–1891), I, 141–143.

4. Account of ketch *Mayflower*, George Corwin Acct. Bk., 1663–1672; John Higginson to son, Aug. 31, 1698, Higginson Family Papers, 1690–1723, JDPL; *Essex Co. Court Recs.*, IV,

rode at anchor there after the turn of the century, and even in 1719 it was not uncommon "to proceed in a shallop on a fishing voyage," as John Croft and Robert Wiger did that November. As early as 1681, however, local merchants and shoremen were turning to larger craft. That year Andrew Tucker and Abraham Ketvill were fighting over a ketch they had purchased in partnership, and Richard Knott had just added another to his existing fleet of shallops. With the passage of time, more and more Marbleheaders consigned their aging boats to the woodpile, and by 1720, if not well before, the majority of professional fishermen were finding berths on deep-sea vessels.[5] Gloucester arrived at a similar point via another route entirely. By 1675, the fishery there had died, and many local residents had turned instead to cutting timber for export. The forests of Cape Ann could not sustain commercial lumbering for long, however, and once the French had been driven from Nova Scotia in 1710, residents of Gloucester returned to the sea in the larger vessels they were able to purchase with their earnings from the timber trade.[6]

Small boats never disappeared from Essex County entirely. Wherever colonists lived within the sound of the surf, they kept shallops, wherries, canoes, and other little craft hauled up on the beach or moored in tidal streams. Youths and older men in particular rowed and sailed the inshore waters—alone or in pairs—fishing for their own tables, for their neighbors, and for nearby markets throughout the period covered in this book.[7]

414, V, 420, 431, VII, 305, VIII, 57, 348, 412–414, IX, 145, 198, 492; *Essex Co. Court Recs.*, *Verbatim Transcriptions*, L, 125 (i); Sidney Perley, *The History of Salem, Massachusetts*, 3 vols. (Salem, Mass., 1924–1928), II, 358–373; James Axtell, "The Vengeful Women of Marblehead: Robert Roules's Deposition of 1677," *WMQ*, 3d Ser., XXXI (1974), 650; accounts of ketches *Dolphin* and *John and Thomas*, John Higginson Acct. Bk., 1678–1689; account of ketch *John*, Philip English Acct. Bk., 1678–1690.

5. On the declining shallop fishery, see *Essex Co. Court Recs.*, VIII, 332; *Essex Co. Court Recs.*, *Verbatim Transcriptions*, XLVI, 85 (i), LV, 1 (i), LVI, 70 (i); Devorix v. Craft & Wiger (1721), Records of the Court of Admiralty of the Province of Massachusetts Bay, 3 vols. (1718–1747), Manuscript Division, Library of Congress, II, 102; Deposition of Magnis Anderson (1715), Box 15, Norden v. Pedrick (1715), Glover v. Statton (1715), Box 16, Rowlands v. Crafts (1716), Box 17, Norden v. Trevey (1723), Box 28, Files ICCP. On the growing importance of larger vessels, see *Essex Co. Court Recs.*, VIII, 231–232, 332; and Russell v. Leeran (1711), Box 13, Norden v. Diamond (1721), Box 26, Stadden v. Stacey (1722), Box 27, Files ICCP.

6. Christine Leigh Heyrman, *Commerce and Culture: The Maritime Communities of Colonial Massachusetts, 1690–1750* (New York, 1984), 39–65.

7. On the survival of small boat fishing at Cape Ann in colonial and early national times,

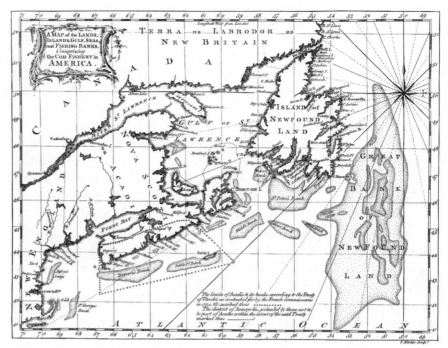

A Map of the Lands, Islands, Gulf, Seas and Fishing Banks, Comprizing the Cod Fishery in America. From William Bollan, *The Ancient Right of the English Nation to the American Fishery . . .* (1764). Courtesy of the Massachusetts Historical Society, Boston

Between 1675 and 1725, however, serious fishermen shifted their major effort from the employment of small vessels inshore to the launching of ketches and schooners in voyages upon the open sea, beyond the coast of Maine to the offshore banks and across three hundred miles of ocean to the Nova Scotia grounds. By 1677 men on "fishing catches about Cape Sable" who came ashore to make (or cure) their fish were running into trouble with the Indians, and within a few years New Englanders could be found at Port La Tour, "Port Muttoone," or any of the other harbors on what they called "the eastern coast." Although the more cautious crews continued to work traditional haunts around Pemaquid, Monhegan, and Casco Bay, the fishery's center was realigning in the last quarter of the seventeenth century toward the north and the east.[8]

see Joseph Reynolds, *Peter Gott, the Cape Ann Fisherman* (Portland, Me., 1856), chaps. 1, 2, 7, 8.

8. Axtell, "Vengeful Women of Marblehead," *WMQ*, 3d Ser., XXXI (1974), 650; *Recs. of*

Year after year fishermen pushed farther into unfamiliar waters—across the sea to Newfoundland and eastward along the Nova Scotia shoreline toward Cape Breton. By 1715 the British governor at Annapolis Royal reported that New Englanders were swarming into every decent harbor between Canso and Cape Sable. "The Fishery on the coast," he observed a bit freely, was "by much the most valuable" in North America. The French minister of marine complained that same year that the harbors of Cape Breton had been invaded by some two hundred "English fishermen of Boston and Accadie." During the 1720s Canso in particular became an important summer base for New England fishermen. Although only a handful of families lived there the year round, several hundred fishermen and shoremen descended on the harbor annually and remained from March until October, erecting flakes, drying fish, reprovisioning themselves from the itinerant merchants who sold supplies from lean-to huts, and blowing a few shillings in the half dozen or so ramshackle taverns. The summer crowd in this boisterous fishing camp was a cosmopolitan one—including mariners from England and France as well as Irish servants—but the greatest part of its fluid population always came from Massachusetts.[9]

For some years after 1675, fishing companies seldom sailed much beyond sight of land and spent much of their time ferrying fish to the shore. The cure they knew was a dry one, and it demanded that catches be landed, dressed, salted, and spread out on flakes as swiftly as possible. A chief advantage of the new and larger vessels, however, was their ability to remain at sea. A banks fishery was now an obvious possibility, and although a new cure would be necessary to ensure that the fish did not spoil before reaching port, the benefits of relocating to the offshore grounds were undeniable. Accordingly, as early as the 1680s merchants began to

Mass. Bay, V, 168; *Essex Co. Court Recs.*, VIII, 193, IX, 145; account of William Cocker, Philip English Acct. Bk., 1678–1690; George A. Rawlyk, *Nova Scotia's Massachusetts: A Study of Massachusetts–Nova Scotia Relations, 1630 to 1784* (Montreal, 1973), 6–7, 18, 34, 42–43, 47–48; Raymond McFarland, *A History of the New England Fisheries* (New York, 1911), 62. Rawlyk and McFarland both claim that fishermen from New England were working in Nova Scotia waters as early as 1640, but I can find no evidence for this.

9. Lt. Governor Caulfield to the Council of Trade and Plantations, Nov. 1, 1715, *CSPC*, XXVIII, 328–329; M. le Comte de Pontchartrain to M. D'Iberville, May 30, 1715, *CSPC*, XXVIII, 197. There is a wealth of material on Canso in *CSPC*, vols. XXIX–XLIII, but the most valuable material on the fishery has been excerpted in H. A. Innis, ed., *Select Documents in Canadian Economic History, 1497–1783* (Toronto, 1929), 154–166.

outfit companies of five to ten men in newer and more substantial craft for voyages of two weeks and longer. Where exactly the vessels were bound is not entirely clear—in large part because fishermen changed their habits frequently and probably tried their luck almost everywhere. At different times after 1675, they worked all the major fishing banks within a thousand miles of Marblehead—Brown's, Sable Island, Banquereau, Green, Canso, and St. Pierre—even the Grand Banks of Newfoundland. The grounds off Nova Scotia were generally their favorites, reported William Douglass in the middle of the eighteenth century, but the men from Massachusetts were quite prepared to go wherever the fish might lead.[10]

Fishing offshore took on a different character from work along the coast. For one thing, at least when the weather held, it was nearly continuous. Most of the day and frequently in turns throughout the night every member of the crew stood at the bulwarks, tending his two lines, hauling up cod from thirty to fifty fathoms deep, and tossing them into the box, or "kid," beside him. Not until the fish began to spill onto the deck did the men leave off fishing, and then only to split and salt away their catch. The routine was similar to that of the inshore fishery, except now the vessel functioned as a floating stage. Part of the crew remained on deck, splitting and cleaning the cod with their "cutthroats" at a waist-high wooden bench, and the others climbed into the hold to receive the fish, salt it, and stow it away in piles. When the decks had been cleared, they all returned to their lines. The only regular breaks the crew enjoyed were mealtimes, the few hours of sleep they snatched every night, and Sundays. Compared with shallop fishermen, who had time to relax in transit to and from the

10. On fishing vessels, see John Robinson and George Francis Dow, *The Sailing Ships of New England* (Salem, Mass., 1924), 22–24, 25–28; and Goldenberg, *Shipbuilding in Colonial America*, 5, 77–79. The momentous task of sorting out the fishing grounds of preference in different decades is not attempted here, but see M. le Comte de Pontchartrain to M. D'Iberville, May 30, 1715, *CSPC*, XXVIII, 197; William Douglass, *A Summary, Historical and Political, of the First Planting, Progressive Improvements, and Present State of the British Settlements in North America*, 2 vols. (Boston, 1749–1751), I, 538; Innis, ed., *Select Documents*, 154; "Marblehead Schooner Taken by the French," Essex Institute, *Hist. Colls.*, LXVII (1931), 304; Jethro Wheeler, Jr., Instrument of Protest, Sept. 3, 1724, Records of the Notary Public, Essex County, Massachusetts, 2 vols., 1696–1768, JDPL, II, 5–6; John Reed, Instrument of Protest, Sept. 7, 1725, *ibid.*, 8–9; Nicholas Girdler, Jr., Instrument of Protest, Aug. 10, 1758, *ibid.*, 115; *Essex Gazette*, Feb. 9–16, 1773. The grounds preferred by colonial New England fishermen are treated more thoroughly in Daniel Vickers, "The New England Fishery in Canadian Waters, 1675–1825" (report prepared for the Canada-France Boundary Arbitration, 1989).

The Bank Hand-Line Cod Fishery. A nineteenth-century representation of traditional practice. From George Brown Goode, ed., *The History and Methods of the Fisheries*, 2 vols. (section V of George Brown Goode, ed., *The Fisheries and Fishing Industries of the United States*, 5 sections in 8 parts [Washington, D.C., 1884–1887]), part iii, plate 23

grounds—between catching and dressing their haul—bankers worked on a more grueling schedule.[11]

The discipline that governed this more demanding workplace was essentially collective. Every voyage had a skipper—usually the eldest or most accomplished fisherman on board—who assembled the crew, guided the vessel to and from the banks, and took charge in heavy weather or other emergencies. Yet the skipper was merely the first among equals. Like his mates, he took a turn at the helm, hauled on the sheets, and tended his lines, and at the end of the voyage he was paid on exactly the same terms they were. A fishery conducted according to a routine understood by the entire fishing community—on vessels of relatively simple rig and driven by the energy of individuals hauling on their own lines—could usually rely on custom to organize most of the work routine, and the skipper rarely

11. Innis, ed., *Select Documents*, 154, 157–158; Capt. Weller to the Council of Trade and Plantations, Dec. 25, 1729, *CSPC*, XXXVI, 566–567; Capt. Waterhous to Mr. Popple, Jan. 22, 1731, *CSPC*, XXXVIII, 20–21; Azor Orne to Major General Lincoln, Oct. 18, 1782, cited in Richard Whiting Searle, "Marblehead Great Neck," Essex Institute, *Hist. Colls.*, LXXIII (1937), 213; Reynolds, *Peter Gott*, 43; G. Brown Goode and J. W. Collins, "The Bank Hand-Line Cod Fishery," in George Brown Goode, ed., *The History and Methods of the Fisheries*, 2 vols. (section V of George Brown Goode, ed., *The Fisheries and Fishery Industries of the United States*, 5 sections in 8 parts [Washington, D.C., 1884–1887]), I, 129–131.

had to intervene. The more grinding but also more productive pace of the banks fishery was sustained by men in partnership.[12]

By combining geographic expansion with technological innovation, fishing companies achieved a century of truly impressive growth. Between 1675 and the outbreak of the American Revolution, the annual catch of a Massachusetts fleet based largely in Essex County ports climbed from about 60,000 to more than 350,000 quintals.[13] Part of this expansion was a straightforward response to unsatisfied demand in the growing markets of the Iberian Peninsula and the West Indies, and part came at the expense of the transatlantic fisheries of Britain and France. In 1675 New Englanders had caught only one-fourth as much fish as their West Country–Newfoundland counterparts, but according to William Douglass, by 1749 this proportion had risen to one-half.[14] The pace of growth was not continuous. It stalled and even reversed itself during periods of war, when the fear of capture or impressment kept fishermen in port, or when access to markets was interrupted, driving down the local price of cod. The conflicts

12. Indeed, not being a master, a skipper lacked the legal authority to intervene. In 1682, when a company of fishermen were washing out their fish in Salem harbor, a crew member named William Russell took a run at the skipper, Thomas Jeggles, with "a Long sharp pointed knife" and tried to stab him in the chest. Although two other hands eventually managed to pull him off, Russell struggled wildly, flinging fish overboard, slashing out at his mates, and "biding the devill & the plaug take them all." What followed from this incident? Not a summary beating at the skipper's hands, as the master of a merchant vessel could have administered, but merely a complaint before the local magistrate! Even with the support of the other crew members, Jeggles knew he did not have the legal authority to discipline the obstreperous Russell personally. Had he tried to do so, he would have laid himself open to countercharges of assault and battery. "Except when he has some order to give in relation to sailing the vessel or catching fish," reported one 19th-century observer, the skipper "has no special authority over the crew, and the respect with which he is treated by the men is only that which his personal character obtains for him." The discipline that governed life in the banks fishery continued to be that of partnership. See *Essex Co. Court Recs.*, VIII, 348. See also *ibid.*, VII, 193, IX, 145; George Brown Goode and Joseph W. Collins, *Fishermen of the United States* (section IV of Goode, ed., *Fisheries*), 8, 97. By way of comparison to the merchant service, see Marcus Rediker, *Between the Devil and the Deep Blue Sea: Merchant Seamen, Pirates, and the Anglo-American Maritime World, 1700–1750* (New York, 1987), chap. 5.

13. See table 4. In the period 1765–1775—for which we possess sufficient data to judge—approximately 75% of the Massachusetts codfish catch was landed in Essex County ports.

14. Douglass, *Summary*, 291; Harold A. Innis, *The Cod Fisheries: The History of an International Economy*, rev. ed. (Toronto, 1954), 102; Order in Council, May 5, 1675, *CSPC*, IX, 226.

with Spain and France, which stretched from 1689 to 1713 and from 1739 to 1763, seriously interrupted the fishery's development (see table 4). In times of peace, when fishermen and shippers regained the freedom of the seas, growth resumed with remarkable speed.[15]

New England's fishery may not have been the largest in the North Atlantic, but it was among the most dynamic. The deepest measure of its success and the economic expression of all the changes described above was the remarkable rise in the output of fishing labor (see table 4). This had probably remained fairly level from the foundation of the fishery through 1675, but as the industry moved from shallop and shore to schooner and banks, the per capita annual landings of cod almost doubled. These gains, it is true, were achieved mainly by the sweat of the fisherman's brow, for doubling the catch in an industry where the essential labor of hauling on hook and line had not changed meant doubling the work load. The intensification of effort was itself an unusual accomplishment, especially since it improved upon a level already competitive with the Newfoundland fishery and since almost all of the gain occurred in the brief fifty years after 1675.[16] Why productivity surged so dramatically, in this particular corner of the New World and of all industries in the fishery, merits explanation.

CLIENTAGE TO FREE LABOR

The shallop fishery of Essex County had been constructed on a foundation of credit. Although the first generation of merchants initially had tried to operate the industry directly with hired hands, the cost and trouble of managing a free labor force on the frontier had forced them to switch strategies. Delegating responsibility over the actual fishery to quasi-independent client operators outfitted on credit, merchants decided to risk their capital only at the point of exchange. Widespread vessel ownership, heavy indebtedness, and the tight interdependence of mer-

15. Innis, *Cod Fisheries*, chaps. 5, 6, 7; Daniel Vickers, " 'A knowen and staple commoditie': Codfish Prices in Essex County, Massachusetts, 1640–1775," Essex Institute, *Hist. Colls.*, CXXIV (1988), 190–194.

16. Annual output per capita in the Newfoundland inshore fishery ranged from 30 to 50 quintals in the 17th and 18th centuries (calculated from Innis, *Cod Fisheries*, 101, 102, 158). At Richmond Island in the Gulf of Maine between 1634 and 1643, mean output per capita for five sample years (calculated from the fisherman's one-third shares, assuming current prices) stood at 42. See *Trelawney Papers*, 39–41, 183–190, 295–298, 344–345.

Table 4. Output of the Massachusetts[a] Cod Fishery, 1675–1775

Year	Fish in Quintals	Men	Vessel Tonnage	Fish (quintals) per Man	Fish (quintals) per Ton Shipping
1675	60,000	1,320	2,640	45	23
1700	50,000				
1716	120,000				
1719	150,000				
1729–1739[b]	47,000	625		75	
1731	230,000				
1741	230,000				
1748	53,000	623	4,450	85	12
1762	240,000				
1765–1775	350,000	4,405	25,630	79	14

[a]Some of these contemporary estimates are for New England; others are for Massachusetts. During the colonial period, these can be treated as roughly equivalent.
[b]Data from Canso only. The actual figures reported an average annual catch of 36,271 quintals and, therefore, 58 quintals per man. Since these did not include the fall fare, which the men carried directly back to Massachusetts, the reported levels have been raised by 30%—to 47,000 quintals and 75 quintals per man.

Sources: Order in Council, May 5, 1676, W. Noel Sainsbury et al., eds., Calendar of State Papers, Colonial Series, America and West Indies, 40 vols. (London, 1860–1939), IX, 226; earl of Bellomont to Lords of Trade, Nov. 28, 1700, in E. B. O'Callaghan and Berthold Fernow, eds., Documents Relative to the Colonial History of the State of New York, 15 vols. (Albany, N.Y., 1853–1887), IV, 790; Mr. Cummings to Mr. Popple, Dec. 15, 1719, CSPC, XXXI, 283; H. A. Innis, ed., Select Documents in Canadian Economic History, 1497–1783 (Toronto, 1929), 158–159; "Report on the American Fisheries by the Secretary of State," Feb. 1, 1791, in Julian P. Boyd et al., eds., The Papers of Thomas Jefferson (Princeton, N.J., 1950–), XIX, 221, 223; "State of the Cod Fishery at Canso," 1739, C.O. 217/8, 54–56, Public Record Office; William Douglass, A Summary, Historical and Political, of the First Planting, Progressive Improvements, and Present State of the British Settlements in North America, 2 vols. (Boston, 1749–1751), I, 537, 538, 540; Lorenzo Sabine, Report on the Principal Fisheries of the American Seas (Washington, D.C., 1853), 131; "Vessels Employ'd in the Fishery in this Province," 1762, Ezekiel Price Papers, 1754–1785, Massachusetts Historical Society, Boston.

chant and producer were the salient features of this system, and the scarcity of capital and labor its source. The triumph of the offshore ketch and schooner fishery after 1675 required that this structure be scuttled. To understand the transformation of this industry, then, requires an examination of how owner operation, credit, and clientage gave way to a new set of organizing principles based on a stricter and simpler division between capital and labor.

The transformation began with a shift in international markets. New England's client-operated shallop fishery had grown up in a period of continuously healthy demand for salt cod, and the high prices that fishermen obtained in the mid-seventeenth century had ensured their quasi independence by inspiring the confidence of their creditors. Then, about 1675, after weathering the general depression of the North Atlantic economy better than most staples, codfish began to drop in value. Following the general direction of world markets, the local price of fish entered a trough that lasted through the middle of the following century. Discounting a few temporary war-induced peaks and the local boom that resulted from the failure of the Newfoundland fishery between 1714 and 1720, it can fairly be said that the price of cod did not regain its seventeenth-century heights until after the Treaty of Paris in 1763.[17]

Although the softening of markets and the rise of the offshore fishery may simply have coincided, there was probably a logical connection between the two. It was much harder to make voyages pay when prices fell, and after 1675 many inshore fishermen went bankrupt. Merchants tightened the flow of credit that had supported the boat fishery because they lost faith in their clients' ability ever to repay. After all, when the returns from the fishery weakened, they, too, were under financial pressure from their creditors (chiefly in Boston and London). Rather than tying up their assets in interest-free personal accounts, it seemed wiser to pare down these debts and reinvest the capital in vessels of their own to prosecute the new and trimmer banks fishery.

None of this would have been possible had the coastal communities of Massachusetts not managed through the years of the client fishery to accumulate an adequate supply of labor and capital. Since the inshore fishery had originally been structured by the very scarcity of those productive factors, its replacement by an offshore fishery required that those scarcities be overcome. That is exactly what happened during the colony's first century.

The development of a resident labor supply hinged first on population growth. As we saw in Chapter 3, fishermen began to drift toward the

17. Vickers, "'A knowen and staple commoditie,'" Essex Institute, *Hist. Colls.*, CXXIV (1988), 194.

Massachusetts coastline to find work in the outports of Essex County in the middle of the seventeenth century. A small but steady portion chose to marry and settle permanently, especially in Marblehead and on the Salem waterfront; as they raised families of their own, the fishing population soared. Marblehead could count only about one hundred souls in 1650, but that figure had risen to six hundred by 1680, and to more than one thousand by the turn of the century. Across the harbor in Salem, members of the seafaring families that dwelt in the narrow lanes leading up from the South River numbered two hundred in 1650 and nearly double that in 1690. Finally, scattered across Beverly, Gloucester, and Ipswich were several dozen fishing households whose members added a few hundred more. At the turn of the century, a French visitor guessed that there were "at Cape Anne some forty fishermen's houses, [and] at Salem four hundred houses, the inhabitants all fishermen and sailors." By 1725, the waterfront population of Essex County stood at nearly four thousand individuals—ten times the level of 1650.[18]

A certain portion of this growth resulted from immigration. The flow of fishing servants from Newfoundland was almost a century old in 1732, and that year British officials in St. John's were still complaining of the "great numbers of seamen" finding passage to New England at the end of the season. Although the navy had been authorized to dam this stream, servants were so bent on shipping southward that they pursued departing Boston and Salem-bound vessels in their fishing boats and even had themselves smuggled aboard the New Englanders' ships, "headed up in hogsheads."[19] By the beginning of the eighteenth century, however, the more important source of population growth within the fishing commu-

18. Heyrman, *Commerce and Culture*, 53n, 213, 245; Evarts B. Greene and Virginia D. Harrington, *American Population before the Federal Census of 1790* (New York, 1932), 20; Christine Alice Young, *From "Good Order" to Glorious Revolution: Salem, Massachusetts, 1628–1689* (Ann Arbor, Mich., 1980), 176, 199n; *Essex Co. Court Recs.*, VI, 400–402. In the calculation of these figures, I used multipliers of 5 for militia totals and 6 for household totals to estimate total population. Maritime Essex County was defined as including all of Marblehead, 20% of Salem, 40% of Beverly, 10% of Ipswich, and 30% of Gloucester. The quotation is from Innis, *Cod Fisheries*, 116.

19. Capt. Kempthorn to Mr. Burchett, May 10, 1715, *CSPC*, XXVIII, 313; Council of Trade and Plantations to the King, Mar. 2, 1716, *CSPC*, XXIX, 37; Capt. Passenger to Mr. Popple, Oct. 1, 20, 1717, *CSPC*, XXX, 50, 76–77; Commodore Scott to Mr. Popple, Nov. 16, 1718, *CSPC*, XXX, 391–392; "Governor Falkingham's Answers to Heads of Enquiry and Instructions," Oct. 4, 1732, *CSPC*, XXXIX, 225.

nities of Essex County was natural increase. As early as 1715, local families in the outports were generating close to two-thirds of each town's fishing labor force, and by the middle of the century that proportion had climbed to three-quarters.[20] The attractions of easy credit that had drawn fishermen to settle in Essex County during the second half of the seventeenth century had begun to bear fruit. Unlike Newfoundland, Massachusetts had acquired by the opening quarter of the eighteenth century a fishery that was demographically self-sufficient.

The growth of wealth within the maritime community was even more dramatic. Not only from the earnings of the fishery but also from the profits of merchants and artisans, property accumulated locally and ever more rapidly as the seventeenth century progressed. In Salem less than £5,300 sterling had been inventoried for probate before 1661, but in the subsequent two decades that sum multiplied twentyfold. Even in per capita terms the mean value of estates nearly tripled. Across the harbor in Marblehead, the process may have been slower; still, the total wealth of all inventoried decedents rose 500 percent and per capita wealth climbed 60 percent between the periods 1640–1674 and 1690–1715.[21] Much of this new wealth accumulated within the merchant ranks of local society, and from the fishermen's perspective this meant primarily a vast broadening in the range of employment and provisioning alternatives that they could pursue. George Corwin, William Browne, Edmund Batter, and Moses Maverick, who had dominated the tight-knit coterie of earlier decades, were

20. Local origin was determined for 1,201 voyages made by colonial fishermen by searching the sources in Appendix 3 for evidence of family names present in town by estimated date of birth. For the 17th century this technique revealed that only 12% of Essex County fishermen could have been born anywhere inside the county. By 1700–1730 close to 60% were fishing out of the port in which they had been born, and by 1760–1774 this percentage had climbed to 73 in Gloucester, 85 in Beverly, and 89 in Marblehead.

21. Donald Warner Koch, "Income Distribution and Political Structure in Seventeenth-Century Salem, Massachusetts," Essex Institute, *Hist. Colls.*, CV (1969), 54, 59. In Marblehead the sum of all inventoried real and personal wealth in estates probated before 1675 was approximately £2,930 sterling and the mean estate value was £95 (N = 31). For the period 1690–1715, total wealth had risen to £14,520 sterling and the mean estate value to £132 (N = 110). These figures were calculated from *Essex Co. Prob. Recs.*, I–II, and Heyrman, *Commerce and Culture*, 415, 416. In Boston, total inventoried wealth climbed very quickly during the same period, marking a roughly fivefold increase between the periods 1640–1664 and 1665–1684. See Gloria L. Main and Jackson T. Main, "Economic Growth and the Standard of Living in Southern New England, 1640–1774," *JEH*, XLVIII (1988), 30, 38.

now joined by a host of powerful competitors, many of whom had had little connection to the fishery before. John Higginson, Timothy Orne, and William Pickering were Salem-born but new to this particular trade, and their neighbors Philip English and Timothy Lindall were actually immigrants. By 1700 a tide of young traders, sea captains, and fish dealers from other towns along the coast and even overseas was sweeping into Marblehead. Most of the important merchant families that the fishing port attracted—the Knotts, Skinners, Nordens, Swetts, Procters, Bowens, and others—arrived during the decades surrounding the turn of the century. All of these new dealers in both towns owned vessels in the fishery and coasting trades, kept stores that were stocked with retail goods, had sizable financial assets, and were ready to deal.[22] In such a world the anxiety of fishermen over security of provisioning was certain to ease.

Of course, rising wealth did not necessarily generate freely circulating capital any more than population growth guaranteed a free labor market. As long as merchants had an interest in cultivating clienteles and fishermen saw an advantage to seeking out patronage, the wealth of the fishery would continue to be buried in the personal accounts of quasi-independent operators and its manpower would be tied into relations of personal dependency. Certainly this was the case in many of the fisheries of eastern Canada and Newfoundland until far into the nineteenth century.[23] The immobilization of labor and capital that was characteristic of all these frontier economies constituted an adaptation to the risks and costs of operating for profit where land was abundant and settlement thin. It follows that their remobilization resulted only when merchants facing depression in the fish trade took steps to reorganize their business.

They managed this by whittling away at the prop that had originally supported the quasi-independent status of inshore fishermen: long-term and interest-free credit. By this means merchants like George Corwin had once delegated control within the industry, but in the last quarter of the seventeenth century his successors started to tighten the pursestrings. From writs entered before the county court, it is clear that the levels of indebtedness fishermen could incur before creditors took them to court

22. Perley, *History of Salem*, I, 152–153, 157–158, 420, II, 298, III, 70; Heyrman, *Commerce and Culture*, 260–262, 357–358.
23. Ommer, "What's Wrong with Canadian Fish?" *Jour. Can. Studies*, XX, no. 3 (1986), 125–128.

Table 5. Indebtedness of Essex County Fishermen, 1660–1775

Decade	Merchant	No. of Fishermen	Persistent Debtors[a] (%)	Balanced Accounts[b] (%)	Persistent Creditors[c] (%)
1660s	G. Corwin	30	60	33	7
1680s	P. English	23	43	57	0
1710s	W. Pickering	23	9	91	0
1740s	M. Ward	32	0	100	0
1770s	W. Knight	35	0	89	11

[a]Fishermen whose accounts continued for at least two years and were always negative in their balance.
[b]Fishermen whose accounts continued for at least two years and were sometimes positive and sometimes negative.
[c]Fishermen whose accounts continued for at least two years and were always positive in their balance.

Sources: George Corwin Account Books, 1658–1664, 1663–1672, Curwen Family Papers, 1641–1902; Philip English Account Books, 1668–1708, 1678–1690, English/ Touzell/Hathorne Papers, 1661–1851; William Pickering Account Book, 1695–1718; Miles Ward Account Books, 1736–1745, 1745–1753, Ward Family Papers, 1718–1945; William Knight Account Book, 1769–1775, all in the James Duncan Phillips Library, Peabody Essex Museum, Salem, Mass.

began to slide about 1675 and then plunged after the turn of the century. In broad terms, the mean litigated sum in debt cases involving fishermen fell from £25 sterling between 1640 and 1700 to £6 sterling between 1701 and 1750.[24] The records of probate mirror the same pattern: the mean indebtedness of fishermen who died in mid-career dropped from £13.5 sterling in the seventeenth century to only £7.5 sterling during the first half of the eighteenth century.[25] The books of fishing merchants, designed to keep track of financial obligation, confirm the picture. The broad chronic indebtedness of the mariners who had dealt with George Corwin is simply not to be found in the accounts of later periods (see table 5).

24. *Essex Co. Court Recs., Verbatim Transcriptions,* I–XLIV; Files ICCP, Boxes 1–150. For 1640–1700, $N = 33$; for 1701–1750, $N = 78$.
25. See Appendixes 1 and 3. For 1640–1700, $N = 41$; for 1701–1750, $N = 12$. Note that dying in mid-career is defined as dying within ten years of one's last recorded voyage.

Underlying the decline of the inshore fishery and the rise of its offshore successor was an undeniably radical credit crunch.

How did this manifest itself? Only a minority of fishermen had their debts actually called in a legal action. Most merchants with a lot of capital tied up in personal accounts preferred to let well enough alone while their customers were still alive and recouped to some extent by insisting on a little extra fishing in the winter or a paring down of store purchases. Philip English called in his indebted hands for frequent reckonings and required them to promise payment "in fish or good pay as the said English shall see."[26] But old obligations died hard, and many men who had been outfitted on credit before 1675 went to their graves well in the red, no matter how long they lived. Suppliers knew that it was easier to delay collection until the client was dead, when they could conveniently demand repayment from the estate—meaning in practice from the legally defenseless and disadvantaged widow.[27] With the slate wiped clean merchants could impose the new, tighter credit rules on the next generation of fishermen and redirect their assets into the purchase of ketches and schooners that would employ the new men on shares.

Take the case of the Salem merchant William Browne and his client fisherman Arthur Kibbins. When Kibbins died in 1685, he was over fifty years of age and probably retired, living in a sparely furnished home that he had purchased about thirty years before. For some time, he had been making ends meet in part with the profits from an ordinary that his wife operated in one of their rooms, in part from the earnings of his children, and in part on credit at the merchant's store. Shortly after Kibbins was buried, however, Browne lowered the boom. Presenting his account for £77 sterling worth of book debts against an estate valued at only £106 sterling, he drove the surviving family for all practical purposes into bankruptcy. The house and its contents were put up for auction; a mere £20 sterling inheritance was salvaged; and the widow with her children left

26. Philip English Acct. Bk., 1678–1690. Many reckonings similar to this in form are scattered through its pages.

27. Of fishermen from the period before 1676, those who died in or after 1676 ($N = 24$) were just as likely as those who died before that date ($N = 24$) to possess a net indebtedness of £7.5 sterling or more at death. In each case, 42% held debts in excess of this sum. By comparison, of those whose documented fishing careers did not begin until *after* 1676 (but who died before 1726 [$N = 26$]), only 19% died more than £7.5 sterling in debt. See Appendixes 2 and 3.

town. By this means, Browne retrieved his capital and was free to invest it wherever he pleased.[28]

As more of these long-standing but outmoded relationships fell to death's ax, merchants also decided it was worth the battle to clamp down on the living. Although fishermen could still obtain short-term credit for gear and provisions, they now periodically had to bring their accounts into a rough state of balance or risk being cut off. After a lean season, or in time of war when the fishery shut down, this could mean tougher times: pottage stretched with Indian meal, more patching on one's britches, fewer pots from the rum keg, making do with worn-out tackle at sea, or even selling one's boat. During the last quarter of the seventeenth century and the first quarter of the eighteenth century, Essex County fishermen gradually ceased to be owners or even renters of the vessels they sailed. Before 1676, 40 percent of those who died in mid-career whose estates were inventoried possessed at least a share in some type of craft, but in the period 1676–1725 that percentage fell to 15; in the fifty years before the outbreak of the Revolution it tailed away to 2.[29] About one skipper in six in the eighteenth century owned the vessel he directed, and some others managed to purchase a one-eighth share therein; among the rest of the crew, however, ownership as a practical possibility vanished.[30]

The very terms on which fishermen negotiated employment were changing. In the inshore fishery a company of three had normally paid a flat "boat hire" and pocketed the entire earnings of the vessel themselves. In the banks fishery that developed after 1675, however, most crews "went on shares," giving up to the merchant owner three-eighths of their net proceeds—"for the vessel" and for the curing of the fish—as a condition of their employment. The remaining balance they normally divided, assuming a rough equivalency of skill and effort, into equal shares. Only the less productive youths had their takes measured daily and were paid by the fish they landed. Occasionally, entire crews would choose to receive their

28. Perley, *History of Salem*, II, 213; *Essex Co. Court Recs.*, VII, 71, 293, 324, IX, 512–513; Sidney Perley, "Salem in 1700, No. 20," *Essex Antiquarian*, X (1906), 120.

29. For 1630–1675, $N = 20$; for 1676–1725, $N = 34$; for 1726–1775, $N = 43$. The sources for active fishermen are listed in Appendix 3.

30. List of Vessels at Canso, 1721, C.O. 217/4, 44, List of Vessels at Canso, 1723, C.O. 217/4, 299–301, List of Vessels at Canso, 1725, C.O. 217/4, 287, Public Record Office. Of the 162 vessels mentioned in these lists, 139 were owned by someone other than the skipper.

shares in this manner—"counting" as it was termed—and then the skipper would have to keep a daily tally of each man's catch so that his individual share could be calculated at the end of the voyage. Under these arrangements, however, the potential for internal competition and dissension was unsettling; counting cut against the natural collective and interdependent grain of seafaring work, so fishermen generally avoided the practice. Insofar as they were sharesmen, regardless of the particulars of division, these mariners did retain some interest in the industry, but a great portion of its risks and opportunities, merchants had now reassumed.[31]

Credit was the financial expression of delegated power. In the past, its price to the fisherman had been loyalty to the store, and outfitters had extended it only to cultivate a dependable clientele. When the same customers or their children discovered that their accounts were being squeezed, that loyalty evaporated. Fishermen, too, began to maneuver openly and to realize that they could slam the door on their merchant creditors and take their business elsewhere without losing much. They might be cut off, but in the stingier atmosphere of the period after 1675, most fishermen probably saw that coming anyway. In their dealings with merchants, it made increasingly good sense to pick and choose. Christopher Battin of Salem fished on William Pickering's sloop the *Content* on every one of its voyages between 1712 and 1717 and, for the last three years, served as the skipper. But only three of the twenty-two other hands who joined him at different times during that period lasted more than a year. The rest served out their

31. One surviving account of 1661 describes payment in shares on what may have been an inshore voyage (see account of Thomas Smith and Company, George Corwin Acct. Bk., 1658–1664); otherwise, all inshore fishermen of the 17th century that I could identify either owned their own boats or paid a flat "boat hire" (see Chapter 3). Payment in shares was the norm in all offshore voyages by 1684, and I infer that as a system it appeared with those voyages in the 1670s. See the accounts of Joshua Connant and Company and Joseph Swazy and Company, both dating from 1684, in Philip English Acct. Bk., 1678–1690. Every set of accounts relating to the 18th-century fishery describes the identical system. See, e.g., Timothy Orne Account Book, 1738–1758, Orne Family Papers, 1719–1899, JDPL; Miles Ward Acct. Bks., 1736–1745, 1745–1753, 1753–1764; William Knight Account Book, 1769–1775, JDPL; and Thomas Pedrick Acct. Bk., 1760–1790. For examples of fishermen working "on their own hook," see Joshua Burnham (1736–1791) Papers, 1758–1817, Box I, Folder 1, and Thomas Davis Account Book, 1771–1778, JDPL. For an interesting account of the difficulties bred by fishing on the "count," see Raoul Andersen, " 'Chance' and Contract: Lessons from a Newfoundland Banks Fisherman's Anecdotes," in Rosemary E. Ommer, ed., *Merchant Credit and Labour Strategies in Historical Perspective* (Fredericton, N.B., 1990), 177–178, 180–181.

Table 6. Continuity of Merchant-Fisherman Clientage, 1660–1775

Merchant	Town	Decade	No. of Fishermen	Clients for 5+ Years (%)
G. Corwin	Salem & Marblehead	1600s	20	40
W. Pickering	Salem	1710s	8	13
M. Ward	Salem	1740s	20	5
W. Knight	Marblehead	1770s	34	6
D. Rogers	Gloucester	1770s	21	10

Note: Clients are defined as fishermen who dealt with a merchant over five consecutive years and fished continuously for him during that period.

Sources: George Corwin Account Books, 1658–1664, 1663–1672, Curwen Family Papers, 1641–1902; William Pickering Account Book, 1695–1718; Miles Ward Account Books, 1736–1745, 1745–1753, Ward Family Papers, 1718–1945; William Knight Account Book, 1769–1775; Daniel Rogers Account Book, 1770–1790, all in the James Duncan Phillips Library, Peabody Essex Museum, Salem, Mass.

initial engagements, took their pay in a combination of goods, money, and notes on other merchants, and then found work on other vessels or even left fishing altogether.[32] This became the common pattern, for no account books of the eighteenth century describe anything like Corwin's stable clientele (see table 6).

Not only did fishermen start to bargain more widely for work, they also shopped around for their provisions. In the years prior to 1675, the act of taking credit had restricted their freedom to deal with whomever they pleased. Between 1675 and 1725 fishermen and their families began to keep tabs all over town and to settle them with cash and notes drawn on the merchant for whom they were currently working. All provisions for the voyage and a fair variety of consumer goods—salt pork, cloth, hard bread, molasses, and so forth—the typical fisherman still obtained from his major outfitting merchant as a matter of both custom and convenience. But now he also spent one-fifth to one-half of his earnings anywhere in town that he pleased.[33]

32. William Pickering Account Book, 1695–1718, JDPL.

33. The exact figure varied considerably from individual to individual, but a sampling of nine fishermen's accounts in merchants' books of the 18th century reveals a mean of 37% of

In the somewhat more anonymous environment of the developed seaport, merchants and others were much quicker to drag indebted fishermen into court and often for far smaller sums. Especially after 1715, when the value of those debit balances was undermined by the accelerating collapse of the Massachusetts currency (printed steadily since 1690 to pay for the colony's military adventures), anxious creditors turned to legal action to recover their money. By the 1720s, a dozen or more fishermen were summoned by writ to every session of the Court of Common Pleas only to default their cases and lose their property unless another merchant or storekeeper agreed to assume their debts. Such obligations had never been this actionable or negotiable in the heyday of the client fishery. There could be no clearer sign that the waterfront world had changed than this flurry of litigation.[34]

Did the credit crunch encounter popular resistance? In the courts, rarely. The cases were usually cut and dried, engineered by merchants to convert book debts of doubtful certainty into written instruments, to collect "damages" to principal wrought by inflation, and to ensure that any credit advanced henceforth would bear interest. Most fishermen could ill afford to miss their fares to pursue legal battles, and thus the majority of suits went uncontested.[35] Still, had the issue been political—had fishermen believed, in other words, that using the courts to enforce debt collection was wrong in principle—they could have acted. Other eighteenth-century Americans—the North Carolina Regulators and the Shaysite rebels in Massachusetts, for example—were quite prepared to interrupt court proceedings with violence when they believed that real justice could only be obtained outside the law. In most instances, however, the legit-

pay taken in cash and notes on other merchants. In the 17th century (see Chapter 3) that figure had been 22%. Accounts of Christopher Battin and Daniel Darling, William Pickering Acct. Bk., 1695–1718; accounts of Samuel Carrill, Abraham Fowler, Michael Smeathers, Nathaniel Yell, and Elezar Giles, Miles Ward Acct. Bks., 1745–1753, 1753–1764; accounts of Ephraim Ireson and James Thompson, William Knight Acct. Bk., 1769–1775.

34. As a proportion of all debt litigation, suits against fishermen stood at 10% in 1665–1673 (N = 235) and climbed to 34% in 1715–1723 (N = 227). See *Essex Co. Court Recs., Verbatim Transcriptions*, X–XX, and Files ICCP, Boxes 16–28. On this issue, see the similar evidence but somewhat different interpretation in Heyrman, *Commerce and Culture*, 231–247, 417.

35. See Files ICCP, Boxes 15–70. The same spurt in debt litigation and the transition from book debt to written instruments are described and explained nicely in Bruce H. Mann, *Neighbors and Strangers: Law and Community in Early Connecticut* (Chapel Hill, N.C., 1987), chap. 1. See, however, my comment in Chapter 5, n. 19.

imacy of debt collection was challenged only when creditors were thought to be outsiders who possessed hidden and sinister links to distant seats of power—links that made fair trials impossible. As long as fishermen were indebted to local merchants with roots in the community, the calling of debts was unlikely to erupt into violence.[36]

Interestingly enough, the one occasion during this period when the fishing community of Marblehead did riot—in 1730 against the new practice of smallpox inoculation—they singled out for abuse a group of merchants who were recent arrivals. Although credit was not the immediate issue in this confrontation, as Christine Heyrman has shown, the resentment of illegitimate power was implicit in the crowd's actions, and more than likely the local people had developed their suspicions of these outsiders from conducting everyday business with them. Merchants like Stephen Minot, whose house was nearly pulled down by an angry crowd of fishermen, were no more inclined than their locally born competitors to sue indebted customers. What made them suspect was their membership in a "small, privileged clique comprised principally of transplanted Bostonians." Indeed, not only were the merchants with local roots exempted from attack; some were later indicted for leading the mob! Debt litigation did not in itself generate resistance from the fishing community.[37]

Fishermen did not object to the stricter credit terms of the eighteenth century in part because balanced accounts made them freer. They also knew that certain inefficiencies within the developing labor market offered them some continued security of employment, for although the market in fishing labor was freer of clientage than it once had been, it was not free in every sense. Above all, it was remarkably local in structure. During the seventeenth century, most fishermen were foreign born and had come to seek work in Massachusetts while circulating in a transatlantic labor pool. By the eighteenth century, merchants and shoremen not only were manning their schooners almost entirely from the New England born; they rarely even looked outside their own town. The actual hiring was usually delegated to the skipper, who, as a member of the local fishing community, selected the crew from among his neighbors and relations.

36. This argument is developed at greater length in Daniel Vickers, "Competency and Competition: Economic Culture in Early America," *WMQ*, 3d Ser., XLVII (1990), 20–22, and n. 46. See also John L. Brooke, "To the Quiet of the People: Revolutionary Settlements and Civil Unrest in Western Massachusetts, 1774–1789," *WMQ*, 3d Ser., XLVI (1989), 425–462.

37. Heyrman, *Commerce and Culture*, 304–323 (quotation on p. 319).

Surviving account books testify to the localism in recruitment that re-sulted. Joseph Orne of Salem took the trouble to record in his account book the hometowns of the fifty-four fishermen who worked for him between 1720 and 1730. Of that crowd, one came from Andover, another from Lynn, four more from Beverly, and the remaining forty-eight lived within Salem itself. At the end of the colonial period, the localism of recruitment was no less remarkable. Between 1770 and 1774 Thomas Davis of Beverly also noted the residences of his sixty fishermen, fifty-five of whom dwelt inside the town, at most four miles from Davis's own house. Remarkably, not one hailed from Salem or Marblehead—towns with hundreds of employable hands, by water less than half an hour away.[38] Using birth in the port of sailing as a somewhat stricter measure of local recruitment demonstrates the same trend. By the 1720s, Joseph Orne already was filling at least 62 percent of his berths with the sons of Salem families, and by the 1750s, his nephew Timothy was finding 79 percent of his hands among the locally born. At the end of the colonial period, 73 percent of the crews hired by John Stevens of Gloucester to man his vessels were from town families, and 85 percent of those hired by the Pedrick brothers were from Marblehead.[39]

Perhaps the most striking illustration of localism in recruitment was the admittedly radical employment practices of William Knight. As the owner and outfitter of two schooners in Marblehead between 1767 and 1775, Knight not only hired 96 percent of his hands from local families, but chose to select a large proportion from among his own relations. Three of his sons—Robert, John, and William, Jr.—combined with an assortment of nephews, in-laws, and even cousins-once-removed filled at least 45 per-cent of his berths. Since Knight was a man of plain origins with deep familial roots in the local fishing community, he may have had obligations to honor that the well-to-do and socially remote Ornes and Pedricks did not. Probably he was typical of the more modest breed of fishing em-ployers whose accounts have mostly been lost but who mattered greatly at

38. Joseph Orne Account Book, 1719–1744, JDPL; Thomas Davis Acct. Bk., 1771–1778. For sources of identification, see Appendix 3.

39. Joseph Orne Acct. Bk., 1719–1744; Timothy Orne Acct. Bk., 1738–1758; John Stevens Account Book, 1768–1775, JDPL; Richard Pedrick Account Book, 1766–1783, Marblehead Historical Society, Marblehead, Mass.; Thomas Pedrick Acct. Bk., 1760–1790. These percentages are calculated from fisherman years (counting each fisherman once for every year he signed on with the merchant in question). For J. Orne, $N = 26$; for T. Orne, $N = 21$; for Stevens, $N = 98$; for the Pedricks, $N = 252$.

the time. In any event, the network of social relations that knit the fishing community together clearly also sustained a protected arena of employment for fishermen who had left the folds of clientage. Without such protection, it is doubtful that a free labor market could have been established at all.[40]

Fishermen had always been poor, though their poverty had once been disguised by the credit that, as laborers in demand, they had been able to obtain. Now, as the formal lines of property grew more distinct and edged inward upon them, the simple pinch of need drove them into regular, paid employment—the marketplace of labor. Similarly, merchants had always been rich, though their wealth had been extended on extraordinarily liberal terms of credit to recruit the help that under frontier conditions was so hard to find. Now, as the need for a stable clientele of fishing companies began to ebb, the invested wealth that had once been tied up in personal accounts was liberated in a marketplace of capital. Throughout the second half of the seventeenth century, wealth and manpower accumulated swiftly in Essex County, just as inexpensive land disappeared. The logic of a cheap but relatively unproductive inshore fishery outfitted on credit and operated by quasi-independent producers slowly ceased to make sense as the coastal economy matured. It took only a fall in fish prices after 1675 and a collapsing currency after 1690 to prompt merchants to discontinue their lending, fishermen to forget their loyalty, and the old relations of clientage to be replaced by those of the open marketplace. With labor and capital thus mobilized, the industry was transformed.

SEAPORT FISHERMEN IN MARBLEHEAD AND SALEM

If maritime Essex County lost its peripheral character between 1675 and 1725, how did this alter the lives and fortunes of ordinary fishermen? Given that the industry made such strides in productivity over that period, one might expect its labor force to have benefited correspondingly. Yet in

40. Out of 112 fisherman voyages, at least 50 were undertaken by relatives or in-laws. See William Knight Acct. Bk., 1769–1775. A rougher and more rapid survey of 77 fishermen in the employ of Thomas Davis in Beverly between 1770 and 1774 revealed that just over half carried the same family name of the outfitter's five skippers or their wives. See Thomas Davis Acct. Bk., 1771–1778. The fishermen were identified using the sources in Appendix 3.

Marblehead and Salem, the traditional centers of the industry, the fortunes of individual fishermen scarcely improved at all. Was it the lot of fishermen always to be poor? Or was there a historically specific logic to their persistent poverty?

As the seventeenth century gave way to the eighteenth, the character of fishermen's physical possessions certainly changed, but fishing families were not broadly better off as a result. A comparison between the periods 1651–1675 and 1751–1775 shows that the median portable estate had inched upward in value from £13 to £15 sterling, and eighteenth-century fishermen generally did own a few more creature comforts than their predecessors had. Featherbeds were nearly universal by the end of the colonial period, and they were now spread with linen or cotton sheets and covered with quilts. Most families had a dining table of maple or walnut in the cooking area as well as maybe a dozen chairs. Along the wall under a framed picture or a mirror stood a chest of drawers and possibly a second table. They served meals on pewter or ceramic plates laid out on a table-cloth, and in the evening they sat in rooms lit by candles set in brass or iron sticks and drank their flip from glassware. But they rarely owned the rooms that contained these furnishings, nor did many of them have guns, woodworking tools, livestock, or boats of their own; their access to the common property of fields and forests was more limited too. The estates of fishing households reflected a shift from productive wealth to consumer amenities, but there were losses as well as gains, and it is not at all clear from the probate records that the standard of living had risen.[41]

Although the range of annual earnings recorded in account books did climb upward across the colonial period—from about £20 sterling in the 1660s and 1670s to £25–£30 sterling on the eve of the Revolutionary

41. These inventories were drawn from the file of active fishermen described in Appendixes 2 and 3. For 1651–1675, $N = 18$, and for 1751–1775, $N = 24$. These figures must be used with some caution, mostly because they do not take into account changes in the prices of inventoried goods. Some representative inventories of active fishermen from Marblehead and Salem with estates of close to median value for the period 1750–1775 are those of John Owen (1757), Probate No. 20312, Benjamin Hendley (1771), Probate No. 13058, Philip Hammond (1772), Probate No. 12260, Robert Allen (1774), Probate No. 496, and James Chapman (1774), Probate No. 503, Essex Co. Prob. Recs. For a different evaluation of similar evidence from across Massachusetts, see Main and Main, "Economic Growth and the Standard of Living in Southern New England," *JEH*, XLVIII (1988), 36, 39–45.

War—the cost of living was rising too.[42] Using the local price of room and board as a rough guide to changes in general, living expenses climbed roughly by half across the century before 1775. House prices in Marblehead traced somewhat the same course, rising by a third between the period 1650–1689 and 1750–1775. It is wrong to be overly precise in these matters, but given the rate at which household expenses seem to have been growing, these money gains possessed little real substance.[43]

The range of store goods that fishing families purchased testifies to certain small improvements in their standard of living. Butter, sugar, coffee, tea, and chocolate were more likely to be found on their kitchen shelves than had once been the case. Fishermen paid for these items with the money they saved on the lumber, bricks, cordage, and canvas that, as renters and laborers, they no longer needed. On balance, however, most of their purchases consisted of the same basic items that storekeepers had been selling them from the time the fishery was founded: salt beef, pork, and mutton; flour and bread; rum and molasses; shoes, mittens, caps, and stockings; woolen and linen goods; and a range of household amenities from wooden pails to metal pins.[44] Essex County fishermen were still better off than most maritime laborers of the day, but their incomes were not rising in tandem with the productivity of their labor. It is this contrast

42. These totals were calculated from George Corwin Acct. Bk., 1663–1672; Timothy Orne Acct. Bk., 1738–1758; Miles Ward Acct. Bk., 1753–1764; and William Knight Acct. Bk., 1769–1775. The figures for the 18th century were adjusted downward by £7 to £12 to account for the fact that by this period (unlike the period before 1675) fishermen had to finance their own outfit and provisions. The cost of these was estimated from William Knight Acct. Bk., 1769–1775.

43. On the cost of room and board in Marblehead and Salem, see *Essex Co. Court Recs.*, III, 332, VI, 51, VII, 145, VIII, 331, 337, 358; *Essex Co. Court Recs., Verbatim Transcriptions*, XLVI, 95 (iii), LI, 28 (i); Croade v. Cooper (1701), Box 5, Holland v. Williams (1720), Box 22, Blackinton v. Egecombe (1721), Box 26, Pierce v. Cenady (1735), Box 63, Flood v. Martin (1736), Box 65, Doke v. Selden (1748), Box 95, Files ICCP; and Estate of Thomas Main (1762), Probate No. 17514, Essex Co. Prob. Recs.; from Gloucester, see account of Stephen Clark, John Stevens Acct. Bk., 1768–1775. On house prices, see Sidney Perley, "Marblehead in the Year, 1700, Nos. 1–9," Essex Institute, *Hist. Colls.*, XLVI (1910), 1–16, 178–184, 221–246, 305–316, XLVII (1911), 67–95, 149–166, 250–252, 341–349, XLVIII (1912), 79–84. Prices were considered only if they referred to the house and lot alone.

44. This can be seen in the many different accounts of individual fishermen in George Corwin Acct. Bks., 1658–1664, 1663–1672, Miles Ward Acct. Bks., 1736–1745, 1745–1753, 1753–1764, William Knight Acct. Bk., 1769–1775, and Daniel Rogers Account Book, 1770–1790, JDPL.

between the successful development of the industry and the stagnating welfare of its hands that we now must explore.

No single family experience can stand for an entire community, but since the Brimblecomes of Marblehead lived through most of the colonial period their history is a concrete illustration of how the transformation of the fishery altered local society. About the year 1660, John Brimblecome left his wife and children in the West Country to work in the Massachusetts fishery. On credit advanced by George Corwin, Brimblecome and two other recent immigrants purchased a shallop and for several years worked the waters off the coast of Maine—delivering their catch to Corwin's wharf in Salem, purchasing provisions at his store, and boarding with fishing families in Marblehead. Meanwhile, Brimblecome had purchased an acre of land in the outport overlooking its harbor (for just under £5 sterling), and on credit wheedled from Corwin he built a house. From this rustic homestead, he sent for his family and, supporting them with what he earned jigging cod and drying fish, he lived out his years on the Massachusetts coast. When John Brimblecome died in 1678, his wife, Tabitha, and their children inherited a small and modestly appointed house with a shed behind, the land they stood on, privileges on the commons, "several lean swine," a share in a cow, and "halfe of a shallop & Connue"—worth altogether £62 sterling.

John's two daughters both married local fishermen, but the house and land were taken over by his only surviving son, Philip. He seems to have become something of a petty shoreman, renting his shallop to fishermen, advancing them credit, and probably drying their hauls. When Philip died in 1692 he had certainly improved upon his father's estate. Not only had he enlarged the family dwelling, but he had furnished it more comfortably too—with added chairs, an extra bed, more pewterware, another spinning wheel, and a new brass kettle. All told, the estate had climbed in value to £110 sterling.

To this point, the fortunes of the Brimblecome family had moved steadily but quietly upward. In the third generation, however, two branches divided and began to follow markedly different courses. Samuel, who was Philip's oldest responsible son (John was older but "wanting in understanding"), began as a fisherman but eventually parlayed his inheritance into a sizable estate. In 1718, while in his early thirties, he purchased a fishyard; by 1735 he had acquired forty-five tons of shipping and an African slave; and at his death in 1762 he was worth about £390 sterling. Each of his sons established a respectable calling on shore: John entered the blockmaker's trade; Thomas built chairs for a living; and both Samuel, Jr., and Seaward purchased schooners and became shoremen like their father. Most of his grandsons did likewise, and some grew wealthier still. The majority probably fished in their youth, but few took it up as a permanent career, and most died in comfort. Of the eight householders from this branch of the family who were listed in the tax valuation of 1771, three owned fishing schooners and four possessed dwellings, an unusual distinction in Marblehead. These Brimblecomes never ranked among the elite of town society, for all performed some manual work in their lives and none was involved in the export trade, where the greatest wealth was amassed. They were, nevertheless, decidedly well-off.

Philip Brimblecome, however, had another son. Like the rest of the family, Philip, Jr., started out as a fisherman, but unlike them he fell into deep financial troubles when he was still a young man. By 1709 "sundry creditors" were pressing him for payment, and although he managed to scrounge the money they demanded from his stepfather, he had to trade away his inheritance in return. Misfortune was followed by disaster when about 1715 he died—probably at sea—leaving behind a wife, Sarah, and two small boys: Philip and Joseph. In hard circumstances, the widow raised them both to manhood, undoubtedly with the help of the money they earned in youthful voyages to the banks. Without a patrimony, how-ever, neither entered adult life on anything like the certain footing of their well-to-do cousins. Both married young and raised families in spare and comfortless quarters. Indeed, when this Philip died in 1743, his family of six was living in a single rented chamber. At meals they ate from a few pieces of "old pewter" while sitting on "old" chairs at an "old" table, and at night the parents slept covered with an "old" quilt as the children huddled together in a trundle bed under an "old" bed rug. Only the cow that they kept chained in the yard gave this Brimblecome family even a hint of independence. Nor were they exceptional, for none of Philip Jr.'s descendants—neither his sons nor their children—managed to acquire any assessable property before 1775. They all apparently lived in rented rooms and supported their families as long as they could, season by sea-son, from their earnings at sea.[45]

45. This history of the Brimblecome family was compiled from "Brimblecome Geneal-ogy," *Essex Antiquarian*, XII (1908), 34–38; *Essex Co. Court Recs.*, II, 208, III, 102, V, 279, VII, 144; Perley, "Marblehead in the Year, 1700, No. 5," Essex Institute, *Hist. Colls.*, XLVII (1911), 90, 92; and Marblehead Tax Valuation Lists of 1735, 1749, 1773, Tax and Valuation

The Brimblecomes' story illustrates nicely the roles that luck and lineage play in family history. Third-generation Samuel's success in business in the opening decades of the eighteenth century created an inheritable fortune that was still enriching his great-grandchildren a century later, whereas his brother Philip's lack of judgment and untimely death condemned his descendants to lives of chronic poverty. More to the point, their tale indicates how the fishing community to which they belonged was reorganized along markedly stricter lines of inequality in the five decades after 1675. For the fortunate few this transformation offered at least an enviable competency and even the opportunity to grow rich; the rest were consigned to lifetime dependency. Thus, although visitors to Marblehead may have been impressed with the few "very grand buildings" that caught their eye, they also had to gape at the jumble of local poverty. The streets, they reported, were "narrow, and rugged, and dirty"; the houses, "Miserable Buildings, Mostly Close in with the Rocks"; the air "Tainted with . . . the stench of the Fish"; and the people "savage in their nature and education . . . [and] very poor in general." Because they "exceed all places in the habit of begging," wrote Simeon Baldwin of Yale College in 1784, "one can hardly ride thro' the Town without being accosted in that way by one half of the old women and children in it."[46] The pens of these genteel travelers often dripped with cultural contempt, but

Lists of Massachusetts Towns before 1776, roll 12. All references to 18th-century Massachusetts tax and valuation lists, unless otherwise specified, are to the microfilm edition compiled by Ruth Crandall and published in 1971 by the Charles Warren Center for Studies in American History at Harvard University, Cambridge, Mass., which filmed the originals. See also Bettye Hobbs Pruitt, ed., *The Massachusetts Tax Valuation List of 1771* (Boston, 1978), 98–101; probate records relating to Brimblecome family, Probate Nos. 3340–3370, Essex Co. Prob. Recs.; Essex Deeds, XXVI, 280, XXIX, 97, XXXIII, 260, XLVIII, 101, CI, 101, CVIII, 141; accounts of John Brimblecome, George Corwin Acct. Bk., 1658–1663; accounts of Thomas and William Brimblecome, Richard Pedrick Acct. Bk., 1766–1783; account of William Brimblecome, William Knight Acct. Bk., 1788–1800; and account of Merritt Brimblecome, Benjamin Knight Account Book, 1800–1833, JDPL.

46. These were the observations of Alexander Hamilton, Francis Goelet, John Adams, Simeon Baldwin, and George Washington, conveniently assembled in George Francis Dow, ed., *Two Centuries of Travel in Essex County, Massachusetts: A Collection of Narratives and Observations Made by Travelers, 1605–1799* (Topsfield, Mass., 1921), 64–65, 76, 88, 96, 167. See also John S. Ezell, ed., and Judson P. Wood, trans., *The New Democracy in America: Travels of Francisco de Miranda in the United States, 1783–84* (Norman, Okla., 1963), 189. Christine Heyrman charts the division of Marblehead into classes in detail in *Commerce and Culture*, chaps. 7, 10.

the sight that Marblehead and the poorer neighborhoods of Salem presented in the eighteenth century was not a happy one. To understand the source of this poverty, we must move beyond their moral judgments to a careful reconstruction of fishing lives.

The eighteenth-century schooner fleet drew most of its hands from local maritime families. "A fisherman's son," as Samuel Eliot Morison put it, "was predestined to the sea."[47] Especially in Marblehead, where so many of their elders would be away handlining for cod on the offshore banks from the waning days of one winter to the first snows of the next, boys grew up knowing that childhood would come to an abrupt end when they made their first voyage sometime in their middle teens. Occasionally, peculiar circumstances could push them to sea at an earlier age. In the spring of 1771, when he was only eleven, Benjamin Salter of Marblehead caught about £5 sterling worth of fish on the Sable Island Bank for his widowed mother's account. James Burrill was a poor fisherman trying to house his growing family in a couple of rooms on the Salem waterfront in 1752 when he sent to sea his eldest boy, Johnny, a mere stripling of eight. Such stories were not common, however. Celebrated as sailor boys have often been in the lore of maritime history, there is little hard evidence to suggest that youths in these larger port towns had acquired any fishing experience, beyond dropping their lines off the wharves and rocks around the harbor, when they first obtained a berth offshore.[48]

By the age of sixteen, however, boys from fishing families were working a steady nine- to ten-month season, and over the next five years they received a working education, signing on with a variety of different skippers and learning from them the fisherman's craft. Two things distinguished them at first from the older members of the crew. As minors, they had to pass all of their earnings on to their parents, and as "cuttailmen," they were paid only by the fish they caught (and marked with an identifying cut from the tail). Within a few years, however, any plucky young fisherman would be able to locate a rope in the dark, find his way at night

47. Morison, *Maritime History of Massachusetts*, 137.

48. For Benjamin Salter, see account of Elizabeth Salter, William Knight Acct. Bk., 1769–1775; and *Vital Records of Marblehead, Massachusetts, to the End of the Year 1849*, 3 vols. (Salem, Mass., 1903–1908), I–II. For Johnny Burrill, see accounts of James Burrill, Timothy Orne Acct. Bk., 1738–1758; Miles Ward Acct. Bk., 1745–1753; and Salem Tax List, 1750, Tax and Valuation Lists of Massachusetts Towns before 1776, roll 8. Samuel Eliot Morison overemphasizes the precocity of boy fishermen, at least those of Marblehead and Salem, in his *Maritime History of Massachusetts*, 137–138.

by the feel of the wind on his face, ease the vessel in a seaway with the slightest movement of his hand, and land as many fish in a day as most of his mates did. When he had persuaded them that he could pull his own weight, he graduated to the status of full sharesman and the skipper ceased tallying his fish apart from those of the other men. At this point, usually toward the end of his teenage years, he became an equal partner with the adult members of the crew. A couple of years later, after attaining at twenty-one the age of legal majority, he could open his own account with an outfitting merchant and negotiate within the fishery as a grown man.[49]

At this point in his career, earning a full share and working on his own account, the young fisherman had reached the peak of his earning potential. And since he did not stand to inherit or hope to acquire anything in the way of housing or productive equipment any time in the near future, there was little to counsel delay in marrying and starting a family of his own. Now was as good a time as any, and eighteenth-century fishermen married at a mean age of twenty-four years.[50] Almost always the spouse was a local girl, usually from another waterfront family, and she was normally two or three years his junior. At the time of their weddings to Salem fishermen in the mid-eighteenth century, Priscilla Woodwell was eighteen, Sarah Masury, nineteen, Hannah Bray, nineteen, Sarah Beckford, twenty, Margaret Lambert, twenty-five, and Elizabeth Foot, twenty-six, and they were all daughters of fishermen, shoremen, mariners, or shoemakers.[51] Like the fishing labor market that defined the social circle

49. Goode and Collins, *Fishermen of the United States*, 51. The payment of youths by the "count" of the fish they caught (e.g., "To the Cuttails 1/2 fish p. fish book") is documented in most of the 18th-century account books listed in Appendix 3, but see esp. accounts of the schooners *Molly* and *Barnard*, William Knight Acct. Bk., 1769–1775. This source also demonstrates well the near-universal opening of individual accounts by fishermen when they reached age 21.

50. Mean age at first marriage for Marblehead and Salem fishermen was 23.9 between 1701 and 1750 ($N = 57$), 23.5 between 1751 and 1775 ($N = 54$), and 23.7 between 1701 and 1775 ($N = 111$). See Appendix 3.

51. The mean age at marriage for women who wed Salem and Marblehead men between 1726 and 1775 was 21 ($N = 48$). See Appendix 3. Of 22 identifiable wives of Salem fishermen, 20 came from Salem families, and in all 7 cases where the head of family's occupation could be discovered, it was a maritime trade. See *Vital Records of Salem, Massachusetts, to the End of the Year, 1849* . . . , 6 vols. (Salem, Mass., 1916–); and Perley, *History of Salem*.

of these families, the choice of spouses was locally defined and occupationally restricted.

That marriage was even a possibility for the great majority of fishermen marked a change from the past, and the presence of women in the fishing communities of the eighteenth century made an obvious difference to the quality of domestic life. Now skilled hands could manage the affairs that the bachelor fishermen of the seventeenth century had either handled clumsily or dropped altogether. In the time they could spare from feeding, cleaning, and disciplining children, waterfront wives chopped wood, tended hearths, sewed new clothes and mended old ones, shopped for provisions around town, paid the rent, and tended to business that could not await their husbands' return. To fishing households all of this represented a clear economic gain. Nonetheless, as time-consuming as these domestic rounds were, the wives of seaport fishermen may have been relatively underemployed. Without animals to raise, field produce to work up for market, or even a shop to assist in, they probably lacked the scope for productive labor that their counterparts in rural settings or craft households enjoyed. In some North American fishing communities, mothers and daughters participated directly in the fishery, taking charge of the cod after it was landed—splitting, salting, and curing it for market. In Salem and Marblehead, however, this was not the case. The splitting and salting were conducted on board the schooner by the fishermen, and the drying was handled in commercial fishyards at home that employed only men.[52] Urban housewives elsewhere spun yarn to knit into caps and stockings for their families or to sell abroad to pay for store necessities, but judging by the rarity of spinning wheels in fishermen's inventories, this

52. Account of Nicholas Merritt, William Knight Acct. Bk., 1769–1775; account of Isaac Needham, Miles Ward Acct. Bks., 1736–1745, 1745–1753; account of Nathaniel Homan, Richard Pedrick Acct. Bk., 1766–1783. For an interesting set of fishyard accounts, although later and from Beverly, see Albert Thorndike, Fish Yard Memorandum Books, 1840–1843, 1844–1850, 1851–1858, Beverly Historical Society, Beverly, Mass. On the role of women in the Newfoundland fishery, see Ellen Pildes Antler, "Fisherman, Fisherwoman, Rural Proletariat: Capitalist Commodity Production in the Newfoundland Fishery" (Ph.D. diss., University of Connecticut, 1982), chap. 4; Marilyn Porter, "'She Was Skipper of the Shore Crew': Notes on the History of the Sexual Division of Labour in Newfoundland," Labour/Le Travail, XV (1985), 105–123; and Sean Thomas Cadigan, "Economic and Social Relations of Production on the Northeast Coast of Newfoundland, with Special Reference to Conception Bay, 1785–1855" (Ph.D. diss., Memorial University of Newfoundland, 1991), chap. 5.

was not common in their households. A few waterfront women ran ordinaries and some may have taken in laundry and lodgers; further, one cannot minimize the work they invested in their households. With more productive wealth to manipulate, however, their energies almost certainly would have been more fully employed.[53]

Some young couples moved in with their parents, but the rooms and cottages they had grown up in generally were crowded enough without having to make space for new families. In fairly short order, therefore, most newlyweds managed to search out rented quarters of their own. In December of 1767 Robert Allen of Marblehead, twenty-two and fresh from his fall fare in William Knight's schooner *Molly*, married eighteen-year-old Deliverance Hooper, Knight's niece and the daughter of a retired banks skipper. As a full sharesman Allen was clearing about £30 sterling a year, most of which went to basic provisions—flour, salt pork and beef, rum, molasses, tea, cloth, lamp oil, and cordwood—or to cash for other purposes. Some supplies Allen bought himself, but his wife visited her uncle's shop even more frequently and each of their mothers was also known to draw on the young man's earnings. Intergenerational dependency, however, did not imply coresidence, and by the spring of 1769, Robert and Deliverance, who was pregnant with twin boys, were living in a chamber they had rented from one of Knight's neighbors, Capt. Thomas Peach. The young couple was able to furnish the home in a modestly comfortable manner with a pair of tables—one made of walnut—a good number of "bowback" chairs, a chest of drawers, a featherbed with a large quilt and an underbed for the twins, a mirror on the wall, and kitchenware sufficient for a small family. But there were no luxuries for the Allens, nor could they realistically hope to accumulate much more, at least until they were well on in years.[54]

53. Laurel Thatcher Ulrich, *Good Wives: Image and Reality in the Lives of Women in Northern New England, 1650–1750* (New York, 1982), chap. 1; Ulrich, "Martha Ballard and Her Girls: Women's Work in Eighteenth-Century Maine," in Stephen Innes, ed., *Work and Labor in Early America* (Chapel Hill, N.C., 1988), 70–105. Of a sample of fishermen's estates inventoried between 1701 and 1775, only 25% (N = 20) contained spinning wheels. The median estate of those with wheels was £19.5 sterling; of those without, £13.5. In 1700, both in Salem and in the rest of Essex County, about 50% of inventoried estates possessed spinning wheels. See Ulrich, *Good Wives*, 17.

54. Account of Robert Allen, William Knight Acct. Bk., 1769–1775; Estate of Robert Allen (1774), Probate No. 496, Essex Co. Prob. Recs.; Philip Chadwick Foster Smith, ed., *The Journals of Ashley Bowen (1728–1813) of Marblehead*, 2 vols. (Colonial Society of

The fortunes of fishing households in Salem and Marblehead did not follow the life cycle that characterized rural New England in colonial times. Granted, families like the Allens could normally expect to acquire some real estate, especially if the father and mother outlived their parents and came into an inheritance. But this did not commonly happen until they were in their forties, and even then they rarely succeeded to more than a little cottage or part of a house. Charles Hooper of Salem, who went fishing as a young man and then quit the sea to take up his father's trade of shoemaking, died at the age of seventy owning half an acre of land and an old house and barn worth £62 sterling—and he was among the more successful. In assembling personal estates, these eighteenth-century fishermen made even less headway. When Robert Allen died in 1774, he owned personal property worth close to the median of £13.5 sterling for fishermen in their twenties; those aged thirty to forty-nine had £14 sterling of personal wealth; and those fifty and older averaged £19 sterling.[55]

The most successful fishermen rose to be skippers and could be counted in the middling ranks of town society. Sometimes, like Robert Knight of Marblehead, they were the sons of vessel-owning shoremen and became partners with their fathers in the schooners they ran. Others employed family name and family property to obtain on credit a minority share from another owner. Samuel Carrill of Salem skippered vessels for Miles Ward in the 1740s and 1750s, fishing on the banks in the warmer months and freighting cod to Spain or the plantation colonies in the winter. In time, Carrill became both a man of property and an entrepreneur in his own right. During the 1750s, Ward advanced him rum and fish to sell in Maryland on his own account; in 1764, in his fifties, Carrill purchased from Ward a one-eighth share in a schooner that Ward graciously named *Hitte* after his shipmaster's second wife. "Captain Carrill," as he now called himself, moved into a comfortable home in Salem's maritime ward and supported himself at least until the outbreak of the Revolutionary War as a petty trader in partnership with the Ward family. This fisherman succeeded where others did not because he managed to break into the export busi-

---

Massachusetts, *Publications*, XLIV–XLV [Boston, 1973]), I, 98; *Vital Records of Marblehead*, I–II.

55. Estate of Charles Hooper (1759), Probate No. 13828, Estate of Robert Allen (1774), Probate No. 496, Essex Co. Prob. Recs. See Appendix 3 for sources on 18th-century Marblehead and Salem fishermen and their inventories. For those aged 20–29, $N = 11$; for those 30–49, $N = 33$; for those 50 and older, $N = 17$.

ness. His story was in no sense typical even among skippers, but it does illustrate the far limits of what talent, ambition, connections, and luck could sometimes achieve.[56]

The more common pattern can be gathered by situating Carrill's life history alongside others who fished with him. Using tax records from eighteenth-century Salem, one can compare the assessable wealth that fishermen possessed (including real and personal estate as well as the assessor's estimate of their "faculty," or earning potential) with the average held by the entire town's population. Indeed, these results roughly mirror those obtained from probate records. Personal peculiarities notwithstanding, the general pattern was for fishermen's taxable worth to climb gradually in the first ten or fifteen years of marriage and to stagnate thereafter (see figure 1). For those who neither owned nor hoped to inherit any real working capital, these curves represent what a family needed to survive, and little more.[57]

Through their late twenties, most of these young husbands and fathers continued to ride out the greatest part of the year at anchor in the North Atlantic, hauling on their lines hundreds of miles from home. Such were the rigors of the banks fishery, however, that the physical capacities of handlining fishermen were outstripped at a fairly early age. Records on the productivity of several dozen fishermen from Beverly who sailed to the banks between 1769 and 1799 make this clear (see figure 2). The

56. Out of 31 skippers who paid taxes in Salem in 1757, none ranked in the top quartile of taxpayers, but 77% paid enough taxes on real property and 90% paid enough taxes on personal property to rank in the second or third quartile of the town's taxpaying population. See Assessment on Fishing, Whaling, and Coasting Vessels, 1757, Salem Tax Lists, 1733–1773, Tax and Valuation Lists of Massachusetts Towns before 1776, roll 8. For Robert Knight, see his account in William Knight Acct. Bks., 1769–1775, 1788–1800; and *Vital Records of Marblehead*, I–II. For Samuel Carrill, see his account in Miles Ward Acct. Bks., 1736–1745, 1745–1753, 1753–1764, 1764–1772; Salem Tax Lists, 1733–1773, Valuation List 3, 1751, Assessment on Whaling, Fishing and Coasting Vessels, 1757, 1758, Tax and Valuation Lists of Massachusetts Towns before 1776, rolls 8, 9; and Pruitt, ed., *Massachusetts Tax Valuation List of 1771*, 148.

57. That laborers in the port of Philadelphia followed the same pattern is clear from Billy G. Smith, "The Vicissitudes of Fortune: The Careers of Laboring Men in Philadelphia, 1750–1800," in Innes, ed., *Work and Labor in Early America*, 221–251. For rural career comparisons, see Jackson Turner Main, *Society and Economy in Colonial Connecticut* (Princeton, N.J., 1985), 140–149, 157–172, and Christopher M. Jedrey, *The World of John Cleaveland: Family and Community in Eighteenth-Century New England* (New York, 1979), 94, 204n.

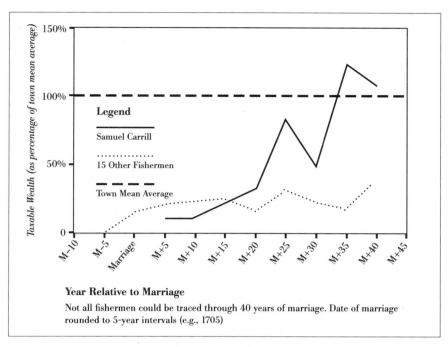

150% —

100% —

Taxable Wealth (as percentage of town mean average)

50% —

0 —

Legend

Samuel Carrill

15 Other Fishermen

Town Mean Average

M-10 M-5 Marriage M+5 M+10 M+15 M+20 M+25 M+30 M+35 M+40 M+45

Year Relative to Marriage

Not all fishermen could be traced through 40 years of marriage. Date of marriage
rounded to 5-year intervals (e.g., 1705)

Figure 1. Taxable Wealth of Eighteenth-Century Married Salem Fishermen

number of fish landed by every man on each of his voyages is expressed as
a percentage of the amount caught by the most successful individual on
that trip. The data demonstrate that although a fisherman's effectiveness
rose through the first ten years of his career, it generally peaked (at the
summit of his physical prowess) about the age of thirty and began to tail
off thereafter.

Not only was work on the banks physically tough, it was also dangerous—far more so than the inshore fishery had ever been. Although the
ketches and schooners that sailed out of Essex County were suited to
heavy weather, storms on the open sea were more severe and shelter
harder to obtain than they were inshore. Lying to in a March gale on the
Sable Island Bank with the rigging encrusted in ice, fishermen had to
keep their craft head on to the wind, or an onrushing wave with its
foaming crest towering over the masthead might bury them forever. And
such disasters did occur. Mortality figures from the nineteenth century in
a fishery that had not changed a great deal show that only one vessel out of
a hundred and four men out of a thousand were likely to be lost in an
average year; but many years defied the norm. In a series of late winter

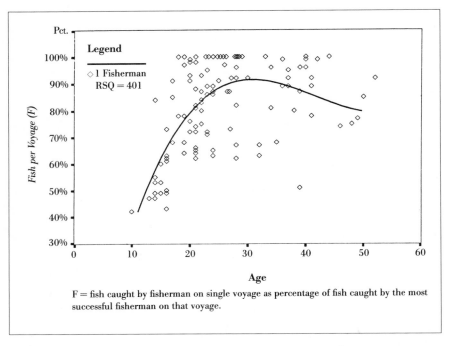

Figure 2. Quantity of Fish Caught by Beverly Fishermen, by Age, 1769–1799

F = fish caught by fisherman on single voyage as percentage of fish caught by the most successful fisherman on that voyage.

gales between 1765 and 1770, at least forty-two vessels from Essex County went down and close to three hundred men drowned. These storms were disastrous, not only for fishermen, but for their families, who depended on the money they earned. As the history of the Brimblecome clan illustrates, the drowning of a household head could cast a shadow of poverty over his family for decades. Although few fishermen spoke openly of the terror of facing death in an Atlantic storm, it undoubtedly preyed on their minds.[58]

58. Between 1830 and 1850, an average of 6.9 fishermen and 2.3 schooners were lost every year from a Gloucester fleet that employed annually 1,300–1,800 hands and 200–275 vessels. See *The Fisheries of Gloucester from the First Catch by the English in 1623 to the Centennial Year, 1876* (Gloucester, Mass., 1876), 73; and John J. Babson, *History of the Town of Gloucester, Cape Ann, including the Town of Rockport* (Gloucester, Mass., 1860), 571, 599. See also *ibid.*, 272n, 380, 381, 382; John J. Babson, *Notes and Additions to the History of Gloucester*, 2 vols. (Gloucester, Mass., 1876–1891), I, 136–137; Joshua Weeks to the Society for the Propagation of the Gospel, Apr. 2, 1770, in William Stevens Perry, ed., *Historical Collections Relating to the American Colonial Church*, 4 vols. (Hartford, Conn., 1870–1878), III, 549; and *Essex Gazette*, Aug. 16–23, 1768, Apr. 11–18, Dec. 26, 1769, Jan.

In quieter times, just living at sea could be a trial. Bankers were crowded, for one thing, and totally lacking in privacy. The summer camps that shallop fishermen had hammered together along the coast of Maine were rude enough, but at least everyone had a chance to stretch his legs, visit among other companies around the harbor, or step into the woods for a quiet smoke. By comparison, nowhere, even on the largest schooners, was it possible to physically distance oneself more than about fifty feet from one's crewmates. Early modern people were accustomed to living cheek by jowl in their indoor space, but not outside and not twenty-four hours a day.

The quality of the food deteriorated, too. Whereas inshore fishermen had kept live hogs, hunted game, and procured fresh water daily, those who worked on the banks were limited in their diet to fish, sea fowl, and whatever could be preserved over a month or two in the hold. Salt beef and pork, hard biscuit, stale water, flour, beans, molasses, tea, and some-times a bit of chocolate—combined in a monotonous daily cycle with the ever-present fish—became the rule for schoonermen. One man remem-bered how Sunday mornings were celebrated with a fisherman's fatcake: "The head was broken out of a flour barrel; the flour scooped out of the centre so as to make a basin-like cavity, sufficiently large for the cooks purpose; he then poured into it a pint of pork fat . . . a quantity of molasses and a little hot water till it was of the proper consistence. It was then taken out in a mass, and baked in a Dutch oven over the fire." Such a concoction would stick to hungry ribs, but as the culinary highlight of the week, "with nearly as many good qualities [it seemed] as Lord Peter's leg of mutton," it reflected poorly on the quality of the regular fare.[59]

Banks fishermen lived with a range of discomforts that worked in sinis-ter combination on their bodies and their nerves. When the fog settled in, as it might for days at a time, obscuring sun, moon, and any trace of other

2, Oct. 23–30, 1770, May 14–21, 1771, Mar. 24–31, 1772, Oct. 27–Nov. 3, 1772, Apr. 12–19, 1774.

59. Provisioning accounts for all periods can be found in each of the account books cited in this chapter, but see esp. Philip English Acct. Bks., 1664–1708, 1678–1690; Miles Ward Acct. Bk., 1745–1753; Timothy Orne Acct. Bk., 1738–1758; and William Knight Acct. Bk., 1769–1775. See also Reynolds, *Peter Gott*, 52–54; Samuel Roads, Jr., *The History and Traditions of Marblehead*, 3d ed. (Marblehead, Mass., 1897), 366–368; Goode and Collins, *Fishermen of the United States*, 90; and Goode and Collins, "Bank Hand-Line Cod Fish-ery," in Goode, ed., *History and Methods of the Fisheries*, 129, 132.

craft, the gloom was palpable. "If there is any situation in the wide world where men feel solitary and alone," wrote a nineteenth-century Cape Ann resident who had talked with colonial fishermen, "it is on the Banks of Newfoundland."

> There you lie, rocking to and fro, and rising and falling with the swelling surges, day after day and night after night; your deck slimy and slippery, the water trickling in streams down the windward face of your mast, and a large drop hangs ready to fall from the loose end of every gasket. . . . When fish are plenty, and the crew take from twenty to thirty quintals a day, the feeling of success enables one to bear the solitude. But when you are doing nothing, or only catching now and then a dog-fish, the feeling of dreariness is sometimes very oppressive.[60]

Drink provided some relief. Every ketch and schooner carried a communal supply of cider, and individual fishermen usually brought along a few extra gallons of rum. Singing, gambling, and storytelling, when fish were not biting or on a calm Sunday, helped as well. Most important were the few minutes every day or so when they hove to alongside other vessels to jaw and exchange news.[61] On balance, however, the banks fishery provided a work environment as trying and tedious as free American colonists anywhere were likely to encounter.

Around the age of thirty, therefore, most eighteenth-century schooner fishermen began to search about for some less strenuous form of work. Crew lists from colonial account books can be combined with evidence from court and vital records to produce age distributions for different groups of fishermen, which can be measured against an age profile of Marblehead males constructed from the 1830 federal census—the closest though still very approximate indication of the population at risk (see table 7). Although one needs to be careful about interpreting these data, it

60. Reynolds, *Peter Gott*, 56–57.

61. From the account books mentioned in n. 59, it is clear that fishing crews departing on four- to eight-week voyages normally carried about 12 gallons of rum and at least 60 gallons of cider (Imperial measure). Among a crew of seven or eight members (including two to four boys), this would amount to roughly a quart of cider and six ounces of rum per fisherman per day. This must be regarded as a minimal estimate since crew members sometimes purchased more in ports closer to the grounds. Suggestive of the camaraderie between vessels, though from a later period, is the log from the schooner *Paragon*, 1830, No. 1824L, Logbook Collection, JDPL.

does seem that crew members were most likely to be under thirty years of age and that middle-aged and older fishermen were more likely to be found ashore than afloat.[62] A small part of the dropout rate resulted from the high mortality that was characteristic of all seaports, especially among those who plied this most dangerous of trades. Part also may have been a function of the limited outmigration that will be treated below. Finally, the rapid drop in the levels of participation for Marblehead fishermen beyond the age of twenty-nine in the pre-Revolutionary years reflects the swift influx of younger hands during a period of rapid development as much as it does the rate of exit from the trade. But as fishermen moved upward in age, participation rates plunged far more precipitously than can reasonably be accounted for by any of these factors, and almost certainly this represented real retirement.[63]

Did fishermen leave the sea by choice? The true answer is hard to determine, and it obviously varied from one individual to the next. Sons of craftsmen sometimes signed onto schooners as young men and then returned to shore after a few years to enter their fathers' businesses or to strike out in other trades. Samuel Reaves sailed to the banks in 1730, when he was twenty-one, but quit to become a heelmaker like his father and later moved to Medford. Skipper John Punchard's son Benjamin fished in his youth, but when he came into his portion at age thirty-two, he was styled a shoreman with a fish house and a small schooner. Like-

62. These calculations are based on the defensible notion that male society in Marblehead was composed almost entirely of people who had passed through the fishery at some time in their lives. If we can assume that between 35% and 45% of the male population in the town was composed of those aged 15–39, we can move from the estimates of 5,000 to 6,000 for the total population in 1765–1775, to an estimate of between 2,500 and 3,500 males during that period, to an estimate of between 875 and 1,400 men aged 15–39. Since we know from table 7 that about 90% of Marblehead fishermen fell between these ages, and since we know from Thomas Jefferson's report on the fisheries of 1791 that there were 1,200 fishermen in Marblehead in 1765–1775, it seems likely that almost all the young men in town were fishermen. On the total population of Marblehead, see Greene and Harrington, *American Population before 1790*, 23, 23n, 31, 31n. On age structure, see U.S. Department of State, *Return of the Whole Number of Persons within the Several Districts of the United States . . . 1800* (Washington, D.C., 1801), 8; and Robert Paul Thomas and Terry L. Anderson, "White Population, Labor Force and Extensive Growth of the New England Economy in the Seventeenth Century," *JEH*, XXXIII (1973), 654. On population of fishermen, see Jefferson, "Report on Fisheries," 223.

63. On seaport mortality, see Maris A. Vinovskis, "Mortality Rates and Trends in Massachusetts before 1860," *JEH*, XXXII (1972), 199–201.

Table 7. Age Distribution of Fishing Population Employed by
Salem and Marblehead Merchants, 1720–1800 (in Percents)

Age of Fishermen	Salem Merchants			
	Corwin[a] 1657–1672 (N = 143)	J. Orne 1720–1730 (N = 37)	Ward 1738–1764 (N = 37)	T. Orne 1751–1752 (N = 19)
10–19	2	5	19	37
20–29	21	46	42	37
30–39	46	43	32	13
40–49	25	5	5	7
50–59	1	0	3	6
60–69	3	0	0	0
70+	2	0	0	0
Total	100	99	101	100

[a]Percentages in all columns save the last have been adjusted to deal with biases introduced by problems in the identification of minors fishing on their fathers' accounts.
[b]Males under the age of 10 have been omitted, since they cannot be considered part of the population at risk.

wise, the offspring of master mariners sometimes used an apprenticeship in the fishery as a springboard into a seafaring career and later the captaincy of a merchant vessel.[64]

The majority of urban fishermen, however, were not so fortunate. Fishing and seamanship were all they knew, and when they relinquished their berths to younger men, steady work became difficult to find. Some floated into the merchant marine and managed to eke out a living for a few years as common seamen, but this too was a hard life and one that was closing

64. For Samuel Reaves, see account of Samuel Reaves, Joshua Orne Account Book, 1719–1744, Orne Family Papers, 1719–1899, JDPL; Perley, *History of Salem*, II, 141; Estate of Cockerel Reaves (1757), Probate No. 23449, Essex Co. Prob. Recs. For Benjamin Punchard, see account of Benjamin Punchard, Timothy Orne Acct. Bk., 1738–1758; Estate of John Punchard (1767), Probate No. 22941, Essex Co. Prob. Recs.; Salem Tax List, 1750, Tax and Valuation Lists of Massachusetts Towns before 1776, roll 8; Perley, *History of Salem*, III, 38; Pruitt, ed., *Massachusetts Tax Valuation List of 1771*, 152; and Sidney Perley, "Part of Salem in 1700, No. 13," *Essex Antiquarian*, VII (1903), 166.

Marblehead Merchants				Census[b]
T. Pedrick 1760–1775 (N = 37)	R. Pedrick 1766–1774 (N = 19)	Knight 1767–1775 (N = 98)	Knight 1788–1800 (N = 138)	Marblehead Males 1830 (N = 1,755)
35	41	36	28	31
40	49	61	38	26
14	10	2	25	16
10	0	0	5	12
2	0	0	3	7
0	0	0	0	5
0	0	0	0	3
101	100	99	99	100

Sources: Fishermen's ages were determined from the sources in Appendix 3. Census data are from U.S. Bureau of the Census, Federal Population Schedule for Marblehead, Essex County, Mass.

off to laboring men as they entered their thirties.[65] Particularly in Marblehead, where the avenues of employment on land were fewer than in Salem, life for a retired fisherman could be very spare. Some may have, as Morison suggested, "puttered about with lobstering, shore fishing, or clam-digging," though almost none owned even a canoe or a wherry. More probably, they spent their days trying to pick up work around the waterfront. Nathaniel Dennen, for instance, who had fished out of Marblehead before the Seven Years' War, cropped up on the eve of the Revolution, working casually by the day in Ashley Bowen's rigging loft. Half of the men whom Bowen employed fixing jib sails or delivering suits of rigging were in their thirties and forties, especially the more regular hands. Nicholas Merritt was an older member of a prolific fishing family in

65. Rediker, *Between the Devil and the Deep Blue Sea*, 156–158, 299–300; Ira Dye, "Early American Merchant Seafarers," American Philosophical Society, *Proceedings*, CXX (1976), 335.

Marblehead, and after quitting the sea, he labored for £14 sterling a year in William Knight's fishyard.[66] Casual employment of this kind is difficult to trace in a systematic manner, and these few examples prove little. But the fact that most fishermen retired in their thirties and yet were called "fishermen" or "mariners" when they died does argue for the difficulty they encountered in mounting second careers.[67]

Part of the problem lay in the aging fisherman's difficulty in competing with the younger and more vigorous men. As we saw earlier, the productivity of fishing hands peaked in their late twenties and then gradually decreased (see figure 2). In fact, since many men in the upper age brackets had stuck to the fishery because they had a gift for it, the pace of decline for their less talented crewmates was probably faster. Thus, any mariner in his thirties or forties who combed the wharves in January or February searching out a berth on the spring fare risked being passed over for a younger man.

By necessity, their families had to depend heavily on the earnings of teenage sons. In the middle decades of the century, between one-third and one-half of the hands on any vessel had yet to come of age, and their shares were credited directly to their parents' accounts. A fisherman who had married in his early twenties hoped by the time he was thirty-five or forty—and probably retired—to have at least one boy old enough to contribute to the support of the household. So important, in fact, were boys' incomes to the family economy that when the great storms of the late 1760s sent many schooners to the bottom, the town of Marblehead had to petition the General Court for a tax abatement. There were now, the selectmen reported, "many Parents deprived of the earnings of their Sons which was their chief support; and . . . many Families since these unfortunate Shipwrecks have scarce any other subsistence than what has come from the Bounty of their charitable Friends and Neighbors."[68] Even in

66. Morison, *Maritime History of Massachusetts*, 138. On Nathaniel Dennen, see "Essex County Notarial Records, 1697–1768," Essex Institute, *Hist. Colls.*, XLVI (1910), 279; and Smith, ed., *Journals of Ashley Bowen*, esp. I, 244, 283–285, 304–310. On Nicholas Merritt, see account of Nicholas Merritt, William Knight Acct. Bk., 1769–1775; and *Vital Records of Marblehead*, I–II.

67. Of 14 fishermen who sailed out of Marblehead and Salem between 1701 and 1775 and died ten or more years after their last recorded voyage (and before 1776), 1 was termed a locksmith, another a heelmaker, 2 were cordwainers, and 10 were still identified as fishermen or mariners when their estates went through probate. See Appendix 3.

68. *Essex Gazette*, June 19–26, 1770.

happier times households so dependent on the earnings of children must have encountered great difficulty making ends meet. Since it is not easy to imagine fathers and husbands subjecting their families to such hardships willingly, one can only conclude that they had no choice in the matter.

Ultimately, the problem that seaport fishing families faced in the eighteenth century, especially in Marblehead, was underemployment. There were too many souls and not enough work. Timothy Dwight was told in 1796 that the fishermen of Marblehead were neither industrious nor thrifty: "In the summer they labor hard in a very toilsome occupation, and frolic away the remembrance of their hardships during the winter." Dwight was only guessing when he attributed the poverty of Marblehead to the moral character of its people, but the lack of gainful employment around that town in the off season was obviously common knowledge.[69] This had not, of course, been a problem for their seventeenth-century ancestors. In the days when maritime labor had been relatively scarce in Essex County, merchants regularly outfitted fishermen who, in their forties, clearly were past their physical prime. By the middle of the eighteenth century, vessel owners had become patently choosier—almost certainly because, confronting an underemployed labor force, they could afford to be. The notion of underemployment, however, is merely descriptive; the last stage in this analysis must be to explain its origins.

The tendency of maritime couples to wed young explains part of the problem. Women in Salem and Marblehead who married fishermen between 1726 and 1775 did so at a mean age of twenty-one—a year or two younger than was common in rural New England. Hence, the number of hungry young mouths and the pressure of youths on the available fishing positions were relatively higher. Marblehead was "Noted for [its] Children and Noureches the most of any Place for its Bigness in North America," observed Francis Goelet in 1750, and many others echoed his judgment.[70] In the federal census of 1790, it was the only town in Essex County where the median age for males was under sixteen. Although the visibility of children also reflected the high mortality of their elders, it served here, as

69. Timothy Dwight, *Travels in New England and New York*, ed. Barbara Miller Solomon, 4 vols. (Cambridge, Mass., 1969), I, 332.

70. See n. 50. On the visibility of children in Marblehead, see Dow, ed., *Two Centuries of Travel*, 76; William Bentley, *The Diary of William Bentley, D.D.*, 4 vols. (Gloucester, Mass., 1962), IV, 514, 544; "Ensign Williams' Visit to Essex County in 1776," Essex Institute, *Hist. Colls.*, LXXXIII (1947), 144–145; Ezell, ed., and Wood, trans., *Travels of Francisco de Miranda*, 189; and Dwight, *Travels*, ed. Solomon, I, 332.

in many of the early modern communities first touched by merchant capital, to exacerbate the pressure of population upon living space, local resources, and available employment. With a residential density that in 1790 exceeded every other town in Massachusetts save Boston, Marblehead was in the most meaningful sense overcrowded.[71]

Rapid natural increase, however, was a feature of New England society everywhere. What ultimately set the fishing community apart was its inability to seize the opportunities of the frontier. As late as 1790, 75 percent of the householders descended from fishermen who arrived in Essex County before 1670 were still living inside the county—chiefly in the coastal villages their ancestors had settled. In contrast, 60 percent of farmers' descendants were scattered by 1790 beyond the county's boundaries all over New England—some elsewhere in Massachusetts but many more outside the state completely.[72] If early America was, in general, an open society, which allowed for mobility and opportunity, these fishing communities followed different rules.

Some contemporaries believed that fishermen and their families stayed in their coastal villages by preference. Back in 1630, John White had argued that "rarely any Fisher-men will worke at Land, neither are Husband-men fit for Fisher-men but with long use and experience." Fifty years later, William Hubbard called the mariners of Marblehead and Salem "a dull and heavy-moulded sort of people," lacking in the enterprise of their landward neighbors. William Bentley suggested in 1791 that Marbleheaders in general lacked personal discipline: "they have so little knowledge of moral life, that they are as profane, intemperate, & ungoverned as any people on the Continent." The habits of the waterfront crowd seemed the antithesis of the self-denial and self-assurance these writers associated with landed independence and the pursuit of opportunity to the frontier.[73]

71. U.S. Bureau of the Census, *Heads of Families at the First Census of the United States Taken in the Year, 1790* (Washington, D.C., 1908), 9, 10.

72. These percentages were based on the 357 householders listed in the 1790 census who were descended from a sample of 23 pre-1670 farmers and fishermen. The individuals in the sample were chosen for the peculiarity of their names and the near certainty that only one person by that name immigrated to Massachusetts in the 17th century. See Appendix 2; U.S. Bureau of the Census, *Heads of Families*; and James Savage, *A Genealogical Dictionary of the First Settlers of New England*, 4 vols. (Boston, 1860–1862).

73. John White, *The Planter's Plea* (London, 1630), in Peter Force, comp., *Tracts and Other Papers, Relating Principally to the Origin, Settlement, and Progress of the Colonies in*

In that Salem and Marblehead possessed a distinctive maritime culture they were correct. Seaport fishermen and their wives were among the minority of New Englanders unfamiliar with rural life and its rhythms. Agricultural skills, patterns of planting and reaping, routines of household production, and all the habits of living that these engendered were foreign to them. They did not possess the same deep roots in reformed Christianity as their Puritan neighbors, and as West Countrymen and Channel Islanders they did not even speak the same dialect. As a community, they drank more heavily, cursed more lustily, and resorted to their fists more readily than rural New Englanders ever did. Coping with life at sea and in port was a hard, even brutalizing, experience, and decades of it bred a peculiar toughness into maritime society. Had a fishing family pulled up roots and tried to move into the town-meeting world of the Massachusetts countryside, one can easily imagine the chilly encounter that might have ensued.[74] A cultural gulf did divide seaward from landward society in colonial New England, and nobody understood this better than the fishermen. When John Robinson of Marblehead appeared before the county court in 1686, claiming that he had been defrauded of his earnings, he introduced himself to the magistrates by addressing what he clearly understood to be prejudice. "A fisherman," he termed himself, "which calling as he humble [sic] conceives is not altogether Unbeneficiall to this cuntrie." No yeoman farmer would have had to justify himself in this manner before the landed society that the bench represented.[75]

And yet there were regions of New England where such cultural division would not have been an issue. Along the Maine shore or in parts of New Hampshire, where the Puritan flame scarcely flickered, where the West Country tongue could be heard abroad, where land was relatively cheap, and where families had traditionally combined farming with fishing, mariners from Marblehead and Salem surely could have found a way of life to their taste. In fact, fishing families were not as culturally committed to place as their critics implied. Many were the sons and daughters or grandchildren of immigrants, and in their seaport domain, governed by

North America, from the Discovery of the Country to the Year 1776, 4 vols. (Washington, D.C., 1836–1846), II, 74; William Hubbard, "A General History of New England, from the Discovery to MDCLXXX," Massachusetts Historical Society, *Collections*, 2d Ser., VI (1815), 635; Bentley, *Diary*, I, 303.

74. Heyrman, *Commerce and Culture*, chaps. 7–9.

75. *Essex Co. Court Recs., Verbatim Transcriptions*, XLVI, 86 (i).

the heaving and pitching of world markets, they witnessed much coming and going all the time. During the hard decade of the 1730s, when a revived Newfoundland fishery had sent world cod prices plummeting, many local families decamped out of desperation. "This town has suffered so much since my coming here," wrote the Anglican minister of Marblehead, "that no less than 300 families have been forced to seek shelter and subsistence elsewhere." Where exactly they went remains a mystery, but it seems unlikely that they headed inland. We can only assume that an ebb in the economic tide had caught and swept them back into the Atlantic to try their luck at some other point around its rim.[76]

Certain episodes reveal the barriers to landward migration with painful clarity. In 1734, at the depth of its economic woes, Marblehead petitioned the General Court for a grant of land "on the Water side or elsewhere" "in consideration of the smallness of their Township and the numbers of their Inhabitants, as also the discouragements they have latterly met with in the Fishery." In a noteworthy reversal of policy (remembering attempts in the seventeenth century to withhold land from fishermen), the court agreed and apportioned a tract six miles square in back of Falmouth, Maine, to "sixty Inhabitants belonging to the Town of *Marblehead*, that are most likely to settle and bring forward a new Plantation, and that most need a Grant of Land." The conditions for becoming a settler were not onerous. One had only to put up £1.5 sterling in cash, move to the township, build a house there, and clear seven acres of land to qualify. Yet when the committee appointed by the court decided on a final list of grantees, it included but a handful of local fishermen. Although a few Marblehead families did move out to the tract—it was about a hundred miles away— not one was connected to the fishery. The original proprietors—chiefly well-to-do artisans and merchants—sold off most of the land in "New Marblehead," or Windham, as it came to be known, to colonists from other parts of New England or forfeited it back to the colony.[77]

Seaport fishermen failed to prosper from the development of their industry because the operation of supply and demand cut against them.

76. Keith Matthews, "A History of the West of England–Newfoundland Fishery" (D. Phil. diss., Oxford University, 1968), 366–367; Mr. Pigot to the Society for the Propagation of the Gospel, May 7, 1736, in Perry, ed., *Historical Collections Relating to the American Colonial Church*, III, 314.

77. *Journals of the House of Representatives of Massachusetts, 1715–1771* (Boston, 1919–), XII, 128–137; Samuel Thomas Dole, *Windham in the Past*, ed. Frederick Howard Dole (Auburn, Me., 1916), 12–14, 33–54.

They failed to prosper from the transformation of the industry after 1675 because, as their numbers rose, their labor grew cheap. This was felt in two important ways: first, through the less favorable terms that fishermen could negotiate with their employers; and, second, in the spread of under-employment throughout their community as a whole. Not only were al-most all of the productivity gains captured by the merchant class, but even the modestly higher earnings of individual fishermen now had to support a much greater number of dependents than had once been the case. The proximate cause of this underemployment was geographic immobility, but the deeper issue in these seaport communities was class. From the very beginnings of settlement the seafaringmen of Salem and Marblehead were the only important occupational group in Essex County to depend on others for access to the means of production. Necessarily, this involved their being both poor in property and cultural outsiders. Had they brought wealth with them or fit comfortably into the New England way, they would have set their sights westward and abandoned the sea before a fishery had ever become established. Rarely did anyone of means remain a career fisherman by choice. The full reality of these productive relations had been masked in the seventeenth century by a credit system that advanced them property on highly conditional terms. But with the credit crunch of 1675–1725, the qualified opportunities of the client fishery were crushed, and the class dependency of fishermen stood fully revealed. Without property, connections, or any real cultural claim on the colonial establishment, they lacked the power to escape their situation. For this reason, an industry that was a cornerstone in the economic development of Massachusetts benefited least those who labored within it.

COTTAGE FISHERMEN ON CAPE ANN

Throughout its first seventy-five years, the Essex County fishery had been based primarily in the seaport towns of Salem and Marblehead. The major new development of the eighteenth century was the rise to competing prominence of a cluster of semirural communities based roughly around the perimeter of Cape Ann. These included the three deep-sea ports of Beverly, Manchester, and Gloucester on the southern flank of the cape, as well as the villages of Sandy Bay, Pigeon Cove, Annisquam, and Chebacco, which stretched around its northern perimeter. Though fronting on the ocean, none had been seaports of importance in the seventeenth century, and their maritime histories were a matter of subsequent development.

The social history of what may loosely be termed the Cape Ann fishery followed, therefore, a course quite different from the pattern in the older ports of Salem and Marblehead.

The modest shallop fishery that Gloucester had harbored in the middle decades of the seventeenth century diminished after 1670, and most of the town's inhabitants turned to farming the cape's reluctant soils. The attractions of the marketplace did not die, however, and after 1690 commercial development began again: first in cutting timber for export to Boston and beyond; then after 1700 in the related business of shipbuilding; and finally, toward the end of Queen Anne's War, in the banks fishery.[78] The town's new fleet—constructed and outfitted by a crowd of local men who had been born into farming families and were only drawn into seafaring commerce in their adult years—boomed after the Peace of Utrecht. Nathaniel Sanders was the skipper of a local sloop that was handlining at Cape Sable as early as 1712, and by the 1720s a host of sloops and schooners, twenty to fifty tons in burden, were sailing from Gloucester harbor and Annisquam to the eastward every summer to follow the fishery. The British colonial authorities recorded that 49 Gloucester vessels manned by 245 men fished at Canso in the years 1721, 1723, and 1725—a higher total than any other port in Essex County.[79] In overall tonnage across the banks, the sum of local vessels was not the equal of the grander fleet at Marblehead; but by 1741 Gloucester was said to possess at least 70 schooners, and this made it the fastest-growing fishing port in New England. The next twenty years, rent by the wars with France, produced little new growth, but during the 1760s and 1770s the town boomed again. By 1775 on offshore banks and inshore waters there were nearly 150 vessels and 900 men hailing from the four different parishes of Gloucester.[80]

78. The history of Gloucester between 1670 and 1713 is well covered in Heyrman, *Commerce and Culture*, 42–59, although the fishery may have persisted after 1670 with slightly more vigor than she allows. See *Essex Co. Court Recs.*, VI, 401–402; and Lane v. Tucker (1699), Box 5, Miscellaneous Papers (1709), Box 12, Files ICCP.

79. Salem had 39 vessels manned by 213 men, and Marblehead had 36 vessels manned by 210 men. See List of Vessels at Canso, 1721, C.O. 217/4, 44, List of Vessels at Canso, 1723, C.O. 217/4, 299–301, List of Vessels at Canso, 1725, C.O. 217/4, 287.

80. Heyrman, *Commerce and Culture*, 59–65; Stover v. Sanders (1713), Box 14, Cogswell v. Denning (1717), Box 17, Smith v. Eveleth (1735), Box 62, Files ICCP; Babson, *History of Gloucester*, 379–381; McFarland, *History of New England Fisheries*, 81–88; "Vessels Employed in the Fishery in this Province," ca. 1763, Ezekiel Price Papers, 1754–1785; Jefferson, "Report on Fisheries," 223.

Ipswich, to the north of Cape Ann, began the century with much the same success. In 1721, 1723, and 1725, the records from Canso counted 29 vessels and 149 men—a banking fleet close in size to those of its Essex County neighbors—and references to local fishermen continued to pepper the court records in considerable numbers until about 1735. Many of these men lived in Chebacco Parish next to the Gloucester line and probably dealt with the merchants on Cape Ann as often as they did with those in the town parish of Ipswich itself. After 1740, however, the local fishery failed to develop further. The schooner fleet had already peaked and numbered no more than a dozen at the end of the colonial period. Although at the outbreak of the Revolutionary War 43 boats moored mainly in the Chebacco River were still working the inshore waters, Ipswich was plainly now a port of the second rank.[81]

Later to launch its fishery but just as enterprising in the end was the town of Beverly. Although numerous fishermen had been making homes there since the seventeenth century, they had usually shipped out of neighboring Salem. There were few fish merchants in town before the Seven Years' War, and references to local vessels from that period are extremely scarce. In 1762, however, 9 local vessels were splitting their time between the fishery and the export trade; by 1772, the Cabots, Thorndikes, Lovetts, and Obers, who now composed Beverly's own merchant class, employed 30 schooners on the banks; and by 1775 the fleet counted 35. When war broke out in April of that year, 300 fishermen—most of the young men in town—were off at sea.[82]

81. On Ipswich's presence in the Canso fishery, see n. 79, above. See also March v. Perkins (1697), Box 4, Lane v. Hossam (1699), Box 5, Perkins v. Robes (1702), Box 7, Johnson v. Standley (1717), March v. Harris (1718), Box 18, Webber v. Holmes (1720), Pearson v. Maybee (1720), Box 22, Brown v. Ringe (1722), Box 27, Wood v. Carter (1729), Box 45, Smith v. Eveleth (1735), Box 62, Files ICCP; Arlin Ira Ginsburg, "Ipswich, Massachusetts during the American Revolution, 1763–1791" (Ph.D. diss., University of California, Riverside, 1972), 129n; Jefferson, "Report on Fisheries," 223; A. Howard Clarke, "Historical References to the Fisheries of New England," in George Brown Goode, ed., *A Geographical Review of the Fisheries Industries and Fishing Communities for the Year 1880* (section II of Goode, ed., *Fisheries*), 685–686. Many of the skippers on Ipswich vessels at Canso in the 1720s bore surnames common in Chebacco Parish. See also the Colonial Office sources in n. 79.

82. Clarke, "Historical References," in Goode, ed., *Geographical Review*, 689–690; "State of the Fishery in this Province," 1762, Ezekiel Price Papers, 1754–1785; Octavius T. Howe, "Beverly Privateers in the American Revolution," Col. Soc. Mass., *Pubs.*, XXIV (1920–1922), 318–322; Jefferson, "Report on Fisheries," 223; Douglas Lamar Jones, *Vil-*

By 1775, the combined fleets of the different towns that clustered around Cape Ann numbered nearly 250 vessels. Many were on the small side, including a host of little boats that worked the waters inshore, and in tonnage and output none of these ports could rival Marblehead. By the outbreak of the Revolutionary War, however, close to 1,500 men from this cluster of communities—more than half of the male working population—were spending part of the year hauling their lines at sea.[83]

The fishing routine followed in these towns was similar in character to that prosecuted by the larger seaports of Marblehead and Salem. Cod was its object, and although some fish was jigged from boats along the coast, the bulk was landed in sizable schooners, fishing on extended voyages to the banks. In the recruitment of its labor force, however, the Cape Ann fishery followed a very different pattern. Marblehead and Salem had always depended on professional fishermen, recruited initially in a North Atlantic labor market and then increasingly among resident New Englanders. By the middle of the eighteenth century, most seaport fishermen had been born into property-poor fishing families, bred to the seafaring life, and were supported in large part by their mariner offspring when they retired. The Cape Ann bankers, by contrast, drew their hands from other sources and by a different logic. William Bentley observed at the beginning of the nineteenth century that the fishermen of Beverly and Manchester "have the mixed life of the seamen, fishermen, artizans, & farmers, & have all the shades of character the various strength of their habits admit." Twenty years earlier, George Grieve had noted that the typical seaman in Ipswich "when on shore immediately applies himself to some handicraft occupation, or to husbandry, and is always ready at a moment's warning to accompany the captain his neighbor, who is likewise frequently a mechanic, to the fisheries." Indeed, this situation had existed

---

lage and Seaport: Migration and Society in Eighteenth-Century Massachusetts (Hanover, N.H., 1981), 17. A single vessel from Beverly fished at Canso between 1721 and 1725. See n. 79.

83. Jefferson, "Report on Fisheries," 223. The claim that half of the male working population were fishermen is based on the following: the reported total of 1,500 fishermen (see *ibid.*, 223); a combined population for Beverly, Manchester, Gloucester, and Ipswich of about 12,000 (see Greene and Harrington, *American Population before 1790*, 23–24, 31–32); the assumption that men accounted for no more than 55% of the population of these towns (see U.S. Dept. of State, *Return of the Whole Number of Persons*, 8); and an estimate that those aged 15–45—i.e., the male working population—accounted for about 40% of all males in these communities (see *ibid.*).

since the beginning of the eighteenth century across the entire cape, for the fishermen there were not, as in Marblehead, drawn from a class of urban maritime laborers. The fishery developed in these newer ports chiefly as an appendage to the rural economy—a cottage industry, as it were, designed to keep diversified family economies viable in the face of population growth.[84]

The men who first organized the Cape Ann fishery after 1700 were not immigrant merchants but resident husbandmen, craftsmen, and mariners. Most had grown up on farms and accumulated the bulk of their capital through their own and their families' labors. Cutting timber, building boats, fishing along the coast, and trading to and from Boston and Salem in vessels they manned themselves, men like Andrew Robinson, Elias Davis, and the Parsons brothers assembled small fleets of twenty- to forty-ton sloops and schooners that they employed on voyages to Canso and beyond.[85] By 1720, however, most budding fish dealers had withdrawn from active seafaring. Once in the business of outfitting voyages and marketing fish, they found they could ill afford to be off at sea and out of touch with the commercial world in which they earned their profits. In any case, it was certainly not the thought of spending summers toiling in the offshore mists for a meager return that had first drawn them into the fishery. A career on the banks was as unattractive to men of means on Cape Ann as to those elsewhere in Massachusetts, and these new entrepreneurs soon preferred to stay at home and mind the store.[86]

Whom then did they hire to crew their vessels? Some of the early recruits were recent newcomers: either refugees, driven out of frontier settlements on the coast of Maine by the threat of Indian attack, or professional mariners drawn from other port towns of New England and even

84. Bentley, *Diary*, IV, 486; Marquis de Chastellux, *Travels in North America in the Years 1780, 1781, and 1782*, ed. Howard C. Rice, Jr., 2 vols. (Chapel Hill, N.C., 1963), II, 627. Grieve visited Essex County at the end of the Revolutionary War, and his observation is contained in a note he appended to his translation of Chastellux at a point in the text where the marquis was passing through Ipswich and observing how easily, during the war, the fishermen had "turned farmers." See *ibid.*, 493.

85. Heyrman, *Commerce and Culture*, 62–64; Babson, *History of Gloucester*, 249–253, 379n. See also n. 79, above.

86. In the Canso fishery of 1721, 1723, and 1725, 88% of Gloucester vessels ($N = 49$) were owned by someone other than the skipper; for Ipswich the equivalent figure was 72% ($N = 29$). Conversely, of 19 Gloucester residents who owned vessels at Canso in those years, only 6 are recorded as having also served as skippers, and none of them owned more than one vessel. See n. 79, above.

from foreign parts by the prospect of employment.[87] A few, like James Farnham "of Boston," lost on the voyage home from Cape Sable in 1716, and Stephen Burns, "drowned at the eastward" in 1718, were merely sojourners who left no further local imprint beyond the record of their employment. More common were those who came to fish but then took up residence in town. Samuel Fleming moved to Gloucester with his wife, Janet, sometime after 1711; when he "drowned on the banks, fishing" in 1730, the two of them had been living with their children in a small house on several acres of land. With a pair of cattle and a pig housed in their barn, and three thousand feet of boards and ship timber stacked elsewhere on their land, theirs was obviously a diversified household. William Coas was a recently arrived English mariner and skipper of the *Greyhound* when he married Mary Gardner in 1723 and settled in a home on the 6-acre lot that he inhabited the rest of his life.[88]

Close to 40 percent of these recent arrivals—a striking proportion—served as skippers and directed the craft on which they worked.[89] This reversed the common pattern in other seafaring industries of the day, where relatives and others with tight personal connections were more likely than newcomers to obtain the mastership of vessels.[90] Probably

87. Of 28 Gloucester fishermen identified from Boxes 1–47, Files ICCP, for the period 1705–1730, 26% had not been resident in the town in 1704. Residence in town as of 1704 was determined from Babson, *History of Gloucester*, 236–237. See also Heyrman, *Commerce and Culture*, 55–57.

88. For Farnham and Burns, see Babson, *History of Gloucester*, 261n, 272n. For Fleming, see *ibid.*, 261n; and Estate of Samuel Fleming (1730), Probate No. 5953, Essex Co. Prob. Recs. For William Coas, see Babson, *History of Gloucester*, 285; List of Vessels at Canso, 1723, C.O. 217/4, 299–301, List of Vessels at Canso, 1725, C.O. 217/4, 287; and Estate of William Coos (1764), Probate No. 6341, Essex Co. Prob. Recs.

89. The reasoning here is as follows. From the sources in n. 87 above, we know that 26% of all Gloucester fishermen in 1705–1730 were recent immigrants (nonresidents in 1704). From the sources in n. 79 and Babson, *History of Gloucester*, 236–237, we also know that 49% of Gloucester skippers at Canso between 1721 and 1725 (N = 35) were immigrants (nonresidents in 1704). In a hypothetical fleet of 20 schooners manned by 100 hands, therefore, newcomers would have accounted for 26 of the crew members and 10 of the skippers, whereas 74 of the crew members and 10 of the skippers would have been locally born. Skippers thus would have comprised 38% of those who had arrived since 1704 and only 14% of those who had been resident before.

90. Ralph Davis, *The Rise of the English Shipping Industry in the Seventeenth and Eighteenth Centuries* (London, 1962), 159–160; Daniel Vickers, "Nantucket Whalemen in the Deep-Sea Fishery: The Changing Anatomy of an Early American Labor Force," *Journal of American History*, LXXII (1985), 284.

merchants ventured less in a relatively short fishing fare than they did in a commercial voyage or a whaling trip, and the need for trustworthy agents to handle their affairs was correspondingly smaller. More to the point in Gloucester, however, was the local shortage in expertise. Since the great majority of local families had earned their living from the soil and the forest, or from training in some craft, the town had no maritime tradition equal to the task of directing the new vessels. The rising group of merchant outfitters had to be on the lookout for potential skippers, which more than any other factor explains the rapid influx of settlers during these decades.[91]

Like the early fishery in Marblehead and Salem, therefore, the Cape Ann fishery depended on professional outsiders for much of its skilled help. Where the cape fishery differed from that of the larger ports was in the degree to which it recruited ordinary hands from among local families that had never been involved in the fishery before. Just over half of the fishermen who sailed out of Gloucester and Ipswich between 1705 and 1730 were born in town, and most of them were descended from the earliest settlers. These families had obtained property in the seventeenth century and managed for two or three generations to provide their children with tracts of farmland and to settle most of them in landward callings. As decade followed decade throughout the colonial period, the land around Cape Ann was granted out and subdivided until most of the local clans no longer possessed enough property to keep their children profitably employed at home. The pace at which this happened varied from family to family, depending on enterprise, demography, and luck; but increasingly, the sons of farmers and craftsmen took to the sea.[92]

For the most part, the first generation of native-born fishermen varied little in origin from the vessel owners who employed them. John Davis, Jr., for example, grew up on a sizable farm near Lobster Cove on the north

91. Heyrman, *Commerce and Culture*, 55–57; Babson, *History of Gloucester*, 239–300, but esp. 259–261.

92. Of the 53 fishermen who sailed out of Ipswich or Gloucester between 1705 and 1730 and who were identified from the sources in Appendix 3, 28 were born in their home port. The diminishing availability of land in eastern Massachusetts during the middle decades of the 18th century is described in Philip J. Greven, Jr., *Four Generations: Population, Land, and Family in Colonial Andover, Massachusetts* (Ithaca, N.Y., 1970), 125–130, 222–227; Kenneth A. Lockridge, *A New England Town, the First Hundred Years: Dedham, Massachusetts, 1636–1736* (New York, 1970), 147–151; and Robert A. Gross, *The Minutemen and Their World* (New York, 1976), 77–78.

side of Cape Ann. In 1716 he was in his mid-twenties and recently married when the sloop he skippered went down in an autumn gale off Cape Sable. Another casualty of that storm was Jeremiah Allen—son of Gloucester's first blacksmith, younger brother of a prominent fish merchant, and but eighteen years of age. Of nine fishermen from the period 1705–1730 whose fathers can be traced to the Gloucester tax list of 1693, six belonged to families whose wealth exceeded the town median. What distinguished them from their neighbors was their youth. Out of eighteen ordinary hands who were locally born and whose date of birth could be determined, sixteen were in their teens and twenties; even among skippers, who tended to be senior to their mates, eight of eleven were under thirty years of age.[93]

Although we cannot know how long the youths of the cape communities planned to stick at the fishery, the logic of their situation and the data presented here suggest that they intended it to be only a stage in life. Voyages to the banks were just as wearing on them as on their contemporaries from Marblehead and Salem, and as soon as they could amass some kind of stake, either by acquisition or inheritance, they probably expected to quit the sea for good. As it was, neither the families they sprang from nor those they founded depended entirely on their earnings. As long as these young fishermen or their fathers owned several acres of tillage and pasture, some livestock, a woodlot, and perhaps a little boat to take winter fishing along the shore, the deep-sea schooner fishery would never be their sole support in the way that it was for the professional fishermen of Marblehead and Salem. With streams where shad and alewives ran annually, nearby marshes in which to cut hay, woods full of berries and small game, and mud flats on which to go clamming, families in these smaller towns could practice a more diversified economy than was possible in the larger ports. For young men raised in such a world, fishing was part of a wider household strategy—a decision to exchange underemployment at

93. For the data on fishermen, see Appendix 3. The skippers referred to were those on Gloucester vessels that fished at Canso in 1721, 1723, and 1725. See the sources in n. 79 and Appendix 3. The 1693 Gloucester tax list was published in Babson, *History of Gloucester*, 213–214. For additional information on John Davis, Jr., see *ibid.*, 76–77, and on Jeremiah Allen, see *ibid.*, 55–56. For Ipswich, the number of identifiable fishermen and the available data on wealth are much thinner, but the number of young fishermen with such family names as Cross, Hovey, Knowlton, and Marshall speaks to a pattern much like that of Gloucester.

home for wages abroad during a time in their lives when dependency was culturally tolerable. Rather than a permanent calling, it was a temporary device to bring in income for the family and to help assemble the patrimony that they hoped would allow them someday to construct independent homesteads. Few ever attained any real competency; the returns from the sea were too meager. But a house and barn with several animals on a few acres of land were not beyond reach, and the fishermen of these early years often managed to move into a brand of hardscrabble farming when they retired from the banks.[94]

As the eighteenth century progressed, however, many Cape Ann families saw the prospect of propertied independence recede even farther. Nowhere is this better illustrated than in the experience of the Ober family. Richard Ober was an enterprising mariner who settled in Beverly in 1669 and became a prosperous shoreman with an estate worth about £470 sterling at his death. This was enough property to enable most of his sons and grandsons to set up in landward trades in town or to migrate westward into central Massachusetts and New Hampshire. In the fourth generation, however, the Obers still living in Beverly returned to maritime work. The pressure of family members against available land resources provided the impetus, and the rapid expansion of the town's fishery after 1765 absorbed it. Captain Benjamin of the third generation had always been a fisherman, so it was no surprise to find his three sons—Francis, Richard, and Samuel—fishing in 1770 on a schooner owned by Joseph Cabot. Five of their cousins, however, also went to the banks in the 1770s, none of whom hailed from seafaring families. Andrew, John, and Hezekiah were born on a farm; Nicholas's father was a weaver; and Richard was a shoemaker's son. All of their parents possessed some productive property, but never enough to employ or settle a houseful of growing children. William Ober, the weaver, had a farm of 20 acres to portion out among his three children, and poor Thomas Ober, the farmer, lived in half a house on only 12 acres of land attempting to raise a family of eleven.

94. For some representative inventories, see Estate of Samuel Fleming (1730), Probate No. 5953, Estate of Richard Rindge (1731), Probate No. 23728, Estate of John Lane (1724), Probate No. 16317, Estate of John Millett (1730), Probate No. 18458, Estate of Charles Byles (1782), Probate No. 4417, Estate of Broster Emmerson (1728), Probate No. 8886, Estate of Jeremiah Foster (1769), Probate No. 9888, Estate of Abraham Robinson, Jr. (1725), Probate No. 23867, and Estate of James Sayward (1737), Probate No. 24929, Essex Co. Prob. Recs. Fishermen were identified from sources in Appendix 3.

These young Obers all came from families whose claim to independence was shaky at best, and they were typical of a class of cottage-fishermen that was emerging around the cape.[95]

Many fishing hands on the Cape Ann bankers of the late colonial period were no older than the Ober boys; with the fishery booming after the Seven Years' War, vessel owners normally rounded out their crews with a number of teenagers. This is why the proportion of younger men in the fishery seems so striking (see table 8). The same data suggest, however, that although most schooners were crewed by men in their teens and twenties, a good number of fishermen were now extending their seafaring lives into their thirties and forties. Particularly in the more established ports of Gloucester and Ipswich, the banks fishery was evolving from a stage of life into a career.

A concrete instance of this development is the story of Aaron Burnham. Born in 1743, he was the youngest surviving son of Jeremiah Burnham, a moderately prosperous farmer with 40 acres and part of a sawmill in Chebacco Parish. As a young man in the 1760s Aaron worked on the banks with his older brother Joshua, a master mariner who divided his time between the fishery and the coasting trades. In 1766 Aaron married and by 1771 had acquired a little house with half an acre of pasture. This was scarcely enough to support a growing family, however, and so he stuck to the fishery into middle age. During the Revolutionary War his older brother gave up the schooner trades, and Aaron and Joshua worked the inshore waters together on shares in a boat belonging to the Gloucester merchant Daniel Rogers. When Aaron drowned in 1782 at the mouth of the Chebacco River—a year short of forty, a time in life when most rural New Englanders had achieved some degree of landed independence—he had made little headway. His property in household amenities did not amount to much more than that owned by seaport fishing families in Marblehead—a room full of assorted furniture, a change of clothing, and

95. Katherine F. Loring and Mary Toomey, "Genealogy of the Ober Family" (1942), typescript at the JDPL; Estates of Andrew, Thomas, and William Ober, Probate Nos. 19901, 19958, 19959, Essex Co. Prob. Recs. The fathers of the Ober sons who fished for Thomas Davis and Joseph Cabot between 1769 and 1775 ranked in the two middle quartiles of the 1772 tax list for Beverly. See Beverly Tax List, 1772, Tax and Valuation Lists of Massachusetts Towns before 1776, roll 10. See also Vickers, "Nantucket Whalemen in the Deep-Sea Fishery," *JAH*, LXXII (1985), 286–296; and Fred Anderson, *A People's Army: Massachusetts Soldiers and Society in the Seven Years' War* (Chapel Hill, N.C., 1984), 28–39.

Table 8. Age Distribution of Fishermen Employed by Beverly
and Gloucester Merchants, 1767–1775 (in Percents)

Age	J. Stevens Gloucester 1767–1773 ($N = 41$)	D. Rogers Gloucester 1769–1775 ($N = 90$)	T. Davis Beverly 1770–1774 ($N = 58$)
10–19	20	28	29
20–29	39	47	50
30–39	6	25	21
40–49	16	0	0
50–59	19	0	0
60–69	0	0	0
70+	0	0	0

Note: Since the data used to calculate the above percentages were drawn from account books, the results had to be adjusted to deal with biases introduced by the difficulty of linking adult fishermen to birth records when no other family members are listed in the account.

Sources: See Appendix 3.

his wife's cooking utensils. True, he owned the cottage his family lived in, and they were able to keep a cow and six sheep besides, but all of this had been financed on credit. When the dust settled, Aaron's estate proved insolvent and had to be sold.[96]

Not all cape fishermen possessed as little as Aaron Burnham, but among the forty-one who could be traced to the provincial valuation list of 1771, he was better off than most. Eleven of the others may have owned entire dwellings, but only four possessed any livestock, and his half-acre of pasture topped everyone.[97] Aaron was luckier than most in that his father,

96. Estate of Aaron Burnham, Probate No. 4055, Essex Co. Prob. Recs.; account of fish landed, fall fare, 1764, Joshua Burnham Papers, 1758–1817, Box 1, Folder 1; account of Aaron Burnham, Daniel Rogers Acct. Bk., 1770–1790; Roderick H. Burnham, *The Burnham Family; or Genealogical Records of the Descendants of the Four Emigrants of the Name, Who Were among the Early Settlers in America* (Hartford, Conn., 1869), 334–335; Pruitt, ed., *Massachusetts Tax Valuation List of 1771*, 78–79; Jedrey, *World of John Cleaveland*, 58–70.

97. The differences between Aaron Burnham and other fishermen were not attributable to age, for Burnham was, at 28 years, exactly on the median for those whose ages could be

Jeremiah—assessed in 1771 for a house, a share in a sawmill, a horse, two cattle, four swine, a small orchard, and 42 acres of land—was a man of some competency. Of the twenty-five other fishermen's fathers who could be traced to the 1771 list, only one possessed wealth of this kind. More typical of the households that spawned fishermen was that of Stephen Bennett, whose three teenage sons worked for the merchant John Stevens between 1768 and 1770. When the elder Bennett was assessed in 1771, he owned only a house in Gloucester with 3 acres of pasture plus a cow, a horse, and a pig; yet even these modest holdings placed him above the median in both real estate value and livestock ownership. Most of these families owned a small dwelling, perhaps one animal, and no pasturage. Few were entirely without property, but almost none could be termed independent.[98]

By the end of the colonial period, therefore, the communities on Cape Ann had arrived by their own path at a point where they, like Marblehead and Salem, possessed a merchant class and an employable labor force. The merchants of Gloucester were neither as numerous nor as wealthy as those of the older seaports, but they nonetheless outfitted close to a thousand men a year in voyages to the banks.[99] Although the cottage fishermen of the cape still had a wider range of property and easier access to common resources than did their seaport counterparts, their families' welfare now depended minimally on their willingness to spend their youths at sea and increasingly on their capacity to last a working lifetime in the trade. This development occurred gradually throughout the eighteenth century—not at all like the experience of Marblehead and Salem, where imported class distinctions had preceded and made possible the establishment of a fishery. On Cape Ann class grew up from indigenous sources along with the fishery. Nevertheless, by 1775 the differences between the working populations of the two fisheries were diminishing.

---

calculated from the vital records ($N = 22$). See Appendix 3, but esp. Pruitt, ed., *Massachusetts Tax Valuation List of 1771*, 77–78.

98. Of the 25 fathers, 14 owned fewer than two animals and 16 owned no pasturage, but only 2 did not own houses. The median rental value of their real estate was less than £2 sterling. If the 5 wealthiest are excluded, none owned more than a house, 10 acres of pasturage, and three animals. See Appendix 3.

99. Compare the valuations of vessel tonnage and merchandise owned by residents of Gloucester, Salem, and Marblehead in 1771 in Pruitt, ed., *Massachusetts Tax Valuation List of 1771*, 48–67, 98–106, 130–155.

In the century from 1675 to 1775 the fishing communities along the North Shore of Massachusetts were transformed. The old inshore boat fishery had given way to the much larger and more productive offshore schooner fishery, and the patron-client relations that drove the inshore fishery had been supplanted by free market relations. The industry had spread, moreover, into a string of new towns around the perimeter of Cape Ann, where young men on small holdings, confronting the specter of underemployment at home, turned to fishing as a way of supplementing household production and assembling competencies that could support them through their adult years.

How are we to understand this complicated transformation? In part it was sparked by outside forces: the depression in fish prices after 1675 drove boat fishermen into insolvency and prompted fish merchants to reorganize the industry around larger and more efficient craft. Falling prices by themselves, however, are hardly the best recipe for development. Many other fisheries along the Atlantic coast have gone through equally difficult times without successfully reorganizing themselves in this manner. There was something different about New England: something that enabled it to gather the charge that the market eventually triggered.

This distinction rested on the fundamental character of the Bay Colony itself—from its very beginnings it possessed a complex and diversified economy, staffed with farmers and waterfront craftsmen who were capable of providing much of the victualing and tonnage that a resident fishery would require. In the seaport towns of the colony, a settled merchant class could use their capital and connections both to link the fishery to this local economic support and to market its produce overseas. No other fishing society in the northeast—Maine, Nova Scotia, Newfoundland, or the Gaspé—was blessed in its early years of development with the instant infrastructure of Massachusetts. Not only could fishermen reasonably settle there, but the business they generated was captured within the colony. Thus it was possible in Essex County for labor and capital to accumulate locally, for the easy availability of land to diminish, and ultimately for the industry to be transformed.

FARMERS

1 7 0 0 – 1 7 7 5

The farming economy of Essex County, unlike its fishing equivalent, experienced nothing during the colonial period that can legitimately be called
a transformation. No dramatic alterations in the markets farmers serviced,
no revolution in agricultural technique, no genuine Malthusian crisis
descended on coastal Massachusetts prior to 1775. Mixed family farming,
the division of labor by gender, and a patriarchal household structure
characterized the rural economy of the region up to the Revolution. Accordingly, the social relations that governed the working lives of men and
boys at the end of the colonial period remained recognizable adaptations
of those that the first generation of New Englanders had established in the
seventeenth century.

And yet it would be wrong to ignore the changes that did occur. For as
the colony matured—as manpower and farm capital accumulated in the
countryside and the supply of unimproved land diminished—the peculiar
ties of exaggerated interdependence that had once bound fathers and sons
together in the tasks of farm formation began to relax. With each passing
decade, as the frontier drifted northward and westward and the countryside behind it was simultaneously improved and subdivided, most

farmers discovered that they could no longer fully employ their sons at home. They slowly carved out an understanding that the path to competency might fairly involve boys in stints of youthful dependency *outside the family*.

This was change of a gradual and strictly measured sort. One cannot point, as with the fishery, to a given year when shifts in the market set local developments in motion. Certain changes discussed in the pages that follow began in the late seventeenth century; others held off until the early eighteenth century; some simply gathered intensity in a gradual fashion through the entire length of the colonial period; and nearly all of them struck different towns at different times. Indeed, the decision to begin this chapter in 1700 is intended mainly to distinguish the second half of the colonial period from the first. And yet it is clear that as the rural economy matured, farm boys realized that their pursuit of competency now dictated less time in farm labor under the paternal eye and more time in paid employment outside the home and often outside agriculture altogether. Although the working lives of male New Englanders were hardly reorganized wholesale during the later colonial period, such changes as we can measure did foreshadow in interesting ways the more revolutionary developments of the industrial century to come.

MARKETS AND PRODUCTION

During the first two hundred years of their history, farming households in Essex County flourished by providing for most of their own needs, swapping goods and services with their neighbors, and learning to deal with eyes open in a regional market. Although historians may pry apart these different spheres of economic activity for the purpose of analysis, early Americans never made such a distinction. Virtually all economic activity had both a personal dimension, which one would expect in a world where people dealt overwhelmingly with others they knew, and the potentially contractual quality inherent in commerce and the pursuit of competency.

Even the closest working relationships—those within the family that operated in normal circumstances by dictate and reciprocity—sometimes acquired a contractual character. John Coy, a householder, had two sons named Caleb and Matthew, who helped him run his little farm in Wenham during the 1720s. During Coy's lifetime, of course, nobody ever took the trouble to spell out the precise nature of the relationship he maintained with his sons. Years later their sister Sarah claimed that Caleb was a full partner to their father in his last years, that he did "Improve . . . John Coys farme to the halves and theay did allways devide what the farme did produce." A neighbor named Benjamin Knowlton, however, was equally certain that Caleb Coy had never shared in the running of the farm, "either by hire, or to the halves." When Knowlton worked for the Coy family, he claimed, it was always father John who had hired and paid him for his work. This lack of precision was not surprising, and nothing would have come of it had John not decided on his deathbed to disinherit Matthew because of his "many miscarriages, & Disobedient actions, Contemptuous abuses, & greivous affronts" and to pass the "Choisest of his Lands" to Caleb. Although bitter about receiving nothing for the years he had invested in the family estate, Matthew chose not to contest the will itself. Instead, the work that he had done out of filial duty he redesignated as wage labor on a farm co-owned by his father and brother; he then computed the value of his "Sundry Services" in an elaborate account and in 1738 sued his brother for £33 sterling in back pay. The jury rejected his argument, and Matthew Coy did not win his case, but the story underlines the potentially contractual character of even the tightest relationships.[1]

The same sort of ambiguity was evident in the lives of the well-to-do. Timothy Pickering owned a large farm on the southern outskirts of Salem and was as well situated to profit by production for sale as anybody in the colony. By his own efforts and with the help of servants and paid labor he bred and slaughtered cattle, swine, and sheep; grew a variety of small grains; cut hay; kept an apple orchard and ground cider; and raised vegetables in his garden. The commercial character of his operations was obvious. The quantities of beef, cider, wool, and hay that he sold about town—sometimes in wholesale lots—suggested as much. So, too, did his meticulous accounting, his familiarity with dealings in cash and written instruments with interest attached, and his frequent appearances in court. At the same time, however, Pickering produced much of what he needed himself and maintained a dense network of exchange with his neighbors—trading sides of beef for carting services, swapping hides for shoes, and pasturing cows and sheep in return for loads of dung. Embedded in his finances were frequent barter entries with no cash value ascribed—with Jonathan Pease in 1743, to take one example, for "making an Axeltree for which he is to Cart me 2 Loads Stones." Pickering's clearly commercial

1. Coy v. Coy (1738), Box 73, Files ICCP. The judgment can be found in the records of the July session, 1738, Inferior Court of Common Pleas, Docket Book, 1736–1740, JDPL.

interests were entwined with neighborly sensibilities, and the distinction between the two is so difficult to draw from his own records that it is hard to imagine he cared about it himself.[2]

This manner of farm operation together with the system of mixed husbandry upon which it rested was inherited from English tradition and given a peculiar American finish by the easy availability of unimproved land. It persisted in its essentials throughout New England until the middle of the nineteenth century, when rural people finally bowed to the pressures of competition from the western states and either converted to specialized market agriculture or quit farming altogether.[3] If the overall structure persisted, however, the balance of its component parts did not. Although most farms continued to be family operated, they altered their operations measurably in response both to market conditions around them and to the press of their own numbers against the land. By disassembling the complex of farm strategies—the interconnected system of home production, neighborly exchange, and market sale—we may consider the changes in each.[4]

In Essex County as elsewhere, full self-sufficiency was neither common nor especially desirable. The wide range of property holdings described in tax valuation lists and probated inventories as well as the diversity of skills within the rural population could have no other meaning. Deficits and surpluses in the different branches of household economy were a part of life.[5] Compare the farms of John Chaplin and Jeremiah Poor, both of whom

2. Timothy Pickering Account Book, 1732–1757, esp. accounts of Jonathan Pease, JDPL; Britton v. Pickering (1735), Box 64, Osgood v. Pickering (1737), Box 72, Pickering v. Shaw (1771), Box 146, Files ICCP; Sidney Perley, *The History of Salem, Massachusetts*, 3 vols. (Salem, Mass., 1924–1928), I, 420–421; Bettye Hobbs Pruitt, ed., *The Massachusetts Tax Valuation List of 1771* (Boston, 1978), 146–147.

3. The broad outline of this story is told most effectively by Howard S. Russell, *A Long, Deep Furrow: Three Centuries of Farming in New England*, abridged by Mark Lapping (Hanover, N.H., 1982).

4. The putative commercialization of rural New England has attracted a great deal of historical attention, and much effort has been spent in attempts to characterize the process and identify the period when the transformation is supposed to have taken place. The many contributions are cited and discussed in John J. McCusker and Russell R. Menard, *The Economy of British America, 1607–1789* (Chapel Hill, N.C., 1985), chap. 14; Allan Kulikoff, *The Agrarian Origins of American Capitalism* (Charlottesville, Va., 1992), chaps. 1, 2; and Winifred Barr Rothenberg, *From Market-Places to a Market Economy: The Transformation of Rural Massachusetts, 1750–1850* (Chicago, 1992), chaps. 1, 2.

5. Bettye Hobbs Pruitt presents this position in "Self-sufficiency and the Agricultural Economy of Eighteenth-Century Massachusetts," *WMQ*, 3d Ser., XLI (1984), 333–364.

lived in Rowley and died in 1774. Undoubtedly the wealthier of the two, Chaplin owned a larger herd of cattle, more than double the pasturage, half a cider mill, a cheese press, and a greater variety of farm implements, which Poor may have borrowed from time to time. For his own part, however, Poor had a set of looms with "warping Bars & reeds" more impressive than Chaplin's; he seems to have raised wheat whereas Chaplin did not; and of the two only Poor owned a gun. Although both men possessed more property than most of their neighbors in Rowley, neither could claim to own everything he needed to provide all of his family's wants. Such comparisons could be multiplied by the hundreds, but they would all confirm the obvious truth that complete self-sufficiency was unknown.[6]

If exchange was ubiquitous, however, its importance and character were by no means constant. Assuming that the network of exchange was determined in large part by the inability of households to provide everything for themselves, it follows that the intensity of that network was largely a function of inequality in specific property types. Farmers with sheep and pastureland but no orchard traded wool for cider; those with tillage land but no oxen traded grain for a plow and team; those poor in land of any sort traded labor for provisioning; and almost everyone tried to raise or fashion something for sale in town. Between the 1680s and 1771 the variation in property holdings from household to household was on the rise, and the network of exchange in which rural families were enmeshed must have deepened too (see table 9). In Salisbury, the only town in Essex County for which valuations from both centuries are available, the coefficients of variation among households rose dramatically for horses, oxen, cattle, and land acreage, remained stable for sheep, and fell only for swine. In considering the other four towns, one has to remember that the seventeenth-century set includes Newbury, where by regional standards property inequality was unusually high.[7] Even so, the same broad pattern of increasing variation among households held: the coefficients rose decidedly for horses, oxen, and sheep, stayed roughly level for

6. Alice Hanson Jones, *American Colonial Wealth: Documents and Methods*, 3 vols. (New York, 1977), II, 630–633, 780–782. Chaplin's estate was assessed with a rental value of £8.1 sterling, Poor's for £6.6 sterling, in the tax valuation of 1771; the town median for Rowley was £5.6. See Pruitt, ed., *Massachusetts Tax Valuation List of 1771*, 122–123, 124–125.

7. David Grayson Allen, *In English Ways: The Movement of Societies and the Transferal of English Local Law and Custom to Massachusetts Bay in the Seventeenth Century* (Chapel Hill, N.C., 1981), 100.

Table 9. Variation Coefficients for Property Holdings by Household
in Selected Essex County Farming Villages, 1681-1771

	1680s			1771		
	Newbury	Topsfield	Salisbury	Salisbury	Rowley	Wenham
Horses	89	68	96	181	97	101
Oxen	103	84	115	179	192	119
Cattle	100	54	62	100	76	88
Sheep	105	119	140	135	118	134
Swine	103	105	146	95	93	92
Acreage	133	88	89	121	109	106
No. of households	220	58	75	330	321	101

Note: Variation coefficients are defined as (standard deviation/mean) × 100 for each type of property in each tax valuation. For a given type of property within a given town, the higher the coefficient, the greater the inequality between households (with zero providing a baseline of absolute equality).

Sources: "Taxes under Gov. Andros: Town Rate of Newbury, Mass., 1688," *New England Historical and Genealogical Register*, XXXII (1878), 156–164; "Taxes under Gov. Andros: Topsfield Town Rate, 1687," *NEHGR*, XXXV (1881), 34–35; George Francis Dow and Mary G. Thresher, eds., *Records and Files of the Quarterly Courts of Essex County, Massachusetts, 1636–1686*, 9 vols. (Salem, Mass., 1911–1975), VIII, 390–393; Bettye Hobbs Pruitt, ed., *The Massachusetts Tax Valuation List of 1771* (Boston, 1978), 120–131, 154–165.

cattle and acreage, and declined only for swine. Bearing in mind that the farmers of the eighteenth century were raising a greater variety of produce than their grandfathers had, especially from the garden and orchard, the problem of balancing the household economy—dealing off excesses and making up deficiencies—must have been growing in complexity.[8]

As even the swiftest pass through eighteenth-century farmers' and mer-

8. Because the coefficient of variation is a function of the standard deviation, it is very sensitive to zero values for the variables concerned. And, in fact, the rising coefficients are mirrored in the rising percentages of households entirely lacking in the different types of property assessed. As is evident from tables 11 and 12, taxpayers without horses, oxen, cattle, sheep, or land were more common in 1771 than they had been 90 years before. On the growing diversity of farm production in eastern Massachusetts in the 18th century, see Sarah F. McMahon, "A Comfortable Subsistence: The Changing Composition of Diet in Rural New England, 1620–1840," *WMQ*, 3d Ser., XLII (1985), 26–65.

chants' accounts demonstrates, rural producers in Essex County coped with these growing imbalances both by going to market and by turning to neighbors. In relative importance commercial dealings beyond one's own community mattered least. The demand for farm produce both from markets overseas and from the seaport towns of the county was certainly rising fast enough. The booming sugar islands were swallowing up more cider, salt beef, and "Surranam horses" than ever, and many schooners from the North Shore made room for these provisions among the hogsheads of fish and the bundles of timber that actually paid for the voyages southward.[9] The seaports they sailed from were also growing in importance. Those that stretched along the coast between Salem and Gloucester probably counted less than 3,500 souls in 1690, but by 1765 their collective numbers had climbed to almost 16,000. In proportionate terms, their population had risen from 26 to 37 percent of the county's total. Counting Newburyport and the maritime population of Ipswich, one can safely estimate that at the opening of the Revolutionary War, nearly half of the households in Essex County had to purchase a significant quantity of the farm produce they consumed. By colonial standards Essex was an unusually urban county.[10]

But did local farmers actively respond to this opportunity? If, indeed, they had been successful in exploiting the commercial potential surrounding them, the composition and value of their farm property would have risen. Here the evidence is less than encouraging. Existing studies of farm wealth in rural New England do not cover Essex County and are not entirely consistent with one another, but they suggest limited per capita improvement in the second half of the colonial period, save in acreage cleared. In Hampshire County, Massachusetts, Terry Anderson found little improvement between 1700 and 1779 in per capita value of livestock holdings, standing crops, or farm tools; across the whole of southern New England, Gloria L. Main and Jackson T. Main found that the value of all physical capital climbed by just about .3 percent per annum between

9. The "Surranam horses" are mentioned in the accounts of Timothy Fuller, Timothy Orne Account Book, 1738–1753, Orne Family Papers, 1719–1899, JDPL; see also James G. Lydon, "North Shore Trade in the Early Eighteenth Century," *American Neptune*, XXVIII (1968), 267, 270; and Russell, *Long, Deep Furrow*, 58, 59, 64.

10. Evarts B. Greene and Virginia D. Harrington, *American Population before the Federal Census of 1790* (New York, 1932), xxiii, 20, 23–24; Max George Schumacher, "The Northern Farmer and His Markets during the Late Colonial Period" (Ph.D. diss., University of California, 1948), 106–109.

1695–1714 and 1765–1774. Only in the value and quantity of cleared land did New England farms mark any real improvement after 1700, and the full meaning of this—given the modest per capita gains in crop and animal output—remains unclear.[11] The land and livestock holdings reported in the tax valuation lists of Essex County record roughly the same pattern of limited intensive improvement (see table 10). Farmers possessed much more cleared land (especially pasturage) in 1771 than they had in the 1680s, but the number of animals they owned had barely increased. In Salisbury, only sheep had risen in importance during the century; horses, oxen, cattle, and swine were all failing to hold their own against the population of adult males. Data from the other towns suggest that elsewhere cattle may have fared better and sheep a little worse, but there is no evidence to suggest that the Essex County countryside could support more livestock per capita in 1771 than it had a century before. In all probability, the growth in acreage represented the addition of newly cleared marginal land to older but well-worked fields, which did not really boost agricultural productivity at all.[12]

Local farmers were probably raising no more for commercial sale at the end of the colonial period than they had a century before. This seems to have been especially true in the case of cereal crops, for although dealers in Salem, Marblehead, and Gloucester were always in the market for grain and flour to provision waterfront families and ships bound for abroad, they obtained comparatively little of it in the immediate hinterland. Owing in part to the spread of black stem rust after 1660, local farmers no longer grew much wheat, and large rural families rarely could spare for sale the corn and rye that had taken its place. Compared with the accounts that George Corwin had kept with his farm customers in the 1650s, which described a flourishing regional trade in all types of grain, those of seaport merchants in the later colonial period scarcely mention grain at all; most

11. Terry L. Anderson, "Economic Growth in Colonial New England: 'Statistical Renaissance,'" *JEH*, XXXIX (1979), 248–255; Gloria L. Main and Jackson T. Main, "Economic Growth and the Standard of Living in Southern New England, 1640–1774," *JEH*, XLVIII (1988), 35–36.

12. See Percy Wells Bidwell and John I. Falconer, *History of Agriculture in the Northern United States, 1620–1860* (Washington, D.C., 1925), 105–113; and Russell, *Long, Deep Furrow*, 82–89. Things may have improved toward the last quarter-century of the colonial period, as has been suggested in Robert A. Gross, "The Problem of Agricultural Crisis in Eighteenth-Century New England: Concord, Massachusetts as a Test Case" (paper presented at the annual meeting of the American Historical Association, Atlanta, Ga., 1975).

Table 10. Farm Property Holdings per Taxable Male in
Selected Essex County Farming Villages, 1681–1771

| | 1680s | | | 1771 | | |
	Newbury (N = 269)	Topsfield (N = 91)	Salisbury (N = 116)	Salisbury (N = 358)	Rowley (N = 269)	Wenham (N = 110)
Horses	1.0	.7	.9	.2	.8	.7
Oxen	1.3	1.3	1.0	.5	1.1	.9
Cattle[a]	2.5	2.3	2.1	1.5	3.0	2.4
Sheep	8.5	3.4	2.3	3.3	6.0	4.5
Swine	1.4	1.1	1.1	.8	1.3	1.1
Land acreage	13.5	10.3	5.6	15.3	30.0	22.0

[a]In the Newbury and Salisbury valuation lists of the 1680s cattle are divided into cows, three-year-olds, two-year-olds, and yearlings. In all the other lists, the assessors appear to have counted only grown cattle, so to preserve comparability, I included only "cows" from the Newbury and Salisbury 1680s lists.

Sources: "Taxes under Gov. Andros: Town Rate of Newbury, Mass., 1688," *New England Historical and Genealogical Register*, XXXII (1878), 156–164; "Taxes under Gov. Andros: Topsfield Town Rate, 1687," *NEHGR*, XXXV (1881), 34–35; George Francis Dow and Mary G. Thresher, eds., *Records and Files of the Quarterly Courts of Essex County, Massachusetts, 1636–1686*, 9 vols. (Salem, Mass., 1911–1975), VIII, 390–393; Bettye Hobbs Pruitt, ed., *The Massachusetts Tax Valuation List of 1771* (Boston, 1978), 120–131, 154–165.

of the bread consumed in the port towns now was made out of flour imported from the Middle Colonies and the Chesapeake.[13] Of course, the county had always been better suited to grazing than to tillage, and the increased emphasis on cattle, sheep, and pasturage represented a switch in strategy from arable to animal husbandry. But given that herds were growing little if any faster than the human population of the county's

13. McMahon, "Comfortable Subsistence," *WMQ*, 3d Ser., XLII (1985), 32–33; David C. Klingaman, "The Coastwise Trade of Colonial Massachusetts," Essex Institute, *Historical Collections*, CVIII (1972), 231, 232. Compare with Darrett B. Rutman, "Governor Winthrop's Garden Crop: The Significance of Agriculture in the Early Commerce of Massachusetts Bay," *WMQ*, 3d Ser., XX (1963), 396–415. None of the 18th-century account books listed in Appendixes 3 and 4 contained as much purchasing of Essex County grain as does the George Corwin Account Book, 1652–1655, Curwen Family Papers, 1641–1902, JDPL.

farming villages, it is hard to imagine much room for commercialization here either.

The timber that had once proved such a valuable by-product of the clearing process—especially boards, shingles, and barrel staves—also diminished in importance as the forests within the long-settled villages of Essex County were gradually cut back. Although builders and merchants in the lumber trades needed more wood than ever, they now found most of it in New Hampshire and along the coast of Maine. Woodlots were still common on local farms, and many householders chose to cut timber and sell it in town. Some of the wood was made into barrels used to ship produce overland. The 992 pounds of salt pork that Oliver Tenney sold to John Stevens in 1769 came in six casks that Daniel Rogers credited to the Rowley farmer's account. Other families in the countryside improved their winters by cutting cordwood and selling it in Marblehead and other towns where forested land no longer existed. Almost certainly, however, commercial lumbering meant less to the region as the colonial period progressed.[14]

Some of the land cleared of standing timber had been replanted in orchards, and cider in particular grew into importance as a commercial product during the eighteenth century. In the Merrimack Valley, farmers grew flaxseed for export to Ireland toward the end of the colonial period, although more was harvested upstream in New Hampshire than in the older towns that flanked the river as it flowed through Essex County. Vegetable production is impossible to measure quantitatively, but the variety of produce expanded somewhat during the eighteenth century. There is little indication of any import or export trade in garden produce, so local farmers probably held their own in this regard. Farmwives may have sent a greater proportion of their butter, cheese, and milk to market than they once had, though any significant development would have swelled the herds of cattle more obviously than was the case (see table 10).[15] Estimating commercial surpluses from the roughest estimates of

14. Charles F. Carroll, *The Timber Economy of Puritan New England* (Providence, R.I., 1973), 101; William Cronon, *Changes in the Land: Indians, Colonists, and the Ecology of New England* (New York, 1983), 117–122; accounts of Oliver Tenney, John Stevens Account Book, 1769–1775, JDPL. References to firewood are ubiquitous in all the 18th-century merchant account books cited in this chapter.

15. Russell, *Long, Deep Furrow*, 71–81; McMahon, "Comfortable Subsistence," *WMQ*, 3d Ser., XLII (1985), 38–43.

production is a risky business since most of this trade connected farmers with butchers, tanners, innkeepers, and carters or directly with customers—almost none of whom kept detailed records. In broad terms, however, it would seem that agriculture in Essex County was no more commercially productive at the end of the colonial period than it had been at the beginning.

If the trade was light in quantity, it was broad in the range of commodities and number of petty suppliers involved. Not only did the produce they bought—live animals, barreled meat, cider, firewood, hay, butter, fruit, vegetables, hides, tallow, and so forth—draw on nearly all branches of local agriculture, but the farmers they dealt with came from every rank in rural society.[16] Between 1769 and 1774, for example, the Gloucester merchants Daniel Rogers and John Stevens dealt with sixteen such customers, fourteen of whom could be traced to the valuation lists of Essex County towns in 1771. Although most possessed somewhat more wealth than the median for rural communities in the county as a whole, there were representatives from every quartile. Among the wealthiest was Oliver Tenney of Rowley. His farm of 53 improved acres—stocked with a team of oxen, eight cattle, twelve sheep, and three swine—had to support a sizable family but was an impressive holding nonetheless and placed him well within the wealthiest quartile of householders at home. Timothy Jackman, who took Stevens and Rogers several cartloads of pork, cider, and peas, owned two oxen, two cattle, ten sheep, and two swine on 29 acres in Rowley—holdings that placed him fairly close to the town median. By contrast, Jonathan Storey of Chebacco, who brought hay and potatoes to Gloucester from a 20-acre farm with no animals, was hardly better off than most cottage fishermen. Although Storey's accounts occupied less space than Jackman's or Tenney's, for he had less to sell, the modesty of his estate did not bar him from the market. Indeed, the range of this business was broad enough to include almost every propertied

16. For some representative evidence on the wide variety of produce, see accounts of Thomas Holt, Jr., of Andover, Daniel Clarke and Jacob Robinson of Topsfield, and Thomas Gage of Rowley, in Timothy Orne Acct. Bk., 1738–1753; accounts of Samuel Procter of Gloucester and Jonathan Storey of Chebacco in Daniel Rogers Account Book, 1770–1790, JDPL; accounts of Enoch Haskell and William Parsons, Jr., in John Stevens Acct. Bk., 1769–1775; and Emerson v. Emerson (1719), Box 22, Webber v. Wallis (1721), Box 27, Webster v. Morse (1767), Box 138, Files ICCP. A good general discussion of the markets for agricultural produce can be found in Schumacher, "Northern Farmer and His Markets."

householder and nearly every type of farm produce to be found in the county.[17]

Some of these relationships turned sour and bred lawsuits that found their way into the court of common pleas. But although many cases pitted farmers against the merchants, traders, shopkeepers, innkeepers, and victuallers with whom they must have dealt commercially, court writs suggest a pattern of litigated indebtedness that did not change much over time. The proportion of all rural litigation that involved these dealers ranged from 22 percent between 1665 and 1673, to 28 percent between 1715 and 1723, to 26 percent between 1765 and 1773. In absolute terms, the sums under litigation dropped from a mean of £19 sterling during the first of these periods to £7 sterling in the second and climbed back up to £16 sterling by the third, but this was true of all litigated debt in Essex County, not just that which set merchants against farmers.[18] As a pattern, it had more to do with the currency depreciation that afflicted Massachusetts between 1670 and 1750 and the stabilization thereafter than with any changes in the network of exchange.[19] Relative to the median

17. For Rogers's and Stevens's 14 customers, the median acreage was 30.5 and the median cattle holding was 4. These individuals were identified from Daniel Rogers Acct. Bk., 1770–1790, and John Stevens Acct. Bk., 1769–1775, and their property holdings as of 1771 were then culled from Pruitt, ed., *Massachusetts Tax Valuation List of 1771*. For my estimation of town medians, see the discussion of the 1771 list in Appendix 4.

18. These figures were calculated from three samples of litigation before the Essex County Inferior Court of Common Pleas: 1665–1673 (235 cases); 1715–1723 (227 cases); and 1765–1773 (452 cases). The data were culled from writs in *Essex Co. Court Recs., Verbatim Transcriptions*, X–XX; and Boxes 16–20, 22, 26, 28, 128, 131, 144–147, 150, Files ICCP. The towns of origin and occupations of the 18th-century litigants were recorded in the writs; equivalent data for the 17th century were determined from the sources in Appendixes 1 and 2. Rural litigants were defined as residents of towns with virtually no merchant presence: Amesbury, Andover, Boxford, Bradford, Haverhill, Lynn, Methuen, Middleton, Newbury, Rowley, Salisbury, Topsfield, and Wenham. Writs record the amount claimed by the plaintiff, not the amount awarded by the court. The latter better reflects the actual sum of the debt under litigation, but only the writs survive in quantity from the 17th century, so they were chosen to measure change over time.

19. In an otherwise exemplary study of legal relations in early Connecticut, Bruce H. Mann neglects currency depreciation as a factor prompting colonists to convert book debts into negotiable instruments. What he interprets as the commercialization of social relations within the region may actually have been largely a practical response to the inflation wrought by the fiscal problems of the colonial government. See his important work, *Neighbors and Strangers: Law and Community in Early Connecticut* (Chapel Hill, N.C., 1987), 30–41, 62–63, and reconsider his findings in light of the material on inflation in

litigated sums for rural communities as a whole, suits involving merchants neither rose nor sank significantly. One has to be cautious about generalizing on the basis of such heavily refracted evidence, but had the flow of commerce between country and town quickened measurably, one would expect the structure of litigated debt to have altered more substantially than it did.

Another index to intensified commercial dealings would be the parallel growth in rural shopkeeping—a form of mercantile specialization that only a greater volume of commerce could sustain. In fact, country stores were rarely part of the rural landscape of Essex County at any point in the colonial period, and their importance did not appreciate over time. According to the valuation lists of 1771, there were entire villages—Methuen, Middleton, and Wenham—composed of householders who possessed no assessable merchandise whatsoever. Rowley, being a larger town, had as many households as those three towns put together, but of its ten residents who owned some stock in trade, only one was assessed at more than £50 worth of merchandise (in Massachusetts currency). Lynn was bigger still, but only two men there were taxed as traders.[20] As litigants in lawsuits with their rural neighbors, village storekeepers were never numerous and probably became less so with the passage of time. Although our occupational data for the seventeenth century are not strong enough to allow comparisons across the whole colonial period, the evidence for the eighteenth century suggests that a minority of those with whom rural residents got entangled in debt litigation were village storekeepers: only 12 percent in 1715–1723 and a mere 7 percent in 1765–1773.[21]

Before claiming that regional commerce in agricultural produce was actually on the decline, one must consider the possibility that Essex County farmers disposed of their surpluses through channels that elude the types of measurement attempted here—they may have sold their cider to innkeepers, their cattle to butchers, and their produce at weekly markets or door to door. There is little evidence to suggest, however, that farmers were more integrated into regional and international markets at

Connecticut in Leslie V. Brock, *The Currency of the American Colonies, 1700–1764: A Study in Colonial Finance and Imperial Relations* (New York, 1975), 43–47.

20. Pruitt, ed., *Massachusetts Tax Valuation List of 1771*, 84–95, 106–115, 120–131, 160–165.

21. The "storekeepers" referred to here are those styled "merchant," "victualler," "trader," or "shopkeeper" in the writs contained in the litigation sample described in n. 18.

the end of the colonial period than they had been a hundred years before. And if it is true that county farms depended increasingly on exchange relations but not necessarily on those of long-distance trade, we can only conclude that they were now more integrated locally. Although this is essentially a piece of deduction, it obtains support from the simple growth over time in the surviving bulk of records that document it. Whereas no farm account books recording local exchange survive from before 1690, a significant number exist for the period thereafter. Possibly the earlier records disappeared—though in the fishing business they did not. It is at least as likely that eighteenth-century farmers actually did keep account books more frequently than their ancestors; with the rising complexity of neighborhood dealings they had more business of which to keep track.[22]

Records of debt litigation suggest the same pattern. In the seventeenth century, the obligations to which neighborly exchange gave rise rarely led to suits at law. Between 1665 and 1673, only 3 percent of all litigated debt within the county involved neighbors suing neighbors in the same or adjoining rural communities; the high amount of the mean litigated sum, £28 sterling, implies that the villagers of the day resorted to legal action only when the debts in question were considerable. By 1715–1723, however, the proportion of legal business involving debt between such neighbors had more than doubled to 8 percent, and the mean litigated sum had fallen to £10 sterling. By 1765–1773, 11 percent of all litigated debt pitted neighbors against one another, and on average £5 sterling was enough to bring disagreements into the courts.[23] Although the relative importance of farming towns within the county was falling slowly over time, rural debt litigation accounted for a growing proportion of court business up to the outbreak of the Revolution.[24]

The origin of these rural debt suits is often impossible to determine. All that remains in the files of most cases are writs and promissory notes, which are seldom specific about the context of the debts in question. The few files that actually describe the background to a case suggest that such

22. The account books in question are listed in Appendix 4.

23. Sums under litigation were drawn from writs. See sources and definition of "rural" in n. 18. See also David Thomas Konig, *Law and Society in Puritan Massachusetts: Essex County, 1629–1692* (Chapel Hill, N.C., 1979), 82–88.

24. As the percentage of the Essex County population resident in seaports rose, the proportion living in rural villages fell. See Greene and Harrington, *American Population before 1790*, 20, 23–24.

litigation usually sprang out of dealings quite within the traditional network of neighborly exchange: lending oxen, passing on parcels of timber, pitching in at harvest, and so on. The wealth holdings of rural litigants in 1771 as measured by town valuations show no consistent difference between creditors and debtors. Likewise, the median age of plaintiffs and defendants who could be traced to the vital records was thirty-nine.[25] Such a pattern is consistent with the broad and ubiquitous network of exchange that seems to have developed in the eighteenth century. In part, of course, the swell in litigation reflected the declining authority of town and church to arbitrate in interpersonal disputes and the growing preference among New Englanders for the formal resolution of disagreement that the courts provided.[26] Almost certainly, however, the rising propensity to turn to the courts arose also from changes in the pattern of exchange itself. We can only conclude, after combining this evidence with the rising variation in property holdings (see table 9), that the network of economic interdependence among rural households was growing in significance as the colonial period advanced.

Although the rural economy of Essex County retained many constant features throughout the colonial period, there were measurable elements of change. Farmers were markedly more immersed in exchange relations in the eighteenth century, but these were more local than regional or international in character. The Massachusetts countryside had always been integrated with the maritime economy of the coast, and this altered little. What was new about the farming villages beyond Salem and Gloucester was the degree to which they were integrated among themselves.

FATHERS AND SONS

"A man must lay upp for posterity," John Winthrop told his fellow passengers on their Atlantic crossing of 1630, "and he is worse than an

25. Mean rental value of real estate was £10.1 for debtors and £12.6 for creditors; debtors owned a mean of 2.8 cattle whereas creditors owned on average 3; and while debtors owned on average 1 oxen, creditors owned a mean of 1.2. The ages of only 20 debtors and 18 creditors could be determined, however. See Appendix 4.

26. Different variations on this argument are found in Konig, *Law and Society in Puritan Massachusetts*; William E. Nelson, *Dispute and Conflict Resolution in Plymouth County, Massachusetts, 1725–1825* (Chapel Hill, N.C., 1981); and Mann, *Neighbors and Strangers*.

Infidell that provideth not for his owne."[27] This understanding of work's purpose—so universal that it rarely had to be made explicit—arrived with the Puritans and governed daily life in rural New England until the age of industrialization. Parents toiled from sun to sun and managed the labor of their children in order to sustain their own households in comfortable independence and to settle their offspring in at least as competent circumstances as they themselves had inherited. What changed across the centuries in question were the strategies that families employed to obtain this end. During the seventeenth century, the first New Englanders had discovered that on the frontier the provision of land for families worked best when the generations combined in tighter bonds of interdependence. Fathers needed their sons at hand because help for hire in this fledgling colony was so scarce; sons agreed to work under paternal authority to the age of marriage and beyond, not because they enjoyed the bark of their fathers' commands, but because the risks of striking out on their own in an economy short of improved land and productive equipment were too great. Very gradually, however, the rise in population and the accumulation of productive wealth during the later colonial period undermined this system and forced New Englanders to readjust the workings of their households to the changing world. Although virtually all relationships within the family had to alter, of primary concern here are those that joined fathers to their sons.

Unfortunately, no single source of information on intrafamily relations as rich as the court files of the seventeenth century exists for the period after 1700. The court records themselves did not diminish in volume; they simply grew less descriptive. With the formalization of legal procedure, the wealth of personal testimony and book accounts that had once filled the court records gave way to a mountain of standardized documents that tell the historian very little about ordinary life.[28] There are new sources for the history of work in Essex County during the later colonial period—a few scattered diaries and a larger number of account books—but these were concerned more with matters between families than within them. Most of what we can say, therefore, about manpower within the farm

27. John Winthrop, "A Modell of Christian Charity" (1630), *Winthrop Papers*, 5 vols. (Boston, 1929–1947), II, 285.

28. This pattern seems to have been general to New England. See Mann, *Neighbors and Strangers*, chap. 1.

family and how it evolved after 1700 has to be pieced together from a variety of documents.

As in the seventeenth century, young boys made their first noteworthy contributions toward the farm economy at about the age of seven. That was the age of Joseph Stickney of Newbury when he and his older brother John were observed helping their father cut thatch and make it up into cocks. The "little boys" who fetched home Zaccheus Collins's barley in the summer of 1739 included Ezra, age ten, and probably Stephen, age six. Richard Sawyer of Salisbury was picking apples with his older brother and helping to plow his grandfather's fields when he was only nine.[29] By their early teens, most sons were pitching in on almost every chore. Abraham Foster, Jr., of Rowley was helping his father with the cart when he was nine, and his older brother Abner was plowing at twelve. More indepen- dent missions began about this time as well. Most of Zaccheus Collins's sons were working and even conducting simple family business by them- selves—grinding malt and carting it to town, for example, or driving cattle to market—by twelve years of age at the latest.[30] By their midteens boys usually knew their husbandry well enough that fathers could hire them out periodically to neighbors—often in teams of two or three supervised by the eldest.[31]

If working by parental command remained the norm for Essex County boys throughout their teens, the same youths began to carve out in their early twenties a novel measure of independence. In certain respects this was traditional enough; what changed in the eighteenth century was the swiftness with which it happened. True, some farms continued to operate as intergenerational partnerships. The Coy family of Wenham had mar- ried sons who continued to work "with and for" their father, and the court records are sprinkled with similar cases. When Jacob Willard of Salem was in his thirties he was "ordered" by his father to make hay every summer;

29. Lunt v. Stickney (1708), Box 11, Files ICCP; entry for Aug. 13, 1739, Zaccheus Collins Diary, 1726–1779, JDPL; accounts of Father Ordway and Reuben French, Josiah Sawyer Account Book, 1736–1793, JDPL.

30. Account of Asa Harriman, Abraham Foster Account Book, 1754–1772, JDPL; en- tries for May 19, 1735, Feb. 24, 1739, Apr. 23, 1744, Apr. 30, 1747, Zaccheus Collins Diary.

31. See, for example, Lunt v. Stickney (1708), Box 11, Files ICCP; accounts of Ephraim Carter and William Persons, Josiah Sawyer Acct. Bk., 1736–1793; account of David Norton and John Gerrish, Josiah French Account Book, 1763–1785, JDPL; account of Eleazar Giles, Robert Hale Account Book, 1723–, Beverly Historical Society, Beverly, Mass.

Samuel Moulton, also of Salem, though he had been married for ten years, reported in 1730 that he had been "employed" at mowing and raking by his father that summer.[32] The once-characteristic interdependence between generations had hardly been overturned. Still, there were changes afoot—almost all of which pointed toward the weakening of paternal control.

One change was the growing tendency of eighteenth-century youths to marry young. Through the end of the seventeenth century and a little beyond, mean age at first marriage for men in most of these rural communities had ranged from twenty-five to twenty-seven years. Beginning about 1730, however, men began marrying earlier, and by the end of the colonial period the mean had fallen by about two years. Fewer men were waiting to marry until their thirties, and more were finding spouses in their early twenties. Age at marriage is difficult to interpret, of course, for it is subject to many influences. Access to means of support is one factor to consider; another is the population balance between the sexes; still another is the values of the partners involved. In this case, any reasonable explanation of the change in Essex County must take account of the fact that age at first marriage began to fall during the middle decades of the eighteenth century on both sides of the Atlantic. Local conditions may have shaped the pattern of change in its particulars, but they could not have prompted it in general. Whatever the causes, these colonial youths were forming families of their own at an unprecedentedly early age.[33]

This squares with a second measure of independence: the faster pace

32. Moulton v. Mackentire (1730), Box 37, Osgood v. Pickering (1737), Box 72, Coy v. Coy (1738), Box 73, Files ICCP.

33. Philip J. Greven, Jr., *Four Generations: Population, Land, and Family in Colonial Andover, Massachusetts* (Ithaca, N.Y., 1970), 117–118, 206–207; Susan L. Norton, "Population Growth in Colonial America: A Study of Ipswich, Massachusetts," *Population Studies*, XXV (1971), 445; Douglas Lamar Jones, *Village and Seaport: Migration and Society in Eighteenth-Century Massachusetts* (Hanover, N.H., 1981), 72–73; Christopher M. Jedrey, *The World of John Cleaveland: Family and Community in Eighteenth-Century New England* (New York, 1979), 199, n. 39. That this was a general trend across New England is confirmed by the work of Daniel Scott Smith, "The Demographic History of Colonial New England," *JEH*, XXII (1972), 177, and Edward Byers, "Fertility Transition in a New England Commercial Center: Nantucket, Massachusetts, 1680–1840," *Journal of Interdisciplinary History*, XIII (1982), 24. That it also held in Europe is clear from E. A. Wrigley and R. S. Schofield, *The Population History of England, 1541–1871* (Cambridge, Mass., 1981), 255, and David Levine, *Reproducing Families: The Political Economy of English Population History* (Cambridge, 1987), 88–91.

with which young men in eighteenth-century Essex County were acquiring farm property. Combining valuation lists with model life tables developed for colonial Massachusetts, it is clear that by the eve of the Revolutionary War, young men, especially those in their early twenties, were measurably more likely to own something worth taxing (see table 11). The shift was not dramatic. Even holdings that caught the assessors' eyes rarely amounted to more than a small house or a couple of animals with a few acres on which to pasture them. Still, the basis for youthful independence was sufficient enough to persuade eighteenth-century town authorities to begin rating most young men for taxes on their own account before they reached the age of twenty-five.

Part of the reason for the more rapid acquisition of property by young people in the later colonial period was a parallel shift in the pattern by which fathers formally passed land and other property to their sons. Informal transfers of the sort that were not legally confirmed until the father's death persisted into the eighteenth century. Thus when John Wilkins of Salem Village died in 1724 and left his son, John, Jr., "the d[w]elling hous wher in he now lives," he indicated that some informal control over the family farm had already changed hands.[34] But the proportion of wills that referred to prior but unregistered transfers dwindled from 23 percent of those probated between 1630 and 1700 to only 7 percent of those probated between 1701 and 1775. Far more important now were transfers of property by deed. During the seventeenth century, only 2 percent of farm fathers had been willing before they died to convey the legally registered ownership of their lands to any of their sons; in the eighteenth century, a full 39 percent chose to grant full title to some paternal land to at least one son, usually within five years of his marriage.[35]

---

34. Estate of John Wilkins (1724), Probate No. 29900, Essex Co. Prob. Recs. For other examples, see Estate of Job Pillsbury (1716), Probate No. 21955, Estate of Walter Phillips (1733), Probate No. 21725, Estate of Timothy Holt (1758), Probate No. 13700, and Estate of Robert Adams (1773), Probate No. 300, Essex Co. Prob. Recs.

35. Testators constituted a random sample of farm householders whose wills survive in *Essex Co. Prob. Recs.*; Essex Co. Prob. Recs.; and Essex Deeds. For the period 1630–1700, $N = 52$, and for the period 1701–1775, $N = 59$. A file was constructed of all testators and the 285 sons mentioned in their wills; the dates of birth, marriage, and death then were collected for all fathers and sons; and finally the county deeds were searched for evidence of formally registered land transfers between the generations. Biographical material was assembled from the sources in Appendixes 1 and 4. For 27 sons of known age who were deeded land by their fathers, the median age was 28. For 24 whose marriage dates are known, 14 married within five years of the first-dated deed.

Table 11. Essex County Males with Taxable Farm Property
by Age Cohort, 1681–1771 (in Percents)

	Taxpayers	Cattle	Horses	Land	Houses	Sheep	Oxen
			17–20 Years				
1680s	1	0	1	0	0	0	0
1771	3	0	0	0	2	0	0
			21–24 Years				
1680s	16	6	7	6	6	5	3
1771	53	14	8	18	12	4	6
			25–28 Years				
1680s	40	36	32	21	23	24	20
1771	77	49	30	42	37	30	23
			29–32 Years				
1680s	72	63	62	53	49	33	43
1771	100	77	43	66	69	42	32
			33–36 Years				
1680s	100	93	85	84	79	67	57
1771	100	77	48	69	73	58	40
			37–60 Years				
1680s	100	96	84	95	90	85	68
1771	100	87	51	84	87	85	43

Note: As in table 1, these are percentages not of taxable householders, but of the
estimated total male population in each age group and, therefore, are intended to be
approximate. The male population in each group was estimated on the assumptions
(1) that all men aged 33 to 60 (1680s) and 29 to 60 (1771) were taxpayers; and (2) that
the life tables given in Robert Paul Thomas and Terry L. Anderson, "White Population,
Labor Force and Extensive Growth of the New England Economy in the Seventeenth
Century," *Journal of Economic History*, XXXIII (1973), 654, are roughly applicable to
rural communities in Essex County for the entire period 1681–1771. For confirmation
that life tables in rural New England did not change dramatically over this period, see

Table 11. (continued)

Jackson Turner Main, *Society and Economy in Colonial Connecticut* (Princeton, N.J., 1985), 15. These percentages should be understood as maxima, since obviously a few men aged 33 (1680s) or 29 (1771) and older were *not* taxpayers, who would raise the number in all age cohorts if they were included in the calculations of estimated men. There were 228 taxpaying householders aged 17 to 60 in the 1680s group and 476 such householders in the 1771 group. The data for the 1680s come from Salisbury (1681), Topsfield (1687), and Newbury (1688). The data for 1771 come from Salisbury, Rowley, and Wenham.

Sources: "Taxes under Gov. Andros: Town Rate of Newbury, Mass., 1688," *New England Historical and Genealogical Register*, XXXII (1878), 156–164; "Taxes under Gov. Andros: Topsfield Town Rate, 1687," *NEHGR*, XXXV (1881), 34–35; George Francis Dow and Mary G. Thresher, eds., *Records and Files of the Quarterly Courts of Essex County, Massachusetts, 1636–1686*, 9 vols. (Salem, Mass., 1911–1975), VIII, 390–393; Bettye Hobbs Pruitt, ed., *Massachusetts Tax Valuation List of 1771* (Boston, 1978), 120–131, 154–165. The ages of these taxpayers were determined from the sources in Appendixes 1 and 4.

This does not mean that most sons obtained land in this manner. Only about half the sons who lived to marriageable age had come into any recognized inheritance by the time their fathers died, and only a portion had a registered deed to prove it.[36] In 1723, the year of his marriage, young Ephraim Brown of Salisbury received a deed for a parcel of family land from his fifty-three-year-old father, but he was the only son to be so favored. Nathaniel had been married a decade before he received title to his land, and Daniel and William obtained nothing of the sort until their father died.[37] Ephraim's early inheritance was far from the universal rule, yet it marked the beginning of a new trend. Sons increasingly assumed

36. Of 82 sons from the sample of 18th-century testators and sons in n. 35 known to have married before their fathers' deaths, 42 came into property—by deed or by simple possession confirmed in the will—when their fathers died. In some cases, young men purchased land from non-family members, but these were rare. Out of 73 Rowley taxpayers aged 20–29 in 1771, 42 were assessed for some real estate, and only 5 of these (Moses Scott, David Todd, Jonathan Pickard, Joseph Nelson, and Phineas Dodge) had purchased the property from non-family members through a legally recorded deed. See Pruitt, ed., *Massachusetts Tax Valuation List of 1771*, 120–131; and Essex Deeds, CXVII, 266, 267, CXXI, 104, CXXVII, 194, 272, CXXVIII, 35, 36, 216, CCXXIX, 33. Ages were determined from the sources in Appendix 4.

37. Estate of Ephraim Brown (1752), Probate No. 3550, Essex Co. Prob. Recs.; Essex Deeds, LIV, 232, LXXIV, 57, LXLVIII, 130, CXIX, 73.

practical and even legal responsibility for the lands they worked while their fathers were still alive.[38]

As adult householders, men pursued farm work with vigor—alone, in the company of kin and neighbors, and later with the help of their maturing sons—into their late forties. About that point (if the descriptions in diaries and court testimony constitute an accurate reflection of the labors in which adults actually engaged) they began, as in the seventeenth century, to gradually withdraw from physical work.[39] This was a relative matter, of course, and one finds scattered examples of older men—even in their early sixties—performing fairly heavy tasks. Henry Silsbee of Lynn, for example, was hauling and freighting hay as well as slaughtering animals for his in-laws in 1758 when he was sixty-three.[40] Most of his contemporaries, however, began to ease off from visible toil when their oldest sons reached their late teens. Naturally men did not cease to manage their property or the labors of their boys, nor did they stop going to market, arranging matters with their neighbors, and doing business for the town.[41] Lighter work around the house would not have placed these older men as much in the public eye but could still occupy a good part of the day. Nevertheless, the gradual retirement from farm work seems to have started about the time that fathers could confidently pass responsibility along to their boys.

This pattern of aging and retirement was rooted in a physiological reality that would have characterized the founding generation as well.

38. This is, of course, Greven's argument in *Four Generations*, chap. 8. Parallel evidence for 18th-century Connecticut can be found in Toby L. Ditz, *Property and Kinship: Inheritance in Early Connecticut, 1750–1820* (Princeton, N.J., 1986), 111–112.

39. The ratio of work performed by males aged 35–44 to those aged 45–54 was 3.2:1, whereas the equivalent ratio within the male population at large was only about 1.5:1. The ratio of work performed by males aged 25–44 to those 45 or older was 2.6:1, whereas the parallel ratio within the male population at large was merely 1.4:1. The data on work are based on 148 instances of adult males of known age performing farm work gathered from testimony contained in Boxes 6–150, Files ICCP, and in the Zaccheus Collins Diary, 1726–1779. The age estimates for the population at large are based on interpolations from Jackson Turner Main, *Society and Economy in Colonial Connecticut* (Princeton, N.J., 1985), 15, and on U.S. Department of State, *Return of the Whole Number of Persons within the Several Districts of the United States . . . 1800* (Washington, D.C., 1801), 8.

40. Entries for Oct. 11, 13, 16, Dec. 2, 1758, Zaccheus Collins Diary, 1726–1779.

41. For a careful analysis of an 18th-century New England farm father and his business, see Thomas C. Thompson, "The Life Course and Labor of a Colonial Farmer," *Historical New Hampshire*, XL (1985), 135–155.

What differed in the later colonial period was the frequency with which physical retirement was followed by the transmission of real and legal authority over the farm. The transfers of land from father to son by registered deed that were so novel to the eighteenth century generally happened when a father was in his fifties or sixties—around the time that his older sons were getting married.[42] Even in the large number of families that did not bother with formalities, older men were readier to part with effective control over their property at the end of the colonial period than in the seventeenth century. In the valuation lists of the 1680s, the mean landholdings of taxpayers tended to rise with each successive age cohort, peaking among those seventy years or older at 33 acres. In 1771, however, the same pattern persisted only until mean acreage topped out at 39 for men in their sixties and then plummeted by nearly half to 24 for those over seventy.[43] Livestock holdings followed much the same pattern. During the seventeenth century, men had been reluctant to give up their animals, but by 1771 rates of ownership had dropped off rapidly among the very old (see table 12). Horses and oxen, especially—working animals whose management was central to husbandry—in the eighteenth century were generally passed on by aging New Englanders to the young.

Before the Revolution, changes in the transmission of property between fathers and sons were gradual and incomplete. In no sense can they be said to have transformed the nature of household production. Without undermining patriarchal power in New England households, however, these changes did mark the gradual dissolution of the exaggerated interdependence between father and son that had prevailed when Essex County communities faced directly on the frontier. That relationship had depended on the authority of fathers to dispose of enough land that sons would be persuaded to delay their independence. Ultimately, that power had rested on control over undivided land resources, which most male householders, by virtue of being town proprietors, possessed.[44] When those resources began to diminish, fathers and sons moved away from the

42. Of 29 deeds from the will and deed sample for the period 1700–1775 in which the age of the father is known, 25 were drawn up when the father was 50–69 years old.

43. For sources, see table 12, below. The ages were determined from the sources in Appendixes 1 and 4.

44. A significant minority of residents in many 17th-century towns were not proprietors, but usually they did not constitute a majority. See John Frederick Martin, *Profits in the Wilderness: Entrepreneurship and the Founding of New England Towns in the Seventeenth Century* (Chapel Hill, N.C., 1991), 197–201.

Table 12. Essex County Males Age Forty and Over with
Taxable Farm Property, 1681–1771 (in Percents)

	Taxpayers	Cattle	Horses	Land	Houses	Sheep	Oxen
			40–49 Years				
1680s	100	100	87	96	92	89	75
1771	100	88	50	86	88	65	44
			50–59 Years				
1680s	100	97	87	100	90	83	70
1771	100	91	57	89	91	69	45
			60–69 Years				
1680s	100	100	88	93	80	82	69
1771	100	95	61	93	95	81	63
			70+ Years				
1680s	100	93	93	92	83	86	80
1771	100	75	38	88	83	60	28

Note: It was assumed that all those 40 years of age and older were taxpayers. Again, as in table 11, these percentages must be understood as maxima, since there must have been some males in both periods who were not taxed. There were 115 taxpayers in the 1680s group and 294 in the 1771 group. The data for the 1680s come from Salisbury (1681), Topsfield (1687), and Newbury (1688). The data for 1771 come from Salisbury, Rowley, and Wenham.

Sources: "Taxes under Gov. Andros: Town Rate of Newbury, Mass., 1688," *New England Historical and Genealogical Register*, XXXII (1878), 156–164; "Taxes under Gov. Andros: Topsfield Town Rate, 1687," *NEHGR*, XXXV (1881), 34–35; George Francis Dow and Mary G. Thresher, eds., *Records and Files of the Quarterly Courts of Essex County, Massachusetts, 1636–1686*, 9 vols. (Salem, Mass., 1911–1975), VIII, 390–393; Bettye Hobbs Pruitt, ed., *Massachusetts Tax Valuation List of 1771* (Boston, 1978), 120–131, 154–165. The ages of these taxpayers were determined from the sources in Appendixes 1 and 4.

frontier principle of strict interdependence and cast about for alternative means of reproducing their families. Of course, this involved changes in strategy for all family members—not just the men—and quite possibly daughters were drawing apart from their mothers under precisely the same logic. Here the problem can be unraveled only in its male dimension, and this necessitates an understanding of how the maturing young men of Essex County managed to support themselves.

SERVANTS AND SLAVES

If sons were emerging more rapidly from paternal control, what were they doing with their time? Could it be that a local market in agricultural labor was developing after 1700, and that sons were finding employment within it? Very little is known about the character and relative importance of extrafamilial work relations in the countryside of colonial New England, and still less about how they changed over time. The picture is complicated, but it can perhaps be simplified by considering the variety of labor forms: indentured servitude, slavery, and hired service, where master and servant dwelt under the same roof; and day labor—paid employment and informal labor exchanges—where the parties in question lived in separate households. Having sorted out the distinctions between these forms of labor and the relative importance of each, the options that maturing farm boys had to confront will be easier to understand.

Although the movement of indentured servants into Essex County had never been more than a steady trickle, these immigrant laborers were a measurable presence through the end of the seventeenth century. Assuming that male servants in general accounted for less than 5 percent of the farm population, that three-quarters of them were immigrants, and that nearly all had bound themselves—either by written contract or informally through an oral pledge—male indentured servants constituted 3 to 4 percent of the population.[45] The founding of Pennsylvania in the 1680s and the rapid development of the Middle Colonies in the early eighteenth century, however, presented emigrant servants from Britain with an alter-

---

45. This figure was calculated from the evidence in Chapter 2, nn. 51, 52, 56. The remaining 1% to 2% of servants would have been locally born and hired in the manner of servants in husbandry. On the informality of some indentures in the early history of another northern colony, Pennsylvania, see Sharon V. Salinger, *"To Serve Well and Faithfully": Labor and Indentured Servants in Pennsylvania, 1682–1800* (Cambridge, 1987), 26–27.

native destination where labor demand was heavier and opportunities brighter. After 1700, therefore, most servants from Britain passed Massachusetts by.[46] The larger farms of Essex County continued to employ the odd immigrant servant, some of whom may have been under indenture. Simeon Arnaudin, who ran away from Dr. Robert Hale of Beverly and drowned two years later at Exeter, New Hampshire, was not a native-born New Englander and may originally have come to Massachusetts under contract. William Brazeal worked for two years on a farm in Lynn as a hired man and, with no family in the colony, could conceivably have been an indentured immigrant. Most of the servants whom Essex County farmers hired during the eighteenth century, however, possessed common New England surnames and were obviously not indentured. Indeed, without a single explicit reference to an actual indenture in any agricultural town after 1700, it can fairly be assumed that as an institution of practical importance, indentured servitude was dead.[47]

To some extent, the limited role of indentured servants in the farm economy of the county had been taken over by African slaves. In Massachusetts as a whole, black bondsmen grew in numerical importance from less than 1 percent of the population in the seventeenth century, to about 2 percent after 1700, to around 3 percent by the middle of the eighteenth century. In Essex County, slaves accounted for about 2.5 percent of the population in 1764, but since most blacks lived in the seaport towns, their proportion of the rural population was undoubtedly smaller— somewhere on the order of 1 percent. Even in the countryside, however, their numbers seem to have been rising.[48] The Quaker Zaccheus Collins

46. Salinger, *"To Serve Well and Faithfully,"* chaps. 2, 3; David W. Galenson, *White Servitude in Colonial America: An Economic Analysis* (Cambridge, 1981), 124–125, 156–157.

47. Account of Simeon Arnaudin, Robert Hale Acct. Bk., 1723–; entries for Apr. 12, 1726, Mar. 9, 1727, Zaccheus Collins Diary, 1726–1779. Bernard Bailyn found that out of 4,472 indentured servants bound for the British American colonies between 1773 and 1776, not one was bound for New England. See Bernard Bailyn, *Voyagers to the West: A Passage in the Peopling of America on the Eve of the Revolution* (New York, 1986), 211, 212–213.

48. William D. Piersen, *Black Yankees: The Development of an Afro-American Subculture in Eighteenth-Century New England* (Amherst, Mass., 1988), 14, 16–17, 164; Greene and Harrington, *American Population before 1790*, 21; Galenson, *White Servitude in Colonial America*, 119; "Number of Negro Slaves in the Province of the Massachusetts-Bay, Sixteen Years Old and Upward, Taken by Order of Government, in the last Month of the

employed a lot of family and non-family labor on his farm in Lynn, but the two men who worked for him the longest were his slaves, Essex and Prince. Even his own sons did not invest as many years of labor in the home farm. According to the accounts of the Dodge family in Wenham, "negroes" commonly earned credits for their masters by doing day labor around town. Jacob Dodge owned a slave; so did each of his brothers, Skipper and William, as well as another neighbor, Edward Waldron. If the men Dodge referred to as Sip, Jack, Bill, and Maxwell were black, then his neighbors had more black servants than white.[49] Wenham had more African bondsmen than most agricultural communities, but when households throughout Essex County were evaluated in 1771, there were "servants for life"—almost all of African origin—working on a scattering of larger farms in every one of its towns.[50] Because blacks served others throughout their working lifetimes, they accounted for more of the dependent labor force at any given time than their relatively small numbers would suggest. Especially for gentlemen-farmers, who needed extra help the year round, the use of African slaves grew increasingly popular up to the outbreak of the American Revolution.

Even if black slaves did replace some of the county's declining population of English-born indentured servants, especially on the larger farms owned by the few who could manage the cost, they were never numerous enough to make up the difference. The total number of bound laborers diminished overall. Pinpointing the transition in time is impossible empirically, but insofar as the drop was driven primarily by the decline

Year 1754, and the Beginning of the Year 1755," Massachusetts Historical Society, *Collections*, 2d Ser., III (1815), 95.

49. Of the nine servants mentioned by name in the Dodge account book, three were black, two were white, and four (those mentioned in the text) were not identified by race; each of their masters, however, was assessed as a slave owner in the tax valuation of 1771. See accounts of Jacob Dodge, Skipper Dodge, William Dodge, and Edward Waldron, Nathaniel Hubbard Dodge Account Book, 1762–1793, Wenham Historical Association and Museum, Wenham, Mass.; and Pruitt, ed., *Massachusetts Tax Valuation List of 1771*, 162–163.

50. Out of 752 male householders in Salisbury, Wenham, and Rowley, 15 (2%) owned "Indian, negro or molatto servants for life, from fourteen to forty-five years of age." In terms of the value of the real estate they owned, 7 of these householders ranked in the top decile of their hometown, 13 ranked in the top quartile, and 14 ranked in the top half. See Pruitt, ed., *Massachusetts Tax Valuation List of 1771*, 120–131, 154–165.

in indentured servitude, it almost certainly occurred between 1675 and 1725. Not only was Pennsylvania then developing into a more attractive destination, but rising real wages in the mother country were simultaneously driving the cost of emigrant servants of all kinds beyond the reach of most Massachusetts farmers.[51] A few of the wealthiest turned to Africans instead, but most of those who needed live-in help recruited chiefly from within the colony.

Their success in this matter hinged, of course, on the willingness of free New Englanders to consider farm service as an alternative to life at home, and past experience provided little indication that they would. Although plenty of servants had accompanied the Puritan fathers to Massachusetts during the 1630s, few remained dependents for long, and the English system of service in husbandry swiftly collapsed. Indentured servants and slaves filled some of the gap, but they were costly, and given the limited profitability of local agriculture their purchase could seldom be justified. To the end of the seventeenth century, as we have seen, most New England families depended almost exclusively on their own children. Not until the second century of settlement did a home-grown institution replace service in husbandry: what came to be called the "hired hand."[52]

Like England's servants in husbandry, New England's hired hands were generally of regional origin. Sometimes a farmer and his man were quite literally neighbors. Timothy Pickering depended heavily on a stream of teenage boys whom he recruited from the families that lived around him in Salem. Richard Dowst and later his widow, Mary, sent both of their teenage sons into Pickering's service during the 1740s. The two boys toiled under the farmer's careful eye and boarded in his house, yet they were close enough to home to stroll over on Sundays for dinner. Just as often, however, hired hands hailed from another part of the village, from across the town line, or even from an area a day's hike away. Caleb Knowlton of Beverly served on a farm in Wenham about four miles from his home; in 1735 William Curtis of Marblehead dispatched his son to live with a certain Isaac Dodge of Boxford, twenty miles overland; and Kneeland Ross, who worked for Abel Waters of Ipswich, was probably from Boston, thirty miles away. Identification of hired hands is sometimes difficult, but 73 percent of those who left some evidence of their service in

51. Galenson, *White Servitude in Colonial America*, 154.

52. For the history of hired hands in the 19th century, see David E. Schob, *Hired Hands and Plowboys: Farm Labor in the Midwest, 1815–60* (Urbana, Ill., 1975).

private or public records can confidently be traced to homes within forty miles of the farms where they worked, and most of the others shared a surname with other New Englanders somewhere in the region.[53]

Unlike servants in husbandry, however, hired hands seldom were retained for the entire year but instead were paid by the month. This apparently was not the case in the seventeenth century, when the majority of servants had either indentured themselves for a period of years prior to emigrating or contracted locally (in the English manner) on annual terms.[54] By the first decades of the eighteenth century, however, more flexibility had crept into these arrangements. Timothy Pickering never hired boys for more than seven months at a time, and most farmers who took in hands considered even half a year to be somewhat extravagant. Thus Jonathan Burton went to work for Ephraim Towne of Topsfield for a two-month stint in July and August of 1756, and John Baker of Ipswich claimed "one months work of Joseph Crol" in return for some weaving and breaking up he had performed for his well-to-do neighbor James Brown.[55] Robert Hale of Beverly hired Simeon Arnaudin to serve him through the winter of 1730–1731 on a carefully structured contract, whereby Arnaudin would lose pay for any time absent. When Arnaudin "went away contrary to Bargain & without my consent" in mid-February, Hale not only docked him eighteen days for his early departure but added on two days that Arnaudin had missed weeks before. "Besides," Hale added ruefully as winter began to relax its hold, "the Dayes being long the Latter part of his Time would have been more gainfull to mee."[56] Although Hale's sense of lost time—construed in this naturalistic way—was quite within New England tradition, the habit of hiring servants for

53. Accounts of Richard Dowst and Mary Dowst, Timothy Pickering Acct. Bk., 1732–1757; account of Capt. John Dodge, Jr., Nathaniel Hubbard Dodge Acct. Bk., 1762–1793; Ross v. Waters (1771), Box 146, Curtis v. Dodge (1738), Box 74, Files ICCP. There were 44 hired hands in this file; see Appendix 4.

54. For examples of longer-term service in the years prior to 1730, see *Essex Co. Court Recs.*, II, 308, VI, 353; Pierce v. Follett and Procter (1722), Box 28, Files ICCP; account of Stephen Barnard, Thomas Barnard Account Book, 1688–1708, JDPL; entries for Apr. 12, 1726, Mar. 9, 1727, Zaccheus Collins Diary, 1726–1779; and Ann Kussmaul, *Servants in Husbandry in Early Modern England* (Cambridge, 1981), 48–51.

55. Account of Jonathan Burton, Ephraim Towne Account Book, 1750–1768, JDPL; account of James Brown, John Baker Account Book, 1769–1834, Baker Library, Harvard Business School, Boston; Pruitt, ed., *Massachusetts Tax Valuation List of 1771*, 70–71, 84–85. On Pickering, see sources in n. 2, above.

56. Account of Simeon Arnaudin, Robert Hale Acct. Bk., 1723–.

briefer terms was not. Closely related to the growing localism of recruitment, it was a reasonable solution to the seasonal demands of prosperous farmers, who could now drum up a certain amount of inexpensive help within the colony.

Some they tapped from traditional sources. In and around Salem, where paid employment had been common from the time of settlement, farmers recruited hands from among the urban poor. James O'Dell, who in 1712 at age eight went to serve on Abraham Pierce's farm, was the son of an immigrant laborer whose estate was worth only a couple of pounds: bedding, clothing, and kitchenware. The Dowst family, who provided Timothy Pickering with teenage help in the 1740s, ranked close to the bottom of the taxable population of Salem even before Richard's death, and they dropped off it completely afterward. Widows in particular had difficulties making ends meet and depended upon their sons' earnings in service. After Henry Cook, a local fisherman, died sometime in the 1750s, his wife, Rachel, moved into a little cottage in Danvers and arranged for her twenty-year-old son Joseph to live with Pickering. Several members of the Torrance family had performed casual labor for Pickering in the 1740s, so when Ruth Torrance was widowed in 1750, the Salem farmer agreed to pay off the debts of her dead husband's estate in return for the service of her son John. Almost every summer Pickering employed one or two hands, and more often than not they were drawn, as many farm laborers in Salem had been since the seventeenth century, from the ranks of the permanently poor.[57]

Across the rest of the county, however, hired men came from a broader range of backgrounds that reflected the overall shape and occupational structure of the towns in which they had grown up. Caleb Knowlton, like the Dowst and Torrance boys, was helping to support a fatherless family.

57. Pierce v. Follett and Procter (1722), Box 28, Files ICCP; accounts of Richard Dowst, Mary Dowst, Mary Neal, Rachel Cook, William Cox, Sr., Widow Munnion, Ruth Torrance, and John Twiss, Timothy Pickering Acct. Bk., 1732–1757. The genealogical, occupational, and economic details on the O'Dell, Dowst, Cook, and Torrance families were reconstructed from Estate of Benjamin O'Dell (1737), Probate No. 19965, Essex Co. Prob. Recs.; *Vital Records of Salem, Massachusetts, to the End of the Year, 1849*, 6 vols. (Salem, Mass., 1916–); Perley, *History of Salem*, II, 44, III, 364; Salem Tax Lists, 1740–1760, Tax and Valuation Lists of Massachusetts Towns before 1776, roll 8. All references to 18th-century Massachusetts tax and valuation lists are to the microfilm edition compiled by Ruth Crandall and published by the Charles Warren Center for Studies in American History at Harvard University, 1971.

But Hathorn Coker of Newbury was the son of a moderately prosperous mason; Daniel Johnson's father was a husbandman in Lynn; and Robert Gilman, who studied with and worked for Dr. Hale in Beverly, came from one of New Hampshire's wealthiest families. Hired men and boys such as these clearly did not constitute a separate class within society.[58] The distinction between the seaport world, where hired labor was partially mediated by class, and the surrounding countryside, where it was not, persisted throughout the county's colonial period.

What was new and striking about the hired hands of the eighteenth century was their youth. The median age of live-in help throughout the county between 1701 and 1775 was seventeen, and 77 percent were under the age of twenty.[59] Fathers and sons equally from a wide variety of families were discovering that from time to time the labor of the younger generation could more profitably be employed with others. When Luke Hovey, an ambitious young husbandman with no grown sons of his own, was assembling one of the largest farms in Boxford, he was constantly short of assistance and persuaded a friend, John Nelson, to help him. When Nelson brought along his thirteen-year-old son, John, Jr., Hovey was impressed enough to approach the boy's parents with an offer. He "then a gread with them for John to live with me from the 1 September-1713 unto the last of May 1714." In return Hovey paid Goodman Nelson £3.6 in the form of hauling, plowing, Indian meal, town rates, a bill with a local shoemaker, and a little more than £1 sterling in cash.[60] The arrangement lasted only for the winter; John then returned to his parents' farm, and although he helped Hovey the following summer on a casual basis, he never lived with him again. In a corner of early America where few farms were large enough to offer sustained employment, this was the normal pattern for most hired hands—a few months away and then home again.

Although young New Englanders were experiencing farm service in greater numbers than those in their fathers' and grandfathers' genera-

58. Account of Capt. John Dodge, Nathaniel Hubbard Dodge Acct. Bk., 1762–1793; entries for Mar. 31, 1727, June 1, Aug. 16, 1728, Sept. 1, 1729, May 20, 1730, Apr. 19, 1734, Zaccheus Collins Diary, 1726–1779; Bickford v. Ruck (1729), Box 44, Files ICCP; accounts of John Gilman, Esq., Robert Hale Acct. Bk., 1723–.

59. Each servant was counted once for every year in service ($N = 52$). Ages were determined as in Appendix 4.

60. Account of Goodman Nelson, Luke Hovey Account Book, 1698–1792, JDPL; *The Hovey Book* (Haverhill, Mass., 1913), 50–55.

tions had, the institution was not measurably more important to the rural economy as a whole. This is apparent from the records that farmers themselves left behind. Jabez True, a man of moderate means, operated a farm in Salisbury with the help of his six sons from about 1710 to 1740. Hardly anywhere in his account book did he mention farm servants. Though well supplied with boys of his own, he never put any of them out to service with another family. And in all the times that neighbors lent him help, only once did they send a hired man. The accounts of Josiah Sawyer—also a father of six boys and also from Salisbury—tell the same story. None of his sons ever went to live on other farms, and only 5 percent of the male help Sawyer employed were the hired hands of other men. For those neighborly dependents whom Jabez True hired, the ratio of sons to hired hands was 6.5:1; at Sawyer's farm, the ratio was 3:1.[61] The wealthiest farmers—Timothy Pickering, Zaccheus Collins, and Robert Hale, for example—may have hired men on a more or less regular basis, but the great majority of independent husbandmen did not. Entire account books—including those kept for different periods between 1720 and 1775 by Jonathan Burnham and Henry Russell of Ipswich, Benjamin Herrick of Beverly, Abraham Foster of Rowley, James Brown of Newbury, and Nehe-

61. Each individual hired by True and Sawyer was counted once for every year in which he was hired. By this standard, there were 44 man years worked on True's farm, and 84 on Sawyer's farm. See Jabez True Account Book, 1710–1741, JDPL; and Josiah Sawyer Acct. Bk., 1736–1793. Winifred B. Rothenberg reports that in a sample of "worker-farmer pairs" 12% of those identified in the 18th-century entries and 22% of those in the 19th-century entries had been hired by the month. Her data suggest a greater significance for hired hands than that presented here, but the discrepancy can be explained. First, many of her 18th-century sources date from after the Revolution, by which time, as she argues, hired hands *were* growing more numerous. Second, by selecting so many 18th-century account books from unusually productive towns, especially in the Connecticut River Valley, she overestimates their importance in Massachusetts as a whole. Finally, by measuring the number of hands that account book keepers, who were disproportionately well off, hired (whereas this study deals with the hired hands their miscellaneous neighbors kept), she focuses on the hiring practices of those in the community who could afford servants. While not disputing her claim for the rising numbers of hired hands, this does call into question their absolute importance within the region of her study. See Winifred B. Rothenberg, "The Emergence of Farm Labor Markets and the Transformation of the Rural Economy: Massachusetts, 1750–1855," *JEH*, XLVIII (1988), 544–545, 562–563, and Winifred Barr Rothenberg, *From Market-Places to a Market Economy: The Transformation of Rural Massachusetts, 1750–1850* (Chicago, 1992), chap. 7.

miah Collins of Lynn—contain a wide variety of individual accounts but no mention of live-in help.[62]

If hired hands played a relatively minor role in the rural economy, many young men served in this capacity for short periods in their lives, which marked at least the beginning of a regional farm-labor market. As long as Essex County husbandmen had been chiefly taken up with the labor consuming but not immediately remunerative process of farm formation, such a market could not have existed. By the second quarter of the eighteenth century, however, the homesteading frontier had moved westward and northward beyond the county bounds. Less strapped for time and often short of productive employment at home, many families now felt they could spare one son for a short stretch of service elsewhere—perhaps in the home of a childless neighbor or with a local farmer who owned enough land to need the help and who could afford the cost. In this way, a thin local market in the labor of young men was cautiously launched.

FREE LABOR AND EXCHANGING WORKS

At the very end of the eighteenth century, an anonymous pamphleteer published in Salem an Address to Farmers, in which he advised his countrymen against the folly of trying to operate a farm with hired help.

The chief use of land, and that which makes it principally beneficial and profitable to a man, is this, it gives him employment: It is of very little advantage or profit to him who does not labor upon it in person. A Farmer should therefore be cautious of hiring too much help; and at no point more than he can fully and profitably employ and readily pay. And to do this, if he hires for a month, or for a year he should endeavour to raise a surplusage of some one, or of several articles to the amount of the laborer's wages at least. And if he does this, even then, he finds that a year's wages are not easily paid: it will take off a considerable part of his corn, flax, dairy, or some other produce.

62. Jonathan Burnham Account Book, 1723–1749, JDPL; Henry Russell Account Book, 1728–1837, JDPL; Benjamin Herrick Account Book, 1759–1790, JDPL; Abraham Foster Acct. Bk., 1754–1772; James Brown Account Book, 1759–1786, JDPL; Nehemiah Collins Account Book, 1756–, Lynn Historical Society, Lynn, Mass.

Farmers would be better advised, he claimed, "to exchange Labor than to hire and pay money." Neighbors with "lands to break up, and teams to connect together," or even those who needed "mowing and hoeing," might "do this business cheaper by exchanging with each other, than by hiring help and cattle." Although most farmers already knew from experience that hired hands could rarely be kept busy enough to pay their way, the temptation to embark on the commercial farming that paid labor made possible must have been there for the pamphlet to address. In light of this, it is worth reconsidering the significance of the author's distinction between wage labor and what he termed "exchanging work."[63]

When trying to characterize the work that farming households in New England performed for one another, historians have tended to privilege one of these two categories over the other. Some argue that farmers were hiring their labor in an increasingly efficient market, which despite regulation and informal social pressure increasingly determined the conditions of employment. Others hold that prior to the capitalist transformation of the countryside, New Englanders did not work for one another on terms set by the price mechanism but rather swapped their labors in an essentially cooperative manner. This incessant lending of hands created obligations that were personal, non-negotiable, and repaid outside of the market entirely.[64] This debate has already been addressed in its seventeenth-century context—though in a preliminary and speculative fashion. Since the surviving records of interhousehold exchange grow more abundant in the period after 1700, the character of the interfamilial labor of the eighteenth century can be dealt with more empirically. By measuring the importance of such labor in rural Essex County, describing the social structures within which it was performed, testing for the negotiability of

63. *An Address to Farmers* (Salem, Mass., 1796), 14–15. This manuscript was published by John Dabney, a Salem bookseller who placed his name on the title page as if he were the author. I doubt very much that Dabney would have possessed the familiarity with farming that the pamphlet displays, and so I prefer to consider it an anonymous work. See Harriet Silvester Tapley, *Salem Imprints, 1768–1825: A History of the First Fifty Years of Printing in Salem, Massachusetts, with Some Account of the Bookshops, Booksellers, Bookbinders, and the Private Libraries* (Salem, Mass., 1927), 172–176.

64. For the clearest statement of the market perspective, see Rothenberg, *Market-Places to Market Economy*, chaps. 1, 2. The clearest statement of the non-market perspective remains Michael Merrill, "Cash Is Good to Eat: Self-sufficiency and Exchange in the Rural Economy of the United States," *Radical History Review*, IV (1977), 52–64.

the obligations it created, and analyzing the wage patterns it generated, one can better understand these work relations.

First, a caveat concerning the overall importance of non-familial help. Certainly, evidence is easy to find. The account books and diaries in which farmers kept track of their business overflow with notations of the carting, planting, mowing, and plowing services that they or their sons either performed for neighbors or hired neighbors to perform for them. These services were also the focus of court testimony, since civil litigation normally arose out of relations between households. One must not, however, overestimate the importance of this highly visible activity. To the end of the colonial period, most householders and their sons spent the majority of their working days on the exploitation and improvement of their own family property. They often may have sold or traded away the fruits of their labor, but they preferred to perform the work itself in settings they controlled. This does not surface directly from the surviving evidence, for there was rarely any need to commit the internal workings of the household to paper. Nevertheless, if one calculates the number of man days in a year that a particular individual employed or spent abroad, the total is generally unimpressive.

Richard Shatswell, Jr., of Ipswich kept a daybook during the last decade of the colonial period describing the work he performed for his neighbors. In 1771 he and his servant, Peter, each performed about forty days of labor around town; averaged across the year that amounted to less than one day a week. Was Shatswell typical? The family farm, which his father owned but he managed, was larger and better stocked than most, so much of the week he was too busy to occupy himself with his neighbors' business. Other farmers may have had more spare time to swap or sell. Yet most of the work Shatswell performed consisted of carting, sledding, and plowing—services that derived from his very ownership of productive wealth. Shatswell, like his neighbors, worked most of the year on property he owned.[65]

Another farmer, Josiah Sawyer of Amesbury, kept accounts that pro-

65. Richard Shatswell Daybook, 1766–1779, Shatswell Papers, 1722–1818, JDPL. The total value of Shatswell's services was actually £16.2 sterling, but since renting the oxen and draft equipment that he or his servant took to the job cost £6.5, the actual value of their labor was only £9.7. On Shatswell's farm, see Pruitt, ed., *Massachusetts Tax Valuation List of 1771*, 72–75.

vide a measure of how often he hired men to assist him. In 1740, at age thirty-one, he managed to get by with thirty-five man days of hired help; three years later he employed only forty. Averaged across the entire year, this meant less than one day's work a week; even during the peak seasons of plowing and hay harvest, when time was often short, Sawyer turned to his neighbors for help at most only a couple of times a week. This is not to say that he lived in self-imposed autonomy. Many types of business— lending oxen, trading hides for leather, and selling wood, for example— did not involve supervised toil and brought Sawyer into regular contact with his fellow townsmen. Seldom, however, did Sawyer call upon others to labor under his direction. This relative self-sufficiency in farm help in no way reflected an abundance of household labor within the Sawyer family; even in 1743 his eldest boy was only six, and Josiah employed no live-in help. By the early 1760s, when he had reached fifty and reared a raft of teenage sons, he employed no day labor whatsoever. Whether he had boys at hand or whether he worked alone, Sawyer never depended heavily on others to manage the regular routine of work on his farm.[66] Account books as carefully kept as Shatswell's and Sawyer's are too un-usual to provide the basis for a confident estimate of the quantitative importance of extrafamilial help. They do, however, suggest that the im-portance of such help for Essex County farmers was not great and raise the possibility that in regard to colonial New Englanders in general the phe-nomenon has often been exaggerated.[67]

To the degree that outside help was necessary to operate farms, how-ever, the logic that drew people into labor relations by the day or the task is important to understand. Except around Salem and possibly the other seaports, class was not a factor. Although obvious inequalities of wealth existed in every town—some tied to the life cycle of property accumula-tion as well as those that sprang from family history, luck, aggressiveness, and skill—these did not divide landowners from laborers in the English manner. Both employers and employees reflected in their wealth holdings the agricultural community at large. The men in Wenham who sought assistance from Jacob Dodge, for example, ranked in every quartile of real

66. Josiah Sawyer Acct. Bk., 1736–1793.

67. Both those who argue for the market orientation of New England farmers and those who believe that exchange was governed by the ethic of reciprocity have, in their enthusi-asm to dismiss the myth of the self-sufficient yeoman, placed too much emphasis on non-familial labor. See, among many others, Rothenberg, *Market-Places to Market Economy*, chaps. 6, 7; and Merrill, "Cash Is Good to Eat," *Radical Hist. Rev.*, IV (1977), 57–59.

property ownership but the lowest, and those who approached Richard Shatswell for help, save only the poorest, were scattered across the wealth spectrum of Ipswich. Abraham Foster of Rowley dispatched his sons to work for an even broader range of fellow townsmen—from Joseph Pike, the youngest taxpayer in town, who owned no property at all, to the venerable John Pearson, whose house and lands were worth more than those of all other householders in Rowley but three.[68] When farmers needed help, they recruited hands from an equally broad selection of neighbors. The men who labored for Jacob Dodge of Wenham in the late 1760s and early 1770s belonged to families of every rank. Jonathan Low, who like most young men in their early twenties owned no assessable property at all, did the odd day's work for Dodge in return for cash and farm produce. But Samuel Quarles also worked for Dodge, mowing fields and carting hay, even though his 50-acre homestead was one of the best-stocked farms in town. Most of the other men who worked for Dodge belonged to families of the middling ranks—they owned a few cows, had less than 50 acres, and swapped produce and favors to meet their own peculiar labor needs.[69]

In general, employers tended to be a little wealthier than employees, but the difference was slight, for both were normally landowners or could expect to be so someday. That is why almost no man in Essex County—in the eighteenth as in the seventeenth century—ever called himself a laborer. Of those who lived in rural communities and were involved in debt

68. Nathaniel Hubbard Dodge Acct. Bk., 1762–1793; Richard Shatswell Daybook, 1766–1799; Abraham Foster Acct. Bk., 1754–1772; Pruitt, ed., *Massachusetts Tax Valuation List of 1771*, 66–85, 120–131, 160–165.

69. Except for three men—Low, Quarles, and Benjamin Edwards—all of those ($N = 15$) who worked for Dodge between 1768 and 1773 and who could be traced (or lived in households that could be traced) to the 1771 valuation list ranked (or lived in households that ranked) between the 30th and 80th percentiles for Wenham in rental value of real estate. Jacob Dodge's records are the best for measuring the wealth holdings of those who worked for others, but scattered references from the accounts of John Baker in Ipswich and Nehemiah and Zaccheus Collins of Lynn suggest the same truth: that Essex County farmers obtained help as they needed it, not from a class of the permanently poor, but from everyone. The median assessed rental value of real estate for households exchanging labor with these three farmers was £4.8 sterling ($N = 18$). This compares with £4.5 sterling in the case of those who dealt with Jacob Dodge. See Nathaniel Hubbard Dodge Acct. Bk., 1762–1793; John Baker Acct. Bk., 1769–1834; Zaccheus Collins Diary, 1726–1779; Nehemiah Collins Acct. Bk., 1756–; and Pruitt, ed., *Massachusetts Tax Valuation List of 1771*, 66–95, 160–165.

litigation during either 1715–1723 or 1765–1773, fewer than 1 percent were styled "laborer" in the issued writs.[70] In no simple sense, therefore, did the ownership of wealth in Essex County divide a class of landowners from those forced by poverty to seek employment.

Neither did age serve in any straightforward way to determine who worked for whom. On a selection of farms in Essex County between 1727 and 1775, male employers and employees in their twenties were less significant than their numbers in the entire population would suggest, for many were still working on family property (see table 13). Men in their thirties and especially those in their forties—the prime farm workers and managers of the day—are heavily represented both as employers and as employees. The data also reflect the general tendency of farmers to begin withdrawing from physical labor and from active management of their property during their fifties and sixties. Most striking, however, is the similarity of age distribution between employers and employees. Work relations between households did not in any consistent manner divide the young from the old.

What, then, did draw farmers into exchanging labor? The anonymous pamphleteer quoted earlier believed that it was chiefly a matter of convenience—the practice he termed "exchanging works." "Through a difference in the situations and soils of farms, though adjoining each other; and through early cultivation in the one, and late in the other, it frequently happens, that the corn, grass, flax, &c. on one, is forwarder and riper by several days, than on the other . . . [and so it was prudent for farmers] to unite their labors and not to hire."[71] Although some of the time this surely happened, the basic structure of labor exchanges derived more from the functional differences among households. Any individual account from the eighteenth century connecting one family to another usually reveals a marked distinction between the debit and credit columns in the types of goods and services recorded. During the 1730s and 1740s, Henry Russell of Ipswich planted, hoed, weeded, and mowed his neighbors' fields, sold them fish in the winter, and wove cloth for them as well. In return, he took

70. The probate records of decedents from farming towns contain just as few. See the Docket Books for 1640–1820, Probate Record Office, Registry of Deeds and Probate Record Office Building, Salem, Mass. Of 48 decedents from farm towns in the county who died in 1774, only one was styled "laborer." See Jones, *American Colonial Wealth*, II, 607–800, but esp. 771–772.

71. *Address to Farmers*, 14.

Table 13. Age Distribution of Agricultural Employers and
Employees in Essex County, 1727–1775 (in Percents)

Age	Employers (N = 235)	Employees (N = 270)
20–29	23	23
30–39	26	29
40–49	28	26
50–59	15	16
60–69	6	5
70+	3	0

Note: Each employer and employee was counted once for every year in which he hired or worked.

Sources: Because some account book keepers were almost exclusively employers and others were mainly employees, the same sources could not be used for both categories. For employers, see Jabez True Account Book (Salisbury), 1710–1741, Zaccheus Collins Diary (Lynn), 1726–1779, Timothy Pickering Account Book (Salem), 1732–1757, Jonathan Burnham Account Book (Ipswich), 1723–1749, James Duncan Phillips Library, Peabody Essex Museum, Salem, Mass.; Nehemiah Collins Account Book (Lynn), 1756–, Lynn Historical Society, Lynn, Mass.; Robert Hale Account Book (Beverly), 1723–, Beverly Historical Society, Beverly, Mass.; and Nathaniel Hubbard Dodge Account Book (Wenham), 1762–1793, Wenham Historical Association and Museum, Wenham, Mass. For employees, see Stephen Little Account Book (Newbury), 1767–1792, Abraham Foster Account Book (Rowley), 1754–1772, Henry Russell Account Book (Ipswich), 1728–1837, Jabez True Account Book (Salisbury), 1710–1741, James Duncan Phillips Library, Peabody Essex Museum, Salem, Mass.; Nathaniel Hubbard Dodge Account Book (Wenham), 1762–1793, Wenham Historical Association and Museum, Wenham, Mass.; and Nehemiah Collins Account Book (Lynn), 1756–, Lynn Historical Society, Lynn, Mass.

his pay in carting and plowing services, horse or oxen hire, and a wide variety of provisions. Almost never was the pattern reversed.[72] Abraham Foster of Rowley was a house carpenter possessed of a sizable young family and a 25-acre farm stocked with cattle and sheep but no oxen. The majority of his accounts between 1760 and 1775 record in one column the Fosters' attempts to procure the use of draft animals, farm produce, and hay and pasturing for their cattle, and in the other column, Abraham's

72. Henry Russell Acct. Bk., 1728–1837.

carpentry work as well as the general farm labor that he and his numerous sons performed about town.[73] During his twenties and thirties James Brown of Newbury made shoes, set glass, hauled dung, performed general labor, and rented out his oxen to others in return for provisioning, rum, and cash.[74] The list could be extended but the point should be clear: day labor was essentially a method of balancing a complicated pattern of interfamilial exchange that reflected the specific advantages or disadvantages of individual farm families in the property and skills they possessed.

The ownership of wealth did shape this pattern somewhat. The better off tended to earn credits by plowing, carting, renting pastureland, hiring out animals, and selling provisions; their poorer neighbors more commonly sold the products of their family's handicraft and did general labor. Age also played a role. Younger men tended to provide general farm labor, planting and reaping the fields of their propertied elders, whereas middle-aged farmers with oxen were more likely to offer plowing and carting services to those who had not yet acquired beasts of their own or had passed beyond their working years. In all of this, it is possible to glimpse the operation of a life cycle in which men moved from doing general labor for their neighbors, through handling draft animals for them, to employing others in turn. But there were too many exceptions—men without sons who hired help all their lives, unsuccessful farmers who moved right through the life cycle without ever acquiring a team of oxen, craftsmen who were too busy in the shop to gather their crops, and cussed old men who were too ancient to work productively but refused to admit it—to accept this as the rule.[75] Of only one generalization can there be any

73. Abraham Foster Acct. Bk., 1754–1772; Pruitt, ed., *Massachusetts Tax Valuation List of 1771*, 126–127.

74. James Brown Acct. Bk., 1759–1786.

75. Historians have recently stressed the correlation between wealth holdings and age, noting that in many New England communities, mean property ownership was generally lowest among young men, progressively higher as they moved into and through middle age, and then lower again as in old age they began to pass land along to their sons. See Main, *Colonial Connecticut*, 374–376; Jedrey, *World of John Cleaveland*, 63–64; Jones, *Village and Seaport*, 15; and Fred Anderson, "A People's Army: Provincial Military Service in Massachusetts during the Seven Years' War," *WMQ*, 3d Ser., XL (1983), 502–503, 518–524. Taking the different forms of farm property recorded for each taxpayer in Wenham, Rowley, and Salisbury in the Massachusetts Tax Valuation List of 1771 and plotting them against the taxpayer's age confirms this generalization. It also reveals, however, for every type of property a considerable degree of variation in property ownership for which the age of the taxpayer cannot account. Although the precise sources of the residual variation

certitude: that the farm economy of colonial Essex County never supported a distinct class or even an age cohort of agricultural day laborers.

How were the terms of these functional labor exchanges set? Michael Merrill has argued that in precapitalist rural economies like that of Essex County, the act of helping one's neighbor created a social obligation that was not negotiable. Since it could not be transferred or paid back in any universal medium of exchange, it was impervious to the play of market forces.[76] Surveying hundreds of individual accounts from the period should persuade anyone that most of the time this was quite true. Not only were cash entries very few, but the transfers of credits and debits to third parties—in the manner that merchants in Salem and Marblehead managed every day—were rarer still.[77] Although accounts were kept in pounds, shillings, and pence and expressed a sense of obligation that was quite precise, these "debts" never collected interest and were to a considerable degree insulated from the world of commercial exchange.

And yet this was not entirely true. Every rural householder in the county felt some obligation to assemble a patrimony large enough to endow his offspring with sufficient property to launch them on the road to comfortable independence. In a society where large families were the rule, moreover, this pressure could be serious enough to provide the organizing principle for a life's work. Farmers managed this by acquiring land and other forms of productive property through several decades of

---

(family of origin, skill, luck, and so on) would be extremely difficult to quantify and measure, they would probably matter at least as much as age does and, therefore, caution against adhering too completely to the notion of the life cycle.

76. Merrill, "Cash Is Good to Eat," *Radical Hist. Rev.*, IV (1977), 55–56.

77. In seven accounts kept by Josiah Sawyer of Amesbury, containing 247 entries over a total period of about 177 person months, there were only two references to cash and six to orders drawn on third-party accounts (one negotiable transaction per account every 31 entries and every 22 person months). In five accounts kept by Jabez True of Salisbury containing 264 entries over approximately 480 person months, there were twelve cash entries and eight orders (one negotiable transaction every 13 entries and every 24 person months). In five accounts kept by Henry Russell containing 186 entries over 369 person months, there were five cash entries and one order (one negotiable transaction every 31 entries and every 62 person months). See accounts of John Easman, Silvanus Carr, Robert Ring, Ebenezer Currier, Daniel Flanders, Gideon Sawyer, and Joshua Clough, Josiah Sawyer Acct. Bk., 1736–1793; accounts of Benjamin Hoyt, Jacob Stevens, Henry Eaton, Nicholas French, and Jeremiah Sheppard, Jabez True Acct. Bk., 1710–1741; and accounts of John Wood, Joseph Bowles, Nathaniel Warner, Benjamin Kimball, and John Smith, Henry Russell Acct. Bk., 1728–1837.

married life and then passing it along to their children in later years. Exactly how they assembled these patrimonies is difficult to know, but by the eighteenth century, when local reserves of unimproved countryside had almost disappeared, land could be had only by purchase, and farmers had to raise something to sell for cash or credit if they were to meet the cost. Either by carrying their surplus to town or by dealing with others who did, they had to scramble—from time to time, at least—for the means to acquire the property that allowed them to fulfill their responsibilities as parents. Squeezing a surplus every year from stony and increasingly barren soil involved a certain degree of hardheadedness in farm management, which demanded among other things some careful attention to neighborly dealings.

Insofar as the seemingly benign business of providing for the next generation forced households to engage in some commerce, the discipline of the market had to intrude upon the system of exchanging works. Two friends who had been swapping favors for some time would certainly have felt it quite improper to haggle over the price of their labor in the open as strangers could, but they surely worried occasionally about whether each was benefiting equally from the exchange. If one decided he was being consistently shortchanged, there were two approaches that he could take. One tack, implicit in the dozens of accounts that trail away to unresolved and unbalanced conclusions and that pepper almost every set of farmers' records, was to cut off the relationship. There was a social cost to be paid here, but through systematic avoidance, persistent begging off, and ceasing to ask for help themselves, most farmers could eventually sever the more problematic connections.[78] The other alternative was to convert the obligation into a formal note or bond that was negotiable, possibly interest bearing, and easily suable in court. Without much fuss, one could turn a relaxed and personal connection that had turned sour into a commercial transaction that operated by stringent and impersonal rules. This happened all the time, and handling the disagreements that arose out of such transformations was among the legal system's most common functions.[79] Neither alternative provided an efficient way of modifying the terms of employment. They were chiefly intended to bring relationships to an end so that others might spring up in their place. Over the long run, however, these options did introduce a degree of flexibility into the system of ex-

78. See Marshall Sahlins, *Stone Age Economics* (Chicago, 1972), 312.
79. Mann, *Neighbors and Strangers*, chap. 1.

changing works, which allowed farmers to respond to the occasional but far from insignificant business of dealing commercially to acquire the means by which the next generation would be settled on the land.

This helps to explain why farm wages continued, as they had in the seventeenth century, to display a marked flatness across the growing season. Mean winter, summer, and harvest wages for ten-year periods between 1695 and 1775 describe a rather monotonous continuation of the annual cycle established at the beginning of settlement, whereby wages rose and fell across the year but only in consonance with the lengthening and shortening of the working day (see table 14). Although the months of hay and corn harvest in Essex County offered about twice as much paid employment as the other months of the growing season, the price of labor did not go up as it did in contemporary England.[80] Unlike the mother country, labor relations among families within New England villages were not mediated by class, and as long as the employment relationship was potentially reversible—if Monday's employer could be Tuesday's employee—the value of a day's work was not worth negotiating. This state of affairs persisted until the commercial character of agriculture began to intensify at the very end of the eighteenth century. Throughout the entire colonial period, as long as the combination of weak markets and rocky soil precluded the sort of specialization that would sustain a major harvest thrust and a laboring class (or even a large crowd of yet-to-be-propertied young men), market forces played only indirectly upon the terms of local employment. And as long as the system of exchanging works continued to answer farmers' limited needs, paid employment in agriculture remained difficult to find.

BY-EMPLOYMENTS

A regional market in free labor was slow to develop in the countryside of Essex County for reasons related to supply and demand. The supply of labor remained limited as long as most families were propertied, for the development of family property possessed first claim on the time of

80. When the 553 instances of paid farm employment during the period 1695–1775 are broken down into monthly percentages, April (8%), May (14%), June (11%), September (12%), and October (7%) were all markedly lower than July (21%) and August (20%). The months from November to March accounted altogether for only 13% of the total. See Appendix 4.

Table 14. Mean Daily Wages by Season in England
and New England, 1695–1775 (in British shillings)

Source	Years	Winter Wage[a]	Summer Wage[b]	Harvest Wage[c]	Summer/ Winter	Harvest/ Summer	N
Essex	1695–1705	.95	1.34	1.62	1.41	1.21	8
County	1716–1725	1.28	1.39	1.48	1.09	1.06	63
account	1726–1735	1.28	1.17	1.21	.91	1.03	139
books	1736–1745	.91	1.01	1.11	1.11	1.10	174
	1746–1755	1.21	1.21	1.41	1.00	1.17	63
	1756–1765	1.29	1.66	1.96	1.27	1.18	77
	1766–1775	1.55	1.57	1.79	1.01	1.14	54
	1695–1775	1.21	1.35	1.46	1.11	1.08	553
English county wage assessments	1700–1778	.58	.67	.95	1.16	1.42	7
Brandsby, Yorkshire, account books	1742–1743	.53	.63	.96	1.19	1.52	1,028

[a]Winter wages were defined in Essex County and in Brandsby, England, as those paid between October and March. In the English magistrates' assessments the definition of winter varied by the assessment.

[b]Summer wages were defined everywhere as wages paid neither in the winter nor at harvest.

[c]Harvest wages were defined in Essex County and in Brandsby, England, as those paid when the monthly average was highest.

Sources: For the Essex County account books, see Appendix 4. For the English wage assessments, see Elizabeth L. Waterman, "Some New Evidence on Wage Assessments in the Eighteenth Century," *English Historical Review*, XLIII (1928), 407; A. E. Bland, P. A. Brown, and R. H. Tawney, eds., *English Economic History: Select Documents* (London, 1914), 546–547; Elizabeth W. Gilboy, *Wages in Eighteenth-Century England* (Cambridge, Mass., 1934), 88–89, 175; and James E. Thorold Rogers, *A History of Agriculture and Prices in England, from the Year after the Oxford Parliament (1250) to the Commencement of the Continental War (1793)*, 7 vols. (Oxford, 1866–1902), V, 610, VII, 499–502.

younger colonists. The demand for labor was equally weak—with limited marketable produce, farmers in the county could not bear the cost of a wage bill. There was plenty of work for family members but little that brought in the cash returns that permitted farming on a scale large enough to support a paid labor force. In short, as long as the frontier remained within practical reach, the logic of farm development on marginal land in a temperate climate generated little in the way of supply or demand for paid help, and a local market in free labor never materialized.

The first limitations to relax were those on supply. As local tracts of undeveloped land were eaten away, young men in these first-settled towns in Massachusetts found less to do at home and began to cast about for other ways of assembling the means to begin householding themselves. There had never been a time in the history of Essex County when this process was not in motion. It was driven by the search for competent livings that had motivated the Great Migration in the first place, and its workings were already manifest in the founding of new towns in the western portion of the county—Topsfield, Boxford, and Bradford—during the middle of the seventeenth century. Nor had there ever been a time when this search for new farmland was not primarily the activity of young families, afraid for their prospects of acquiring landed independence in the settled neighborhoods in which they had grown up.[81] What changed during the colonial period was the context of authority within which migration occurred. From the earliest decades, young couples with ideas about moving out—to a far corner of their parents' lands, to another part of town, or to a new community entirely—had necessarily invested much of their young adulthood in preparation. In the seventeenth century, however, this had mostly involved the development of nearby lands that their fathers controlled, either by ownership or by influence in town government. By the eighteenth century, local reserves of land had been largely exhausted, and young people could no longer look to their parents for the same sort of beneficence or leverage. Independence in the town of their birth was not out of the question, but it now had to be bought. Out-migration was another possibility, but it, too, had to be financed. Although parents could help, much of the responsibility for assembling the means to a competency fell on the shoulders of the maturing children themselves,

81. Jedrey, *World of John Cleaveland*, 164–165; Darrett B. Rutman, "People in Process: The New Hampshire Towns of the Eighteenth Century," *Journal of Urban History*, I (1975), 277–278.

and this task demanded that they bring in some income from outside the parental home. In a rural economy with so little agricultural potential, this was no easy business. Commercial farmers wanting hired hands or landlords requiring tenants were no more common at the end of the colonial period than they had been at the beginning. How, then, as the logic of toiling on family land under paternal direction diminished, did colonists who were facing the specter of chronic underemployment begin to reorganize their working lives?

Since there was no single obvious solution to this problem, most young men attempted to cobble together a remedy from a variety of sources. Military service was one brand of employment that surfaced from time to time and plainly possessed some attraction for rural youth. Soldiers' wages were anything but handsome, but the work was steadier than day labor in farming and the combination of monthly pay and enlistment bounties compared favorably with what a colonist might alternatively earn as a hired hand in agriculture—if such employment could even be had. During the Seven Years' War soldiers were paid at a monthly rate calculated on the basis of two shillings a day over a six-day work week. A hired hand at home earned a monthly wage that assumed a higher daily rate—two to three shillings, depending on the season—but only about three to four days of work a week. Thus it was a fortunate farmhand who made even £11 sterling in the course of a year, whereas a volunteer in the provincial expeditions against New France who enlisted for eight months could expect to earn at least that much from pay alone and anywhere from £2 to £20 sterling more in bounty.[82] In the Seven Years' War, and probably in most of the eighteenth-century expeditions against the French, the vast majority of provincial recruits were young men aged thirty and under. This made sense, in part because their youth enabled them to better withstand the rigors of campaigning in the wilderness. Military service also corresponded, however, with the real needs of maturing youths. A soldier who saved £20 or £30 after a couple of years' service could purchase an acre or two of cleared land and a yoke of oxen; more practically,

82. Fred Anderson, *A People's Army: Massachusetts Soldiers and Society in the Seven Years' War* (Chapel Hill, N.C., 1984), 38–39, 225. Compare these with the payments to hired hands recorded in the accounts of William Cox, Sr., Richard and Mary Dowst, Widow Munnion, Rachel Cook, and Widow Mary Neal, Timothy Pickering Acct. Bk., 1732–1757; and the accounts of Nathaniel Caswell, Timothy Elet, John Merrill, Moses Chase, Jr., Stephen Chase, Moses Cooper, Jr., Edward Mordain, and Joseph Conner, Moses Little Account Book, 1724–1778, JDPL.

the possession of that much provincial scrip made one a better risk in the eyes of potential creditors. In any event, cash was scarce in the rural economy of provincial Massachusetts, and given the chance to earn some as a soldier, those with worries about setting themselves up seized it.[83]

Even in a century studded with colonial conflicts, however, military operations were not a regular occurrence. Prior to the Seven Years' War, the opportunity to serve for pay arose only with sporadic expeditions. True, hundreds of colonists took part in such early colonial adventures as William Phips's 1690 assault on Quebec and the capture of Port Royal in 1710; four thousand volunteers joined in the major operation against Louisbourg in 1745. Only for the comparatively brief period of the Seven Years' War, however, did military service become an annual possibility. Although the British military commitment in North America rose over the course of the eighteenth century, military earnings provided nothing more than an occasional quick fix to the problem of rural underemployment.

Those who lived in towns along the coast had the obvious option of going to sea, and the eighteenth-century banks fishery recruited many of its hands among the sons of small-holding farmers in Ipswich, Gloucester, and Beverly. By the end of the colonial period, hundreds of families were settled around the perimeter of Cape Ann trying to patch together some sort of a competency from a combination of dependent labor in the fishery and self-employment at home. And other types of work on the coast besides fishing—sailoring to the West Indies, for example, or working by the day in a fishyard—played a role in the cottage economy of the time. Rural New Englanders in the seventeenth century—even those who lived within a few miles of the coast—had mostly managed to avoid the dependency of maritime employment. By the second quarter of the eighteenth century, however, boys growing up in the seafront villages of the county normally expected to spend some of their youth at sea. During the last decade of the colonial period, when the surviving data on the fishery allow a degree of precision, more than half of the men in their twenties who lived in the towns that ringed Cape Ann spent several months a year on the banks. Even by the most conservative estimate, most men in coastal communities must have spent part of their youths at sea to man the vessels that sailed out of these harbors with locally born crews. This was mainly a feature of coastal life, for the network of recruitment did not extend very

83. Anderson, *People's Army*, 28–39.

far inland. Even in a town such as Topsfield, from which one could actually make out the spires of Marblehead, the ocean was unfamiliar and maritime labor was something few boys ever took up. Close to the Atlantic shore, however, where farms were smallest and the cottage economy predominated, seafaring was the primary antidote to youthful under-employment.[84]

More important than either military service or seafaring in the struggle to sustain one's family in some degree of competency was the developing practice of by-employment in craft manufacture. In its nineteenth-century context, this is a well-known story. With the elaboration during the early republic of regional and national markets in manufactured goods, young men and women discovered that by turning their hands to the fashioning of shoes, hats, shirts, pieces of furniture, and bolts of cloth, especially during the long, inclement winter, they could profitably improve days that would otherwise have lain idle.[85] What is less clear is when and how by-employments first appeared. For most women, the generalized calling of housewife had always involved a multitude of tasks, and

84. The estimates of male participation in the fishery are based on the assumption that men in their twenties accounted for 40%–50% of all fishermen and roughly 10% of the population as a whole. The towns around Cape Ann were Beverly, Manchester, Gloucester, and Ipswich. See Jefferson, "Report on Fisheries," 223; Robert Paul Thomas and Terry L. Anderson, "White Population, Labor Force and Extensive Growth of the New England Economy in the Seventeenth Century," *JEH*, XXXIII (1973), 654; U.S. Dept. of State, *Return of the Whole Number of Persons*, 8; Greene and Harrington, *American Population before 1790*, 23–24, 31–32; and table 8, above. On coastal recruitment in another colonial New England maritime industry, see Daniel Vickers, "Nantucket Whalemen in the Deep-Sea Fishery: The Changing Anatomy of an Early American Labor Force," *Journal of American History*, LXXII (1985), 286–295.

85. Blanche Evans Hazard, *The Organization of the Boot and Shoe Industry in Massachusetts before 1875* (Cambridge, Mass., 1921), chap. 3; Nancy F. Cott, *The Bonds of Womanhood: "Woman's Sphere" in New England, 1780–1835* (New Haven, Conn., 1977), 26–28; Mary H. Blewett, *Men, Women, and Work: Class, Gender, and Protest in the New England Shoe Industry, 1780–1910* (Urbana, Ill., 1988), chaps. 1–4; Thomas Dublin, "Women and Outwork in a Nineteenth-Century New England Town: Fitzwilliam, New Hampshire, 1830–1850," in Steven Hahn and Jonathan Prude, eds., *The Countryside in the Age of Capitalist Transformation: Essays in the Social History of Rural America* (Chapel Hill, N.C., 1985), 58–63; Gregory H. Nobles, "Merchant Middlemen in the Outwork Network of Rural New England," in Rosemary E. Ommer, ed., *Merchant Credit and Labour Strategies in Historical Perspective* (Fredericton, N.B., 1990), 333–347; Christopher Clark, *The Roots of Rural Capitalism: Western Massachusetts, 1780–1860* (Ithaca, N.Y., 1990), esp. 93–105, 176–190.

working life amounted to a complex of by-employments throughout the preindustrial age. For male New Englanders, whose careers had been framed by a more specialized sense of occupational calling, the decision to branch out into a second trade represented a more visible break from tradition. When did the practice of by-employments among men emerge in Essex County, and how did this phenomenon spring from the larger developments charted in this chapter?

These questions are easier to pose than to answer, mainly because it is difficult to distinguish between husbandmen who practiced a craft on the side and artisans who also farmed. Throughout the countryside there had always been blacksmiths, house carpenters, wheelwrights, and masons whose holdings of land and livestock were similar to those of their neighbors who called themselves husbandmen or yeomen. Zaccheus Collins of Lynn, for example, was an eighteenth-century blacksmith who worked actively at the forge into at least his sixties but was also among the most substantial farmers in town.[86] Conversely, all farming households practiced some manufacturing activities in addition to the basic work of agriculture. At the very least, the raw material of agriculture had to be processed for home consumption, and women's work especially fell mainly into this realm. In rural New England, the specialized craftsman who did no farming and the professional husbandman who eschewed manufacture had never existed, and since all households pursued a mix of activities, any judgment on the importance of by-employments has to be relative.[87]

In these terms, the first hundred years of settlement in Essex County were comparatively poor in home manufacture. The probated inventories filed for farming householders before 1730—meaning chiefly those of the first settlers and their children—contained land, animals, the basic implements of husbandry, and a few rough carpentry tools, but they generally lacked the implements that might have enabled farmers to practice a specialized handicraft on the side. Looms, shoemaking equipment, and fishing boats, for example, were relatively scarce; even spinning wheels were by no means universal. Orlando Bagley, a well-to-do farmer in Amesbury, died in 1728 with an estate valued at about £400 sterling,

86. Zaccheus Collins Diary, 1726–1779; Pruitt, ed., *Massachusetts Tax Valuation List of 1771*, 90–91.

87. This point is well developed in Eric Guest Nellis, "Communities of Workers: Free Labor in Provincial Massachusetts, 1690–1765" (Ph.D. diss., University of British Columbia, 1979), 47–98.

which included oxen, cattle, sheep, swine, all sorts of farming gear and kitchen utensils, and more than a hundred acres of land; aside from a pair of linen and woolen wheels and a set of basic woodworking tools, however, he and his family, like most of their contemporaries, were not set up for specialized manufacture. One can only assume that Bagley and his neighbors either sailed down to Ipswich or Salem to buy dry goods, metalware, and shoes or did without.[88] The first generation of settlers and their children were essentially planters who focused their energies on clearing land, feeding themselves, and raising small surpluses of grain or meat to take to market and sell for the imported manufactures—especially cloth—that they did not yet have the time or the equipment to manufacture themselves. That is why so few took the trouble to identify themselves by occupation in the public records of the county. The English emigrants in the 1630s, judging by the lists of ships' passengers during the Great Migration, usually styled themselves by the trades they had practiced at home. In the forests of the New World, however, occupational titles lost their significance, and when the first planters went to court or had their estates administered, they generally went by their surnames alone. Since there was normally little that was individually specific in the generalized business of homesteading, these were quite appropriate.[89]

All of this began to change in the early decades of the eighteenth century as the third- and fourth-generation descendants of the original planters, finding themselves less wholly occupied with the work of farm formation, began to take up by-employments to improve their spare time. One indication of this is the gradual increase in the intermingling of craft tools and farm implements in the inventoried estates of farming householders. Judging from a random sample of such estates, the proportion of farmers who possessed any tools definitely connected to fishing, weaving,

88. Estate of Orlando Bagley (1728), CCCXVI, 294, Essex Co. Prob. Recs., BV. Farming households are defined here as those that owned farming implements, land, and livestock. Laurel Ulrich suggests that the equipment rural women employed was more common than this, but her figures do not distinguish, as mine do, between families that farmed and those that did not. See Laurel Thatcher Ulrich, *Good Wives: Image and Reality in the Lives of Women in Northern New England, 1650–1750* (New York, 1982), 15–17.

89. This is a general impression derived from searching the numerous public records described in Appendix 1. Curiously, the early deed books of the county constitute a partial exception to this rule, for they style individuals more commonly by their occupation than do the records of the quarterly courts or the administration of estates. Even so, only about half the grantors and grantees of the 17th century were identified by calling, and a good many of those simply termed themselves "planter."

shoemaking, tanning, milling, or metalworking—tools that could easily be identified by trade—climbed from 22 percent between 1660 and 1675, to 34 percent between 1710 and 1725, to 50 percent by 1760–1775.[90] More and more frequently, rural householders were setting up looms in their kitchens, building woodworking or shoemaking shops alongside their homes, constructing fishing boats, and investing time or capital in the construction of mills. If Orlando Bagley was representative of rural householders who lived most of their lives in the seventeenth century, Jonathan Hutchinson, yeoman, of Andover was more typical of their eighteenth-century descendants. Valued at £360 sterling with a variety of livestock and acreage that was quite similar to Bagley's, Hutchinson's farm was different in that a shop equipped with a set of shoemaker's tools adjoined the house. The farm of husbandman David Tuxbury was about half the size of Hutchinson's though similarly furnished with livestock and the necessary tools of husbandry. In addition, however, this Amesbury resident owned "a weavers loom and all Things belonging" as well as a small share in a local sawmill.[91]

Although probated inventories describe precisely enough the range of handicrafts that these rural New Englanders were beginning to pursue, they distort the timing of their first appearance. The looms and the shops that appraisers noted as they toured the farms of men like Hutchinson and Tuxbury had been purchased or constructed earlier. Thus the diversification that inventories begin to measure in the 1730s must have started some years before. Dating the shift in the work habits of the living is not easy, but one indication of change may be the parallel changes in habits of self-identification. As late as the 1670s, court records rarely styled either plaintiff or defendant by trade, whereas by 1700 the practice was com-

90. These inventories were sampled from *Essex Co. Prob. Recs.*, vols. I–II; and Essex Co. Prob. Recs., BV, vols. CXI, CXVI, CXIX, CXX, CXL, CXLIII, CXLV, CXLVIII. For 1700–1729, $N = 25$; for 1730–1739, $N = 17$; and for 1760–1775, $N = 46$. Farm inventories were defined as in n. 88, above.

91. Estate of Jonathan Hutchinson (1768), CCCXLV, 136–138; Estate of David Tuxbury (1769), CCCXLV, 329, Essex Co. Prob. Recs., BV. James A. Henretta identifies the same development of rural handicrafts throughout the colonial north, though he dates its appearance to the period after 1750 and analyzes it as a species of proto-industrialization in "The War for Independence and American Economic Development," in Ronald Hoffman, John J. McCusker, Russell R. Menard, and Peter J. Albert, eds., *The Economy of Early America: The Revolutionary Period, 1763–1790* (Charlottesville, Va., 1988), 51–58. See Jacob M. Price's survey of the problem in "Reflections on the Economy of Revolutionary America," *ibid.*, 308–315.

mon, and by 1715, customary. Almost immediately these occupational labels began to reflect a broad range of callings. Now there were joiners in Wenham, clothiers in Newbury, housewrights in Topsfield, weavers in Rowley, fullers in Salisbury, locksmiths in Ipswich, and shoemakers in Haverhill.[92] These were almost certainly the sons and grandsons of the older generation, whose deaths in the 1730s revealed the spread of rural manufacturing. The very tools that were listed in their fathers' inventories were likely those with which these young men had first learned their crafts. Around the turn of the century, therefore—about the time the third generation of colonists was reaching adulthood—home manufacture began to blossom in a way that encouraged rural householders in Essex County to identify themselves by the trades they followed.[93]

Although at first glance one might be tempted to believe that this pattern reflected a trend toward individual specialization within the rural economy, such was not the case. Not only did almost all of these "craftsmen" also farm, but a great many treated their craft status as a transitory feature of young adulthood. Moses Hopkinson, born in 1700, called himself a blacksmith in his twenties but a yeoman or husbandman in his thirties and forties. Stephen Mighill, born in 1707, was a wheelwright until age thirty-six, a yeoman or husbandman until he was fifty-one, and a gentleman thereafter. Mark Cressey, born in 1734, was a cordwainer until age thirty-four, a yeoman at thirty-six, and a gentleman by forty-eight.[94] Not everyone passed through this cycle. When he bought his first piece of land in 1749 at age twenty-two, Moses Clark styled himself a yeoman, as he did three decades later at fifty-three. During the eighteenth century, however, his became the exceptional path to follow. By the end of the colonial period, most men in the farming villages of the county styled themselves craftsmen into their thirties, and husbandmen, yeomen, or even gentlemen thereafter.[95]

92. Harris v. Ring *et al.* (1701), Wainwright v. Harris (1702), Box 7, Osgood v. Hutchins (1716), Box 16, Symonds v. Fairfield (1719), Box 19, Lindall v. Averill (1722–1723), Box 26, Calfe v. Easman (1723), Box 28, and many others in the same boxes, Files ICCP.

93. For the maturation of the third generation, see Greven, *Four Generations*, 117.

94. George Brainard Blodgette and Amos Everett Jewett, *Early Settlers of Rowley, Massachusetts* ... (Rowley, Mass., 1933), 87, 164, 238; Essex Deeds, LI, 192, 193, LXXI, 245, LXXII, 192, 193, LXXXV, 236, LXXXVII, 114, 115, XCIX, 19, CIII, 151, CIX, 142, CX, 59, 60, CXXVII, 123, 162, 166, 168, 172, CXLI, 10, CXLII, 70, 71, CXLIII, 151, 152.

95. Working from those rural litigants in the writ sample for 1765–1773 whose ages could be determined, 12 of 13 craftsmen and 4 of 13 farmers were 35 or younger, but not

One should not interpret this to mean that at the onset of middle age, men laid down their tools and took up the plow instead. The precise shift in the way they styled themselves reflected the much more gradual process by which rural householders slowly acquired the property that enabled them to support themselves as independent farmers. Trades such as woodworking and weaving probably occupied less of their time with the passage of years and the accumulation of agricultural responsibilities, but they were seldom dropped entirely. James Brown continued to install windows for his neighbors in Newbury even as he assembled his own farm during his twenties and thirties. Abraham Foster of Rowley combined house carpentry with farming into his forties and fifties. Both men, however, called themselves yeomen once they had, largely by dint of their manufacturing labors, assembled a competency.[96]

In one obvious sense it would be wrong to confuse this type of rural manufacture with the various forms of outwork that began to envelop the northern countryside of the early republic. Virtually all of it was custom production for a limited circle of people whom the producers knew as friends and acquaintances, and merchant capital had little to do with its development. In another sense, however, the line between the rural industries of the nineteenth century and their colonial predecessors was less distinct. Even when home manufacture was first spreading across the countryside, men considered the focus on handicrafts to be less an end in itself than a stage in their careers. Building a chimney or repairing a cartwheel for a friend was never the mark of dependency that stitching together sale shoes for a local dealer at a predetermined price came to be. But whether they plied a trade to help a neighbor or to earn cash in a wider market, successful men in rural communities generally outgrew their reliance on manufacture as they accumulated land. Always, it was an activity most proper to youth and the early years of married life.

In colonial Essex County, mastering a craft and plying it around the neighborhood enabled young men of the third and fourth generations to employ themselves productively in a period when the pressure to assist

one out of 9 gentlemen was. Expressed differently, 75% of those in the above occupations aged 21–35 identified themselves as craftsmen ($N = 16$); only 5% of those aged 36–70 styled themselves so ($N = 19$). See Pruitt, ed., *Massachusetts Tax Valuation List of 1771*; Boxes 144–147, Files ICCP. Ages were determined from the sources in Appendix 4.

96. James Brown Acct. Bk., 1759–1786; Abraham Foster Acct. Bk., 1754–1772; Estate of Abraham Foster (1796), Probate No. 9799, Essex Co. Prob. Recs. A copy of the inventory made of James Brown's estate, dated 1789, is contained in his account book.

their families in clearing land and building farms was diminishing. As working fields multiplied and the tracts of forest between them were steadily trimmed, there was simply less to do on family lands; for young men who did not yet possess the means to strike out for a less developed town in the New England interior as well as for those who simply preferred to make a go of things closer to home, the pursuit of by-employments became a critical element of household strategy. The scarcity of land did not throw these young men into a labor market, for as craftsmen they sold a service whose performance they controlled. But they were forced to find their own way, as artisans in their own right with a degree of independence from their fathers, earlier in life than had once been the case. In this way extrafamilial employment became part of growing up—a custom of youth that the merchant capitalists of the early republic later would be able to exploit.

In the Anglo-American world of the early modern day, production was normally accompanied by some form of social dependency. The relationship could be of several types—class, gender, age, ethnicity, and so on—but absolute individualism and wholesale cooperation among equals were almost nonexistent. Throughout this book the aim has been to view the relations of production comparatively across time and space and to distinguish the forms that dependency assumed. In the countryside of Essex County, the tight generational interdependency that had once served the purposes of frontier development began to relax as the local economy matured. By the eighteenth century, when farm formation was playing a progressively smaller role in the working year, fathers no longer needed the help of all their maturing boys, and few sons could find enough to do in helping to work paternal lands. Although this did not prompt a general crisis in the local economy, it did push young men to search for other employment away from home or outside agriculture. Since inheritance now meant less to the achievement of landed competency and purchase meant more, families had to look beyond their own lands for the property needed to properly endow their offspring—sons and daughters alike. Much of this new responsibility passed to the boys themselves.

In this way the habit of working for others outside the family and learning a trade on the side gradually insinuated itself into the rural economy, not as proletarianization, but initially during the eighteenth century as a stage in growing up: a means to the ultimate end of recapturing the comfortable independence of the parental farm. As a strategy it adapted the pursuit of competency and yeoman status to the changing balance in the factors of production—that is, the growth in labor and capital relative to land. Most young men probably bore these years of dependency and manufacture easily enough. After all, a skilled craft was a respectable calling—especially if one could expect to outgrow it—and many young men who went to sea or joined the army were probably relieved to escape temporarily the confines of home and village. In time, this same habit of youthful dependency would be mobilized by industrial capitalism under different terms—about which young men would feel considerable ambivalence—but in the colonial years nobody could have anticipated the transforming developments to come.

FISHERMEN, FARMERS, AND MANUFACTURES

1 7 7 5 – 1 8 5 0

During the half-century that followed American independence, Essex County began to industrialize. In some degree, this transformation had its roots in recent developments: the contemporary industrialization of England, the creation of a national market in America, and the commercial integration of the North Atlantic. In other ways, it owed something to such traditions as the security of property, the idealization of competency, and the tradition of moderate state intervention—all of which had developed in the old country before a single Englishman had set foot in Massachusetts.[1] Still another condition of Essex County's early industrialization, however, and one closest to the subject matter of this book, was the region's own history. For it was during the colonial period that the North

1. All of this is traditional ground that historians have mapped reasonably well. A good, brief summary is Stuart Bruchey, *The Roots of American Economic Growth, 1607–1861* (New York, 1965).

Shore of Massachusetts—like much of New England and the rest of America's northeast—acquired most of the social underpinnings necessary to support industrialization.

One of these was the development in the North Shore's seaport towns of a resident merchant class. Not merely retailers, warehousers, or local agents but real "traders by sea," launching transatlantic voyages with their own capital in their own vessels, such merchants were more plentiful in the northern colonial ports than anywhere else in Britain's North American and Caribbean possessions.[2] Another was the settlement and growth of a resident population characterized by impressive occupational diversity. Most of this consisted initially in the presence of skilled housewives and some urban craftsmen, but in the eighteenth century, when cottage farmers began taking up by-employments, the same diversity spread among the county's male population as a whole. This heterogeneity gave rise to a dense network of local and regional exchange, a striking capacity for import substitution, and a range of business opportunities for locally resident merchants. Although none of this marked off Essex County from the rest of New England or from the Middle Colonies, it did distinguish the American northeast from the simpler export-driven societies elsewhere in the New World.

Still another precondition for industrialization was the accumulation of manpower and productive wealth within the county and the consequent development of local free markets in capital and labor. In the fishery, where profits could sustain the cost of supporting a paid labor force, these markets began to replace clientage as the medium for the mobilization of labor toward the end of the seventeenth century. In agriculture, where commercial production could not support a paid labor force, no similar markets ever developed during the colonial period and the pressure of numbers against the land was felt chiefly in out-migration and the development of by-employments. Both the maritime and the rural economy, however, had matured by 1775 to the point where men and women throughout Essex County were ready to look outside the family for profitable employment—at least as a temporary expedient—were such employment available. Productive relations in Essex County had acquired thereby a flexibility that systems of servitude and peonage denied to other colonies. With a resident merchant class and a population of skilled producers,

2. Jacob M. Price, "Economic Function and the Growth of American Port Towns in the Eighteenth Century," *Perspectives in American History*, VIII (1974), 138.

connected throughout by a series of incipient if as yet incompletely elaborated markets, the different communities on the North Shore were as well situated as any to imitate England's industrial example.

To argue this is not to suggest that working people in Essex County regarded the prospect of industrial development as an unalloyed blessing. During the period of the early republic, the future course of capitalist development presented a cloudy amalgam of vague opportunities and indistinct dangers. Insofar as it meant a quickening of demand for local manufactures and for the produce of land and sea as well as a broader range of paid work for young people thinking about founding independent households, industrialization was welcome. Yet any development that concentrated power in the hands of the few and threatened to drive small-scale self-employed producers out of business was simultaneously worrisome. For women, who had never shared fully in the benefits of household independence, there were obvious advantages to the emerging order of things that probably outweighed their anxieties. But for men, the disappearance of a household economy that had traditionally supported their power as patriarchs and their independence as propertied producers presented something of a crisis. Independence, enhanced in value by a revolutionary war fought in part to preserve it, remained a powerful force in men's minds into the nineteenth century, one that did not lend itself easily to industrial employment.

The persistence of competency as an ideal in plain tension with the realities of population growth and the possibilities of paid employment gave a particular shape to Essex County's first wage labor force. Capitalism was a powerful developmental force during the period but not an immediately transforming one; it built upon the assumptions of an earlier world—assumptions that died hard. By following the evolution of the region's fishing and farming economies into the age of industrialization, it is possible to see how older patterns of male employment influenced the creation of a labor force in the new manufacturing economy.

FISHING

At the end of the colonial period, two types of maritime community within Essex County were pursuing the same cod fishery. The first had come into being after 1640 when a crowd of North Atlantic maritime laborers— attracted by favorable terms of credit and the possibility of secure provisioning—settled on the ocean periphery of Massachusetts at Salem and

Marblehead. Chronically poor in property, they had always constituted a laboring class, driven into working for others by the pinch of need. The other community materialized at the beginning of the eighteenth century when the pressure of numbers against the limited fertility of Cape Ann pushed underemployed young men from several previously agricultural villages stretching from Beverly to Chebacco into part-time fishing. Combining voyages to the banks with small-scale farming and craft employment, these cottage fishermen pursued complicated multi-occupational strategies to keep their households economically afloat.

By 1775 the cod fishery was providing a cash income to thousands of coastal New Englanders. Some salted the money away in savings; many more spent it as soon as it was earned. But in a part of New England where the threat of underemployment now hung over most people's heads throughout much of the year, families depended on income from the fishery. As a form of employment, however, fishing left much to be desired. It was brutal work, exhausting at the best of times and perilous at the worst; like all seafaring labor it was hard to reconcile with the normal run of pleasures and obligations—at home, in church, or simply around the neighborhood—that New Englanders enjoyed. As a source of earnings, fishing was decidedly seasonal, notoriously unpredictable, and seldom a route even to the most modest brand of prosperity. To this day, fisheries economists ponder the poverty that seems to have accompanied fishermen from biblical times, and the colonists knew as well as anyone that fishermen seldom grew wealthy.[3] Men who experienced the numbing cold of handlining for cod in subfreezing temperatures, the boredom of midsummer days spent shrouded in fog, and the fear of riding out a November gale in the blackness of night—all in the knowledge that their best efforts might not be rewarded with an adequate catch or a decent market—could easily have been drawn into other lines of work, had the opportunity existed. In the nineteenth century, when the growth of manufacturing finally presented the fishing communities of Essex County with exactly this alternative, most of them abandoned the sea without a murmur, and the fishery retreated to its final home in Gloucester.

Revival

With the outbreak of the Revolutionary War in 1775, many decades of vigorous expansion for the cod fishery came to an abrupt end. With the

3. H. Scott Gordon, "The Economic Theory of a Common-Property Resource: The Fishery," *Journal of Political Economy*, LXII (1954), 124–142.

New England Restraining Act, passed by Parliament in March of that year, all vessels owned in New England were banned from the offshore fishing grounds, and after the few companies that had ventured out on spring fares returned in June or early July, hardly a fishing vessel stirred from any Essex County port until peace was concluded in 1783. Schooners that were not converted to privateers or some sort of naval purpose lay silently at the wharves or hauled up on shore. By October of 1775, with many fishermen "in the army & the Rest . . . out of Employ," Marblehead was reported to be "dirty, disagreeable," and in such "great Distress" that hungry children filled every house and swarmed in the streets, being "forc'd [to] beg of all they see." Muttered one disturbed visitor, "I do not want ever to see such another place." At Gloucester the grass was soon "growing upon the wharves, and many of the larger class of fishing vessels were rotting at their moorings." The seafaringmen of Beverly and Salem survived the war better than their neighbors—but only by converting their sloops and schooners into privateers.[4]

The Revolutionary War took a tremendous toll on the fishery. By the early 1780s only a few dozen serviceable fishing schooners were still afloat. In Marblehead the fleet had dwindled from 7,500 tons before 1775 to 1,509 tons in 1780, and around Cape Ann the banks fishery had given way to a mere scattering of small boats working inshore. Joshua Burnham of Chebacco, who before 1775 had been skipper of his own schooner and a trader to the Chesapeake, by the war's end was handlining with his neighbor from a two-man boat in Ipswich Bay.[5] And Burnham was a survivor. Before 1783 many skilled fishermen had either died in combat

4. Raymond McFarland, *A History of the New England Fisheries* (New York, 1911), 121–125; Samuel Roads, Jr., *The History and Traditions of Marblehead*, 3d ed. (Marblehead, Mass., 1897), 123–157; James Duncan Phillips, *Salem in the Eighteenth Century* (Boston, 1937), 372–379; "Revolutionary War Manuscripts Copied from the Originals in Possession of the Marblehead Historical Society," Essex Institute, *Historical Collections*, LXXV (1939), 15–22, 382–392; "Ensign Williams' Visit to Essex County in 1776," Essex Institute, *Hist. Colls.*, LXXXIII (1947), 144–145; Joseph Reynolds, *Peter Gott, the Cape Ann Fisherman* (Portland, Me., 1856), 128–129, 148; John J. Babson, *History of the Town of Gloucester, Cape Ann, including the Town of Rockport* (Gloucester, Mass., 1860), 440; Octavius T. Howe, "Beverly Privateers in the American Revolution," Colonial Society of Massachusetts, *Publications*, XXIV (1920–1922), 318–435.

5. Jefferson, "Report on Fisheries," 223; Lorenzo Sabine, *Report on the Principal Fisheries of the American Seas* (Washington, D.C., 1853), 174, 202; accounts of Joshua Burnham, Solomon Allen, Ebenezer Burnham, and Abraham Wharff, Daniel Rogers Account Book, 1770–1790, JDPL.

or perished in British prison hulks. Gloucester is said to have lost 357 seamen to the war, Beverly counted 190 widows by 1780, and so heavy were the casualties among Marblehead fishermen that the selectmen listed 866 fatherless children in a petition submitted to Congress in 1790. Many fishermen who returned from privateering or from service in the army had aged too much or been injured too severely to return to the rigors of their trade, and for nearly a decade no youngsters had been trained to replace them. All the fishermen Daniel Rogers of Gloucester had shipped before the war were less than forty years old, and three-quarters were under thirty; by the early 1780s a full half of his men ranged in age from thirty to fifty-five. At the conclusion of peace in 1783 merchants and fishermen alike knew that tonnage and trained fishermen were in equally short supply.[6]

The demand for their hauls, however, had never been healthier. All of the major national cod fisheries had shrunk during the Revolutionary War, and prices around the North Atlantic had climbed to historically high levels. In Boston, Jamaica fish was selling for $3.67 a quintal in the winter of 1783–1784—more than even the highest grades of fish had ever commanded.[7] With remarkable speed, responding to prices and availing themselves of the credit that this healthy market called forth, merchants and fishermen began to reconstruct the fleet. By 1784 a visitor reported sixty schooners at anchor in Marblehead, and toward the end of the decade scores of small boats were fishing out of the several harbors around Cape Ann. Taking the Essex County fleet as a whole, by 1786–

6. Babson, *History of Gloucester*, 440; Howe, "Beverly Privateers," Col. Soc. Mass., *Pubs.*, XXIV (1920–1922), 378; "Report on the Fisheries: Editorial Note," in Julian P. Boyd et al., eds., *The Papers of Thomas Jefferson* (Princeton, N.J., 1950–), XIX, 148. For the age profile of Daniel Rogers's hands, 1769–1775, see table 8, above. For the period 1780–1783 (after adjusting for the bias toward identification of minors, since the given names of both fathers and sons were recorded in his accounts), 11% were aged 10–19, 39% were 20–29, 31% were 30–39, 14% were 40–49, and 6% were 50–59 (N = 56). See Daniel Rogers Acct. Bk., 1770–1790, and Appendix 3.

7. For prices, see Ruth Crandall, "Wholesale Commodity Prices in Boston during the Eighteenth Century," *Review of Economic Statistics*, XVI (1934), 182; Selwyn H. H. Carrington, *The British West Indies during the American Revolution* (Dordrecht, 1988), 113; Earl J. Hamilton, *War and Prices in Spain, 1651–1800* (Cambridge, Mass., 1947), 250–253; Harold A. Innis, *The Cod Fisheries: The History of an International Economy*, rev. ed. (Toronto, 1954), 285; and Anne Bezanson et al., *Wholesale Prices in Philadelphia, 1784–1861* (Philadelphia, 1936), 45.

1790 both tonnage and annual catch had regained more than 70 percent of their pre-Revolutionary levels. Prices dipped somewhat when the European fisheries reorganized in the later 1780s, but they began to climb again during the French Revolutionary Wars, and production rose with them. Tonnage for the entire state climbed from 19,185 in 1789, to 42,746 in 1798, to 69,306 in 1807; exports of codfish in quintals per annum climbed from an average of 250,650 between 1786 and 1790 to 523,440 between 1803 and 1807; close to three-quarters of this gain went to the outports of Essex County.[8] Political conditions sometimes prevented local fishermen from exploiting this boom to the fullest. The British West Indies, most notably, were closed to American fish between 1783 and 1797. But the free access to European and colonial markets outside the British Empire that New England had obtained as a result of the Revolution more than made up for these inconveniences. As rising population around the North Atlantic drove the demand for fish upward, the privilege of supplying war-torn Europe as a neutral outsider provided New England's fishing industry with a striking opportunity. Jefferson's embargo of 1807 would interrupt the boom, and the War of 1812 would shut it down entirely, but until then the local fisheries enjoyed unparalleled prosperity.[9]

In certain ways the conditions of the early national period re-created those of the 1640s, when the local fishery had first been constructed. Once again both productive equipment and manpower were scarce in a context of high prices and the disruption of transatlantic fisheries. True, the scarcities were less acute than at the beginnings of settlement, and every fishing port now possessed a class of property-poor fishermen accustomed to dealing with a variety of merchant outfitters through local labor markets. Both in human casualties and in the destruction of shipping, however, the fishery had lost enormous ground during the Revolutionary War,

8. John S. Ezell, ed., and Judson P. Wood, trans., *The New Democracy in America: Travels of Francisco de Miranda in the United States, 1783–84* (Norman, Okla., 1963), 189; "Report on the Fisheries: Editorial Note," in Boyd *et al.*, eds., *Jefferson Papers*, XIX, 145–146, 148; Jefferson, "Report on Fisheries," 223; McFarland, *History of the New England Fisheries*, 136–138; Sabine, *Report on Fisheries*, 176. My estimate that close to three-quarters of the Massachusetts fishery was located in Essex County during this period is based on Jefferson, "Report on Fisheries," 223, and on the treatment of the different town fisheries in McFarland, *History of the New England Fisheries*, 143–150.

9. Gerald S. Graham, *British Policy and Canada, 1774–1791: A Study in Eighteenth Century Trade Policy* (London, 1930), 64; Innis, *Cod Fisheries*, 220–224.

and the task of rebuilding the fleet from scratch required merchants and fishermen to revert to some of the strategies that had worked a century and a half earlier.

Given the shortage of tonnage and trained men, merchants thin on resources but eager to profit from high prices were only too happy to allow certain fishermen to invest their earnings either in vessels of their own or in the materials to build them. And fishermen knew that with their services in demand, they could obtain the credit necessary to finance these purchases. The degree to which fishing was once again credit driven is mirrored in the records of probate. The proportion of active fishermen who owed money at their death climbed from 19 percent in 1726–1775 to 46 percent between 1783 and 1812. Credit could be used for many purposes, but generally speaking those who assumed the most debt had done so to purchase or construct their own craft.[10]

In Marblehead and Beverly, two ports that followed the banks fishery, a sizable minority of the men—mostly skippers—acquired shares in or the outright ownership of schooners. Edward Hammond of Marblehead died in 1812 at the age of forty-four possessing half a schooner and a small fishyard; the wife of twenty-three-year-old Daniel Haskell of Beverly collected $102 of insurance when the vessel he skippered was lost in 1800. Among active fishermen whose estates passed through probate in these two towns, the proportion of those who owned vessel tonnage when they died climbed from 3 percent in 1726–1775 to 17 percent in 1783–1812. Since those with probated estates were commonly the older and more established fishermen who had succeeded in becoming skippers, their holdings are not typical of those of all crew members. Yet insofar as skippers possessed few special perquisites and were generally recruited from the fishing community at large, their fortunes did represent a standard to which fishermen of talent could reasonably aspire. The revival of vessel ownership among them reflected a revival of opportunity in general, and the achievements of Hammond and Haskell suggest a potential for advancement that their fathers and grandfathers had never experienced.[11]

10. See Appendix 3. For 1726–1775, $N = 52$; for 1783–1812, $N = 35$. The four most seriously indebted estates during the second period all belonged to vessel owners. See Estates of John Garner (1791), Probate No. 10675, Edward Hammond (1812), Probate No. 12247, William H. Lovett (1805), Probate No. 17163, and Ebenezer Gott (1797), Probate No. 11326, Essex Co. Prob. Recs.

11. Estate of Edward Hammond (1812), Probate No. 12247, Estate of Daniel Haskell

In Gloucester and Ipswich, easy credit meant something different. "We were told at Cape Ann," wrote William Bentley in 1793, that the merchants there "could with difficulty provide hands for their bankers, from the general persuasion that the Bay boats were more lucrative." Before the War of Independence, fathers had sent their sons down from the coves and hamlets around the cape to the harbor at Gloucester to ship out on schooners for the banks; now they commonly constructed smaller craft for themselves and employed their offspring closer to home. The workhorse of this new inshore fleet was the chebacco boat—a craft of less than thirty tons with a foremast stepped nearly in its stem and a cuddy forward in which two or three men might sleep overnight. Narrower, sharper, and normally large enough to carry a crew of five or six were the pinkies and jiggers developed shortly after the turn of the century. For families with farming interests settled along the coast, these nifty and flexible craft were well suited to a few weeks' fishing here and there—in May once the crops were in the ground or in October after harvest.[12]

Typical of the cottage fisherman who prospered in these flush times was John Wheeler of Sandy Bay. About 1803 he died owning "half of a dwelling . . . two stories high" with privileges in the fireplace, oven, well, garden, lane, back room, and cellar. His home was probably similar in appearance to others in the village: "small . . . & generally painted," with doors on the side "so as to afford a good front room & back kitchen, with a bed room back of the front entry." Included in his holdings were an acre of land, a fish house by the harbor, and half of an old, modestly fitted two-masted boat moored to a "stump & stone" by the shore. In addition, his wife tended a pair of cattle, he kept "a parsel of old husbandry & farming tools In and about the Dwelling house," and there were three guns in the

(1802), Probate No. 12716, Essex Co. Prob. Recs.; account of schooner *Hawk*, John Lovett Account Book, 1797–1801, Beverly Historical Society, Beverly, Mass. The calculations for all probated active fishermen were based on 37 cases from 1726–1775 and 23 cases from 1783–1812. An active fisherman was one who died within ten years of his last recorded voyage. See Appendix 3. In 1805 17% of Marblehead skippers owned a controlling interest in the schooner they commanded, though the rate among all fishermen was considerably lower. See Marine Ledger B: Abstracts of Registers, Fishing Licences, 1800–1805, Marblehead Customs House Records, JDPL.

12. William Bentley, *The Diary of William Bentley, D.D.*, 4 vols. (Gloucester, Mass., 1962), II, 8, 304; Howard I. Chapelle, *The History of American Sailing Ships* (New York, 1935), 252; Babson, *History of Gloucester*, 571; J. P. Brissot de Warville, *New Travels in the United States of America, 1788*, ed. Durand Echeverria (Cambridge, Mass., 1964), 366.

back room. When Wheeler died, leaving a young family, the estate that supported this diversified household economy was valued at $600. During the extraordinary boom that framed the turn of the century, the brand of credit-driven quasi independence that Wheeler represented enjoyed one final revival.[13]

Were fisherman and outfitter linked together by the same ties of client-age that had organized the industry in the seventeenth century? Here the evidence is ambiguous. The account books of William Knight in Marblehead suggest that credit did have a price: some fishermen lost some of their freedom to bargain as the network of indebtedness spread. The proportion of fishermen who returned to Knight for five consecutive years after their first voyage rose from 6 percent among those who began between 1767 and 1770 to 28 percent among those who started between 1788 and 1795. The terms that Daniel Rogers struck with his hands at Gloucester harbor scarcely changed, however, with the proportion of five-year hands edging upward but only slightly, from 10 percent among those who signed on with him in 1770 to 12 percent among those he hired between 1784 and 1786.[14] The most likely setting for the revival of client-age lay in the more remote parishes of Cape Ann. Where cottage fishermen retained some independence and were difficult to recruit either as suppliers of fish or as paid employees, outfitters might be forced to stake a prior claim over their labor by using credit in this way. In small communities dominated by a couple of dealers, moreover, such a policy could work. The semifictional tale *Peter Gott, the Cape Ann Fisherman*, written by Joshua Reynolds, a local doctor familiar with these communities, described a fish dealer from this period who lived in Sandy Bay and operated in precisely this manner.

> In addition to the real estate which Mr. Dennis had accumulated on shore, he owned a large share of five or six schooners, whose outfits he furnished, and whose proceeds he received and marketed. The crews for these vessels, consisting of eight or ten hands each,

13. Inventory of John D. Wheeler, Probate No. 29450, Essex Co. Prob. Recs. On Sandy Bay, see Bentley, *Diary*, II, 304, 305, IV, 478–479. A "stump & stone" was constructed from a tree stump rammed up through a large flat stone with a hole bored in the middle and then set on the bottom of the harbor.

14. For Knight, 1767–1770, $N = 34$; for Knight, 1788–1795, $N = 46$; for Rogers, 1770, $N = 21$; for Rogers, 1784–1786, $N = 69$. See William Knight Account Books, 1769–1775, 1788–1800, JDPL; Daniel Rogers Acct. Bk., 1770–1790.

were usually shipped in the winter. From the time they were shipped, Mr. Dennis supplied them and their families with groceries, shoes, and most of their clothing. After the vessels put to sea, he continued to supply the families during the spring and summer. If the vessel was doing well, he continued to supply them till she was hauled up, late in the fall; but if she did not make good fares, he refused to supply them at an early day in the fall. It very often happened that strong and active men, after having labored hard through the season, had not a dollar coming to them when the voyage was settled, with which to supply the wants of their families through the winter. This was owing, in part, to the want of economy in their families, and in part to the high prices which they had to pay for everything that he furnished them. Mr. Dennis always considered it an object to bring about this result. Even if they owed him a few dollars at the settlement, it was all the better, for then he was sure of their services the next year. Thus they were bound to him by a bond which they found it very difficult to break. He had all their earnings in his hands, and paid for them in goods at his own price, and how could he fail but grow rich, or they to remain poor? He had several men who had been in his employment from twenty to thirty years and had rarely, if ever, been out of his debt.[15]

Whether Mr. Dennis represented a historical character is impossible to know. The power he was said to possess does seem a bit exaggerated, for any of his young clients who really wanted to escape the relationship could have marched overland to the harbor at Gloucester, found a berth on a banker or on a voyage to the West Indies, taken cash or a note for his earnings, used it to pay off Dennis, and then started afresh with another dealer. Even in the seventeenth century this had happened often enough. Reynolds also neglected to mention that fishermen often employed the credit they obtained in productive ways. Though sometimes a trap, it could also help the cottage fishermen of Cape Ann to retain a modicum of independence. Indeed, Peter Gott, the hero of Reynolds's tale, began climbing the ladder of success when Mr. Dennis invited him to purchase on credit one-third of a new fifty-ton schooner and to serve as her skipper.[16] Although few of Gott's neighbors were nearly as successful, credit at

15. Reynolds, *Peter Gott*, 29–31.
16. *Ibid.*, 162–163.

Dennis's store and elsewhere around the village enabled them to purchase salt, timber, wool, and fodder and otherwise make their petty farming and fishing operations work.

These truly were the halcyon days of the cod fishery. Two hundred small boats were said to be working out of Gloucester by 1804; nearly one hundred schooners took out licenses in Marblehead the following year, as did a further sixty from Salem and Beverly, and Newburyport sent out fifty-five or sixty sail the year after.[17] Many vessels continued to work the traditional grounds off the coast of Nova Scotia, but others set out to try waters that New Englanders had never fished before. About 1790, some passed through the Strait of Canso to test the hitherto unexploited banks and bays around the Gulf of St. Lawrence. By 1797 thirty-five American vessels were drying fish on the Magdalen Islands, and after the turn of the century three hundred New England vessels reportedly were working throughout the gulf. A smaller number even chose to sail beyond Newfoundland to catch and dry their fish along the coast of Labrador. As early as 1792, American fishermen were accused of driving British fishermen from these shores, and by 1805 one British official believed that "not less than 900 sail of American vessels" were trading and fishing between Anticosti Island and the Davis Strait.[18]

Throughout these years the Massachusetts fishery, based predominantly in Essex County, was a magnet for local labor. At its peak on the eve of Jefferson's embargo, it employed close to ten thousand men and boys—more than twice the number that had sailed from the same ports before the Revolution. Such a rate of growth, exceeding that of the state or county population by about 25 percent, testifies clearly to the extraordinary good health the industry enjoyed between 1783 and 1807.[19] As the

17. Babson, *History of Gloucester*, 571; Abstracts of Licences Granted to Enrolled Vessels in the District of Marblehead for Carrying on the Cod Fishery, 1805, Marine Ledger B: Marblehead Customs House Records; List of Allowances to Fishing Vessels for the Year 1805, Fishing Vessel Accounts: Lists of Bounty, Box 28, Salem Customs House Records, JDPL; McFarland, *History of the New England Fisheries*, 147. Many of the customs house records used in this study have since been reorganized and transferred to the National Archives Depository in Waltham, Mass.

18. Innis, *Cod Fisheries*, 222–223; McFarland, *History of the New England Fisheries*, 152–154; log of the schooner *Nancy*, 1795–1796, No. 1795N, log of the schooner *St. Peters*, 1793–1794, No. 1793S, Logbook Collection, JDPL.

19. The number of fishermen rose from about 4,400 in 1765–1775 to about 10,000 in 1805 (2.3% per annum); the population of Massachusetts rose from 235,308 in 1770 to 381,000 in 1810 (1.2%); the population of Essex County rose from about 43,000 in 1765 to

annual earnings fishermen could reasonably expect climbed from the $100–$200 that had prevailed at the end of the colonial period to the $200–$300 that was normal by the opening years of the nineteenth century, teenagers and married small holders flocked to the wharves to be outfitted and berthed for voyages to the banks. Some had grown up in families without the resources to launch them in any other career; others were the sons of farmers and artisans anxious to save money toward launching a household of their own; still others were small holders trying to eke out a living from any source that presented itself. A mixture of traditional motives—little changed from the eighteenth century—pushed men into this trying line of work, and for a time the local markets in fishing labor could happily absorb them.

Diversification

Benjamin Webber of Gloucester was among those who prospered from the fishing boom of the early republic. His father, a mariner with a tiny farm on the outskirts of town astride the road to Manchester, first shipped Benjamin and his younger brother Joseph on voyages to the banks in the 1770s, when they were in their teens. On schooners owned by Daniel Rogers at the harbor, Benjamin spent five years fishing offshore and coasting to Virginia to pay the debts on his father's account until the outbreak of the Revolution closed down the fishery. Both boys then enlisted and served at Bunker Hill, in the navy, and on privateers. Benjamin must have acquired quite a reputation locally, for in 1781 he was commissioned as commander of a Gloucester brigantine, the *Ruby*. After the war ended, he married his cousin Betsey and became a property owner—partly on credit and partly from his wartime earnings—purchasing a few parcels of land around his father's property, some trading stock, and a chebacco boat. By 1792, he owned a rugged little farm with several buildings and a few head of livestock, as well as sixty-seven tons of shipping—probably a small schooner in addition to his fishing boat. For twenty years, this merchant

---

61,000 in 1800 (1.2%). See Innis, *Cod Fisheries*, 222, 223; Series A195–209, "Population of States, by Sex, Race, Urban-Rural Residence, and Age: 1790 to 1970," and Series Z1–19, "Estimated Population of American Colonies: 1610 to 1780," U.S. Bureau of the Census, *The Statistical History of the United States from Colonial Times to the Present* (New York, 1976), 29, 1168; Evarts B. Greene and Virginia D. Harrington, *American Population before the Federal Census of 1790* (New York, 1932), 21; U.S. Department of State, *Return of the Whole Number of Persons within the Several Districts of the United States . . . 1800* (Washington, D.C., 1801), 8.

View of the Town of Gloucester, Mass., by Fitz Hugh Lane (1836). Courtesy of the Peabody Essex Museum, Salem, Mass.

mariner enjoyed success commanding vessels to the West Indies, trading there on his own account, and running a store in town.[20]

After 1807 his affairs began to sour, however, and the problem was debt. The same advances that had underwritten his successful ventures during the French Revolutionary and Napoleonic Wars were now called in. One by one, Webber had to sell off his assets—first the shop in town, then his fish houses, wharf, and right in the commons, and finally his dwelling house with the largest part of the farm—all to satisfy his creditors. In 1830, the government judged him needy enough to deserve a pension, which he received until he died in 1841. Benjamin Webber lived his roller-coaster career in higher style than most who had begun their working lives hand-lining for codfish, but his history illustrates as well as any both the oppor-

20. Accounts of Benjamin Webber, Daniel Rogers Acct. Bk., 1770–1790; George Walter Chamberlain, *Descendants of Michael Webber of Falmouth, Maine, and Gloucester, Massachusetts* (Wellesley Hills, Mass., 1935), 23–24, 29–37; Bettye Hobbs Pruitt, ed., *The Massachusetts Tax Valuation List of 1771* (Boston, 1978), 48–49; entries for Benjamin Webber, Gloucester Tax Valuation Lists, 1784, 1791, 1792, JDPL.

tunities that plucky fishermen seized during the period prior to Jefferson's embargo and the mounting problems that confronted them thereafter.[21]

What brought on Webber's financial ruin? Although he undoubtedly made many personal errors, a host of more general problems struck the entire cod fishery after 1807, and Webber was merely one of many who succumbed. Initially, the industry's troubles were political. The Embargo Act of 1807 prevented any vessel from shipping produce out of an American port, and within a year exports of dried codfish had dropped from 473,924 to 155,808 quintals. Business picked up a little between 1809 and 1811, but the outbreak of war with England in 1812 dealt the fishery a further blow, and by the following year the British navy had bottled up New England shipping and killed the export trade in fish. In themselves, however, these difficulties were hardly terminal. With the return of peace in 1815 prospects for fishermen seemed as good as ever, and the fleet was rapidly rebuilt. In the summer of 1816, William Bentley recorded that Marblehead was rising again and that at Beverly there were "several fields replanted with flakes, which had been divided for house lots." On Cape Ann, he caught sight of "boats building for the bay fishery not only at every landing place but in the yards of the farmers." In tonnage if not in exports the whole American cod fishery regained its pre-embargo levels by 1817.[22]

Peace did not prove an unqualified blessing, for with it came trouble in international markets. The boom of the early republic had hinged on the havoc that war had wrought among New England's competitors—especially the French—and with their revival after 1815 prices started to drop. The settlement of Newfoundland during the war period—fed by high prices and the difficulties of carrying on a transatlantic fishery prey to privateering—had created a huge resident fishery on that island, whose product further depressed the market. During the 1820s, moreover, cheap Norwegian fish (dry cured without salt) began to arrive in quantity at Bilbao and other Spanish ports, driving the American product from the field entirely.[23]

21. Chamberlain, *Descendants of Michael Webber*, 29–37.

22. Sabine, *Report on Fisheries*, 176; McFarland, *History of the New England Fisheries*, 138–139; Bentley, *Diary*, IV, 219–220, 400, 403, 406, 423, 478–479.

23. Shannon Ryan, *Fish out of Water: The Newfoundland Saltfish Trade, 1814–1914* (St. John's, Nfld., 1986), chaps. 3, 4, esp. 105–106; Bezanson *et al.*, *Wholesale Prices in Philadelphia*, 45; Innis, *Cod Fisheries*, 285.

Fortunately for local fishermen, however, the formation of the United States had begun to provide a protected and rapidly growing domestic market that they could exploit instead. The Impost Act of 1789 placed a tariff of fifty cents a quintal on dried fish and a dollar a barrel on pickled fish, and prohibitive duties remained in place, though altered in particulars, until the Reciprocity Treaty of 1854. With the country's population climbing at about 3 percent per year between 1790 and 1850, the creation of a protected national market presented a grand opportunity. The cod fishery of colonial times had been wholly export driven, but in 1817 William Bentley was noting in his diary the sale of fish via Albany to markets in the Mississippi Valley, and by 1840 three-quarters of the New England catch was consumed inside the United States.[24]

The codfish had no time-honored hold upon the tastes of American consumers, however, and when its price dropped after 1815, merchants and fishermen in several Essex County ports began to consider diversification into other species. Haddock, pollock, hake, and halibut teemed alongside the cod in the waters directly off the Massachusetts coast; landed fresh, any of them could find a ready sale in the growing port towns of the New England seaboard. By the opening decade of the nineteenth century, a haddock trip in springtime, a pollock voyage in the autumn, and "haking" in the winter were all legitimate alternatives to the traditional cod fares. By 1830, some of the more adventurous crews began to chance the dangerous, shallow waters of Georges Bank to handline for halibut that could be carried into Charlestown and "traded off to the farmers for produce" or hawked in the fish markets of Salem and Boston. Enterprising merchants meanwhile had uncovered an even larger market among middle western farmers and southern slave owners for salt fish— cod, of course, but also "Quoddy" pollock and especially barreled mackerel.[25]

24. Sabine, *Report on Fisheries*, 158, 164, 175, 176; Innis, *Cod Fisheries*, 324, 351; "Area and Population of the United States, 1790–1970," Series A1–5, U.S. Census Bureau, *Statistical History*, 8; Bentley, *Diary*, IV, 514; McFarland, *History of the New England Fisheries*, 168, 169; Louis McLane, ed., *Report of the Secretary of the Treasury, 1832: Documents Relative to the Manufactures in the United States*, 22d Cong., 1st sess., H. Doc. 308, I, 241, hereafter cited as McLane, *Report*.

25. The best description of the hake, haddock, and pollock fisheries is Reynolds, *Peter Gott*, 98–99, 101–106, 120–122. On the Georges Bank fishery, see James B. Connoly, *The Port of Gloucester* (New York, 1940), 160–169; Richard Rathbun and Joseph W. Collins, "The Sea Fishing-Grounds of the Eastern Coast of North America from Greenland to

So popular was mackerel that during the 1820s and 1830s it became in certain ports the prime commercial fish. Although New Englanders had always landed some of this fish, which they either used for bait or shipped to the West Indies, it had never amounted to much of a business before 1800. In the eighteenth century contemporaries had estimated the annual take of New England mackerel at between 5,000 and 20,000 barrels—in value perhaps one-tenth the worth of the cod fishery—and almost all of this had been landed at Cape Cod or in Boston. In the second and third decades of the nineteenth century, a remarkable succession of years followed, when oceans of mackerel migrated in vast numbers past the Massachusetts coast, and the fishermen of Essex County were finally prompted to launch voyages in pursuit of this species alone.[26]

At its inception the new fishery employed small companies of at most six men on week-long trips directly off the Massachusetts coast. "Mackerel-catching" was always thought to be something of a lottery. As a species, the fish congregated in schools that were often enormous but also unpredictable in their movements and difficult to find. Furthermore, even when lured around the vessel with bait ground up by the men and cast overboard, the fish might be unwilling to take the hook. Then suddenly and for no clear reason the entire school would surge madly after the numerous lines draped over the sides of the vessel, keeping every man frantic for hours drawing up the mackerel, ripping them from the hooks, and tossing them into barrels. This might continue for only a few minutes, or it could last for hours or even days at a stretch, while the men stood blear-eyed at

Mexico," in Richard Rathbun, ed., *The Fishing Grounds of North America* (section III of George Brown Goode, ed., *The Fisheries and Fishery Industries of the United States*, 5 sections in 8 parts [Washington, D.C., 1884–1887]), 74–75; Sabine, *Report on Fisheries*, 197; and G. Brown Goode and J. W. Collins, "The Fresh-Halibut Fishery," in George Brown Goode, ed., *The History and Methods of the Fisheries*, 2 vols. (section V of Goode, ed., *Fisheries*), I, 29–35. On coastal fish markets, see Bentley, *Diary*, II, 203, IV, 453; George H. Procter, *The Fishermen's Memorial and Record Book* (Gloucester, Mass., 1873), 65, 72, 73; and Babson, *History of Gloucester*, 571. On the marketing of fish in the interior, see Sabine, *Report on Fisheries*, 173, 197; Procter, *Fishermen's Memorial*, 67; Babson, *History of Gloucester*, 573–575; and McFarland, *History of the New England Fisheries*, 166–169.

26. G. Brown Goode and J. W. Collins, "The Mackerel Hook-Fishery," in Goode, ed., *History and Methods of the Fisheries*, I, 298–302; "State of Fishermen of North America, 1764," Chatham MSS 30/8:81, 191, Public Record Office; Ezekiel Price Papers, 1754–1785, folio 17, Massachusetts Historical Society, Boston; Procter, *Fishermen's Memorial*, 61, 63.

the rail, forgoing sleep to tend their lines while the picking was good. And then, just as quickly and unaccountably, as if by common signal, the fish would cease biting and vanish—perhaps for good. The men had to pull in their lines, tally up their individual hauls, and dress the catch. After heading and gutting the fish, washing them out, rolling them in salt, and laying them in barrels to be stowed away, the crew (along with "the deck, the tubs, and everything near") were drenched "with blood and garbage." When the job was done and both vessel and crew had been scrubbed down with seawater, the men finally dropped into their berths for a well-earned rest. This was demanding but profitable work, and it rapidly became the fishery of preference for the most skilled and best-connected fishermen in the state.[27]

By the middle of the nineteenth century, Essex County possessed a complicated mix of fisheries that could keep an enterprising individual busy throughout most of the year. The work was no easier, and the pay was not much better, but in towns with a range of fisheries the feasibility of combining them into steady employment the year round made fishing a viable career.

Growing Gray in the Service of the Sea

During the early national period, the capital of innovation within the New England fishery moved to Cape Ann. With a longer tradition in the short and midrange fisheries and more local experience in handling different craft, the fishermen of Gloucester and the neighboring hamlets that ringed the cape—close to the shoals and ledges where mackerel, hake, haddock, and pollock were most readily caught—were better poised to capture the new opportunities than their counterparts in Beverly, Salem, and Marblehead. By 1820 Gloucester fishermen were following all of these species in a complicated annual cycle, and the development of the town's fisheries in the nineteenth century was founded on the increasingly diverse catch that its eastward perch encouraged (see table 15). Furthermore, the same geographic factors that advantaged Gloucester's inhabitants locationally in the new fisheries also disqualified them from competing in New England's

27. Sabine, *Report on Fisheries*, 181–186; Goode and Collins, "Mackerel Hook-Fishery," in Goode, ed., *History and Methods of the Fisheries*, 283–287; Reynolds, *Peter Gott*, 164–176; A. Howard Clarke, "Fisheries of Massachusetts," in George Brown Goode, ed., *A Geographical Review of the Fisheries Industries and Fishing Communities for the Year 1880* (section II of Goode, ed., *Fisheries*), 152–153; Babson, *History of Gloucester*, 599.

Table 15. Landings (in Pounds), Tonnage, and Employment
in the Gloucester Fisheries, 1786–1859

	1786–1790	1827	1837	1847	1859
Cod[a]	4,256,000	7,407,000	6,180,000	7,088,000	12,773,000
Mackerel[a]		5,445,000	8,787,000	9,356,000	11,933,000
Halibut				3,380,000	4,500,000
Pollock				919,000	
Hake				736,000	
Total catch[b]	4,256,000	12,852,000	14,967,000	21,479,000	29,206,000
Total value[b]	$114,240		$522,082	$589,354	$1,276,704
Vessel tonnage	3,600		9,824	12,354	23,882
Men	680		1,580	1,867	3,434
Catch/Man	6,259		9,428	11,505	8,186
Value/Man	$168		$330	$306	$368

[a]Codfish weights were converted from quintals (112 lbs.) to pounds; mackerel weights
were converted from barrels (200 lbs.) to pounds.
[b]Neither total catch nor total value includes fish oil or other species of fish.

Sources: "Report on the American Fisheries by the Secretary of State," Feb. 1, 1791,
in Julian P. Boyd *et al.*, eds., *The Papers of Thomas Jefferson* (Princeton, N.J., 1950–),
XIX, 223; A. Howard Clarke, "Historical References to the Fisheries of New England,"
in George Brown Goode, ed., *A Geographical Review of the Fisheries Industries and
Fishery Communities for the Year 1880* (section II of George Brown Goode, ed., *The
Fisheries and Fishery Industries of the United States*, 5 sections in 8 parts [Washington,
D.C., 1884–1887]), 691; John J. Babson, *History of the Town of Gloucester, Cape Ann,
including the Town of Rockport* (Gloucester, Mass., 1860), 599.

changing landward economy. Cape Ann was too rocky to farm sensibly in
the more competitive rural economy of the nineteenth century and too
remote from the developing centers of manufacture to allow fishermen to
slip easily into industrial employments. For all of these reasons, Gloucester
outlasted every one of its neighbors throughout the nineteenth century as a
serious fishing port.

As Cape Ann came to depend ever more strictly upon the sea, the
cottage component of local society began to diminish. Seafaring families
of the eighteenth century had often owned a few head of livestock, a
woodlot, or a parcel of arable land. Their nineteenth-century descen-

dants, however, owned little productive property beyond what they needed to fish. The minority who had real estate possessed little besides housing for their families, the habit of keeping animals had almost vanished, and few fishermen owned tools of husbandry or any landward craft. Even shoemaking was not the common by-employment it was almost everywhere else in Essex County. Indeed, the very "boots and shoes used in Gloucester," Henry Field told the U.S. Treasury Department in 1832, "are made principally . . . in other towns." True, there was always work to be had in sail lofts, fishyards, boatyards, and a variety of local stores. A number of granite quarries were opened around Cape Ann after 1824, and the business they generated eventually employed a few hundred men. The work of fishing wives centered increasingly on what they could sew, knit, cook, or clean, and now they often performed these services for boarders as well. In general, however, the local economy had come to be focused as never before on a single industry. Field put it plainly in 1832: "nineteen-twentieths of the business of Gloucester is in fishing."[28]

As Gloucester grew steadily more specialized, the ownership of fishing craft passed almost entirely out of the hands of active fishermen. The story of Benjamin Webber, whose turn-of-the-century affairs collapsed under the pressures of war and softer markets, was repeated many times after 1820. The proportion of Gloucester vessels under twenty tons of which a skipper owned the majority interest dropped from 69 percent in that year, to 38 percent in 1830, to only 30 percent by 1840. Among vessels over twenty tons such owner operation was rarer still—encompassing by 1840 only 17 percent of Gloucester's deep-sea fleet. Assuming that only the skipper would be the managing owner of a vessel—invariably the case with schooners and usually so with smaller boats—by 1840 a mere 3 percent of Gloucester fishermen owned the vessels they sailed.[29]

28. This characterization of the local householding economy is based on the probated inventories of active fishermen described in Appendix 3; a sample of 171 fishermen from U.S. Bureau of the Census, Seventh Census of the United States, 1850, Population Schedules for Gloucester, Mass., Microcopy 432, roll 315; Pruitt, ed., *Massachusetts Tax Valuation List of 1771*, 48–67; Babson, *History of Gloucester*, 576–577; and McLane, *Report*, I, 220–221. Of the 10 fishermen who died in mid-career between 1701 and 1800, 6 owned livestock, whereas only 1 of the 16 who died between 1800 and 1855 had an estate containing animals. Of fishermen age 30 or older, 78% of those who fished between 1767 and 1775 and who could be traced to the Massachusetts Tax Valuation List of 1771 ($N = 9$) owned real estate, but only 49% of those listed in the 1850 census sample ($N = 86$) did so. Almost no one under 30 owned real estate in either period.

29. Summaries for 1820, 1830, 1840, Abstract of Licences Granted to Vessels under 20

Table 16. Age Distribution of Gloucester Fishermen, 1767–1850 (in Percents)

Age	1767–1775 Fishermen from Account Books[a] (N = 131)	1830–1849 Fishermen from Drownings in Vital Records (N = 60)	1850 Fishermen by Occupation from Census[b] (N = 171)	1850 Males, 10+ Years of Age from Census[b] (N = 151)
10–19	26	20	14[c]	28
20–29	43	37	36	30
30–39	19	23	25	17
40–49	5	13	13	13
50–59	6	5	9	7
60–69	0	2	2	3
70+	0	0	0	2

[a]Where the data used to calculate the percentages for 1767–1775 were drawn from account books, the results had to be adjusted to deal with biases introduced by problems in the identification of minors who were fishing on their fathers' accounts.
[b]This constitutes a random sample.
[c]These results were adjusted to correct for the bias introduced by the fact that those under 15 were not required to report their occupation for the 1850 census.

Sources: Daniel Rogers Account Book, 1770–1790, John Stevens Account Book, 1769–1775, James Duncan Phillips Library, Peabody Essex Museum, Salem, Mass.; *Vital Records of Gloucester, Massachusetts to the End of the Year, 1849,* 3 vols. (Topsfield, Mass., 1917–1924); George H. Procter, *The Fishermen's Memorial and Record Book* (Gloucester, Mass., 1873), 9–14; U.S. Bureau of the Census, Seventh Census of the United States, 1850, Population Schedule for Gloucester, Mass., Microcopy 432, roll 315.

The decline of Cape Ann's cottage economy and the concentration of vessel ownership among Gloucester's merchant elite continued the process whereby fishing was transformed from a youthful stage of life into a working career. This had begun in the eighteenth century, but voyaging to the banks had still been overwhelmingly a young man's occupation through the end of the colonial period (see table 16). In the aftermath of the Revolution, when a near-decade of inactivity had left the fishery short

Tons, 1815–1841, vol. 167, Summary for 1840, Abstract of Codfish Licences, 1834–1842, vol. 153, Gloucester Customs House Records, JDPL. Converting the percentage of vessels that were owned by skippers and masters to the percentage of fishermen who owned vessels assumes a ratio of four men to a boat and eight men to a banker.

of hands in their teens and twenties, fishing crews had to be assembled
from older men. Nor was there any reversion in the nineteenth century to
the earlier pattern. If one compares the age distribution of nineteenth-
century fishermen to that of the adult male population of Gloucester as a
whole in 1850, the fit is reasonably close—at least among those aged
twenty to sixty-nine. Dependent labor, which had begun in colonial times
as part of a family strategy to sustain household independence, had developed for the most part into a lifetime profession.

Through midcentury, Gloucester boys still signed on in droves every
season, but now they were likely to sail with men their fathers' ages or
older. When the *Golden Fleece* foundered in the frigid waters of Georges
Bank in the March gale of 1852, she took with her a crew of nine—seven of
whom can be traced to entries in the manuscript census of 1850. Sylvester
Rust, the skipper, was twenty-nine years of age—at the prime of his productive career—with a wife and two small children housed in rented
quarters in Gloucester. That year he brought with him on the winter
fishery his teenaged brother Samuel, who still lived at home with their
father, Moses. Two other boys also sailed on the *Golden Fleece:* fifteen-
year-old George Blaisdell, the son of a stonemason from Amesbury, and
seventeen-year-old Samuel Jackman, a shipmaster's boy from Newburyport. The rest of the company, however, were middle-aged. Edmund
Cook, Samuel Atwood, and James Norwood ranged in years from thirty-
nine to forty-five, each rented living quarters in Gloucester, and each left
behind a widow with children to support. Naturally, the makeup of different Gloucester fishing companies varied more than this single example
suggests. Among fishermen from the 1850 census were immigrants from
Denmark and Portugal; single men supporting their widowed mothers;
grandfathers with no children left at home; businessmen's sons; and even
one businessman's father. Most Gloucester schoonermen of the mid-
nineteenth century, however, retained little or nothing of the albeit modest independence that their grandfathers had once enjoyed. Poor in property, they depended entirely on paid employment on the banks. As Samuel
Eliot Morison once observed, they now indeed "grew gray in the service of
the sea."[30]

30. Procter, *Fishermen's Memorial,* 16; U.S. Census Bureau, Seventh Census, Population
Schedules for Gloucester, Mass. For the sources of the 1850 sample, see n. 28, above. The
quotation is from Samuel Eliot Morison, *The Maritime History of Massachusetts, 1783–
1860* (Boston, 1979), 138.

Elsewhere in Essex County, fishing history took a different turn; indeed, it was coming to an end. The first two ports to drop out were Salem and Ipswich. In 1794 Salem's schooner fleet had nearly regained its pre-Revolutionary size when the outbreak of European war began to deflect the attention of merchants and seafaringmen to the profits and wages to be earned in neutral shipping. By 1801 William Bentley was noting in his diary that with merchant voyages to Europe and the East Indies commanding most local capital, Salem was withdrawing from the fishery. Fitfully, the schooner fishery diminished, until by 1844 only three local vessels were sailing annually to the banks.[31]

The fishermen of Ipswich also recovered rapidly from the Revolutionary War. Although few schooners ever sailed from the town proper anymore, according to Jefferson's report to Congress fifty-six small craft were based in Chebacco Parish during the late 1780s, outfitted mainly from Gloucester, and they conducted their business along the same lines as the boat fishery elsewhere around Cape Ann. This little fleet seems to have been prospering even at the turn of the century. One contemporary later remembered "forty sail of boats from this place . . . engaged in the fishery on the eastern shore [and] a few . . . employed in the Bank fishery" about that time. But after 1812, the succession of war and falling prices began to sap local interest in this taxing work, and with the growth of a local shipbuilding industry after 1815, most fishermen quit the sea for more comfortable and remunerative work closer to home.[32]

Three other towns in Essex County maintained an active interest in the fisheries until well into the nineteenth century: Beverly, Newburyport, and Marblehead. Beverly had been a latecomer to the industry, but the schooner fleet based in that harbor grew steadily from nineteen vessels at the end of the 1780s, to over forty in 1832, to about seventy-five by 1850. At the end of the eighteenth century, Bentley heard along the waterfront that whereas "the Marblehead fishermen accustomed to Grand banks wait there for fish . . . the Beverly fishermen take advantage of less fre-

31. Bentley, *Diary*, II, 373; A. Howard Clarke, "Historical References to the Fisheries of New England," in Goode, ed., *Geographical Review*, 701–702.

32. Jefferson, "Report on Fisheries," 223; Joseph B. Felt, *History of Ipswich, Essex and Hamilton* (1834), cited in Clarke, "Historical References," in Goode, ed., *Geographical Review*, 693. In 1803, Bentley noted that Ipswich was in decay, with no fishery or foreign trade; he meant the town parish, however, and not Chebacco. See Bentley, *Diary*, III, 44.

quented places"; especially in their push into the Gulf of St. Lawrence, Beverly skippers were, indeed, among the more innovative fishermen of the new republic. After the financial crisis of 1857, however, the local fishery entered a tailspin from which it never recovered. At the end of the Civil War only twenty to thirty Beverly vessels were still sailing for the banks, and by 1879 that number had dwindled to fifteen.[33]

Newburyport followed a similar curve. Prior to the Revolution, few local merchants had any experience with either the fishery or the fish trade. After 1796, however, the development of West Indian connections—especially with the boom in neutral trade—created a local demand for low-quality cod and prompted a handful of active fishermen to launch voyages to the hitherto unexploited Labrador coast, where small fish suitable for cheap markets abounded. By the beginning of the nineteenth century, hundreds of Newburyport fishermen in dozens of schooners were catching and curing cod on those northern shores through the warmer months and then carrying their product southward to the sugar islands in the winter. After 1804, the diversion of Merrimack Valley produce to Boston via the Middlesex Canal robbed Newburyport of its traditional hinterland and forced local merchants to depend even more heavily on the fishery for business and exportable cargoes. As foreign shipping fell into eclipse during the 1820s and 1830s, merchants turned to outfitting vessels in the chase for mackerel, and with 166 vessels under license Newburyport briefly rivaled Gloucester as the premier fishing port of New England. With the construction of five steam-powered cotton mills in the 1840s, however, alternative employment lured manpower and capital from the local fishery, and the fleet gradually decreased in tonnage from 8,385 in 1835, to 6,012 in 1851, to about 1,000 tons by 1874. The industry had seen Newburyport through a difficult period, but the return of prosperity spelled its demise.[34]

The most striking story of any nineteenth-century fishing community, and ultimately the most significant, was that of Massachusetts's oldest outport—Marblehead. Staggered by war yet again in 1812, the town re-

33. Clarke, "Fisheries of Massachusetts," in Goode, ed., *Geographical Review*, 180; Clarke, "Historical References," *ibid.*, 694; Bentley, *Diary*, I, 368.

34. Jefferson, "Report on Fisheries," 223; Clarke, "Historical References," in Goode, ed., *Geographical Review*, 682–684; Benjamin W. Labaree, *Patriots and Partisans: The Merchants of Newburyport, 1764–1815* (Cambridge, Mass., 1962), 7, 97–98, 131–132; Stephan Thernstrom, *Poverty and Progress: Social Mobility in a Nineteenth Century City* (Cambridge, Mass., 1964), 9–15.

View of the Town of Marblehead, Massachusetts. From Gleason's *Pictorial*, VI (1854). Courtesy of the Peabody Essex Museum, Salem, Mass.

covered one last time during the difficult period of the 1820s and by 1837 had assembled probably the greatest fishing tonnage in its history—an achievement all the more remarkable given the town's single-minded focus on traditional grounds and the traditional cod. The mode of hand-line fishing had not changed, nor had the practice of salting the fish at sea, washing it out in the harbor at home, and drying it on flakes in the town's many "fences," or fishyards. Marblehead schooners were now somewhat larger, could stow more fish, and made but two or three fares a year—remaining at sea for months at a time. The quality, the kind, and the quantity of fish that a man could land in a given year had not changed much from colonial times, but within these technological limits, the local fleet had risen again.

Yet fortune reserved for this community a final blow. On a September evening in 1846, a thousand miles to the east of Marblehead, the sun was setting on one of the finest evenings local fishermen could ever remember on the Grand Banks of Newfoundland. As the light began to vanish from the sky and the several hundred vessels of various sizes and rigs from fishing ports all around the North Atlantic had finished stowing away their gear after the day's work, a front of black thunderclouds suddenly broke over the horizon, and in less than an hour the ocean was plunged into darkness. By midnight a heavy gale had begun to batter the fleet, and by the following morning a hurricane was kicking up mountainous seas, knocking vessels on their beam ends, smashing masts, and tearing sails to ribbons. All day, except in the direst extremities, nobody dared venture on deck. "One moment we were on the very top of the highest wave," remembered one fisherman, "and the next would be dashed down apparently hundreds of feet . . . as if one were suddenly thrown from a precipice into a pit of seething, angry waters." Nothing could describe, he continued, "the agonizing fear that beset us all during the hours in which we were compelled to sit idly in that cabin, silently waiting what seemed inevitable destruction." When the winds finally abated that night, the ocean was littered with the remains of the ruined fishery: "Barrels, spars, firkins, parts of vessels, even the three masts of a ship with all the rigging attached to them were floating about." Wrecks covered the waters, the *Salem Gazette* reported, and dead bodies were "continually being washed up on shore." For weeks, wives and children in the fishing towns of Essex County strained their eyes to the eastward for any sign of returning craft. When survivors did limp into port, some minds were set at rest, but the tales they brought with them—of finding ghostly schooners riding shattered and empty on the ugly swell or of hauling brine-bloated corpses out of submerged cabins—scarred the collective memory of this outport community for years. "My fishing days," wrote skipper John Procter, "ended with that trip."[35]

Procter was not alone, and this time Marbleheaders remembered their resolve. As before there was some talk in the gale's aftermath of reorganizing the fishery, but—for the first time in the town's history—nothing came of it. By 1856 just forty-three Marblehead vessels were still actively fishing the banks; by 1860 the number had fallen to thirty-five; by 1865 there were only twenty-one; and in 1879 a single banks schooner rode to anchor in the harbor. The town that in colonial times was the greatest fishing port in the New World had turned its back on the sea altogether.[36]

If the sixty-three Marblehead men who drowned in those dreadful twenty-four hours mirror the fishing community they belonged to, it is not hard to understand why the great gale of 1846 tipped the local fishery into terminal decline. The estates they left behind displayed little real improvement from the colonial period. Active fishermen whose personal

35. *Patriot and Terra Nova Herald*, Sept. 30, 1846; *Salem Gazette*, Oct. 6, 9, 13, 16, Nov. 10, 1846; Roads, *History and Traditions of Marblehead*, 372–373.

36. Clarke, "Historical References," in Goode, ed., *Geographical Review*, 707–708.

wealth approximated the median for the period 1840–1855 ate food prepared on stoves rather than over fires and served on crockery instead of
pewter; they sat on furniture more often made of mahogany than of maple
and pine and decorated their rooms with clocks, mirrors, pictures, and
plaster ornaments. But as in the past, bedding was still the most valuable
possession of the fishing family, and their dwellings continued to be furnished mainly with simple inexpensive items of wood and cloth.[37] The
credit-funded revival of owner operation during the French Revolutionary and Napoleonic Wars had died with the subsequent collapse in fish
markets, and by 1846 few local fishermen owned even part of the vessels
on which they worked. Among the probated casualties of the great gale,
Sans Standley, Jr., whose wife collected the insurance on his quarter-
share of the schooner he skippered, was the lone exception to this general
rule.[38] The estates of active fishermen did mark some gain in home ownership; nearly half possessed real estate—usually part of a house and the
lot it stood on—when they died. Yet the true reason for this change was
that fishing companies were no longer predominantly composed of the
young (see table 17). The seven crew members of the *Zela*, all casualties of
the gale, ranged in age from twenty-four to thirty-eight, and five of them
were married; most of the vessels that foundered that day carried hands
who were even older. In Marblehead, as in Gloucester, working on the
banks retained little appeal for younger people and became largely the
preserve of a shrinking minority of career fishermen.[39]

Unlike their Gloucester counterparts, however, the young men of Mar-

37. The median portable estate of active Marblehead fishermen between 1840 and 1855
($N = 20$), converted from dollars into pounds sterling (multiplying by a factor of .3), was
£16—virtually unchanged since the end of the colonial period. See Chapter 4 and Appendix 3. For examples, see Estates of Edward F. Trefry (1852), Probate No. 55644, Samuel
Dodd (1847), Probate No. 37415, and Edward Humphries (1847), Probate No. 43067,
Essex Co. Prob. Recs.

38. The percentage of skipper-owned bankers in Marblehead dropped from 17 in 1805,
to 10 in 1820, and to 4 in 1840–1841. This translated into a fall in rate of ownership for *all*
Marblehead fishermen from 2.2% in 1805 to .5% in 1840–1841. See Abstracts of Licences
Granted to Enrolled Vessels in the District of Marblehead for Carrying on the Cod Fishery,
1805, Marine Ledger B; Abstract for 1820, Marine Ledger D, 1818–1830, and Cod Fishing
Licence Bonds, Apr. 11, 1840–Apr. 7, 1841, Marblehead Customs House Records.

39. The names of all those known to have drowned in the great gale of 1846, complete
with age, marital status, and the vessels they served on, are listed in the *Vital Records of
Marblehead, Massachusetts to the End of the Year 1849*, 3 vols. (Salem, Mass., 1903–1908),
II, by surname.

Table 17. Age Distribution of Marblehead Fishermen, 1760–1850 (in Percents)

Age	1760–1775 (N = 154)	1788–1800 (N = 138)	1801–1850 (N = 171)	1846 Gale[a] (N = 63)
10–19	36	28	16	10
20–29	54	38	31	27
30–39	2	25	24	24
40–49	6	5	20	30
50–59	1	3	6	6
60–69	0	0	2	3
70–79	0	0	1	0

[a]Fishermen who drowned in the great gale of 1846 form a subset of all fishermen active between 1801 and 1850 (in previous column).

Sources: Thomas Pedrick Account Book, 1760–1790, Richard Pedrick Account Book, 1766–1783, Marblehead Historical Society, Marblehead, Mass.; William Knight Account Books, 1767–1775, 1788–1800, Benjamin Knight Account Book, 1800–1833, James Duncan Phillips Library, Peabody Essex Museum, Salem, Mass.; *Vital Records of Marblehead, Massachusetts to the End of the Year, 1849*, 3 vols. (Salem, Mass., 1903–1908), II. Ages were calculated from the sources in Appendix 3.

blehead could find other work. Some was in the traditional waterfront trades: the town possessed in 1832 a cooperage, a cod-line manufactory, and two ropewalks employing 56 men and boys. In other shops around town 16 of their neighbors worked at making cigars, furniture, tinware, soap, and visiting cards. Overwhelmingly, however, the youth of Marblehead was turning to the manufacture of footwear. The rising shoe city of Lynn stood right next door, and after 1815 increasing numbers of men and women began to make and bind shoes for the larger firms there or for the smaller dealers in their hometown. By 1832, close to 350 men as well as 325 women and girls were making shoes in Marblehead, and dozens of families had moved from there to Lynn or Salem to work at this and other trades. Compared with the 412 men and boys following the fishery, these numbers clearly indicate a shift in the town's economic base.[40]

Terrible as the great gale of 1846 may have been, therefore, it did not drive the fishery from Marblehead unaided. The town on the rocks had always rebounded from other storms. What had changed, and this is

40. McLane, *Report*, I, 238–241; Roads, *History and Traditions of Marblehead*, 261, 279–282.

clearest when one views all of the Essex County fishing ports together, was not the fishery but the nature of the society surrounding it. Put simply, the economic developments of the nineteenth century—first in overseas trade and then in manufacture—presented merchants and seamen in Marblehead and most of the county's traditional fishing ports with the opportunity to make better money at a smaller human cost on shore. An industry that in 1850 was still powered by wind and human muscle—as yet barely touched by the technological and organizational genius of industrial capitalism—could retain neither the financial backing nor the manpower to survive, except in Gloucester, where proximity to the grounds and distance from other work continued to focus men's energies on harvesting the sea.

Before they retreated to their final haven in Gloucester, however, the fisheries of Essex County evolved into an industry that consumed not merely the youth but the entire productive lives of those who labored within it. In Marblehead, where earning a living had always meant primarily fishing, this was not a great change. But in the towns that stretched north and east around the perimeter of Cape Ann, where fishing had once been a cottage industry pursued mainly by younger men, often in tandem with petty agriculture and landward crafts, it clearly was. From a stage in life to be left behind when an inheritance or at least the prospect of a more lucrative and less strenuous trade presented itself, fishing became a career that few men outgrew. As dependent labor on the banks evolved from a youthful expediency into a working lifetime, the sons of Yankee householders abandoned it for more desirable lines of work.

FARMING

During the colonial period the agricultural economy of Essex County never managed, as its fishing counterpart did, to generate a local labor market. Farmers knew that paid labor would cost sums of money they could not always realize from the sale of their own produce, and so they sensibly operated within the limits that family help (with some neighborly assistance) defined. The difficulty was not that of weak demand for what they raised. No part of the county lay more than a long day's ride by cart or boat from populous seaports that also furnished access to distant markets. Labor scarcity had been a problem in the first century of settlement when the task of farm formation absorbed the energies of otherwise employable men, but by the end of the colonial period chronically underemployed youths interested in earning money could be met at every turn. The reason a farm labor market failed to develop in Essex County before the Revolution was the mediocre quality of the soil. New Englanders, like other New World colonists, had responded to the prospect of seemingly limitless land with an exploitative style of agriculture that eventually diminished the fertility of the country. Mature fields could not produce enough grain, hay, or vegetable crops to exceed the basic needs of families that owned them, nor did such fields serve well for pasture. And without sufficient cash from the sale of surplus produce, few farmers were foolish enough to take on a wage bill they could not pay.

When independence came and Essex County was incorporated into a national American market, local farmers altered some of their ways, but the social relations of agricultural production were not transformed. Although new consumers in the booming seaports and among the growing manufacturing population provided an opportunity to expand commercial production, the possibility of restructuring agriculture along capitalist lines, given the limited potential of most farms, simply did not exist. In the short term, Essex County farmers responded to industrialization by adapting their practices to dodge competition from the more productive agricultural regions of the Midwest and by focusing their energies on the few branches of the business where they possessed some natural advantages. In the long term, the great majority abandoned agriculture altogether. Like fishing, serious farming survived industrialization only in a few select corners of the county.

Markets and Production

The farmers of Essex County survived the Revolutionary War in far better shape than did the fishermen. Although the War of Independence broke out in Lexington, half a day's march from the western border of the county, no real fighting ever took place within its bounds. Dozens of young men from places like Rowley and Topsfield enlisted in the revolutionary struggle, and the rest of the rural population had to endure currency disruptions, price controls, shortages of imported goods, and the heaviest taxes in New England's memory. With the fishery shut up in port and overseas commerce at a near-standstill, farm families suffered from the decline of seaport demand for their surplus produce. Nevertheless, communities that normally provided most of their own needs and were battling chronic underemployment before the war were not likely to be overwhelmed by such difficulties. On balance, relative to other regions of early America and even to the maritime towns along its own coastline, this particular stretch of American countryside weathered the period with little serious disruption.[41]

With the return of peace in 1783 farmers took up roughly where they had left off in 1775. Military purchasing had come to an end, and the maritime trades were in the process of rebuilding, so the commercial demand for agricultural produce was not especially healthy at first. Still, prices for farm produce were higher in the 1780s than they had been before the Revolution, and since the farmer's margin of surplus had always been narrow at best, softer markets could be borne for some time without much alteration in farm practice. The traditional difficulties remained, of course. Essex was an old county, and as population grew the proportion of families with any claim to true landed independence shrank. The disruptions of the Revolution had widened the gap between those who profited from speculation or military supply and those who had not; accordingly, the number of property-poor young families forced to make shift through part-time wage work, manufacture, and seafaring was slightly higher in 1790 than it had been in 1775. Now "all the farmers in these parts are either sailors or shipbuilders," observed Brissot de Warville in 1788 as he rode northward from Newburyport into New Hampshire. Commonly too, single people and young couples were pulling up stakes and moving townward to hunt for paid employment or migrating westward toward the Appalachians and beyond in search of land. Yet even these strategies were variations on those traditionally employed for household survival, and the rural economy of the immediate post-Revolutionary years reflected little real structural change.[42]

41. Ronald N. Tagney, *The World Turned Upside Down: Essex County during America's Turbulent Years, 1763–1790* (West Newbury, Mass., 1989), 265–266, 291–297, 335–345; Howard S. Russell, *A Long, Deep Furrow: Three Centuries of Farming in New England*, abridged by Mark Lapping (Hanover, N.H., 1982), 123–128; Christopher M. Jedrey, *The World of John Cleaveland: Family and Community in Eighteenth-Century New England* (New York, 1979), 136–144; Paul G. Faler, *Mechanics and Manufacturers in the Early Industrial Revolution: Lynn, Massachusetts, 1780–1860* (Albany, N.Y., 1981), 12–13. Jedrey believes that labor shortages were yet another problem for farmers during this period, but this does not square with the drop in real farm wages during the Revolutionary War reported in Winifred Barr Rothenberg, *From Market-Places to a Market Economy: The Transformation of Rural Massachusetts, 1750–1850* (Chicago, 1992), 177.

42. Jedrey, *World of John Cleaveland*, 163–165; Winifred B. Rothenberg, "A Price Index for Rural Massachusetts, 1750–1855," *JEH*, XXXIX (1979), 983; Arlin Ira Ginsburg, "Ipswich, Massachusetts during the American Revolution, 1763–1791" (Ph.D. diss., University

When Britain declared war on the French republic in 1793 and launched Massachusetts on a short but highly profitable career as the key neutral carrier in the North Atlantic, agriculture showed signs of emerging as a profitable business. With the surge in maritime enterprise, the Essex County seaports boomed. The proportion of county residents who lived in Salem, Marblehead, Beverly, Gloucester, or Newburyport climbed from 38 percent in 1784 to 49 percent in 1800, and nearby Boston nearly doubled in size.[43] Prices for agricultural produce shot upward in the mid-1790s, and the burgeoning urban market of maritime Massachusetts provided farm families with a variety of commercial opportunities. Not only was there new trade in furnishing garden vegetables, firewood, and cider to the townspeople, but as ocean-bound voyages multiplied, so did the demand for salted meat, turnips, potatoes, and other ships' provisions. These had to be barreled, moreover, which required a steady supply of staves, hoops, and heads. Carting the hogsheads from warehouse to ship, returning with landed cargoes, and then distributing them around the region demanded horses and quantities of fodder as well. No rule forced port dwellers to purchase supplies from local farmers, but it was a natural relationship, and the numbers of "market people . . . carrying their commodities from house to house" were plain to see.[44]

At the beginning of the nineteenth century, Timothy Dwight called Essex the most urbanized county (excluding Philadelphia and New York) in the United States. By 1800 two-thirds of the region's inhabitants, in his estimation, supported themselves from "commercial and fishing" pursuits. Here, indeed, was a swelling market for farm produce.[45] Between 1807 and 1814 embargoes and war temporarily complicated Massachusetts's overseas commerce and choked off the demand for rural produce that it had nurtured. Businessmen soon adjusted to the interruptions in British trade by launching industrial ventures on American soil, however,

of California, Riverside, 1972), 201–205; Robert A. Gross, "Culture and Cultivation: Agriculture and Society in Thoreau's Concord," *Journal of American History*, LXIX (1982), 56; Brissot de Warville, *New Travels*, ed. Echeverria, 366.

43. Labaree, *Patriots and Partisans*, 62–63, 94–100, 106, 131–133; Morison, *Maritime History of Massachusetts*, chaps. 3–12; Greene and Harrington, *American Population before 1790*, 40–41, 46; U.S. Dept. of State, *Return of the Whole Number of Persons*, 8.

44. Rothenberg, "Price Index," *JEH*, XXXIX (1979), 983–984; Russell, *Long, Deep Furrow*, 136–140, 144–146, 181; Timothy Dwight, *Travels in New England and New York*, ed. Barbara Miller Solomon, 4 vols. (Cambridge, Mass., 1969), I, 323.

45. Dwight, *Travels*, ed. Solomon, I, 334–335.

and the mill towns that sprang up across the New England countryside through subsequent decades multiplied the demand for whatever farmers could raise and manufacture for sale. Since Essex County lay mostly below the fall line, it possessed little potential waterpower and was not seriously touched by industrialization before the arrival of steam manufacture in the 1840s. Although the population of Lynn rose from 4,500 to 10,000 between 1820 and 1835, Salem marked time through this period, and Newburyport actually shrank. One did not have to ride far beyond the boundaries of the county, however, to find booming mill towns like Waltham, Dover, and Lowell, and as the administrative and commercial hub of New England, Boston was adding thousands to its population every year. The founding of Lawrence in the 1840s and the transformation of Lynn, Haverhill, Newburyport, and Salem into small industrial cities around midcentury extended the urban market into the heart of Essex County—to the local farmers' own doorsteps.[46]

At first, farm families responded to commercial opportunity by stepping up agricultural production. The operations of a midsized Rowley farm, chronicled in the diary of Caleb Jackson, Jr., at the opening of the nineteenth century, reflected precisely this strategy. The Jacksons had bought their 50-acre property in 1786, and in 1802, when fifteen-year-old Caleb began to keep a diary of events on the farm, the family consisted of himself, his father and mother, and his two younger siblings—Sally and Samuel. Much of the time the Jacksons concentrated on subsistence production. Caleb, Samuel, and their father broke up the soil, sowed crops and reaped them, fenced fields, tended cattle, sheared sheep, slaughtered hogs, cut timber, and dug cellars, among dozens of other tasks, while Sally and her mother complemented this intricate pattern of mixed agriculture with their own labors in the barn, the dairy, the garden, and the house. None of this work routine had altered significantly in more than a century.[47] Caleb's diary also catches his family, however, in the process of

46. Robert Greenhalgh Albion, "From Sails to Spindles: Essex County in Transition," Essex Institute, *Hist. Colls.*, XCV (1959), 125–136; Faler, *Mechanics and Manufacturers*, 42, 88–89; Thernstrom, *Poverty and Progress*, 9–12; Morison, *Maritime History of Massachusetts*, 124, 225.

47. Caleb Jackson Journal, 1802–1806, JDPL. See also Laurel Thatcher Ulrich, "Martha Ballard and Her Girls: Women's Work in Eighteenth-Century Maine," in Stephen Innes, ed., *Work and Labor in Early America* (Chapel Hill, N.C., 1988), 70–105; and Ulrich, *Good Wives: Image and Reality in the Lives of Women in Northern New England, 1650–1750* (New York, 1982), 13–34.

A View of the Jewett House (built in 1785). Diversified farming in Rowley, Massachusetts. Photograph courtesy of the Society for the Preservation of New England Antiquities, Boston

intensifying their involvement in the regional market network. Every spring, for example, Caleb helped his father set out new apple trees in the family orchard, and one September evening in 1802, with the help of a dozen neighbors, the two of them raised a new and bigger cider mill to better supply the taverns of Salem and Newburyport. The whole family went cherry picking at the end of summer, for in town, Caleb claimed, "cherries . . . are ready cash." Potatoes were growing in popularity, both in Essex County and along the Atlantic seaboard, so the Jacksons began to plant and harvest them, too. Apples, cherries, and potatoes were not new crops. They had been grown in Rowley for generations, and with the rise of urban demand the Jacksons simply pushed themselves to plant and pick more. Chopping firewood and hauling it to Ipswich; carting butter, eggs, or corn to Salem market; driving calves and steers to the butcher: in these and other ways the Jacksons prospered by working their farm more intensively.[48]

In time, however, the opportunities that developing urban markets afforded families like the Jacksons were matched and offset in certain

48. Entries for Sept. 6, 7, 10, 23, Oct. 23, Nov. 5, 1802, May 26, 27, June 21, Aug. 26, 27, Nov. 8, 1803, May 7, June 1, July 5, 1804, Jan. 7, May 8, Sept. 27, summary for Sept., 1805, Caleb Jackson Journal. A Rowley neighbor named Amos Jewett planted 7 bushels of red potatoes in 1816, sent 41 bushels to market in 1819, and had raised production to 254 bushels by 1829. See Russell, *Long, Deep Furrow*, 162, on potatoes, and chaps. 18–22 on the intensification of market production across New England during this period.

branches of their business by rising competition from farmers in the newly settled areas of the Midwest. Grains and barreled meat could be produced more cheaply in the Great Lakes and Ohio River basins, and when they invaded New England markets, especially after 1820, Essex County farmers responded by experimenting with some specialization rather than attempting to cover all branches of husbandry equally. This did not substantially alter the patterns of domestic farm production. As the improver Henry Colman observed critically in 1837, local agriculture was still largely geared to self-sufficiency, and most farms continued to raise the diversity of crops and animals they needed at home.[49] But whereas most farmers once had depended on vending the surplus of *all* their farm produce, more now focused on a smaller range of specifically commercial items. Thus the sort of orcharding the Jacksons practiced rose in importance; dairy farms catered to rising urban demand; and some families planted root crops, such as potatoes and onions, for a cash return.[50]

The most patently commercial new strategy adopted by Essex County farmers in the first half of the nineteenth century, however, was to plant worn-out arable fields with grass and to market hay in town. In coastal Ipswich the acres under tillage fell between 1771 and 1831 by 15 percent, but the "English upland" sown with imported grasses high in nutrients and suitable for commercial sale rose by 105 percent; in upcountry Middleton, tillage fell by 9 percent and English mowing land rose by 88 percent. Significantly, the quantity of salt marsh and fresh meadow, where farmers cropped lower-quality natural grasses for their own animals, did not increase substantially. Across the county, between 1801 and 1831 salt marsh declined in acreage by 3 percent and fresh meadow by 11 percent. By contrast, the quantity of English upland sown with commercial grass jumped by 40 percent. In 1837 Henry Colman claimed that the great objective of county farmers was to crop the land repeatedly with hay and sell it to jobbers, who crisscrossed the landscape in horse carts picking up fodder to sell in the city markets of Salem, Boston, and Lowell. Ipswich was the center for this business. Not only did it possess more acreage in mowing land than any other town, but also merchants there specialized in

49. Henry Colman, *First Report on the Agriculture of Massachusetts, County of Essex, 1837* (Boston, 1838), 36.

50. Colman, *First Report*, 36, 40, 61; "Report of the Committee on the Best Cultivated Farms," *Massachusetts Agricultural Repository and Journal*, X (1831), 285–291; *The Essex Memorial for 1836* (Salem, Mass., 1836), 91, 196, 224, 274.

Newburyport Marshes, by Martin Johnson Heade (probably 1863–1865). Bequest of
Maxim Karolik. Courtesy of Museum of Fine Arts, Boston

buying up hay from the surrounding villages and shipping it into the
cities. The very town that in 1650 Edward Johnson had praised for its
ability to "feed, at the latter end of Summer, the Towne of Boston with
good Beefe" in 1836 was said to be furnishing the city market annually
with "one thousand tons of English hay."[51]

To say that farmers were somewhat more deeply involved in regional
markets and that they had chosen to specialize in certain commercial
products is not to argue that the agricultural economy of Essex County had
been substantially transformed. The shift was merely one of degree. A few
farmers had taken an interest in changing how they did things: enough to
inspire them to join the Massachusetts Society for Promoting Agriculture
after its incorporation in 1792 and to form a number of local societies in
subsequent decades.[52] Real improvement, however, demanded more than

51. Ginsburg, "Ipswich during the American Revolution," 241n; Pruitt, ed., *Massachusetts Tax Valuation List of 1771*, 112–115; Colman, *First Report*, 12, 16–19, 135–136; Percy
Wells Bidwell and John I. Falconer, *History of Agriculture in the Northern United States,
1620–1860* (Washington, D.C., 1925), 105; Henry Colman, *Essex Agriculture* (n.p., 1839),
102–103; *Essex Memorial*, 131; Patrick Shirreff, *A Tour through North America Together
with a Comprehensive View of the Canadas and United States, as Adapted for Agricultural
Emigration* (Edinburgh, 1835), 43.

52. Bidwell and Falconer, *History of Agriculture*, 184–190; Russell, *Long, Deep Furrow*,
130–131, 198–200. By the 1820s, agricultural fairs sponsored by local societies were popular enough to draw farmers and hands from all over the county. See entries for Oct. 1, 1829,

curiosity and rhetoric. It required technical innovation that took time to master, nerve to risk, and money to afford; in most parts of the county, farmers seldom possessed either the capital or the potential fertility of soil to encourage such experimentation. The vast majority retained oxen as their principal draft animal, corn as their staple grain crop, meadowland for hay, and a diversity of livestock through the early national period until the Civil War. The quality and quantity of their farming tools were probably somewhat greater than those of their colonial ancestors, and they tended to store a wider variety of produce in their barns and cellars. In Henry Colman's opinion, however, local farmers were nearly all traditionalists with "a great want of system . . . [and] no regular plan of cultivation or regular rotation of crops." Sheep, cattle, and swine were grazed, but not systematically fattened. Manure was saved, but not very carefully. Fences were of stone, but in "wretched" condition. Colman may have been a little harsh, but in 1815, when the Danvers Agricultural Society was asked whether it could report any local improvements "in dairies . . . the quality of butter and cheese . . . the tools of husbandry . . . new and valuable fruits or productions . . . the breed of cattle . . . [or] in any branch of agriculture," even this presumably progressive group of farmers on the outskirts of Salem had to answer in the negative. Colman argued that agriculture in Essex County was governed by custom, exploitative of its resource base, and seldom pursued in a businesslike manner "with a main view to pecuniary advantage"—and his judgment rang true. In the spirit and conduct of their farming practice, these New Englanders were, indeed, wedded to the past.[53]

Sept. 29, 1831, Abijah Northey, Journal of Boxford Farm, 1828–1832, 1832–1836, Northey Family Papers, 1688–1964, Box 1, JDPL, hereafter cited as Northey Journals.

53. Colman, *First Report*, 14, 16–17, 40, 43, 46, 65, 66; Colman, *Essex Agriculture*, 102–112; Henry Colman, *Hints Addressed to the Farmers of Essex* (Salem, Mass., 1830), 7–11; Andrew Nichols, Secretary, Danvers Agricultural Society, to Massachusetts Society for Promoting Agriculture, Jan. 14, 1815, *Mass. Agric. Rep. and Jour.*, III (1815), 348–349. The best modern discussions of change in New England agriculture during this period are Gross, "Culture and Cultivation," *JAH*, LXIX (1982), 48, 49, 57–61; Sarah F. McMahon, "A Comfortable Subsistence: The Changing Composition of Diet in Rural New England, 1620–1840," *WMQ*, 3d Ser., XLII (1985), 43–65; Russell, *Long, Deep Furrow*, chaps. 21, 22, 26, 27, 29; Rothenberg, *Market-Places to Market Economy*. All four of these authors emphasize change. My point is to remind the reader of basic general continuities and to suggest that a shift in emphasis within the available crop and livestock mix constitutes a change in the tactics, but not in the overall character, of husbandry. Thus, although

Relations of Production

Although the techniques of production in agriculture remained essentially unaltered, the social relations that mobilized them did begin to shift around the turn of the century in novel and measurable ways. The great majority of farm households still began with very little land and never accumulated more than 100 acres—a size that a family with teenage children and additional help at harvest could quite easily handle.[54] Caleb Jackson of Rowley, for instance, recorded the activities of 669 working days between 1802 and 1806, and mentioned extrafamilial farm labor only on about 70 of them.[55] The brief diary of Moses Porter records the same

---

Russell loved to celebrate Yankee innovation, even this unabashed farm booster had to admit (1) that as late as 1825, "tillage methods had not changed much since the Revolution, nor the tools that did the work"; (2) that "carelessness in conserving and returning fertility" was still widespread; and (3) that oxen persisted as the prime draft animal and Indian corn as the staple grain into the middle of the 19th century. See Russell, *Long, Deep Furrow*, 172, 176, 202, 213. Rothenberg's view that Massachusetts agriculture was transformed during the early national period is similarly hard to accept. By relying mainly on account books (kept disproportionately by the well-to-do—her arguments to the contrary are not persuasive) and the estate records of men whose property was worth the trouble of going through probate, she has written mainly a history of agricultural improvers. Her best evidence on the rising productivity of agriculture, the rise in real wages over the period in question, is convincing; but she exaggerates the rate of growth by taking the abnormally low values of the Revolutionary period (when real wages were low because prices had temporarily soared) as her conceptual starting point. Using her data and comparing the average real wage for 1752–1771 with that for 1846–1855, one obtains a net growth of only 18%, which works out to a compound annual rate of growth of only .2%. That the improvements she describes took place is true enough; that they extended to the entirety of farm society and can be termed a transformation, I doubt. See Rothenberg, *Market-Places to Market Economy*, 65–68, 115–119, 168–173, 176–179. For a more measured view, stressing gradually accelerating change after 1820, see Clarence H. Danhof, *Changes in Agriculture: The Northern United States, 1820–1870* (Cambridge, Mass., 1969), chap. 1.

54. Colman, *First Report*, 14; Nichols to Massachusetts Society for Promoting Agriculture, Jan. 14, 1815, *Mass. Agric. Rep. and Jour.*, III (1815), 338; Daniel Vickers, "Competency and Competition: Economic Culture in Early America," *WMQ*, 3d Ser., XLVII (1990), 4, 8–9; Gross, "Culture and Cultivation," *JAH*, LXIX (1982), 44. On a 70-acre farm in Pembroke, just south of Boston, one farmer and his 16-year-old boy did all the men's work with the additional input of about 40 "man days" of paid labor. See "Report of the Committee on the Best Cultivated Farms," *Mass. Agric. Rep. and Jour.*, X (1831), 357–363; and Danhof, *Change in Agriculture*, 137.

55. The 70 days is an estimate, since in about 10 cases it was impossible to distinguish between work that Caleb was performing for neighbors and work that he was performing for his father on land *rented* from neighbors. See Caleb Jackson Journal, 1802–1806.

preference for internal family help in the more commercial environment of Danvers, a two-hour walk from Salem. Porter was twenty-two and single—still working on his father's farm but with a field of his own that also needed attention. Between the beginning of January and the beginning of May 1817—admittedly the slack end of the year—Porter described 94 working days, only one of which he spent working for anyone other than himself or his father, and only three of which involved the employment of neighbors.[56] Like most other farm accounts of the early nineteenth century, neither Porter's nor Jackson's mentioned hired (live-in) hands.[57] In the technologically stable agriculture of the early republic, family operations continued to predominate.

Yet insofar as the rising demand for farm produce gave some impetus to specialization and economies of scale, large farms did become more numerous. Though still outnumbered easily by homesteads of 80 acres or less, a scattering of truly substantial landholdings began to catch the attention of travelers through Essex County, and in subtle ways they influenced the rural economy as a whole. William Bentley toured the region often in these years, and some of the agricultural operations he described were quite impressive. Browne's Farm in Lynn, 375 acres in size and "very flourishing" when Bentley visited in 1790, had almost 50 acres under the plow, and the tenant in residence kept a herd of twenty-nine dairy cattle. Timothy Dwight traveled through the county at the beginning of the next century and was particularly struck by a number of handsome farmhouses with fine meadows and large barns he discovered in Andover. Some years later Erastus Ware rented a 428-acre farm outside of Salem that won a prize from the state agricultural society—largely on the strength of its dairy. During the first quarter of the nineteenth century, George Choate of Ipswich owned 180 acres of land in Chebacco Parish, part of which he rented out and part of which he ran himself, raising commercial loads of hay and keeping sheep and cattle. Farms of this size would have been unusual in pre-Revolutionary times, but not by the 1820s. Gentlemen like Choate, who owned more than 100 acres, several teams of oxen, and at

56. Moses Porter Diary, 1817–1822, JDPL.

57. See, e.g., Caleb Jackson Journal, 1802–1806; Moses Porter Diary, 1817–1822; Israel Sawyer Account Book, 1774–1819 (Salisbury), JDPL; Merrill Family Account Book, 1775–1834 (Salisbury), JDPL; Enoch Follansbee Account Book, 1820–1865 (West Newbury), JDPL; Moody Jacques Account Book, 1814–1827 (West Newbury), JDPL; Asa Perkins Account Book, 1803–1851 (Topsfield), JDPL; and Brackenbury Prince Account Book, 1807–1832 (Beverly), JDPL.

least a dozen cattle, cropped up in the probate records of this period more frequently than they had a half-century before.[58]

The gradual spread of farming on this scale placed a somewhat greater demand on the available labor supply. The tenant at Browne's Farm in Lynn had ten children, so he and his wife may have been able to manage without much paid assistance. But Erastus Ware had six hands working and boarding with him throughout most of the year, and George Choate normally employed at least two or three men on his estate.[59] An Ipswich farmer named John Baker kept accounts that monitor the growing importance of hired help throughout his neighborhood between 1769 and 1834. Like other farmers, Baker sometimes needed assistance from those who lived near him; when they could not spare the time themselves, they sent along one of their dependents. Normally these were their own sons, of course, but by the end of the eighteenth century the number of "hands" and "men" in proportion to all dependents (including sons) that were dispatched Baker's way had begun to rise—from 25 percent before 1790 to 44 percent afterward. According to the accounts of Christopher Howe of Methuen, by the 1820s and 1830s some farmers were in the habit of repaying their debts by lending out their hired men. When one remembers how often, even in the 1790s and 1800s, farmers had discharged the same obligations with the labor of their sons, the rising importance

58. George Francis Dow, ed., *Two Centuries of Travel in Essex County, Massachusetts: A Collection of Narratives and Observations Made by Travelers, 1605–1799* (Topsfield, Mass., 1921), 108; see also *ibid.*, 119, 130–131; Dwight, *Travels*, ed. Solomon, I, 286, 290; "Report of the Committee on the Best Cultivated Farms," *Mass. Agric. Rep. and Jour.*, X (1831), 285–291; George Choate Account Book, 1789–1823, JDPL; and Estate of George Choate (1826), Probate No. 5340, Essex Co. Prob. Recs. In Chebacco, where Choate lived, a farm of this size would have ranked among the five wealthiest owned by the parish's 205 ratepayers in 1771 (and Chebacco possessed more large farms than most towns in the county). See Pruitt, ed., *Massachusetts Tax Valuation List of 1771*, 76–81. Choate's estate was inventoried at $7,848, and in a sample of farm inventories drawn from across the county during the period 1817–1824, 11 out of 38 estates were evaluated at $7,000 or more. See Essex Co. Prob. Recs., BV, vols. 391, 393, 394, 398, 401, 403. On the concentration of farm property ownership elsewhere in Massachusetts, see Gross, "Culture and Cultivation," *JAH*, LXIX (1982), 56, 57. Choate's estate contained more land, more cattle, and more total wealth (deflated using tables in Rothenberg, "Emergence of Farm Labor Markets," *JEH*, XLVIII [1988], 564–565) than any of the 35 farm inventories for Essex County transcribed in Alice Hanson Jones, *American Colonial Wealth: Documents and Methods*, 3 vols. (New York, 1977), II, 607–800. One 1774 farmer owned more oxen than Choate did, and four owned more sheep.

59. See sources in n. 58, above.

of hired men is undeniable. By the 1840s, most householders who did enough business to necessitate keeping accounts employed a farmhand or two on a regular basis. Abraham Dodge, one of Wenham's largest farmers at midcentury, had one teenage son but usually boarded a hired man the year round and an additional couple of hands through the summertime. The Ferguson family—composed of a widowed mother, two grown sons, and a daughter—managed a farm of middling size in Newbury in the late 1840s with the help of Josiah Tilton, a shoemaker who lived with them for several years and paid for his board in farm labor, as well as a variety of other hands hired by the month at mowing time. John Plummer Foster of North Andover paid out the equivalent of ten to fifteen man months of wages per year for help to run his farm between 1849 and 1854.[60]

Throughout eastern Massachusetts, the number of propertyless households inched steadily upward during the first half of the nineteenth century, and farmers with sufficient land who were confident of seeing some cash return for their produce could usually find someone willing to sell his labor by the month. By 1850—according to the first census that permits the precise identification of hired hands—male hands probably accounted for between 5 and 10 percent of the county's farm population. In comparison to the seventeenth century, when the equivalent figure had been less than 5 percent, this signified real if measured change. At Topsfield in 1687, the ratio of menservants to sons in a population given over almost entirely to farming had been less than 1:5; by 1850, counting only farming households, that proportion had doubled to 2:5. In rugged Manchester the 1850 ratio stood at 2:3, and in fertile, progressive West Newbury, it was practically even.[61] The largest properties of 1850 were no bigger than

60. The data from Baker's accounts are based on a survey of 32 different accounts; those from Howe on 12 different accounts. See John Baker Account Book, 1769–1834, Baker Library, Harvard Business School, Boston; Christopher Howe Account Book, 1825–1830, JDPL; E. P. Ferguson Account Book, 1848–1853, JDPL; John Plummer Foster Account Book, 1842–1856, JDPL; and Abraham Dodge Account Book, 1829–1871, Wenham Historical Association and Museum, Wenham, Mass. See also Farmer's Almanack belonging to Daniel Hale of Byfield, Massachusetts Society for the Promotion of Agriculture Papers, Drawer A, Folder 1, Massachusetts Historical Society, Boston. Biographical material was drawn from the sources in Appendix 4.

61. See Chapter 2; "Taxes under Gov. Andros: Topsfield Town Rate, 1687," *New England Historical and Genealogical Record*, XXXV (1881), 34–35; and U.S. Census Bureau, Seventh Census, Population Schedules for Topsfield, West Newbury, and Manchester, Mass., Microcopy 432, roll 315. The obvious problems in comparing figures derived from court and tax records of one century with those obtained from the manuscript census of another

those of the 1680s, and few farm households employed more than a couple of hands. But clearly more farmers were doing business on a scale that required live-in help.[62]

At first, the demand for labor that larger farms generated fell predominantly on the young. When farmers like George Choate went looking for hands, the individuals he hired were usually—like David and William Low or Ebenezer Andrews—a few years either side of marriage. Most of the men who worked on Christopher Howe's farm in Methuen were, indeed, still single when they entered his service.[63] By the beginning of the nineteenth century, however, more hands than ever before were married men with families, often newcomers to the towns in which they dwelt as laborers. James Nutter was already on the road when he arrived in Ipswich en route from Hamilton to marry Mehitable Burnham in 1805, and he must have been well into middle age when he started working for John Baker in 1822. John Mears was another outsider, but he had lived in

---

should caution against assuming too much precision here. In the case of Topsfield in 1687, only taxable sons and servants were listed, whereas in the census of 1850 all household members were enumerated. Since the former would omit younger teenagers who, although of working age, were more likely to be living at home, the reported figures probably *understate* the rising importance of hired help. Comparing the two periods is complicated further because in 1850 the rural population was only partially agricultural, and selecting households headed by "farmers" excludes "shoemakers" and "blacksmiths" who may have farmed part-time. The calculations for 17th-century Essex County included all those who did any farming whatsoever—admittedly a somewhat different criterion. A final caveat is that the 1850 figures were derived from a sample: 169 members of farming households in Topsfield; 199 in West Newbury; and 111 in Manchester. Rothenberg believes that hired hands ("contract laborers," as she terms them) grew rapidly in numbers and significance during the early national period (*Market-Places to Market Economy*, chap. 7); I am arguing for less dramatic change.

62. In the 17th century, half of the servants worked for households that can be placed within the top decile of wealth holders in the town in which they lived. In 1850, half the hired men lived with families that can be placed within: (1) the wealthiest 35% of farm households in Topsfield; (2) the wealthiest 26% of those in West Newbury; or (3) the wealthiest 9% in Manchester. In 42 farm households with hired men, randomly selected from the 1850 census for these three towns plus Danvers, 3 households contained more than two such hands (six, four, and three, respectively), and the remaining 39 contained only one or two. See the sources in n. 61, above; U.S. Census Bureau, Seventh Census, Population Schedules for Danvers, roll 310; and the 17th-century tax lists for Newbury, Topsfield, and Salisbury listed in Appendix 1.

63. Accounts of Thomas Low, William Low, and Ebenezer Andrews, George Choate Acct. Bk., 1789–1823; accounts of Samuel C. Butrick, Pebody Gonrin, Benjamin Philpott, Oliver J. Philpott, and Sterling Kimball, Christopher Howe Acct. Bk., 1825–1830.

Ipswich as a married man for seventeen years when he leased a cottage on George Choate's estate in 1816. Out of his earnings as a hired hand he paid the annual rent of $15 a year, wintered his animals on Choate's land, and bought fodder, wood, and provisions from him.[64] Both Nutter and Mears were old enough to have sons of working age, and in both cases father and son went to work together, sharing a dependent status. Each of these families probably hoped to cobble together a stake, purchase land of their own, and escape the lot of the laboring poor. Perhaps they did—though many others did not. A sample drawn from the 1850 census for Essex County reveals that by that date farmhands were decidedly older than their colonial counterparts (see table 18). Indeed, they came close to mirroring the age structure of the surrounding rural population.[65] What in colonial times had been a gully of dependency to be bridged with a few years of youthful labor was now a valley from which many New Englanders never emerged.

Characterizing the development of this real but thin labor market more precisely is difficult. Winifred Rothenberg has found that daily wages of farm laborers in eastern Massachusetts began to converge around a regional mean about 1800.[66] Comparing harvest wage rates with those that prevailed during the rest of the summer confirms this. Prior to the Revolution, seasonal wage patterns seem only to have reflected the lengthening and shortening of the working day. After 1796, however, the daily rate of pay began to swing up and down more vigorously throughout the year (see figure 3). As farmers focused more of their energies on commercial production—especially of hay—they needed more help at harvest, and they began to compete more vigorously and widely for that help. More often than in previous centuries, the men they hired were laborers on the English model, who confronted their employers across lines of class and were quite prepared to bargain openly over the value of their time. Although it is difficult to know the origins of the earliest participants in this labor market, the population schedules of the seventh census, which list occupations and places of birth, provide exactly this information for 1850. In Topsfield not only had a full 94 percent of farmhands been born

64. Account of James Nutter, John Baker Acct. Bk., 1769–1834; account of John Mears, George Choate Acct. Bk., 1789–1823.

65. U.S. Bureau of the Census, *Seventh Census of the United States: 1850* (Washington, D.C., 1853), 48.

66. Rothenberg, "Emergence of Farm Labor Markets," *JEH*, XLVIII (1988), 543, 546–548.

Table 18. Age Distribution of Male Farmhands
in Essex County, 1630–1850 (in Percents)

Age	1630–1700 ($N = 44$)	1850 ($N = 108$)
0–14	16	11
15–24	61	47
25–34	20	21
35–44	0	6
45–54	2	4
55–64	0	7
65+	0	3
Total	99	99

Note: The 1850 percentages were based on a sample of hired hands in Danvers, Manchester, Topsfield, and West Newbury. Hands were identified as those who: (1) owned no property; (2) were listed in the same family as a farmer; (3) were styled either as laborer, farmer, or with no occupation; and (4) possessed a different surname from the family head.

Sources: On the seventeenth-century servants, see Chapter 2, n. 55. For 1850, see U.S. Bureau of the Census, Seventh Census of the United States, 1850, Population Schedules for Topsfield, Manchester, West Newbury, and Danvers, Mass., Microcopy 432, rolls 310, 315.

outside of town, but 42 percent were either from out of state or foreign born. In West Newbury just as many were from outside town, and a striking 59 percent hailed from other states and beyond. Over time, under the pressures of commercialization, a farm labor market that reached across New England and overseas had come into being.[67]

As a market, however, it was not exactly dense. Even in 1850, most farm households in the county did not take on farmhands, and all but the largest operations depended predominantly on family help.[68] The degree

67. For Topsfield, $N = 31$; for West Newbury, $N = 56$. See Population Schedules for Topsfield and West Newbury, Seventh Census, roll 315; *Vital Records of Topsfield, Massachusetts to the End of the Year 1849*, 2 vols. (Topsfield, Mass., 1903–1916); *Vital Records of Newbury, Massachusetts to the End of the Year 1849*, 2 vols. (Salem, Mass., 1911); and *Vital Records of West Newbury, Massachusetts to the End of the Year 1849* (Salem, Mass., 1918).

68. In a sample of 132 farm households drawn at random from the 1850 manuscript census for Manchester, Topsfield, Danvers, and West Newbury, only 32% contained any non-family male members. See sources in nn. 61 and 62, above.

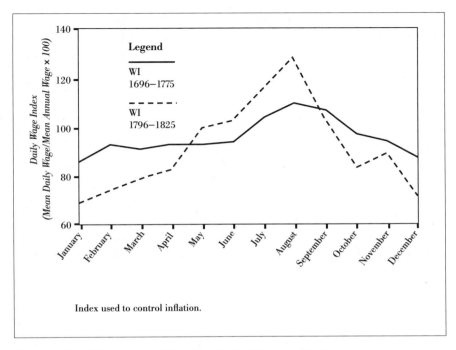

Figure 3. Farm Wage Levels in Essex County by Month, 1696–1825

of commercialization that had occurred did mobilize some labor, but the limited productivity of the land prevented the development of anything resembling a farm proletariat. A class of laborers who were poor in property and thus forced to sell their labor for a living was emerging in Essex County during the nineteenth century, but only a small number found or even sought employment in agriculture.

The Northey Farm

The persistent logic of family farming is nowhere better illustrated than in the experience of Abijah Northey—a gentleman-farmer who tried to farm without children. In 1828, at the age of fifty-four, Northey retired from business in Salem and bought a 100-acre estate in Boxford. On March 27, he traveled up to the farm with his wife "to take charge"; because he had no practical experience as a farmer himself, taking charge meant hiring hands. The domestic chores he must have left to his wife's management, for he made almost no reference to them in subsequent years. The outdoor work was his responsibility, however, and after two days of asking about for names and the customary rates of pay, he hired a thirty-one-year-old local man named Isaac Spofford at $13 a month, "the same as Mr. Eaton pays." Within a week Northey had hired a second man, Samuel Allen, to assist Spofford; with the help of a local mason and carpenter the two hands began making repairs to the property and preparing for planting.[69]

Although the farm that Northey ran was unusually large, it nonetheless resembled others across the region in its diversity. In 1828 and following years, his men planted a selection of peas, beans, lettuce, cabbage, squash, beets, potatoes, onions, turnips, and parsnips in the garden; sowed corn, wheat, oats, and barley in the fields beyond; cropped hay from the meadowland; picked apples and pears in the orchard; calved, pigged, and lambed animals in the spring and butchered them at the end of the year; and cut wood in the winter—to name only the most prominent of tasks. Some of the produce was for home consumption, but much of it was for sale, and Northey frequently rode to market in Andover and Salem with live animals, meat, potatoes, hides, and apples. This was the sizable surplus of a traditional farm, for although Northey took some interest in innovation—mentioning new varieties of apples and peas when they were planted, for example—the core of his agricultural regime followed customary ways.[70]

A gentleman beyond his physical prime, Northey depended exclusively on hired help. Through the entire year he invariably kept one man in his employ; during the summer, there was always a second and sometimes a third hand to lend assistance; and at mowing time a few neighbors or their hands usually helped out as well. To the extent that a regional labor market was coming into existence in Northey's day, his journal provides a window on its character. Only a few of the farmhands that worked for him had grown up in Boxford. Isaac Spofford worked for Northey from 1828 to 1831 and then left to try his luck on a farm of his own. By December of 1834, however, he had "failed . . . had everything attached," and he returned to his former employer the following March. Jonathan James Porter, his twenty-one-year-old replacement, and John Perly, who in Nor-

69. Entries for Mar. 27–Apr. 8, 1828, Northey Journals. Northey previously had been a successful shipmaster, merchant, and president of the Essex Marine Insurance Company. See the biographical information in the introduction to the Northey Family Papers.

70. Northey Journals, but esp. entries for Mar. 29, Apr. 3, 1828, Apr. 28, 1829, Mar. 11, 30, Apr. 16, Oct. 5, 21, 25, Nov. 1, 1830. For sources of biographical material on all of Northey's hands, see Appendix 4.

they's opinion "bid fair for becoming a good member of society," had also been born in Boxford. Three hands were local teenagers: Francis Swan, whom Northey labeled a "lazy gormandiser" and fired within three weeks; Samuel Foster, who worked the summer of 1830 but quit in October after a dispute with Northey over the beating of a horse; and Charles Foster, who "came to stay" in the winter of 1832 and left again four days later. Another local fellow named Moses Kimball—thirty-one years old but single—did a month of haying in July of 1828 and occasional work for Northey in the years thereafter.[71] The rest of Northey's help, however, hailed from out of town. Spofford's first assistant, Samuel Allen, was a migrant laborer with a brother in Boston but no ties to Boxford; another boy, John Wiggins, came to Northey by way of the Salem workhouse; Peter Bohannon was a young Irishman who had previously lived in Lowell; and several other hands were recruited across the town boundaries in Rowley, Haverhill, Andover, and Bradford.[72] The word-of-mouth network that drew men into Northey's employ stretched across eastern Massachusetts, but it worked most efficiently within a day's walk of the farmhouse door.

The same network, of course, lured them away again. Northey may have been a difficult man to work for, but the turnover of help on the farm was nonetheless remarkable. Occasionally, the journal suggests where his hands went; Moses Kimball left in the spring of 1829, for example, "to work on the roads."[73] For the most part, however, Northey did not care where they were bound and was only concerned with finding replacements. When Frazer Foot, a hand whom Northey once described as "good for nothing, a purfect eye servant," quit on the eve of mowing time in 1831, the farmer was strapped to find another man; after the hay was in he remarked: "I missed it this year in hireing a man that was sickly: just as the hot weather came on and the work began to crowd us, he was taken sick; it was then difficult to get another man; the consequence was that I had to pay a dollar a day for what I did hire and my corn and potatoes was left to take their own course over run with weeds."[74] For lack of other help,

71. Entries for Mar. 29, July 3, 1828, Mar. 21, May 9, 25, June 1, Oct. 19, 27, Nov. 6, 1829, Feb. 8, 12, Mar. 20, 1832, Apr. 1, Nov. 6, Dec. 29, 1834, Mar. 7, 1835, Northey Journals.

72. Entries for Aug. 23, 29, Nov. 19, 1828, June 9, July 6, 1831, Feb. 25, Mar. 26, Sept. 8, Nov. 17, 30, Dec. 1, 1832, Mar. 19, Apr. 5, Nov. 16, 1833, Aug. 6, 1834, Mar. 21, 1835, Northey Journals.

73. June 1, 1829, Northey Journals.

74. Aug. 1, 1831, Northey Journals.

Northey turned to Foot a second time the following winter, but then in February, calling him "the poorest hand that I ever had," Northey fired him for good. Once again, finding someone to fill Foot's place proved quite a headache. Northey "went after Mr. Holt to come and live with me but could not get him"; two weeks later he rode to Andover "to see a man at Mr. Jacob Osgoods," but they could not settle on terms either. Only the following day was Northey finally able to get another hand, and he had to cross the Merrimack to find him. Winter was an idle time in Boxford, and it is hard to imagine a scarcity of potential hands, but few seemed eager to work for Northey.[75]

This particular farmer bargained vigorously with his men over the terms of employment. He was an outsider in Boxford, as were most of them; in confronting one another not as neighbors, but as employer and employee, negotiation over terms was clearly the norm. Samuel Allen left Northey in 1828 because "he wanted more rum and more wages." Peter Bohannon only agreed to the $10 a month he was offered in 1832 when Northey agreed "if he does well to add 50c."[76] The following year, the situation was even worse. "Labour is uncommon high this spring," he wrote, "such men as you could hire last year for $10.50 a month are now offered $13." Complaints about the price of labor were nothing new in the history of New England, but the context in which they arose was different. It was not the prospect of independence that was drawing men away from farm employment, but rather, as Northey observed, "the demand for labour on the Railroad & the Factories." In another decade, industrial employers would draw heavily on immigrant labor, but in the first great boom of mill and rail construction, the demand for manpower presented itself chiefly to the native-born—many of them small holders—the very men whom Northey was trying to hire.[77] "Labor" *in the abstract* was being

75. Oct. 17, 1831, Jan. 30, Feb. 8, 24, 25, 1832, Northey Journals.

76. Apr. 16, 1828, Mar. 26, 1832, Northey Journals.

77. Mar. 27, 30, 1833, Northey Journals. On the social origins of the first generation of Yankee millhands, see Jonathan Prude, *The Coming of Industrial Order: Town and Factory Life in Rural Massachusetts, 1810–1860* (Cambridge, 1983), 92–96; and Christopher Clark, *The Roots of Rural Capitalism: Western Massachusetts, 1780–1860* (Ithaca, N.Y., 1990), 112. Female mill operatives came mostly from the poor to middling ranks of rural New England, according to my reading of Thomas Dublin, *Women at Work: The Transformation of Work and Community in Lowell, Massachusetts, 1826–1860* (New York, 1979), 33–35. That nominal and real farm wages were rising throughout the period 1825–1850 is evident from Rothenberg, "Emergence of Farm Labor Markets," *JEH*, XLVIII (1988), 541, 565.

drawn off—not by the frontier or for some temporary emergency, but because the world around and inside Essex County was beginning to industrialize.

By the spring of 1833, Northey was reconsidering his rural experiment. Having lived in the country "long enough to form a pretty correct opinion of the profits of farming," he had "found from actual calculations that the proceeds of a farm will not pay for the expense of carrying it on where you pay for all the labour." It was simply "impossible for a man to earn for you the amount of his wages and board." For two more seasons he tried to make a go of it, but in the fall of 1835 he finally gave up, sold the farm for $4,500, and returned to Salem.[78] Northey was probably not the most efficient of agriculturalists, but neither was he the only New Englander of his time to abandon farming for the city. From one perspective, he was merely following his own men. Professional farmers who worked the fields themselves with the help of unpaid family members—all of whom could pursue some sort of by-employment—outlasted Northey by several decades by exploiting themselves and their lands to exhaustion. But even those who owned enough property to support themselves had to wonder whether their energies and their capital were being employed to the best advantage. In reality, Abijah Northey had not failed at farming; he had simply given it up. Like many of his men, he was moving to town.

MANUFACTURE

The transformation of Essex County into a manufacturing region during the first half of the nineteenth century has received a good deal of attention from other historians and is not the subject of this book.[79] Where those studies begin, this one concludes. Clearly, however, the cultural and behavioral patterns that had structured work in the old rural and mar-

78. Mar. 27, 1833, Aug. 31, Oct. 14, Dec. 22, 1835, Northey Journals.

79. See esp. Donald B. Cole, *Immigrant City: Lawrence, Massachusetts, 1845–1921* (Chapel Hill, N.C., 1963); Thernstrom, *Poverty and Progress*; Alan Dawley, *Class and Community: The Industrial Revolution in Lynn* (Cambridge, Mass., 1976); Faler, *Mechanics and Manufacturers*; and Mary H. Blewett, *Men, Women, and Work: Class, Gender, and Protest in the New England Shoe Industry, 1780–1910* (Urbana, Ill., 1988). A brief but convenient overview of the whole county can be found in Albion, "From Sails to Spindles," Essex Institute, *Hist. Colls.*, XCV (1959), 115–136.

itime economies did not disappear immediately with industrialization. The manufacturing industries of Essex County recruited their first labor force within a society in which adult men continued to believe that working for others was demeaning. By the beginning of the nineteenth century they and their families were hungry for the sort of full employment that the rural and maritime economies could no longer provide, yet most regarded wage labor as a temporary expedient—a means to the further end of sustaining themselves in some degree of competency. Farmers and fishermen—who formed the majority of the male population of the North Shore of Massachusetts when the United States came into being—carried these assumptions in their breasts. How their behavior shaped the development of New England's first industrial labor market is the point at which this study ends.

The development of Essex into a manufacturing county was an extended event. It began with the founding of the colony in the 1630s, when immigrant artisans first settled in the seaport towns and the wives of Puritan farmers carried their skills in domestic manufacture into the countryside. A further step came in the opening decades of the eighteenth century, when the quantity of uncleared land began to dwindle, the obvious task of farm building began to relax, and the practice of manufacturing as a by-employment spread among young men in rural districts. The final stage in the transformation, however, began with the American Revolution. When trade with Britain was complicated by non-importation after 1768 and then shut down by the Revolutionary War after 1775, the supply of overseas manufactures evaporated, and men and women throughout Essex County were rudely introduced to the necessity of large-scale import substitution. Although this immediate burden weighed on New Englanders until the conclusion of peace in 1783, it also provided a forcible education about the ways in which their handicraft skills could be turned to production for other than local and regional markets. Fishermen's wives sewed sailcloth into tenting, weavers turned out hundreds of blankets, a few farmers set up gunpowder mills, and shoemakers fashioned cartloads of boots—all for the Continental Army. Working people struck few bonanzas answering what were chiefly state-ordered requisitions, but many did a reasonable business servicing the civilian market by manufacturing goods their countrymen could no longer import. In Essex County, shoemakers in particular seem to have profited by the interruption in British supply; the small-holding families of Lynn turned to the trade with such enthusiasm that the town's annual output of shoes rose to a hundred thousand or more by the war's conclusion.[80]

The restoration of peace in 1783 brought an end to the shortage of imported goods and to the business of manufacturing substitutes for them under the odd protection of Britain's naval blockade. In New England as a whole the reappearance of English woolens, china, shoes, and metalware in local markets met with broad relief, but for craftsmen who had grown accustomed to servicing civilian and military demand this was the beginning of a difficult period that lasted through the 1780s. The expectations and innovative thinking that the wartime emergency had awakened, however, were not easily put to rest. During the 1780s, some merchants and artisans with an eye for business met British competition by reorganizing local families into larger networks of production and aggressively marketing their wares up and down the Atlantic seaboard. Some of these ventures actually borrowed from the British example by introducing mechanized technology. With government assistance but mixed success, groups of merchants established a cotton mill in Beverly, a woolen mill in Ipswich, and a sailcloth manufactory in Haverhill—all of which were by 1792 in fitful production. Much more impressive was the growth of domestic industry. In Ipswich, women and girls were turning out close to 40,000 yards of lace and edging by 1790. In Lynn, a number of entrepreneurs furnished local shoemakers with leather on credit and marketed the finished shoes in Philadelphia, Baltimore, and Savannah. When George Washington passed through the town in 1789, he learned that about four hundred local workmen and a good many of their wives—

80. Tagney, *World Turned Upside Down*, 342–343; Russell, *Long, Deep Furrow*, 124, 127–128; Robert A. East, *Business Enterprise in the American Revolutionary Era* (New York, 1938), 53–54, 238; James A. Henretta, "The War for Independence and American Economic Development," in Ronald Hoffman, John J. McCusker, Russell R. Menard, and Peter J. Albert, eds., *The Economy of Early America: The Revolutionary Period, 1763–1790* (Charlottesville, Va., 1988), 71–73; Victor S. Clark, *History of Manufactures in the United States*, rev. ed., 3 vols. (Washington, D.C., 1929), I, 222. Paul Faler claims that shoe production in Lynn climbed from 80,000 pairs in 1768 to 400,000 by 1783, but estimates for the late 1780s place annual output at 100,000 to 175,000; Faler's figures, drawn from a local historian, may be exaggerated. See *Mechanics and Manufacturers*, 12; Donald Jackson and Dorothy Twohig, eds., *The Diaries of George Washington, 1748–1799*, 6 vols. (Charlottesville, Va., 1976–1979), VI, 483; and Brissot de Warville, *New Travels*, ed. Echeverria, 362.

comprising most of the households in town—were turning out 175,000 shoes a year.[81]

The shipping boom that framed the turn of the century reinforced the development of local manufactures. Shipbuilding—ruined by the Revolutionary War and slow to recover in the 1780s—surged with the expansion of neutral carrying trades after 1795. In most towns along the coast vessels of all sizes were under construction. Salisbury had been "deserted by the carpenters and ship-wrights" as late as 1785, but a decade later Timothy Dwight observed that "together with the mechanical arts which it involves," vessel construction gave the town a striking "appearance of life and activity." Danvers was also developing a reputation for shipbuilding, as was Chebacco Parish in Ipswich, and the cottage fishermen of Cape Ann, spurred on by the rising price of fish, were building boats by the dozen. All this meant casual employment for any farm boy who could turn his hand to carpentry, and work for rural craftsmen who could provide the iron fittings, blocks, cordage, sailcloth, and barrels that new vessels required.[82] The boom in North Atlantic shipping also broadened the network of business connections among the states and extended the markets to which local craftsmen had access. Granted, the vessels that sailed out of Salem, Newburyport, and Boston continued to fill their holds mostly with local fish, timber, and reexported products from other ports, but local manufactures were now competing for carrying space. Locally made furniture, hats, rum, and flannel cloth played a small but growing role in the development of coastal commerce, and the shoe trade blossomed. By the

81. Jackson and Twohig, eds., *Washington Diaries*, VI, 485–486, 492; Thomas Franklin Waters, *Ipswich in the Massachusetts Bay Colony, 1633–1917*, 2 vols. (Ipswich, Mass., 1905–1917), II, 627–628; George Cabot to Tench Coxe, Jan. 24, 1791, Joseph Dana to George Cabot, Jan. 24, 1791, in Arthur Harrison Cole, ed., *Industrial and Commercial Correspondence of Alexander Hamilton, Anticipating His Report on Manufactures* (Chicago, 1928); Faler, *Mechanics and Manufacturers*, 13–21; Blewett, *Men, Women, and Work*, 17; Marquis de Chastellux, *Travels in North America in the Years 1780, 1781, and 1782*, ed. Howard C. Rice, Jr., 2 vols. (Chapel Hill, N.C., 1963), II, 628n.

82. Douglas S. Robertson, ed., *An Englishman in America, 1785, Being the Diary of Joseph Hadfield* (Toronto, 1933), 198; Dwight, *Travels*, ed. Solomon, I, 316, 326; Bentley, *Diary*, II, 8, IV, 478–479; Dow, ed., *Two Centuries of Travel*, 111–112; Robert G. Albion, William A. Baker, and Benjamin W. Labaree, *New England and the Sea* (Middletown, Conn., 1972), 62–63; James Duncan Phillips, *Salem and the Indies: The Story of the Great Commercial Era of the City* (Boston, 1947), 158, 161; Morison, *Maritime History of Massachusetts*, 101; Dana Story, *Frame-Up! The History of Essex, Its Shipyards and Its People* (Barre, Mass., 1964), 2–3.

1800s, the annual output of Lynn shoemakers had doubled the levels of 1790, and in 1804 the merchants of that town claimed to have done $500,000 worth of business in the American South alone.[83]

After 1807, the special advantages enjoyed by the American merchant marine gradually disappeared. First the embargo, then the War of 1812, and finally the revival of European shipping cut into the profitability of the carrying trades and slowly persuaded merchants to redirect the considerable capital they had been accumulating since the 1790s into other channels. In New England, this meant manufacturing, and by the 1830s Essex County had become one of New England's leading centers for the manufacture of leather, woolen cloth, sailing vessels, cigars, hats, combs, and especially shoes. The McLane Report of 1832 enumerated close to 13,000 people within Essex County employed in these and other manufacturing trades. During the 1840s, textile mills of truly industrial proportions were constructed at Lawrence on the Merrimack and in the old seaports of Salem and Newburyport. Even the most agricultural of towns had become hives of rural industry, and by 1850 there was hardly a spot in the region where the majority of men were not artisans or industrial laborers—save the fishing port of Gloucester. Essex was no longer an agricultural and maritime county but a manufacturing one.[84]

Especially at first, the growth of manufactures took place within the traditional structure of independent household production, combining farming or fishing with the processing of farm produce and the practice of artisanal by-employments. Thus Israel Sawyer, who operated a small farm in Salisbury during the 1780s and 1790s, became a cooper every winter, making barrels for his neighbors in which to cart surplus produce across the river to sell in Newburyport. Moody Jacques of West Newbury owned enough land during the 1810s and 1820s to require assistance at mowing time and harvest (he being the first Essex County farmer to pay by the hour), but he also found time in the spring to net shad and alewives in the

83. Labaree, *Patriots and Partisans*, 98, 131–132; Phillips, *Salem and the Indies*, 63, 68, 316; Clark, *History of Manufactures*, I, 423, 473, 561; Faler, *Mechanics and Manufacturers*, 17–19; Dwight, *Travels*, ed. Solomon, I, 333–334.

84. McLane, *Report*, I, 210–259. In a random sample drawn from the manuscript census for 1850, the proportion of all males 16 and older who designated themselves craftsmen or industrial laborers was 74% in Georgetown ($N = 47$), 60% in Marblehead ($N = 57$), 52% in West Newbury ($N = 44$), 50% in Topsfield ($N = 48$), but only 11% in Gloucester ($N = 38$). See the population schedules for those towns in U.S. Census Bureau, Seventh Census, rolls 310, 315.

Merrimack River for sale in Newburyport; in the winter he made shoes. By combining a range of commercial activities with improvement of their home farms and "exchanging works" with their neighbors, Sawyer and Jacques were trying to sustain their own competencies and to pass them along to their children in the most conventional manner.[85] As late as 1830, the agricultural improver Henry Colman insisted that no man was more independent than he "who, to the advantages of a well-managed farm, adds the profits of some handicraft trade, which gives him employment in inclement weather."[86]

Still, there can be little doubt that in the first half of the nineteenth century, this tradition was in slow decline. For one thing, fewer farmers owned craft equipment than had been the case in colonial times. In a sample of farm inventories from the period before the Revolution, 50 percent of the estates contained looms, shoemaking kits, tanyards, mills, or smithing implements; after the War of 1812, the equivalent proportion had dropped to 35 percent. Likewise, few rural craftsmen now practiced agriculture as they once had. Among shoemakers and housewrights who had made their homes in the countryside and whose estates had passed through probate between 1725 and 1775, 81 percent owned farm equipment or livestock; by the period 1800–1840, only 53 percent could claim the same. The tradition of by-employments survived but in weakened form. As commercial agriculture and the market for manufactures developed, the degree of technical expertise and organizational efficiency necessary to compete and survive began to climb as well, and the old occupational diversity of households gradually diminished.[87]

The really dynamic elements in the industrial transformation of the county in the nineteenth century were three in number: the expansion of shops; the extension of outwork; and the construction of mills. All of these required labor; all involved employment of a plainly dependent sort; all recruited hands within a labor market that adult men were reluctant to join; and all relied to a great extent in their early years on women and young men. Indeed, it was in large part the ability of all three sectors to

85. Israel Sawyer Acct. Bk., 1774–1819; Moody Jacques Acct. Bk., 1814–1827.

86. Colman, *Hints Addressed to the Farmers of Essex*, 12–13.

87. For farm inventories (defined as those containing farm implements, land, and livestock), $N = 46$ for 1760–1775 and $N = 37$ for 1815–1820. For rural craftsmen (defined here as housewrights and shoemakers dwelling in rural communities), $N = 32$ for 1725–1775 and $N = 38$ for 1800–1840. These inventories were sampled from the Essex Co. Prob. Recs. See the discussion of this point earlier in this chapter.

recruit among the traditionally dependent population of Essex County that enabled them to grow at all.

The intensification of small-scale manufacture, frequently overlooked in treatments of industrialization, mattered enormously in Essex County. In Salem, Newburyport, and around Cape Ann, cooperages, ropewalks, and sailmakers began to expand in size and number during the prosperous years of the 1790s and 1800s. In Ipswich's Chebacco Parish (incorporated as Essex in 1819), shipbuilding replaced fishing as the town's primary maritime industry and was employing hundreds of men in a dozen or so yards by the 1830s. In Lynn and Haverhill shoemakers added to their "ten-footers" to make room for additional hands, and in the surrounding towns a host of new tanning and currying establishments sprang up in response. By 1832 Essex County contained scores of small businesses: building furniture, ships, and carriages; manufacturing paper and shoes; tanning, currying, and dressing leather; twisting rope and working tin.[88]

Although the central figure in these shops continued to be the master craftsman—now sometimes straddling the line between artisan and manufacturer—such workplaces grew in size by dividing the production process into several stages and assigning each to a different type of worker. Physically less demanding parts of the labor process could be handed to women, unskilled work delegated to younger and untrained men, and the simplest of tasks assigned to children. Ambitious artisans could recruit these hands at low rates of pay and concentrate on business, management, and the more complex elements of the craft. Predictably, shops with women and children on the payroll tended to be larger than those without. Among operations identified in the McLane Report of 1832, those in which all the workers were adult males employed an average of 4.4 hands; those which also hired women and children employed 9.1.[89] Tanyards,

88. In the 149 different firms that can be separately identified from McLane, *Report*, I, 210–259, the median number of employees (including the proprietor) was 16. Since in several towns the enumerators grouped smaller firms together (e.g., "Tanning and currying of leather, by 6 persons or firms," employing a total of 13 hands in Bradford [*ibid.*, I, 216–217]), they are underrepresented here, and the actual median size must have been smaller.

89. McLane, *Report*, I, 210–259. For the purpose of this calculation, the 37 distinct firms employing fewer than 20 hands and not involved in shoemaking (where the "firm" incorporated several distinct and separately owned workshops and many individual shoebinders) were defined as shops.

cigar manufactories, ropewalks, and the like reorganized traditional crafts to raise output and lower costs.

An interesting case in point was the horn-comb manufacturing business of the lower Merrimack Valley. Unimportant before the nineteenth century, combmaking boomed after the War of 1812, when a small number of craftsmen in West Newbury sensed the possible demand for inexpensive mass-produced combs and reorganized their business toward that end. The raw materials were South American cattle horns, landed in a decomposing state at the mouth of the Merrimack and then carted overland in a cloud of stench to the shops in West Newbury. Softened by being soaked in boiling water and hot oil, the horns were then pressed in molds of the desired shape until they cooled. The teeth were marked and laboriously cut out with a thin saw, and finally the whole comb was polished for sale. During the first half of the century the cutting and polishing processes were mechanized, and the lathes and polishers were sometimes connected to treadmills driven by horses that labored in the shop basements, but there were no genuine comb factories in West Newbury before 1850.[90]

How comb manufacturers organized work in their expanded shops cannot be known precisely, but the surviving evidence suggests that labor was almost certainly divided by gender and age. The manufacturers themselves were not wealthy men; the most prosperous was worth no more than a gentleman-farmer, and most probably worked alongside their employees. Together with a few journeymen—sometimes English emigrants but more frequently native New Englanders—manufacturers performed the difficult task of preparing the horn and pressing it into shape. Heavy work, loading and carting the horns and combs, was undoubtedly delegated to younger and brawnier hands, often their sons, but the bulk of the labor in combmaking lay in the endless cutting and polishing of teeth, hundreds each day, performed it would seem almost entirely by women and children. In 1832, close to twenty manufacturers employed sixty-five men and more than a hundred women and children. Whereas the men

90. John J. Currier, *History of Newburyport, Mass., 1764–1905*, 2 vols. (Newburyport, Mass., 1906–1909), I, 179; Wilbur E. Rowell, "The Merrimack River," Essex Institute, *Hist. Colls.*, LXXXII (1946), 17; George Ripley and Charles A. Dana, eds., *The American Cyclopaedia*, 16 vols. (New York, 1883), V, 133; Mary Musser, "Massachusetts Horn Smiths: A Century of Combmaking, 1775–1875," *Old-Time New England*, LXVIII (1978), 59–68; McLane, *Report*, I, 220–221, 246–247, 258–259. There were also a few combmaking shops in Haverhill and Newburyport.

were paid about eighty cents for a day's work, the women and children were fortunate to earn even thirty-five. By dividing labor to exploit the abundance of culturally dependent and inexpensive help, the comb-makers of West Newbury were able to turn out several hundred thousand cheap combs annually for sale up and down the American coast.[91]

Even more dynamic in Essex County's transformation into a manufac-turing region, however, was the extension of outwork.[92] This process began at the end of the eighteenth century when merchants, storekeepers, and enterprising artisans discovered that underemployed people across the county could be recruited into networks of domestic production for market sale. Advancing them on credit the raw materials with which to fashion standardized commercial manufactures, these entrepreneurs bought back the finished products for a prearranged price and then sent them to market. Although the outwork system eventually dominated a number of industries—lacemaking in Ipswich and cigar rolling in Saugus are two good examples—its greatest impact on the regional economy was through the reorganization of the shoe industry.[93] During the Revolution-ary years, shoes took over from ships as the premier manufacture of Essex County, and 64 percent of the county's manufacturing labor force were employed in this industry by 1832. Down to the outbreak of the Civil War, no other manufacture within the region rivaled shoemaking in impor-tance, and throughout the entire antebellum period, the bulk of produc-tion within the industry was performed on the laborers' own premises through credit-driven outwork arrangements.[94]

Although as a system outwork developed gradually from the long tradi-tion of by-employments, it worked on somewhat different principles. An independent craftsman produced work that was recognizable, on which

91. See the sources in nn. 89 and 90, above. Some of the social division of labor was inferred from the entries for adult male combmakers in the Population Schedules for West Newbury, Seventh Census, 1850, microcopy 432, roll 315.

92. Insofar as the expansion of small shops frequently depended on merchant credit, the distinction between the expansion of small shops and the development of outwork is not easy to draw. The chief distinction is that in the former a manufacturer—usually with some practical experience as a workman himself—organized the division of labor, whereas in outwork a merchant, without the same practical experience, oversaw the system.

93. McLane, *Report*, I, 256–257; Waters, *Ipswich in Massachusetts Bay Colony*, 534, 628.

94. McLane, *Report*, I, 210–259; Albion, "From Sails to Spindles," Essex Institute, *Hist. Colls.*, XCV (1959), 130–131, 133–134.

his reputation depended. Even when his wares were to be shipped abroad, he and the exporting merchant could negotiate their price as equal partners in a commercial bargain that did not compromise the independence of either party. In shoemaking and other forms of outwork, the advance of raw materials on credit fixed the price that the producer received and effectively standardized the character of the product. An outwork shoemaker was in no position to bargain on an equal footing with a shoe merchant boss—his indebtedness prevented it. Not only did this sort of work involve long hours and tedious repetition, it also bore no individual stamp and carried little if any pride in achievement. Between the independent artisan and the dependent outworker, of course, there was no clearcut distinction; most working people had characteristics of both. During the first half of the nineteenth century, however, outworkers constituted a progressively larger fraction of the labor force.

That the outwork system in shoemaking exploited the dependency rooted in gender—specifically the willingness of mothers and daughters to add commercial shoebinding to their list of domestic chores—is well established and has recently been reaffirmed in the work of Mary Blewett.[95] The manner in which the same system also built on the relative dependency of young men demands recognition in its own right. The experience of the Jackson family of Rowley illustrates this point exactly. In 1803 Caleb Jackson presented his two sons, Caleb, Jr., and Samuel—aged sixteen and twelve, respectively—with enough cut leather to fashion seven pairs of trial shoes. He took the finished footwear to a local agent for the larger shoe dealers of Newburyport and Lynn, who was pleased enough to ask the Jacksons to produce a hundred more before spring. Every winter thereafter, Caleb, Sr., contracted with a local agent to buy leather, which his sons stitched and made into shoes. As in most tasks, the two boys toiled for their father within the framework of household production, but as Caleb, Jr., recorded in his diary, making shoes for sale was drudgery— something "we have got to [do]," language that he never applied to husbandry. A few custom jobs—such as the pair of "thin shoes" that he fashioned for his mother in February of 1805—were noted in his diary with obvious satisfaction. The 226 "pistareen" (two-bit) pairs that he and

95. Blewett, *Men, Women, and Work*, chaps. 1–3. On female outwork in hatmaking and spinning, see Dublin, "Women and Outwork," in Hahn and Prude, eds., *Countryside in the Age of Capitalist Transformation*, 58–63; and Cott, *Bonds of Womanhood*, 26–28.

his brother made for Mr. Solomon Stickney that year, however, merited little more than a cursory entry every few days, even though the two were hard at it most of the winter. The Jacksons were in general agreement that sale shoemaking was a useful way of improving the otherwise idle days of winter and thereby obtaining the means of settling retail accounts with local shopkeepers. But it never commanded the dignity of independent farming. There is no evidence that Caleb, Sr., ever stitched, lasted, or bottomed a single shoe. He passed the awl to his sons in exactly the same way that early American farmwives delegated spinning and hatmaking to their daughters—as an occupation proper to dependency.[96]

The final branch of manufacture to develop in the early nineteenth century by employing the traditionally dependent was factory production. Essex County lagged here because most of its territory lay along the coastal plain and lacked the waterpower to support much large-scale production. True, a pair of cotton mills had been constructed in Ipswich and Methuen during the 1820s, the lower Merrimack Valley between Andover and Salisbury was by 1832 the center of America's factory-woven flannel industry, and Salem possessed by that date a ropewalk that employed 118 hands. But as late as the 1830s, most local manufacturing took place on a small scale in shops, shipyards, and farmhouses scattered across the region.[97] With the arrival of steampower during the 1840s, however, the number of truly industrial establishments began to multiply. By mid-century, the biggest employers in Newburyport and Salem were large textile firms that combined spinning and weaving in a single mill. Businessmen were carving up the fields of Andover and Methuen alongside the Merrimack into the new industrial city of Lawrence. By 1859, the two largest firms there employed 1,700 and 2,200 hands, respectively. About the same time shoe manufacturers in Lynn and Haverhill purchased sewing machines and initiated the long but successful struggle to centralize production into factories.[98]

96. Entries for Jan. 15, Dec. 3, 1803, Feb. 20, May 8, Dec. 7, 1804, Jan. 3, Aug. 10, Dec. 10, 1805, Jan. 10, 16, 1806, summaries for Feb. and Apr. 1805, Caleb Jackson Journal, 1802–1806. On custom work, see entries for Dec. 7, 1804, Jan. 3, 5, 14, 15, 19, 23, 26, Feb. 2, 9, 19, 1805, summaries for Feb. and Apr. 1805, *ibid.* On Caleb's distaste for shoemaking, see Jan. 15, Mar. 29, 1803, Jan. 3, 1805, *ibid.*

97. McLane, *Report*, I, 210–259; Clark, *History of Manufactures*, I, 238–239, 567.

98. Albion, "From Sails to Spindles," Essex Institute, *Hist. Colls.*, XCV (1959), 129, 134–135; Blewett, *Men, Women, and Work*, 97–105, 142–153. On a smaller scale, even lighter

In their early development, factories depended chiefly on female and child labor. In five of the seven firms described unambiguously in the McLane Report of 1832 as employing at least fifty hands under one roof, women and children composed more than half the labor force. At the New England Lace Company in Ipswich, a cotton mill in Ipswich, another in Amesbury, and a cigar factory in Salem, they accounted for 80 percent of the employed hands. At the woolen mill in Amesbury the equivalent figure was 55 percent; only at the Salem ropewalk and a woolen mill in Saugus did the proportion fall below half. Since the larger of these seven establishments hired the fewest men, about 80 percent of the employees in these seven factories were women and children.[99] No doubt women played this role because some of the skills that the new industries required (especially stitching) lay within their traditional province, and children fitted in because much of the labor in the mills required little strength and minimal training. What women and children shared, however, was their political weakness and its consequence—that they commanded less pay. As long as adult men could practicably resist wage employment, family dependents would provide the bulk of the factory labor force.

Factory employment, outwork, and paid labor in shop manufacture had originally appeared around the turn of the century as a form of part-time employment suited to those in Essex County—women, children, and younger men especially—who were less than fully independent. More than class, therefore, gender and age first directed certain people into the employ of capital. Toward the middle of the century, however, the balance shifted, and nothing more defined the constitution of this labor force by 1850 than its lack of property. As the most dynamic sector within the regional economy, manufacturing certainly continued to recruit younger people, and the industrial labor force in 1850 was still composed primarily of the young. Less and less, however, did it form a stage in life or a by-employment to agriculture. This seems generally to have been the case in factory production throughout New England, but even within the smaller-

---

industries with fewer power requirements were growing in scale. By 1848, for example, a single Newburyport factory employed 100 men and women rolling out six to seven million cigars a year. See Clark, *History of Manufactures*, I, 488.

99. In manufacturing as a whole, women and children (16 years of age or under) accounted for 47% of all employees, but only 21% of those working in the 30 distinct establishments described as having fewer than 10 employees. See McLane, *Report*, I, 210–211, 222–223, 242–243, 250–251, 256–257.

scale operations that were more typical of Essex County, dependent employment in the service of capital was becoming a career.[100]

By midcentury, for example, combmaking had acquired most of the trademarks of a small-scale capitalist business. In 1850 West Newbury had twenty-one comb manufacturers. Many still worked with their hands, and a good number were sending their sons through a practical apprenticeship in the shop, but they nonetheless formed a very different group from the majority of their employees. Preeminently, of course, they were adult males, which distinguished them from the women and children who composed most of their labor force. Yet even between the shopowners and the men who worked under them, a clear social gap now existed. Of those who identified themselves as combmakers in the 1850 census, a full 35 percent were foreign born: a large contingent of chiefly single young Irishmen; a smaller group of mostly older and married Englishmen; and a twenty-four-year-old Scot. Almost none of these immigrants owned any real property, and the majority boarded with local families. Even native New England combmakers, however, constituted a class apart from their employers. In this industry men (and probably women) did not outgrow wage labor; male combmakers outnumbered manufacturers in every age cohort, and the age distribution of employees listed in the 1850 census mirrored that of adult New Englanders in general. The older hands were likely to have acquired some real estate, but those short of fifty years were in general propertyless. Even though combmaking as a business depended in the first instance on the labor of women and children, it eventually capitalized on the swelling number of adult male New Englanders who preferred wage employment to hardscrabble farming on a few acres of exhausted soil. They had become combmakers for life.[101]

100. For comparative studies of other New England regions, see Dublin, *Women at Work*; Dublin, "Women and Outwork," in Hahn and Prude, eds., *Countryside in the Age of Capitalist Transformation*, 51–69; Prude, *Coming of Industrial Order*; Gregory H. Nobles, "Commerce and Community: A Case Study of the Rural Broommaking Business in Antebellum Massachusetts," *Journal of the Early Republic*, IV (1984), 287–308; and Clark, *Roots of Rural Capitalism*.

101. Among married combmakers ($N = 58$), mean value of real estate was $516, and 62% owned no real estate at all; among married comb manufacturers ($N = 20$), mean real estate holdings amounted to $2,655, and only 5% owned no real estate. These findings are based on the listings of all 21 comb manufacturers and 91 combmakers contained in the Population Schedules for West Newbury, Seventh Census, 1850, microcopy 432, roll 315. For comparative age distributions for all Massachusetts males, see U.S. Census Bureau, *Seventh Census of the United States: 1850*, 48.

The same pattern held increasingly true in the outwork industries. At the beginning of the century Caleb Jackson, Jr., had turned to the manufacture of sale shoes in his spare time as a means of sustaining both the family of his birth and the family he hoped one day to head in some degree of comfortable independence. Indeed, when he grew up he took over the operation of the family farm, and after his father died he inherited it. At midcentury, his lands were valued at $4,000, and when he died in 1867, the farm had grown to nearly 200 acres and was thought to be worth more than $7,000.[102] But how common was Jackson's story? Among those who remained in the countryside, there were undoubtedly many who aimed in the traditional manner to succeed their fathers on the land, and many did. Regardless of the trades rural men of Jackson's generation had followed in their youth, nearly half of those enumerated in the census of 1850 called themselves farmers and assigned to their lands a mean value close to that of Jackson's property.[103] At the same time, however, such outwork clearly was not serving this function everywhere. By midcentury a great many shoemakers lived in urban settings such as Lynn and Haverhill, where farmland was scarce and shoemaking had turned into a lifetime occupation. Even in the rural precincts of Essex County a fair number of older shoemakers and a crowd of younger ones had no real property and little chance of acquiring any, except possibly a small house and lot.[104] Whereas country shoemakers in the pre-Revolutionary period whose estates passed through probate had owned on average 18 acres of

102. See entry for Caleb Jackson in the remarkable card index to the 1850 Census for Essex County, housed in the Lynnfield Public Library, Lynnfield, Mass.; and Estate of Caleb Jackson (1867), Probate No. 43409, Essex Co. Prob. Recs.

103. In a sample of 359 men aged 15 years or older from West Newbury, Danvers, Bradford, Georgetown, Middleton, and Topsfield who reported occupations, 66 were 50 or older; 29 (44%) of these termed themselves farmers, and the mean value of their real estate was $3,952. See the population schedules for these towns in Seventh Census, 1850, microcopy 432, rolls 310, 315.

104. The same sample described in n. 103 contained 110 shoemakers with a median age of 27. Among those 40 or older ($N = 20$), the mean value of real estate was $628, and 60% owned none at all. Among those under 40 ($N = 90$), the mean value of real estate was only $90, and a full 82% owned nothing at all. Mary Blewett's sampling of 255 Lynn shoemakers from the 1860 census suggests that urban shoemakers were older but just marginally more likely to own property. The mean age of Lynn shoemakers in 1860 was 34; that of 1850 rural shoemakers was 26. In Lynn, 28% of shoemakers owned real estate; in rural communities, only 22% did. See the sources listed in the previous note, and Blewett, *Men, Women, and Work,* 332.

farmland and five head of livestock, their nineteenth-century successors possessed only 7 acres and seldom more than an animal or two.[105]

Painting the picture in its broadest strokes, therefore, industrial capitalism invaded Essex County by first mobilizing the labor of those who, chiefly because of age and gender, came from the ranks of the traditionally dependent, and then transforming employment into the lifetime condition of a working class. The early recruits, especially those in industries where the division and mechanization of labor were most advanced, were undeniably women and young people. By the middle of the century, however, the manufacturing population of the county was no longer particularly young. What had begun as a means to economic independence had turned into a defining condition of proletarian dependency.

In 1775, the dependency of class had dominated production in Essex County only within the maritime economy—and imperfectly even there. Throughout the rural economy, labor was organized overwhelmingly within structures of age and gender-determined power internal to the family. By 1850 this was no longer the case. In town and country most people either worked for wages or toiled at outwork where the terms were largely imposed upon them. That capitalism had begun to effect a structural transformation of the deepest sort upon the region goes almost without saying.

Like every transformation, however, it could only build on preexisting materials, and, indeed, the form that it first assumed retained important continuities with the colonial past. As long as most adult men clung to a notion of personal respectability in which landed independence mattered, and as long as that ideal retained any plausibility within or beyond the county, the practice of working for pay *outside* the family spread first among those with the longest tradition of dependence *inside* the family. During the first half of the nineteenth century, the only period when native-born Yankees provided the labor necessary to capitalist development, it was thus the traditionally dependent portion of the population— women, children, and younger men—who provided the bulk of that labor.

105. This is based on two samples of rural shoemakers culled from Essex Co. Prob. Recs.: one drawn from 1725–1775 ($N = 17$); the other from 1800–1840 ($N = 19$). In the first sample, the 17 estates contained together 78 animals; in the second, the 19 estates contained only 28.

During colonial times class had been the prime agency for the mobilization of labor in only a few of the seaport towns. When capital began to reorganize the economy that prevailed in the rest of the county, therefore, it did so first by exploiting the age and gender-specific dependency that still dominated that world.

By the middle of the nineteenth century, this pattern was losing its grip on the region. For men in particular, dependent employment was turning from a phase in life into a lifetime fate. The rising tide of immigration that began after 1845 only compounded this development by providing New England with dependents of all ages and both genders, who had little choice but to sell their labor for a living. And as families in general—men and women, young and old—leaned more and more heavily on paid employment and raised their children to do the same, the social foundations of a working class came into being.

CONCLUSION

The industrial transformation of New England in the nineteenth century was itself the product of earlier transformations, without which industrial development would never have begun. These earlier changes were not as wrenching and total as those the region experienced in the nineteenth century, but they mattered subsequently and must be understood. The key to such an understanding is to recognize in the development of Essex County and the surrounding region both what was new and what was English.

The quality that the Puritan settlements of the seventeenth century shared with every European colonization venture was their newness. Expansion was in itself no novelty. Like most Europeans, the English had been trying to conquer territory beyond their borders for centuries, and the notion that colonization was the surest way to retain a conquest had been accepted wisdom since the 1570s. What distinguished settlement in the New World was the manner in which epidemic disease among the native population and the social disruption that followed cleared the country of effective opposition. Consequently, when the Puritan colonists arrived in Massachusetts Bay they found the terms of economic life to be the reverse of what they had known at home. Whereas labor and capital had been the cheapest factors of production in the Old World, they were the dearest in the new. This forced New Englanders, as well as their counterparts in Virginia and the West Indies, to reorganize their economic lives. With dependent labor and productive wealth in short supply, they could only secure the competencies they sought when they found a way to control the risks and costs that these twin scarcities imposed. The particular solutions that the farming and fishing populations of Essex County seized upon, outlined in the first half of this study, were distinctively rooted in the peculiarities of the region. They shared with other colonial ventures, however, this principle: that frontier settlement proceeded most successfully when those who directed production and those who performed it were tied in the tightest bonds of interdependence. The strict intergenerational dependency that suffused the New England countryside and the reins of clientage that ran throughout the fishery may have been closer to the English experience than was an institution like slavery, but like all colonial labor systems, they responded to the inadequacy of free labor on the peripheries of settlement.

New England was exceptional not in its newness, but in its conscious and relatively successful imitation of England. The Puritan founders were serious in their intention to construct a commonwealth pleasing to God, and this meant a purified form of the English model that in their imagination was the only one God could possibly favor. Hence, they chose to settle a stretch of the hemispheric coastline that from all reports resembled the mother country, and they brought along everything they could—from land systems and political structures to printing presses and colleges— cleansed of corruption, but English in spirit. Above all, they carried with them their reformed Protestant faith and their families. The two were intimately related. God wanted to be worshiped by the faithful in their families; the failure of many other colonies was rooted, the Puritan founders knew, in the failure to take this point seriously. Self-consciously, the founders set out to recruit exactly the diversity of households, possessed of all the skills—male and female—that would enable a new England to survive in America. In the temperate climate of the American northeast, where English crafts and agriculture made geographic sense and where there was little to encourage specialization in anything else, the diversity quite unself-consciously survived. New England was born, therefore, with a degree of instant infrastructure and local integration that other colonies lacked; much of the business that one portion of the economy could generate, other sectors could capture. To coordinate and profit from this complex network of local exchange, merchants came and stayed on New England's shores, and the returns they reinvested within the region planted more business in turn.

Gradually and unevenly throughout the economy, wealth and manpower accumulated, and the frontier adaptations of the earlier years were shaken off. Fishermen and farmers found increasingly that economic survival, let alone prosperity, demanded they spend part of their youth and increasingly their adult years as well in the employ of others. These people did not seize upon waged labor with enthusiasm; the energy that both landsmen and seamen poured into the establishment of competent or semicompetent households during the seventeenth century is proof of that. But in time, as labor and capital accumulated within the colony and the easy access to uncleared land diminished, recourse to paid employment became a necessity—either as a means to establishing one's independence in later life or, for the less fortunate, as a permanent condition rooted in lifetime poverty. Thus an internal market in labor gradually came into being. This did not cause the industrial revolution in New England, but it allowed Yankee entrepreneurs of the early republic to successfully imitate what was in essence another English model.

The colonial experiment that spread outward from Massachusetts was not exceptional in its novelty. The first generation of settlers had to grapple with a new environment, but so did colonists everywhere. In this regard, the story told here is a variation on a theme common to all the Americas. What distinguished the Puritan colonists was the determination with which they re-created so quickly so much of the Old World in the new. For that reason they termed themselves "New Englanders." Serious people, they would expect us to listen.

APPENDIXES

This study is based primarily on a series of files containing several thousand cases of work performed. Since they were all constructed on common principles, which would be tedious to repeat from footnote to footnote, I have decided to describe them here, first in general terms and then, chapter by chapter, in their specifics.

Every file was organized around the act of work itself. Rather than rely on occupational designations, I began by recording instances of labor performed—crew lists, for example, or pieces of court testimony describing the mowing of a field—and then attempted to reconstruct the social context that surrounded them. Each case amounted to a snapshot of working life, and, assembled in different ways, they enabled me to reconstruct the social relations of production and their evolution over time. There are several points to be made about a research strategy of this sort. First, since each case in every file related to a piece of work performed, certain individuals surfaced more often than others and play a greater role in the data base. This gave a more accurate sense of how the work force was structured but also forced me to be careful about not allowing a few people's experiences to dominate the statistics. Second, as a result of being scrupulous about including as fishermen or farmers only those whom I had "caught in the act," my population sizes were often smaller than I would have wished. This gave a degree of precision to my research, but again, reminded me not to conclude too freely from limited numbers. Finally, since almost every case contained some missing data, the reported population size for different calculations based on the same file could vary, depending on how many cases in the file in question possessed the specific type of data (age, marital status, and so on) being analyzed.

Chapter 2 is based on five separate files: master/servant; day labor; land-lord/tenant; father/son; and undirected labor. In every case I recorded the names of the parties in question, the dates that framed the work or tenancy relationship, and the details of that relationship. The cases were drawn from George Francis Dow and Mary G. Thresher, eds., *Records and Files of the Quarterly Courts of Essex County, Massachusetts, 1636–1686,* 9 vols. (Salem, Mass., 1911–1975); Archie N. Frost, comp., *Verbatim Transcriptions of the Records of the Quarterly Courts of Essex County, Massachusetts, 1636–1694,* 57 vols. (Salem, Mass., 1936–1939); Files of the Essex County Inferior Court of Common Pleas, property of the Supreme Judicial Court, Division of Archives and Records Preservation, on deposit at the James Duncan Phillips Library, Peabody Essex Museum, Salem, Mass., Boxes 1–34, 1694–1725; and Thomas Barnard Account Book, 1688–1708, James Duncan Phillips Library.

For the individuals in each case, I attempted to discover their town of residence, age, birthplace, parents' names, date of marriage, spouse's name, date of death, and property holdings (if any) at the time the work was performed. The last was measured from surviving tax and probate records, which were taken as valid evidence only if the individual had been taxed or inventoried within five years of performing the work in question. The sources used to compile this biographical data were those mentioned in the preceding paragraph; James Savage, *A Genealogical Dictionary of the First Settlers of New England,* 4 vols. (Boston, 1860–1862); George Francis Dow, ed., *The Probate Records of Essex County, Massachusetts, 1635–1681,* 3 vols. (Salem, Mass., 1916–1920); Probate Records of Essex County, Massachusetts, Probate Record Office, Registry of Deeds and Probate Record Office Building, Salem, Mass.; "Taxes under Gov. Andros: Town Rate of Boxford, 1687," *New England Historical and Genealogical Record,* XXXIII (1879), 162–163; "Taxes under Gov. Andros: Town Rate of Newbury, Mass., 1688," *NEHGR,* XXXII (1878), 156–164; Ipswich town rate, 1648, in "Ipswich Proceedings," *NEHGR,* II (1848), 50–52; Ipswich town rate, 1679, in Dow and Thresher, eds., *Essex Co. Court Recs.,* VIII, 309–311; Salem town rate, 1683, in Sidney Perley, *The History of Salem, Massachusetts,* 3 vols. (Salem, Mass., 1924–1928), III, 419–422; "Salem Town Rate, 1689," typescript at the James Duncan Phillips Library; "Taxes under Gov. Andros: Topsfield Town Rate, 1687,"

NEHGR, XXXV (1881), 34–35; Gloucester town rate, 1693, in John J. Babson, *History of the Town of Gloucester, Cape Ann, including the Town of Rockport* (Gloucester, Mass., 1860), 213–214; "Settlers to Whom House Lots Were Given prior to 1662 and the Sizes of Their Lots," table 4 in Philip J. Greven, Jr., *Four Generations: Population, Land, and Family in Colonial Andover, Massachusetts* (Ithaca, N.Y., 1970), 46; Salisbury town rate, 1681, in Dow and Thresher, eds., *Essex Co. Court Recs.*, VIII, 390–393; "Ancient Tax List of the Town of Rowley," *NEHGR*, XV (1861), 253–254; Perley, *History of Salem*, I, 454–465; the list of Marblehead landowners in 1638 in William P. Upham, ed., "Salem Town Records, 1634–1659," Essex Institute, *Historical Collections*, IX (1869), 63; the 1648 and 1676 lists of householders with common rights in Marblehead in William Hammond Bowden, ed., "Marblehead Town Records," Essex Institute, *Hist. Colls.*, LXIX (1933), 211, 272–282; and the local history and genealogical collection at the James Duncan Phillips Library. Useful for comparisons to the probate wealth structure for the county as a whole was Donald Warner Koch, "Income Distribution and Political Structure in Seventeenth-Century Salem, Massachusetts," Essex Institute, *Hist. Colls.*, CV (1969), 59.

APPENDIX 2

Chapter 3 is based on a file of Essex County fishermen from the period 1640–1675. In every case I recorded the name of the fisherman and his outfitting merchant (if evident), the details of their relationship, and the year(s) of the voyage(s). The cases were drawn from George Francis Dow and Mary G. Thresher, eds., *Records and Files of the Quarterly Courts of Essex County, Massachusetts*, 9 vols. (Salem, Mass., 1911–1975), I–VIII; George Corwin Account Books, 1758–1664, 1663–1672, Curwen Family Papers, 1641–1902, James Duncan Phillips Library, Peabody Essex Museum, Salem, Mass.; Edward E. Hale, ed., *Note-Book Kept by Thomas Lechford, Esq., Lawyer, in Boston, Massachusetts Bay, from June 27, 1638 to July 29, 1641* (American Antiquarian Society, *Transactions and Collections*, VII [Cambridge, Mass., 1885]); and William B. Trask, ed., *Suffolk Deeds*, 14 vols. (Boston, 1880–1906).

For each fisherman, I constructed a biography including information on his place of origin, town of residence, date of birth, date of arrival in the colony, length of residence in the colony, parents' names, marital status, date of marriage, spouse's name, church membership, vessel ownership, taxable estate, court presentations, date of death, estate at death, and any other seemingly relevant material from court testimony and town records. This information was drawn from the sources mentioned in the preceding paragraph as well as from William Hammond Bowden, ed., "Marblehead Town Records," Essex Institute, *Historical Collections*, LXIX (1933), 207–329; George F. Dow, ed., *The Probate Records of Essex County, Massachusetts, 1635–1681*, 3 vols. (Salem, Mass., 1916–1920); James Savage, *A Genealogical Dictionary of the First Settlers of New England*, 4 vols. (Boston, 1860–1862); Charles Edward Banks, *Topographical Dictionary of 2885 English Emigrants to New England, 1620–1650* (Baltimore, 1957); John J. Babson, *History of the Town of Gloucester, Cape Ann, including the Town of Rockport* (Gloucester, Mass., 1860); Sidney Perley, *The History of Salem, Massachusetts*, 3 vols. (Salem, Mass., 1924–1928); Richard D. Pierce, ed., *The Records of the First Church in Salem, Massachusetts, 1629–1736* (Salem, Mass., 1974); Archie N. Frost, comp., *Verbatim Transcriptions of the Records of the Quarterly Courts of Essex County, Massachusetts, 1636–1694*, 57 vols. (Salem, Mass., 1936–1939); William P. Upham, ed., "Town Records of Salem, 1634–1659," Essex Institute, *Hist. Colls.*, IX (1868), 1–242; the entire Essex Institute *Historical Collections* series; and the local history and genealogical collection at the James Duncan Phillips Library.

APPENDIX 3

Chapter 4 and part of Chapter 6 are based on a file of Essex County fishermen from the period 1676–1855. As in Appendix 2, for every case I recorded the fisherman's name, his outfitting merchant's name, the details of the relationship between them, and the dates of any voyages described. The cases were drawn from Archie N. Frost, comp., *Verbatim Transcriptions of the Records of the Quarterly Courts of Essex County, Massachusetts, 1636–1694*, 57 vols. (Salem, Mass., 1936–1939), XLVI–LVII; Files of the Essex County Inferior Court of Common Pleas, property of the Supreme Judicial Court, Division of Archives and Records Preservation, on deposit at the James Duncan Phillips Library, Peabody Essex Museum, Salem, Mass., Boxes 1–150; and numerous manuscript sources. At the James Duncan Phillips Library, I used the Joshua Burnham Ac-

count Book, 1763–1790, Joshua Burnham (1736–1791) Papers, 1758–
1817; Burnham Papers, Box 1, Folders 1–4; Cabot Family Papers, 1712–
1862, vol. 1, Commercial, 1742–1773; Thomas Davis Account Book,
1771–1778; Derby Family Papers, 1716–1921, vol. 28; Philip English
Account Books, 1664–1708, 1678–1690, 1699–1718, English/Touzell/
Hathorne Papers, 1661–1851; Fishing Accounts, Beverly, Mass., 1816–
1848; John Higginson, Jr., Account Book, 1678–1689; Benjamin Knight
Account Book, 1800–1833; William Knight Account Books, 1769–1775,
1788–1800; John and Jonathan Lovett Papers, Miscellaneous, 1778–
1803; Joseph Orne Account Book, 1719–1744, Timothy Orne Account
Book, 1738–1758, Orne Family Papers, 1719–1899; William Pickering
Account Book, 1695–1718; Joseph Procter Account Book, 1783–1806;
Daniel Rogers Account Book, 1770–1790; John Stevens Account Book,
1768–1775 (and in the same volume, Samuel Whittemore Accounts,
1787–1807); Miles Ward Account Books, 1745–1753, 1753–1764, Ward
Family Papers, 1718–1945; and log of unidentified vessel (1828), No. 1828,
log of unidentified vessel (1825–1833), No. 1825, log of schooner *Paragon*
(1824–1827), No. 1824L, log of schooner *Nancy* (1795–1796), No. 1795N,
Logbook Collection. I also used the Thomas Pedrick Account Book, 1760–
1790, and the Richard Pedrick Account Book, 1766–1783, at the Marblehead Historical Society, Marblehead, Mass.; the Daniel Rogers Account
Book, 1790–1800, at the Cape Ann Historical Association, Gloucester,
Mass.; and the John Lovett Account Books, 1793–1796, 1797–1801, at the
Beverly Historical Society, Beverly, Mass. To these were added the names
of fishermen who drowned in the course of their work and whose deaths
were recorded in the Marblehead, Salem, Beverly, Manchester, Gloucester, Essex, and Ipswich volumes of the published vital records to the end of
the year 1849 and in George H. Procter, *The Fishermen's Memorial and
Record Book* (Gloucester, Mass., 1873), 8–18.

The biographies assembled for these fishermen were briefer than those
for the period before 1676, mostly because the court records, which had
served as the main biographical source in Chapter 3, were unindexed
from 1687 onward. The information collected for the period after that
date thus was limited to place and date of birth, parents' names, town of
residence, date of marriage and spouse's name, marital status, vessel ownership, taxable estate, date of death, and estate at death. This information
was culled from the sources in the paragraph above as well as from George
F. Dow, ed., *The Probate Records of Essex County, Massachusetts, 1635–*

1681, 3 vols. (Salem, Mass., 1916–1920), III; Probate Records of Essex County, Massachusetts, Probate Record Office, Registry of Deeds and Probate Record Office Building, Salem, Mass.; Bettye Hobbs Pruitt, ed., *Massachusetts Tax Valuation List of 1771* (Boston, 1978); Salem town rate, 1683, in Sidney Perley, *The History of Salem, Massachusetts*, 3 vols. (Salem, Mass., 1924–1928), III, 419–422; Salem Tax and Valuation Lists, 1689–1773, Marblehead Tax and Valuation Lists, 1734–1776, Beverly Tax Lists, 1735–1779, in Ruth Crandall, comp., Tax and Valuation Lists of Massachusetts Towns before 1776, microfilm edition (Charles Warren Center for Studies in American History, Harvard University, Cambridge, Mass., 1971), rolls 8, 9, 10, 12; Gloucester Town Rates and Valuation Lists, 1784, 1791, 1792, microfilm copy in possession of the James Duncan Phillips Library; Manuscript Census of 1850, Card File of Essex County Residents, Lynnfield Public Library, Lynnfield, Mass.; Perley, *History of Salem*; John J. Babson, *History of the Town of Gloucester, Cape Ann, including the Town of Rockport* (Gloucester, Mass., 1860); Philip Chadwick Foster Smith, ed., *The Journals of Ashley Bowen (1728–1813) of Marblehead*, 2 vols. (Boston, 1973); the Essex Institute *Historical Collections*; and the local history and genealogical collection at the James Duncan Phillips Library.

APPENDIX 4

Chapter 5 and part of Chapter 6 are based on a file of farm work experiences covering the period 1700–1855. In each case I recorded the nature of the work and the terms on which it was performed, the date, the town, and the names of the two parties. The cases were drawn from numerous manuscript sources at the James Duncan Phillips Library, Peabody Essex Museum, Salem, Mass.: Abraham Adams Account Book, 1746–1842; Thomas Barnard Account Book, 1688–1708; James Brown Account Book, 1759–1786; Capt. Jonathan Burnham Account Book, 1723–1749; George Choate Account Book, 1789–1823; Zaccheus Collins Diary, 1726–1779; E. P. Ferguson Account Book, 1848–1853; Enoch Follansbee Account Book, 1820–1865; Abraham Foster Account Book, 1754–1772; James and Aaron Foster Account Book, 1798–1816; Jonathan Foster Account Book, 1797–1829; Joseph Plummer Foster Account Book, 1842–1856; Josiah French Account Book, 1763–1785; Josiah Gerrish Account Book, 1827–1835; Benjamin Herrick Account Book, 1759–1790; Luke

Hovey Account Book, 1698–1792; Christopher Howe Account Book, 1825–1830; Caleb Jackson Journal, 1802–1806; Moody Jacques Account Book, 1814–1827; Joseph Jewett, 3d, Account Book, 1811–1819; Stephen Kent Account Book, 1805–1841; Moses Little Account Book, 1724–1778; Stephen Little Account Book, 1767–1792; Merrill Family Account Book, 1775–1834; Thomas Nelson Account Book, 1692–1741; Abijah Northey, Journals of Boxford Farm, 1828–1832, 1832–1836, Northey Family Papers, 1688–1964, Box 1; Asa Perkins Account Book, 1803–1851; Timothy Pickering Account Book, 1732–1757; Jonathan Porter Account Book, 1818–1828; Moses Porter Diary, 1817–1822; Brackenbury Prince Account Book, 1807–1832; Joseph Rawlings Account Book, 1790–; Henry Russell Account Book, 1728–1837; Israel Sawyer Account Book, 1774–1819; John Sawyer Account Book, 1771–1833; Josiah Sawyer Account Book, 1736–1793; Richard Shatswell Day Book, 1766–1779, Shatswell Family Papers, 1722–1818, Folder 1; Ephraim Towne Account Book, 1750–1768; Jabez True Account Book, 1710–1741. I also used the Robert Hale Account Book, 1723–, at the Beverly Historical Society, Beverly, Mass.; the Amos Breed Account Book, 1763–, Jonathan Buffum Account Book, 1775–, and Nehemiah Collins Account Book, 1756–, at the Lynn Historical Society, Lynn, Mass.; the Nathaniel Hubbard Dodge Account Book, 1762–1793, and Abraham Dodge Account Book, 1829–1871, at the Wenham Historical Association and Museum, Wenham, Mass.; the John Baker Account Book, 1769–1834, at the Baker Library, Harvard Business School, Boston; and the Files of the Essex County Inferior Court of Common Pleas, property of the Supreme Judicial Court, Division of Archives and Records Preservation, on deposit at the James Duncan Phillips Library, Boxes 5–150.

As in Appendix 3, the biographical material assembled for the different parties to these work relationships was more limited than for those of the seventeenth century. In each case, I tried to determine the relationship between the two parties, their place of origin, parents' names, dates of birth and marriage, spouse's name, and taxable estate. In the case of hired hands, I also searched the probate records for inventoried estates. This information was culled from the sources in the paragraph above as well as from Bettye Hobbs Pruitt, ed., *Massachusetts Tax Valuation List of 1771* (Boston, 1978); Probate Records of Essex County, Massachusetts, Probate Record Office, Registry of Deeds and Probate Record Office Building, Salem, Mass.; Salem Tax and Valuation Lists, 1689–1773, in Ruth Crandall, comp., Tax and Valuation Lists of Massachusetts Towns before 1776, microfilm edition (Charles Warren Center for Studies in American History, Harvard University, Cambridge, Mass., 1971), rolls 8, 9; Manuscript Census of 1850, Card File of Essex County Residents, Lynnfield Public Library, Lynnfield, Mass.; the published vital records to the end of the year 1849; and the genealogical and local history collection at the James Duncan Phillips Library.

INDEX

Adams, Abraham, 65

Age: coming of, 67–68, 138, 174; of active fishermen, 89, 135, 173, 182–186, 198, 200, 201, 266, 281–282, 287–289; of free laborers, 242, 243, 244; of indentured servants, 58; of rural manufacturers, 256–257; of servants, 235, 302, 303, 304; of soldiers, 250

Agricultural fairs, 297n

Agriculture: capital in, 43–46, 211–212; commercial, 47, 54, 207, 210–219, 247, 250, 279, 291–297, 299, 302, 303, 306; dairying, 58, 214, 295, 299; farm construction and maintenance, 7, 22, 43, 45–46, 50, 63, 258; for home consumption, 208–209, 295, 306; grains, 45, 50, 63, 212, 214, 297, 306; hay, 50, 66, 295–296, 297, 299, 303; in England, 32–41; in Midwest, 290, 295; land clearing, 3, 43, 45, 49, 212, 258; livestock, 23, 33, 34, 44, 46, 50, 67, 69, 212, 213, 224, 227–228, 297, 306; livestock ownership by farmers, 68–69, 209–210, 223–224, 227–228; livestock ownership by fishermen, 168, 198, 201–202, 269, 273, 279–280; livestock ownership by manufacturers, 314, 323; orchards, 103, 111, 202, 214, 306; productivity of, 48, 211–212, 296–297, 297n–298n; seasonal patterns of, 34, 42–43, 50–51, 62; specialization

in, 295; technique in, 33–35, 42–45, 46–47; vegetables, 214, 294, 306

Alcohol: consumption of, among fishermen, 93, 96–97, 114, 126, 127, 128, 133, 140, 182, 189

Allen, David Grayson, 33n

Allen, Jeremiah, 198

Allen, Robert, 176–177

Allen, Samuel, 306, 307

Allerton, Isaac, 92, 93

Amesbury, Mass., 55n

Andalusia, Spain, 87n

Anderson, Terry L., 211

Anderson, Virginia DeJohn, 33n

Andover, Mass., 2, 25, 299

Andrews, Ebenezer, 302

Annapolis Royal, N.S., 149, 251

Annisquam, Mass., 191, 192

Anticosti Island, 272

Arnaudin, Simeon, 230, 233

Artisans. *See* Manufacture

Atkinson, John, Jr., 66

Atwood, Samuel, 282

Bagley, Orlando, 254–255, 256

Bailyn, Bernard, 136n

Baker, John, 233, 241n, 300, 302

Baldwin, Simeon, 172

Baltimore, Md., 311

Banquereau Bank, 150